1. dream it
2. hold it
3. go for it

Petzl

www.petzl.com

David Atchison-Jones
Chief Editor & Photographer
Carrie Atchison-Jones
Climber & Photographer

PORTUGAL - Sport onsight & Bouldering
Jingo Wobbly – Topo Guides
First Published in April 2004
By Jingo Wobbly Euro Guides
(An imprint of Vision PC).
Holmwood House, 52 Roxborough Park,
Harrow-on-the-Hill, London. HA1 3AY, Great Britain

Copyright © David Atchison-Jones
Graphics by Botticelli
Image Scanning – Professional Film Company, London
Printing – Fratelli Spada SPA, Roma.

All rights reserved. No part of this publication may be reproduced, stored in a retrieval system, or transmitted in any form or by any means, electronic, mechanical, photocopying, recording or otherwise, without prior written permission of the copyright owner.

A CIP catalogue record is available from the British Library

ISBN   1-873 665 51-2

This book by definition is a climbing guidebook, and not a climbing safety book, and has no instructions or directions with regard to any safety aspect of climbing or general safety in climbing areas. Please seek professional safety advice before ever entering any climbing environment.

A climbing guidebook, is a collection of past climbing knowledge from a variety of sources. It cannot be regarded as either fact or fiction, since the information has been generally handed down across the generations, and is always open to the interpretation of the reader. We do of course however, make every effort to ensure that the information included in the guidebook is as up to date, and as accurate as possible at the time of going to press, but we unfortunately cannot guarantee any complete accuracy. Any information included within the advertisements, are the sole responsibility of the advertiser. The publisher and editor cannot accept responsibility for any consequences arising from the use of this book, and do not accept any liability whatsoever for injury or damage caused by anyone arising from the use of this book.

The inclusion of any cliff in this guide, does not mean that anybody has any right of access whatsoever. All climbers and visitors should be aware that there may be strict access and conservation issues at any of the cliffs included in this guide, and should read and understand all notices, before climbing.

If there is any information that you feel is improper, or that you feel could be updated, please write to us or email us (info@jingowobbly.com) at our publishing address, where we will gladly collect the information for future editions.

Up to date latest information can be found at www.jingowobbly.com

Top photo: TRAVESSIA 7a,
Farol da Guia; Carrie Atchison-Jones
Left photo: NEW WAVE 6a,
Sintra; José Teixeira
Right photo: MISSÃO CUMPRIDA 7b+,
Poios; Ben Moon

Top photo: KIND OF MAGIC 7c+,
Farol da Guia; Miguel Loureiro
Lower photo: Desert sector,
Pedra do Urso; Jerry Moffatt

PORTUGAL

ON-SIGHT & BLOC

DAVID & CARRIE ATCHISON-JONES

GUIDEBOOK TRADE DISTRIBUTORS

BRITISH ISLES & GENERAL WORLD
CORDEE
3a De Montfort Street,
Leicester. LE1 3HD, Great Britain.
Tel: 0116 254 3579   Fax: 0116 247 1176
sales@cordee.co.uk
www.cordee.co.uk

PORTUGAL – Main Distributor:
VERTICAL
R. Gen. Alves Roçadas, 10 – Loja 5
2710 SINTRA, PORTUGAL.
Tel: 00 351 219 243 885
www.vertical-outdoor.com

BERGVERLAG ROTHER
Haidgraben 3,
D-85521 Ottobrunn (München),
DEUTSCHLAND
distributor-publisher as
Licensed by Jingo Wobbly-Euro Guides for
Deutschland, Österreich, Schweiz, Italia(South Tyrol).

FREYTAG & BERNDT - PRAHA
Na Florenci 19, budova C
CZ-11286 Praha 1
CESKA REPUBLIKA
distributor-publisher as
Licensed by Jingo Wobbly-Euro Guides for
Ceska Republika, Slovenska Republika, Hungary.

FRANCE – Main Distributor:
RANDO diffusion IBOS
4, rue Maye Lane, F 65420 IBOS-TARBES,
tél; 00 33 5 62 90 09 96
RANDO diffusion PARIS
2bis, place du puits de l'ermite, F75005 Paris.
tél; 00 33 1 44 08 78 10

NETHERLANDS – Main Distributor:
NILSSON & LAMM
Pampuslaan 212, Postbus 195
1380 AD Weesp (NL)
www.nilsson-lamm.nl
00 31 294-494 949

JAPANESE AGENCY:
Sport Climbing Center PUMP
Frontier Spirit, Inc.
2-20-10 Higashimotomachi Kokubunzi-shi,
Tokyo, Japan.
www.pump-climbing.com
Tel/fax 0081-42-324-6762

JINGO WOBBLY SERIES OF CLIMBING BOOKS

Learning series; climbing books from beginner to expert.
Euro-guides; a complete overview of a country & Europe.
Topo-Guides; Individual topo illustration in fine detail.

Please contact our distributors for the latest list of titles that we publish. Complete details on all books and distribution from our website

www.jingowobbly.com

Contents

Acknowledgements/Sponsors - 6	Salir - 47	Clubs - 277
Jingo Wobbly Sport Vertical - 7	Alte - 50	Appendix I
Preface- UK/8 - P/9	Setúbal - 72	Limestone-Calcaire - 278
Introduction - English - 10	Serra da Arrábida - 73	Appendix II
Introduction - Portuguese - 14	Guincho - 96	Complete icons - 282
Introduction - Deutsch - 18	Cascais - 97	Scrapbook - 286
Introduction - Français - 22	Sintra - 145	Funny page - 287
Introduction - Spanish - 26	Obidos - 185	Travel checklist - 288

Rocha da Pena

SOUTH
Faro - region
Rocha da Pena - 31

Lagos/Sagres - region
Sagres - 65

Capuchos

CENTRAL
Leiria - region
Reguengo do Fétal - 188

Coimbra - region
Redinha - 210
Poios - 225
Buracas do Cagimil - 240

SOUTH LISBOA
Setúbal - region
Fenda - 75
Outão - 90

WEST LISBOA
Sintra - region
Farol da Guia - 95
Baía do Mexilhoeiro - 128
Sintra - 143
Capuchos - 159
Peninha - 166
Malveira - 174
Praia do Cavalo - 178

NORTH LISBOA
Alenquer/Santarem - region
Montejunto - 180

Pedra do Urso

Farol da Guia

CENTRAL EAST
Guarda/Covilhã - region
Pedra do Urso - 252
Penha Garcia - 274

Buracas do Cagimil

Acknowledgements & Advertisers

I dedicate this book to the memory of Paulo Alves, a climber I met on my first visit to Portugal who typified a friendly and welcoming nature, so common in Portugal. He unfortuntely died of a cardiac problem at the young age of 34.

I have to thank Carrie for her wonderful support, and brilliance as a climbing and photographing companion. Also, for putting up with my endless hours on a computer to generate this book. I have to thank many other climbers for the great trips that I have had in Portugal, and others who have commented on routes, grades, wobbly icons etc; André Neres, Ben Moon, Fred Silva, Jerry Moffatt, José & Alda Teixeira, Matthias Berndt, Miguel 'Mikey' Loureiro, Ulrike Burkert.

Obviously the collection of material for a new guide like this takes several years, and I am very thankful to many climbers who were enthusiastic with their climbing, but also in writing down the names of routes to be kept, and past on for historic correctness, also their help with being able to find all the different climbs and generally enjoy climbing, and nearly always – a fantastic input into the heart of Portuguese climbing; Alex Rebelo, Américo Pedrosa Santos, André Neres, Andy Reid, Bruno Mendes, Carlos Pereira, Eduardo Costa, Estoril-Cascais Tourist Office, Francisco 'Chico' Ataíde, Filipe Costa e Silva, Oldemiro Lima, Nuno Soares, José Maria Oliveira, José Teixeira (FPME), Luis Pinheiro, Mário Carvalho, Miguel 'Mikey' Loureiro, Nuno Seabra, Ricardo 'Macau' Alves, Rui Carvalheira, Sandra Seabra, Secçao de Montanhismo do Clube de Campismo da Covilhã, Sérgio Martins.

My thanks to everyone who helped with the photographs, and especially all the belayers. My regrets to any of the photos that we didn't have room to fit into the book, but here are thanks to those whose names we managed to remember; Ana Coelho, Antonio Gonzales Gonzales, Bruno Coelho, Candida Duxa, Carla Duarte, Cosme Aldazabal, Diogo Paulo, Diogo Serrano, Emilio Andrade, Esther Zaragoza, Gerado Pradilla, Ian Darley, José Manuel Armario, Juan Manuel Perez, Leopoldo Faria, Luis Asensio, Manuel Franco, Mariá Garcia Campos, Mário Albuquerque, Mario Santos, Miguel Angel, Miguel Suarez, Nuno Neves, Nuno Pinheiro, Paulo Alves, Ricardo Belchior, Rui 'Pop' Appolinari, Rui Rosado, Sandra Albuquerque, Sonia Afomso; and a special thanks for Andy Reid and his photos of Sagres.

My thanks to all the people who have helped out with the different translations in an assortment of languages, and in particular to Mário Carvalho, for the overall editorial control of the Portuguese sections; Alda Vieira, Américo Pedrosa Santos, Carlos Pereira, José Maria Oliveira, Mário Carvalho, Miguel Loureiro, Nuno Seabra, Sandra Mendes, Virgine Percival, Rudiger Jooss, Maria Jose Marchena

I have to thank Len Worrall and Paul Hooper at PFC, for the delicate task of taking the images on film and creating digital photos that reflect with clarity, the beauty of the Portugal. I must thank also Marco Marziale and everyone at Spada in Roma, for looking after the printing of our books.

David Atchison-Jones   May 2004

Petzl Distribution Sport, Zone Industrielle, 38920 Crolles, France.
Tel: #33 (0) 4 76 92 09 00
www.petzl.com

Beal (Page 227)
Beal Cordes, 2 rue Rabelais,
B.P.235 38201 Vienne
Tel: #33 (0) 4 74 78 88 88
www.beal-planet.com

Lyon Equipment, (Page 227)
Dent, Sedbergh, LA10 5QL, GB
Tel: #44 (0) 15396 25493
www.lyon.co.uk

Peglers (Page 34)
69 Tarrant Street, Arundel, West Sussex. BN18 9DN. GB.
Tel: # 44 (0) 1903 883 375
www.peglers.co.uk

Vertical (Page 147)
R. Gen. Alves Roçadas, 10 – Loja 5
2710 SINTRA, PORTUGAL.
Tel: 00 351 219 243 885
www.vertical-outdoor.com

Boreal
P.Altos Condomina 15 –P.O.Box 202, 03400 Villena, España.
Tel: # 34 965 800 589
www.e-boreal.com

Expedição (Page 98)
Rua Joao Seraiva, 34 A-B
1700-250 Lisboa
Tel: #351 21 843 55 80

Tecniaventura (Page 191)
Tel: TLM; 917 54 85 82
www.tecniaventura.pt

INTRODUCING
' THE HOLIDAY PLANNER'

If you want to know about, all the other areas in Europe to climb, try out our Europe - Sport Vertical guidebook. We give full climbing details to 2600 different cliffs, all located by our 96 - easy to use, colour maps. We show the quality of local climbing guidebooks available & where to buy them. Campsites included. Each cliff is indicated with number of routes, heights, altitude, sun aspect, style of climbing etc.

There are over 350 breathtaking colour photograps to illustrate the superb cliffs of Portugal, Spain, France, Italy, Suisse, Austria, Germany, Czech Republic, Belgium, England, Wales and Scotland.

EUROPE - SPORT VERTICAL
A guidebook to the best rock climbing sites in Europe
How to plan your perfect climbing trip

If you get more than one weeks climbing holiday a year, you most probably browse the web, looking for ideas. Now you can have the whole of Europe at your fingertips in an instant, all with superb quality information and details that you can trust. It is the classic Jingo Wobbly size, so you can carry it with you to the Alps or anywhere, fits into the top of your rucksack or the car glove compartment. It works in 7 languages using special climbing icons. You will never want to leave home again - without it.

EUROPE SPORT VERTICAL 384 pages, colour, **£ 19.95 - 32.50 Euros**
Flexibound,   210mm x 151mm (A5)   **ISBN: 1-873-665-21-0**

Preface

Why don't you write a climbing guidebook? A question that I had never thought of until some 5-6 years ago at the London Book Fair, when a friend of mine suggested that I put something back into climbing; a pastime that I loved, and got a huge amount out of. I tried to argue my way out – but was unsuccessful; so much - that this is my third topo guidebook. I was very fortunate in starting climbing at a very early age, and zoomed into top level climbing and instructing by the age of 18. From then on, I certainly never needed a guidebook to anywhere. What was the point of knowing about climbs before you did them, surely it would spoil the adventure? For many years, I climbed a great deal of first ascents, travelled around the Alps, and simply climbed up mountains and rock faces that I liked the look of. Other climbers would look in complete disbelief when they questioned me about the route I was on – I didn't even know, and had never seen a guidebook to the area! Ironically, I was in a very safe position, since I knew exactly what I was getting myself into – just by looking and assessing myself. To that end, I had always been suspicious about guidebooks - which took less experienced climbers into highly dangerous places, and with little, or no room for error. Maybe though as you get older, you get fairer and less pompous, and can see that other people just don't have the huge amount of time that I enjoyed as a teenager, to get highly skilled at climbing. I now appreciate that climbing guidebooks are of fantastic benefit to a huge amount of climbers, and it does allow a 'quick ticket' to some spectacular climbing, and then can usually forecast a quantifiable level of danger. Taking a decision to write climbing guidebooks was complicated enough, but that leaves me with a far greater dilemma – what to actually put into a guidebook.

With 25 years of climbing experience across the whole of Europe, I enjoy a wide knowledge and perspective on the whole climbing game. I have seen just about everything from remote and quiet little boulders; up to the hundreds - if not thousands of people queuing on the climbs of Mont Blanc. I have seen that a large concentration of climbers, is one of the real problems in climbing. Over popularity is often generated by magazine publicity or singular books, about individual routes or individual cliffs. When I write a guidebook, I try to put as many different cliffs and routes in the guidebook as possible. This way, you spread all the climbers out across a whole area, and do your utmost to relieve crowding in any one particular spot. Enjoyment from the freedom of travel today around Europe is fantastic, and I know that incredible areas like Fontainebleau and Finale, have opened up their climbing areas for everyone to enjoy. I know from talking to many Portuguese climbers, that they would like to be as reciprocal. I feel that European integration can work, and is of great benefit; but only if people respect local cultural ways. I hope that the different languages and icons can make everything available to all, and communicate to everyone, the wishes of local people and climbers. We try to highlight any particular problems that 'visiting climbers' must be made aware of.

Guidebooks in many areas, evolve from one edition to another edition, yet this book is most probably the first ever climbing guidebook written to Portugal. I have hopefully 'propelled' Portuguese guidebook culture, into the fast lane of the 21st century with our glossy and zippy design. We have used many of the latest computer graphics techniques, to make presentation of the information, amusing and colourful. It is obvious that you don't need to carry the guide with you on the climbs here – they're short - so it can be a nice A5 size – and with plenty of information on each page. I also believe that modern guidebooks can serve both as a guidebook when you are at the cliff, and as a lovely photographic climbing book that you treasure in your book collection. That is exactly why our books are printed on exceptionally high quality paper, are properly sewn bound, and now enjoy 'collectors' status. If you want a cheap guide - the internet fully provides for instant free downloads of topos, and I love it for that purpose. But a book is a lot more than a download, it is a personal view on a whole area. The book should be representative, but it can also be relative. For this reason, I try to climb every route, and of course, draw every topo myself. I try to make the whole guidebook as evenly balanced from cliff to cliff, and on a scale that will relate to the rest of Europe. You should find that grade 5b here, will be the same as in Vienna, Rome, Marseille or Stuttgart. It is a personal guidebook with 'intended humour' – varying from appraisal to condemnatory; it is a book with a soul and a life. I simply hope the book gives something back to the climbing of Portugal - with the principle that I've had great enjoyment, and I would love to share it with others.

Preface

Porque é que não escreve um guia de escalada? Um assunto em que nunca tinha pensado até à 5-6 anos atrás, quando na feira do Livro de Londres um amigo me sugeriu que devolvesse alguma coisa à Escalada; uma paixão do passado a que me entreguei com grande intensidade. Ainda tentei esquivar-me – mas sem sucesso; de tal forma que este é o meu terceiro topo guia. Tive muita sorte em ter começado a escalar muito jovem, e ter atingido um nível superior de escalada e ensino aos 18 anos. Desde então, nunca precisei dum guia de escalada fosse para onde fosse. Qual era a ideia de conhecer as vias antes de escalá-las? Com certeza estragaria a aventura! Durante vários anos, fiz muitas primeiríssimas, viajei pelos Alpes e escalei montanhas ou paredes rochosas, simplesmente por gostar do aspecto delas. Os outros escaladores olhavam para mim completamente incrédulos quando perguntavam em que via é que eu estava … e eu nem fazia ideia, nem nunca tinha visto um guia da área! Ironicamente, era seguro, uma vez que sabia em que é que me estava a meter – bastando olhar e avaliar-me. Sob esse ponto de vista sempre desconfiei dos livros – pois conduziam escaladores menos experientes para lugares muito perigosos, com pouca ou nenhuma margem para erro. Talvez a idade nos torne mais razoáveis e menos afectados, permitindo-me compreender que outras pessoas não têm o tempo imenso que eu tive enquanto jovem, para se tornarem altamente eficientes na escalada. Hoje acredito que os guias de escalada constituem um benefício fantástico para uma quantidade enorme de escaladores, pois dão acesso imediato a algumas vias espectaculares, e permitem prever habitualmente um nível de risco quantificável. Tomar a decisão de escrever guias de escalada já foi bastante complicado, mas deixou-me num dilema ainda maior – o que incluir num guia.

Com 25 anos de experiência de escalada por toda a Europa, possuo um vasto conhecimento e uma perspectiva abrangente em matéria de escalada. Já vi quase tudo, desde pequenos blocos tranquilos e afastados, até filas de centenas ou milhares de pessoas para escalar o Mont Blanc. Compreendi que uma grande concentração de escaladores constitui um problema real para a Escalada. O excesso de popularidade é geralmente provocado pela publicidade em revistas ou por livros excepcionais, sobre determinadas vias ou escolas. Quando escrevo um guia, tento incluir tantas escolas e vias quantas possíveis. Desta forma, distribuem-se os escaladores por uma área mais vasta e evita-se ao máximo sobrelotar um determinado local. A liberdade que hoje existe de viajar por toda a Europa é extraordinária, e sei que áreas tão incríveis como Fontainebleau ou Finale foram abertas a toda a gente. Por conversas que tive com muitos escaladores portugueses, fiquei a saber que gostariam de oferecer alguma reciprocidade. Sinto que a integração Europeia é boa, que pode funcionar, e que pode ser muito benéfica; mas apenas se respeitar a identidade cultural de cada membro. Espero que as várias línguas e símbolos possam tornar tudo acessível a todos, mas permitam também comunicar-lhes os desejos dos naturais, escaladores e pessoas em geral, sublinhando quaisquer problemas específicos de que os "escaladores visitantes" devam estar conscientes.

Em muitas regiões, os guias vão-se sucedendo de edição em edição, mas este é provavelmente o primeiro guia de escalada escrito para Portugal. Espero ter impulsionado a cultura portuguesa de guias para a via rápida do século XXI, com o nosso design vistoso e cheio de energia. Usámos muitas das técnicas mais recentes de desenho por computador, para apresentar a informação de forma divertida e colorida. É óbvio que não precisa de levar o guia consigo para as vias – que elas aqui são curtas – por isso este pode ter um belo formato A5, com montes de informação em cada página. Também acredito que os guias modernos podem servir, tanto de guia quando se está na falésia, como de álbum fotográfico de escalada para guardar religiosamente na nossa colecção. É por este motivo que os nossos guias são impressos em papel de qualidade excepcional e devidamente encadernados, merecendo o estatuto de "para coleccionadores". Se o que pretende é um guia barato, vá à Internet; está cheia de topos para download imediato, e para esse fim agrada-me sobremaneira. Mas um livro é muito mais do que um download, é uma visão pessoal de uma região inteira. O livro deve ser representativo, mas também pode ser relativo. Por isso, tento escalar todas as vias, e está claro, desenhar eu mesmo todos os topos. Também tento que o guia no seu todo seja uniformemente equilibrado de escola para escola, e numa escala que se compare com o resto da Europa. Deve sentir que o 5b daqui, é semelhante ao de Viena, Roma, Marselha ou Estugarda. O guia é pessoal com um "humor intencional" – variando desde a aprovação à condenação; é um livro com vida e com alma. Espero simplesmente que ele devolva alguma coisa à Escalada de Portugal – considerando que me tem dado um enorme prazer, e que adorava partilhá-lo.

Welcome to this book about the climbing in Portugal. You must be someone who is stirred by curiosity – thankfully, since Portugal is not famous for any Alps or gigantic, deep canyons. However, it certainly does have a good selection of small cliffs, and worthwhile bouldering areas. These have given a lot of fun and superb climbing enjoyment, to a lot of people. The most relevant part of getting to know a new climbing area, is to place it in the right perspective for yourself, and appreciate how extensive and useful it will be to you. Portugal is not, a 'full on' climbing destination; where you have mile after mile of routes. It just doesn't have the geographic make up to produce such cliffs. Portugal on the other hand, is one of the most perfect holiday destinations in Europe - with some very respectable climbing areas, just a short drive away from superb beaches and surfing spots. If you want to go on holiday, have a great time with friends, family etc; and do some excellent climbing as well, then carry on reading.

Landscape and climate

Portugal is a long thin country of hilly ground, with the occasional mountain range of 'hills,' up to nearly 2000 metres. It has a huge variety of weather patterns, and it is impossible to give any general climatic assessment. In a nutshell, it is warm, but seemingly never too warm, and is highly influenced by the Atlantic Ocean. Any weather front zooming in on the prevailing westerlies, is going to dump big time on Portugal. However, because it is wide open to the Atlantic, bad weather tends to blow through very quickly and sunshine returns. You are also a long way south, hence the sun is powerful and dries everything superbly quickly. It's a windy place too, where everything dries - radically quickly. It is an ever changing country, where you can have monsoon rain one afternoon, then glorious sun and perfect climbing conditions the following morning.

Cliffs & climbing

You don't have any giant cliffs in Portugal like Céüse or Ailefroide, but you do have small cliffs of very high quality, and sectors that would not be out of place, on either of those 2 great cliffs. You get a completely mixed bag of locations and heights.

In the far south of the Algarve you have Rocha da Pena, which is a lovely limestone ridge of about 10 different small buttresses. Only a handful of routes on each, but in a beautiful setting that is just far enough from the busy holiday resorts to be in complete rural quietness. Around Lisbon, you have a superb selection of coastal limestone bouldering and small sea cliffs; then only a short drive up into the hills, you have the white granite of Sintra. Here the cliff is rewarded with staggering exposure, whilst lurking in the forest are some excellent granite bouldering spots. In the more central area of Portugal, there are the high limestone ridges of Montejunto and Redinha, short cliffs with wonderful views and beautiful situations. For the aggressive hard climber, the small gorges of Reguengo, Poios and Buracas, will offer very steep routes on top quality limestone, and very much in a scenic setting. Not to be missed of course is the wilderness bouldering area of Pedra do Urso, high up above the town of Covilha in the mountains of Serra da Estrela. Here the temperature is cooler, and the granite has superb friction. The shapes of the boulders are beautiful and we have only covered one of its many areas in this guidebook. There remain many unsolved problems – such as the Cannonball boulder; come and try your luck on it. The want will be there, it's only your skin that will prevent you climbing non-stop for a week. In the far north there are many other areas that are being developed, and we have included as much information as possible – that has been kindly made available to us by the FPME & the local Portuguese climbing clubs. There are also areas of traditional-classic style climbing in the North of the country; explore further, and find even more cliffs and boulders to climb.

Travel

Most people will choose to fly to Portugal and use the airports at the major cities of Lisbon, Oporto and Faro. You can hire cars fairly easily from all of these airports and the prices compare very favourably with more expensive countries like France. Portugal is a very hilly country, and there are a lot of ancient roads that twist and turn forever. Fortunately, over the last 15 years, a superb network of toll motorways have been built, which allows for easy coverage of long distances. The tolls do not take credit cards, so make sure you are loaded with cash euros, for your fast escape from the airport. The traffic on the motorways, in returning to Lisbon airport can be very bad – so leave plenty of time. Tip; if a route is jammed up, consider using the wider ring road of the A9, to go around the city for another route to the airport. For anyone not able to hire a car, trains go to Cascais, and local buses go to the camping at Guincho, and past the cliff of Farol da Guia. Trains also go to Sintra, but the mountain can attract iffy weather, and it is not therefore the best place to base yourself.

Beaches & surfing

Portugal has a huge expanse of coastline that is exposed to the wild ravages of the Atlantic, which 'ain't' nothing like the Mediterranean. Here you get big waves, and surfing is hugely popular on the long, golden, sandy beaches. Check out your surf guide since some of the waves here are pretty big to handle. The sea is cool (freezing in my opinion), and wet suits are the order of the day. The wind blows, yes it blows – 364 days a year! You are well advised to site your tent with respect to the wind, and if you are coming during the Easter or October gales, bring a substantive and gale proof 'erection.' If you are into windsurfing or kitesurfing, it's the number one spot in Europe. Some of the popular beaches are enormous and even have walkways over the sand to get to the sea. In other areas, you can find lovely small coves, that are completely deserted. Nearly all of the climbing areas are within half an hour of some superb beaches (some are only minutes away).

Portugal is pretty hot in the main holiday month of August, and it is very busy. You have to get up very early not to get roasted on the rock at this time of year. But, even so – under the forest canopy of Sintra, or high up in Pedra do Urso, you can still enjoy your summer cranking. Sept-Oct & then May-July are the best months to visit and have a great holiday combination of warm weather and good climbing days. During this time, you will

Rocha da Pena, Algarve; you need an umbrella here - for the sun.

find it a lot easier to book accommodation, and the camping sites are 'enjoyably' busy. During March and April you will certainly get a lot more rain, but you also get some brilliant spells of fine weather, so it is a practical Easter destination. November to February is not the recommended time – it really is wet (maybe not the Algarve though). There are no shortage of superb travel guidebooks, which help you appreciate the wonderful food, traditions and historic culture of Portugal. The big cities have a lot of sights to offer, as well as museums, concerts and lively bars. Most of the tourist restaurants are yum - lavish, and often have great views over the sea; but seek out the local ones inland a bit, and you will be fabulously rewarded. Most cliffs have nice picnic areas very near, and are quite practical for a family who wants to do a bit of sport climbing and bouldering. Even with toddlers, you can get a lot out of a visit here.

How To Use - Jingo Wobbly Topo Guides

Jingo Wobbly Topo guidebooks are certainly no ordinary climbing guidebooks. We produce climbing guidebooks for climbers who want the most detailed and specific guidebook to a whole region. They can be more than invaluable if you don't climb in the very top grades, and rely on the information from more experienced climbers. Our books may seem expensive, compared to other cheap photocopy topos; but we are fully committed to producing enticing guidebooks, with hundreds of colour photographs, and try to achieve top quality reproduction, printing and robust binding.

The heart of any topo guidebook is obviously in the actual topo's included, but we hope to go a lot further with our guides. Our series is dedicated to areas that you would actually go to on holiday and spend a reasonable amount of time. This is why we designate any extra space that we have in our guidebooks to relevant information of things to do on your rest days – or when it is just too hot to climb. We also may jog your mind to all the lovely rural things an area has to offer, and illustrate the depth of culture and relaxation to be had on a climbing holiday. We can never replicate the wealth of accommodation information given by a local tourist office, but we do try to give as much information on all the possible camping venues in a given area. We try to visit every campsite and illustrate their best points. We give different colours to our camping icons from yellow the most simple (like the climbing grades) – up to purple for a campsite with amazing swimming pool, lush deep grass, gastronomic restaurant etc. Prices we feel are academic, since you nearly always get what you pay for.

Navigation around the guidebook is simple, there is a map of all the climbing on the inside front cover, and a cliff comparison chart on the inside rear cover. Running down the side of the book, are the different areas included in the guide; and on the relevant page, they are marked with colour. Here we use yellow to indicate morning sunshine, red for afternoon sunshine, and blue for no sun at all. You can easily find any cliff in the guidebook, and immediately know if you will get boiled, or end up shivering - especially useful when you don't know an area well. Each cliff has an introduction in English and Portuguese, for those visiting any area for the first time. We then supply 2 maps generally; one to get you to the parking for the cliff, from the local campsite - and the other usually for locating the cliff. Please park your car with consideration, and check that you obey any climbing or parking notices of restrictions that are currently applicable.

We layout every cliff from left to right, regardless as to where you approach from. At the bottom of each topo is a crag navigation bar, indicating all the sectors on a crag and the specific topo highlighted in yellow (red for bouldering). The topo will have a quick height indicator for the height of the cliff at that sector, and time information to the parking, and the next sectors in either direction. If we have space we give each topo a quick résumé as a general character introduction. Our topo's are some of the most detailed in climbing history. Each route is numbered and illustrates difficulty in colour, bolt placements, top lower off. The two most important icons that we use in the guidebook are the red Jingo, and a yellow Wobbly. These are placed where you have a particularly hard move. Jingo stands for pure strength where brains have little effect, you just need the ability to crank. Wobbly is used to illustrate a highly difficult technical move, or a section where skill and ingenuity can easily replace strength. We also use a reach ruler to indicate if a move particularly demands a long reach. Often at the bottom there is a warning triangle for a high position of a first bolt; 1- you might break a wrist; 2 – you may break ribs or your back; 3 – possibly terminal!

Our grading system looks complex at first, but is far more informative and useful to visiting climbers. All routes are graded first by colour to show the hardest bouldering move on a climb – there is an index on the inside back flap, to show the corresponding Fontainebleau or V grade. (The colours are also the same as that you find on the circuits at Font; and also ascend in the same colour scheme that skiing uses.) Each bouldering grade has a comparative sport grade. If the climb has a lot of hard moves of the same standard, then it will most probably get a higher sport grade – but still only the lower colour for the hardest move (even though it feels harder because you are tired). We find most climbers

MOON ARÊTE 7c+ (1st Ascent), Peninha; Ben Moon

like this, because they are usually more limited by strength and power to do a move, than stamina. We use an additional blue flash, if the climb has moves that are fairly easy to read, and should be enjoyable to climb onsight. We use a redpoint icon, if the climb has hidden holds, or very tricky moves that need to be practised first. We give each climb its name, stars for quality, length, a short description, and the type of limestone found on the route (Index in the appendix at the rear of the book). We use a system of icons to represent the style of climbing on each climb, angle of route, individual desperate stopper (bloc) moves. We also give you a flight indication in the event of a fall; Helicopter - Hover by the bolt; Fighter plane – for a 1-2 metre quick flight; 747 – for a transatlantic 2-4 metre flight; Rocket for a flight that may take you on a galactic trip. We also often show the number of quickdraws, which should relate to the flight indicator. If there are more, then we either made a mistake, or the route has been re-equipped. Because climbers need to plan climbing, in or out of the sun, we give a sunshine indicator for every route in the guidebook (almost), and it shows the time that the sun is on the route. We also have little morning and afternoon sun indicators, and if there is green on them, then you are likely to be in the shade in summer. Always remember though, that all climbing guidebooks are a representation of past experience, but certainly not a prediction of future condition that the routes may be in!

Sejam bem-vindos a este guia de escalada em Portugal. Esta é a primeira vez que se reúne num único livro tanta informação sobre escalada no Centro e Sul de Portugal. Conhecem-se muitos pequenos guias locais, relativos a esta ou aquela falésia, quase sempre elaborados por quem equipou as vias ou quem as conhece muito bem, e que em muitos casos foi o primeiro a encadeá-las. Estes escaladores, por todo o país, estão orgulhosos das vias que equiparam, sendo tradição na escalada que quem encadeia a via pela primeira vez tem o privilégio de lhe dar um nome. Alguns nomes serão elegantes, outros ridículos ou divertidos. Uns e outros são, em todo o caso, uma parte importante da história da escalada. Na concepção deste completo guia, com tantas falésias distintas, foi feito um grande esforço para manter os nomes originais correctos, assim como tentar apresentar a história da escalada em Portugal da forma mais correcta possível.

Este livro cobre todas as falésias onde se pratica maioritariamente escalada desportiva. Nesse terreno as vias são preparadas previamente. Em terreno de aventura os escaladores procuram formas possíveis de escalar uma determinada parede. Depois utilizam fixações removíveis colocadas em fendas ou buracos. Em zonas mais compactas poderá colocar-se uma protecção de expansão num furo feito na rocha, de forma a aumentar a segurança em caso de queda. Na escalada desportiva as vias são todas preparadas previamente, colocando fixações de aço inoxidável nos seus pontos-chave. Nenhuma destas protecções é utilizada para auxiliar a progressão, estão lá apenas para segurança de quem as queira usar. A colocação destas protecções é bastante trabalhosa e demorada e deve ser efectuada com o máximo cuidado e atenção. Tendo as falésias portuguesas sido equipadas ao longo dos últimos 20 anos, haverá muitas pessoas diferentes responsáveis pela sua colocação, muitas vezes pagando-as do seu bolso. Todos nós lhes devemos estar gratos por terem visto as vias antes de elas existirem. Recentemente, várias organizações locais e clubes de escalada, nomeadamente em Sintra e Cascais, juntaram esforços no sentido de equipar falésias inteiras com equipamento de grande qualidade. Devemos agradecer a generosidade dos escaladores e clubes locais por nos darem a oportunidade de usufruirmos dessas vias. Suportando os clubes locais, que mantêm as falésias, estamos a contribuir para o futuro equipamento e a manutenção de todas as falésias de Portugal.

Clima e paisagem

Temos muita sorte por ter em Portugal um clima que nos permite escalar praticamente todo o ano, mesmo quando uma grande parte da Europa enfrenta temperaturas gélidas e vê as suas falésias cobrirem-se de neve. Claro que é difícil escalar no Algarve em pleno Verão, mas é possível encontrar em Portugal locais com boas condições climatéricas praticamente em qualquer altura do ano, desde que se esteja disposto a viajar um pouco. A Serra da Estrela tem bastantes vias clássicas, mas também excelentes e modernos problemas de bloco nos seus esculpidos calhaus que, mesmo no Verão, poderão estar bastante frios ao final do dia. Uma das principais características do clima em Portugal é o vento. Apesar de chover bastante, o que torna a rocha molhada e impraticável, o vento sempre dá uma ajudinha a secar tudo rapidamente. Raramente haverá dias em que o vento não seque a rocha em apenas algumas horas, podendo voltar-se a escalar pouco tempo depois de ter terminado a chuva.

Falésias e escalada

Não há escolas de escalada em Portugal que sejam consideradas Mecas mundiais, o país simplesmente não tem esse tipo de orografia. Mas encontram-se pequenas falésias que são excelentes tanto para iniciados como para escaladores experimentados. No Sul do país, no Algarve, têm a Rocha da Pena, uma adorável falésia de calcário, com cerca de 10 sectores. Cada um deles tem apenas uma mão cheia de vias, mas num local paradisíaco, suficientemente afastado dos locais de veraneio para que se sintam numa total quietude rural. Nas imediações de Lisboa, poderão encontrar uma soberba selecção de pequenas falésias costeiras e de zonas de bloco. Têm ainda o granito branco de Sintra. Aqui a falésia é premiada com uma paisagem de rara beleza, enquanto dentro da floresta poderão encontrar algumas excelentes áreas de boulder em granito. Mais para o Centro de Portugal, têm as paredes de calcário de Montejunto e Redinha, pequenas falésias rodeadas de paisagens fabulosas, em locais muito calmos e aprazíveis. Para os escaladores mais desportivos, existem as falésias

Introdução

MISSÃO CUMPRIDA 7b+, Poios; Ben Moon

do Reguengo, Poios e Buracas, que oferecem vias de grau mais alto, em calcário de excelente qualidade, contudo em locais de grande beleza paisagística. A selvagem zona de bloco da Pedra do Urso é um local a não perder, na Serra da Estrela, relativamente perto da Covilhã. Aqui a temperatura é mais fria, e o granito tem uma soberba aderência. As formas dos blocos são belíssimas, apenas estando ilustrada neste guia uma das suas muitas áreas. Podem-se lá encontrar muitos problemas por resolver, tais como o Cannonball. Venham tentar a vossa sorte. A motivação não vos faltará, apenas a fraqueza da pele impedirá uma semana consecutiva de escalada. Mais para Norte há inúmeras áreas que estão a ser desenvolvidas tendo-se incluído o máximo de informação possível – disponibilizada pela FPME e pelos clubes de escalada locais. Existem também muitas zonas de escalada clássica no Norte de Portugal. Explorem mais fundo e encontrarão sempre mais falésias e blocos.

Esperamos que este guia ajude a encontrar as muitas possibilidades disponíveis para se divertirem escalando em Portugal. Se é um escalador inexperiente, por favor contacte um clube local para saber mais sobre a escalada na sua área. Poderá desconhecer alguns dos procedimentos de segurança que os escaladores utilizam, e pior, poderá pensar que está seguro, não o estando totalmente se não cumprir com aqueles procedimentos. Contactar com outros escaladores é divertido, e20é importante para todos nós manter as falésias sem acidentes, para todos os escaladores que as utilizam. Poderá visitar o site http://www.fpme.org e poderá encontrar todos os clubes locais e conhecer mais gente. Esperamos que este livro vos inspire e conduza para que o vosso nível de escalada melhore. Portugal é apenas uma pequena parte do continente europeu, onde existem milhares de outras falésias. Aprendendo bem as técnicas e procedimentos nas vossas falésias locais, poderão viajar confortavelmente para Espanha, França e outras regiões para desfrutarem de escaladas semelhantes. Divirtam-se.

Os topo-guias Jingo Wobbly são seguramente guias de escalada fora do vulgar. Produzimos topo-guias para escaladores que pretendem o guia mais detalhado e específico para a totalidade de uma região. Podem ser mais do que inestimáveis se não escalar graus elevados e tiver de contar com a informação de escaladores mais experientes. Os nossos livros podem parecer caros se os comparar com topos ordinários, fotocopiados; mas estamos totalmente empenhados em produzir guias atraentes, com centenas de fotografias a cores, e esforçamo-nos por atingir uma qualidade superior de reprodução, impressão e encadernação.

O coração de qualquer topo-guia reside óbviamente nos próprios topos nele contidos, mas temos esperanças de ir muito mais longe com os nossos guias. A nossa série é dedicada a áreas onde normalmente se vai de férias e onde se passa um período de tempo razoável. É por isso que preenchemos qualquer espaço adicional que exista nos guias, com informações relevantes para ocupar os seus dias de descanso ou passar o tempo quando estiver demasiado calor para escalar. Também podemos espicaçar a sua atenção para todas aquelas coisas típicas e encantadoras que qualquer área tem para oferecer, e ilustrar a dimensão cultural e recreativa de que se podem revestir umas férias de escalada. Nunca poderemos reproduzir a riqueza de informação sobre alojamentos fornecida por um posto de turismo local, mas tentamos fazê-lo para todos os parques de campismo disponíveis numa dada área. Tentamos visitar cada um deles e apresentar os seus pontos fortes. Atribuímos cores diferentes aos nossos símbolos de acampamento desde o amarelo que é o mais simples, (tal como o grau das vias de escalada), até ao púrpura que caracteriza uma área de acampamento com piscina assombrosa, relvado exuberante, restaurante

FOTOGENICA 7a, Redinha; Jerry Moffatt

gastronómico, etc... Achamos que os preços são meramente teóricos, já que quase sempre se tem aquilo que se está disposto a pagar.

A navegação através do topo-guia é simples. No verso da capa, há um mapa com todas as escolas e no verso da contra-capa um quadro comparativo das mesmas. Descendo ao longo da frente do livro estão identificadas todas as escolas nele incluídas e na página respectiva está marcada a exposição ao sol com a cor correspondente: amarelo para indicar sol de manhã, vermelho para sol de tarde, e azul para as zonas sem sol. Deste modo poderá encontrar fácilmente qualquer escola no topo-guia, e saber imediatamente se vai assar ou ficar arrepiado – o que é particularmente útil se não conhecer bem a área. Cada escola tem uma introdução em inglês e em português, dirigida a quem a visita pela primeira vez. Habitualmente fornecemos dois mapas: um para o orientar desde o parque de campismo local até ao estacionamento da escola – outro para localizar a escola própriamente dita. Por favor estacione a sua viatura com civismo, respeitando sempre as restrições eventuais ao estacionamento e à escalada propriamente dita.

As paredes são apresentadas sempre da esquerda para a direita, independentemente do lado por onde se faz a aproximação. No rodapé de cada sector existe uma barra de navegação contendo todos os sectores da zona, apresentando-se o sector corrente destacado a amarelo (ou vermelho no caso do Bloco). Para cada sector indicamos também a altura da parede bem como o tempo de aproximação desde o estacionamento e dos sectores adjacentes. Quando o espaço disponível o permite, fazemos um pequeno resumo a título de introdução de carácter geral. Os nossos topo-guias são dos mais detalhados na história da escalada. Cada via é numerada, a sua dificuldade assinalada a cores, e inclui também a localização das protecções e do "top". Os dois símbolos mais importantes que utilizamos no topo-guia são o Jingo vermelho e um Wobbly amarelo, colocados onde exista um passo particularmente duro. O Jingo assinala um passo de força pura em que os miolos têm pouco efeito e só é preciso habilidade para dar à manivela. O Wobbly é usado para ilustrar um passo técnico de grande dificuldade, ou uma secção onde a perícia e a criatividade podem substituir facilmente a força. Também usamos uma regra de alcance para indicar se um passo exige um lançamento longo. Frequentemente usa-se um triângulo de advertência para a altura da primeira protecção: 1 – Pode partir um pulso; 2 – Pode partir as costelas ou as costas; 3 – Provavelmente pode morrer!

O nosso sistema de classificação ao princípio parece complexo, mas é de longe mais informativo e útil para os escaladores visitantes. Todas as vias são classificadas em primeiro lugar com uma cor que assinala o passo mais duro de bloco – na aba traseira interior foi incluída uma tabela de correspondência para os sistemas de graduação Fontainebleau e V. (As cores são também as dos circuitos de Fontainebleau, e sobem de acordo com o mesmo esquema de cores que se usa no esqui.) Cada graduação de bloco tem uma graduação desportiva correspondente. Se uma dada via tiver muitos passos duros do mesmo nível, terá provavelmente um grau superior de desportiva – mas manterá a cor inferior do passo de bloco mais duro (apesar dele parecer ainda mais duro devido ao cansaço). Acreditamos que a maioria dos escaladores gosta deste sistema, porque, frequentemente, a força e a potência necessárias para executar um movimento limita-os mais do que a continuidade. Utilizamos ainda um raio azul adicional para assinalar as vias com movimentos de leitura fácil, presumivelmente agradáveis para escalar "à vista". Usamos um ponto vermelho se a via tiver presas escondidas ou movimentos muito intricados que exijam ensaio prévio. Para cada via indicamos o nome, a qualidade (por meio de estrelas), o comprimento, uma breve descrição e o tipo de calcário que a constitui (a tabela de correspondência faz parte do apêndice e encontra-se no fim do livro). Usamos um sistema de símbolos para representar o estilo de escalada, o ângulo da via, e os passos individuais de bloco mais violentos. Indicamos igualmente o tipo de voo na eventualidade duma queda: Helicóptero – suspenso pela protecção; Caça – voo rápido de 1-2 metros; 747 – voo transatlântico de 2-4 metros; e Foguetão – voo que o pode transportar numa viagem inter galáctica. Também lhe mostramos com frequência o número de expressos que deveria estar relacionado com o indicador de voo. Se houver mais, ou nos enganámos ou a via foi reequipada. Porque os escaladores precisam de planificar a escalada em termos de sol ou sombra, incluímos um indicador de exposição solar (quase) para cada via, mostrando a que horas o sol lhe bate; também foram incluídos outros mais pequenos para informar se a via fica ao sol de manhã ou à tarde – se estiverem verdes significa que poderá ficar à sombra no Verão. Contudo, lembre-se sempre de que todos os guias de escalada representam uma experiência passada e não uma previsão das condições futuras em que as vias se poderão encontrar.

Herzlich Willkommen zu diesem Buch über das Klettern in Portugal. Du scheinst ein eher neugieriger Mensch zu sein – zum Glück, denn Portugal ist nicht bekannt für alpine Gebirge oder gigantische, tiefe Schluchten. Dennoch bietet das Land einige sehr gute kleinere Kletter- und Bouldergebiete, in denen viele Leute bereits herrliche Klettertage verbracht haben. Das wichtigste beim Entdecken eines neuen Klettergebiets ist zu erkennen, wie ergiebig und erlebnisreich es für einen selbst sein wird. Aufgrund seiner Geographie bietet Portugal nicht ‚Kletterkonsum pur' mit massenhaft Felsen an denen ein kilometerlanges Routennetz besteht. Dafür gilt Portugal als eines der besten Urlaubsländer Europas – mit einigen sehr lohnenden Klettergebieten die nahe bei hervorragenden Bade- und Surfstränden gelegen sind. Wer Urlaub machen will, um mit Freunden, der Familie usw. Spaß zu haben und zudem einige schöne Klettertage erleben möchte, sollte unbedingt weiterlesen.

Landschaft und Klima

Portugal ist ein langgestrecktes schmales Land mit einigen Höhenzügen die bis gegen 2000 Meter Meereshöhe aufragen. Da das Wettergeschehen regional stark variiert, ist eine einheitliche Klimabeschreibung nicht möglich. Kurz gesagt ist es warm aber scheinbar nie zu warm, da das Klima stark durch den Atlantik geprägt ist. Jede von den vorherrschenden Westwinden herangetragene Schlechtwetterfront trifft Portugal mit voller Wucht. Da die Wolken jedoch nicht durch ausgeprägte Höhenzüge aufgestaut werden, ziehen die Fronten in der Regel sehr schnell durch und lassen die Sonne wieder herauskommen. Durch die Lage weit im Süden ist die Sonnenstrahlung sehr intensiv und zudem ist es recht windig, sodass alles sehr schnell abtrocknet. Das Wettergeschehen ist insgesamt sehr wechselhaft, ein Nachmittag mit monsunartigen Niederschlägen gefolgt von einem wunderschönen sonnigen Morgen mit perfekten Kletterbedingungen ist keine Seltenheit.

Felsen & Klettern

Es gibt in Portugal keine so gigantischen Felsen wie in Céuse oder Ailefroide aber dennoch bieten die kleineren Felsen hier sehr gute Kletterei und manche Sektoren könnten sich genauso gut in einem der beiden großen Gebiete befinden. Das Spektrum an Felsen im Hinblick auf Lage, Größe und Höhe ist insgesamt sehr groß. Ganz im Süden der Algarve liegt Rocha da Pena, ein wunderschönes langgestrecktes Kalkgebiet, das aus etwa 10 kleineren Massiven besteht. Sie bieten jeweils nur eine Handvoll Routen doch lockt die reizvolle Lage in ländlicher Abgeschiedenheit abseits der stark besuchten Ferienorte. Die Gegend um Lissabon bietet eine faszinierende Auswahl an Boulderfelsen und kleinen Klettergebieten im Kalk der Küstenfelsen und, nach einer kurzen Fahrt ins hügelige Hinterland, dem weißen Granit von Sintra. Hier beeindrucken die Felsen durch ihre schwindelerregende Ausgesetztheit während sich im Wald einige exzellente Boulderblöcke verstecken. Im zentralen Teil Portugals erheben sich die Kalk-Höhenzüge von Montejunto und Redinha die eher niedrige Felsen in reizvoller Landschaft mit wunderschöner Aussicht bieten. Ambitionierte Kletterer werden in den kleinen Schluchten von Reguengo, Poios und Buracas, mit ihren stark überhängenden und sehr schön gelegenen Kalkgebieten, voll auf ihre Kosten kommen. Auf keinen Fall sollte man einen Abstecher in das wildromantische Bouldergebiet Pedra do Urso versäumen, das hoch über der Stadt Covilha in den Bergen der Serra da Estrela liegt. Dort oben ist es immer etwas kühler und die Reibung des Granit an den skurril geformten Blöcken ist perfekt. Wir haben nur eines der vielen Gebiete in den Führer aufgenommen. Es warten noch viele ungelöste Boulderprobleme auf ihre Erstbegehung – wie z.B. der Kanonenkugel-Boulder, kommt und versucht Euer Glück. Der Wille wird sicher da sein doch macht die Haut hier eine Boulderwoche ohne Ruhetage nicht mit. Im Norden des Landes werden viele Gebiete gerade erst erschlossen. Darüber geben wir so viele Information wie möglich, die uns der FPME und lokale portugiesische Kletterclubs zur Verfügung gestellt haben. Im Norden kann man auch klassisch-traditionell klettern und es warten noch viele Felsen und Boulder darauf entdeckt zu werden.

Reisen

Die meisten Leute fliegen nach Portugal und kommen in einer der größeren Städte Lissabon, Oporto oder Faro an. Mietwägen bekommt man an allen Flughäfen problemlos und die Preise sind im Vergleich zu teureren Ländern wir Frankreich erfreulich niedrig. Portugal ist ein sehr hügeliges Land mit vielen alten und kurvenreichen Straßen. Glücklicherweise wurde in den letzen 15 Jahren ein vorbildliches, gebührenpflichtiges Autobahnnetz gebaut, das eine deutlich schnellere Fortbewegung ermöglicht. Kreditkarten werden dort nicht akzeptiert, für einen schnellen Start vom Flughafen weg sollte man mit genug Euro-Bargeld anreisen. Der Verkehr auf den Autobahnen kann bei der Rückfahrt zum Flughafen von Lissabon sehr stark sein – ausreichend Zeitreserven sind einzuplanen. Kleiner Tipp: Sollte die Autobahn völlig verstopft sein, kann es besser sein den äußeren Ring der A9 zu benützen, Lissabon zu umfahren und sich dem Flughafen von der anderen Seite zu nähern. Wer kein Auto mieten möchte, kann mit dem Zug nach Cascais gelangen, örtliche Busse fahren den Campingplatz von Guincho an und weiter zu den Felsen von Farol da Guia. Per Zug kann man auch nach Sintra fahren, da in diesen Bergen jedoch gern schlechtes Wetter hängt ist dies nicht gerade der beste Ausgangspunkt.

Strände & Wellenreiten

Portugal verfügt über sehr viel Küste gegen die der wilde Atlantik donnert. Die Brandung ist im Vergleich zum Mittelmeer viel stärker und daher ist Wellenreiten an den langen goldenen Sandstränden sehr beliebt. Ein Führer ist ratsam, da die Wellen an manchen Stränden recht anspruchsvoll sein können. Weil das Meer eher kühl ist (meiner Meinung nach eiskalt) sind Neoprenanzüge an der Tagesordnung. Es ist windig, sehr windig sogar – 364 Tage im Jahr! Man ist gut beraten das Zelt nach dem Wind auszurichten und wer in der Zeit der Oster- oder Oktoberstürme kommt, sollte ein absolut sturmfestes Zelt dabei haben. Für Wind- und Kitesurfer ist Portugal der beste Ort in ganz Europa. Einige der beliebten Strände sind so breit, dass Stege gebaut wurden, um die Überquerung des Sandes zu erleichtern. In anderen Gebieten findet man kleine beschauliche Buchten, die völlig menschenleer sind. Fast alle Klettergebiete sind innerhalb einer halben Stunde von herrlichen Stränden aus zu erreichen (manche sind sogar nur ein paar Minuten entfernt).

Urlaubstipps

Zur Hauptreisezeit im August ist es in Portugal heiß und es ist sehr viel los. In dieser Jahreszeit muss man sehr früh aufstehen wenn man nicht am Fels verschmoren möchte. Aber selbst dann kann man im Schatten der Wälder von Sintra oder hoch oben in Pedra do Urso hochsommerliches Klettern genießen. Die besten Monate sind Sept.- Okt.& Mai-Juli mit einer sehr angenehmen Urlaubsmischung aus warmem Wetter und guten Kletterbedingungen. In dieser Zeit ist es zudem viel einfacher eine Unterkunft zu buchen und die Campingplätze sind erträglich voll. Im März und April regnet es zwar immer wieder mal aber die ebenfalls auftretenden Schönwetterperioden machen Portugal zu einem durchaus geeigneten Ziel für den Osterurlaub. Von einem Besuch von November bis Februar ist abzuraten – es regnet sehr viel (mit Ausnahme der Algarve vielleicht). Es mangelt sicher nicht an sehr guten Reiseführern die das wunderbare Essen, die Traditionen und die historische Kultur Portugals näher bringen. Die großen Städten bieten eine Menge an Sehenswürdigkeiten, Museen, Konzerte und lebendigen Bars. Die meisten Touristen-Restaurants servieren ausgesprochen leckeres Essen - zu gehobenen Preisen – und oft mit sehr schönem Meeresblick. Doch wird auch der reichlich verwöhnt werden, der sich die Mühe macht und etwas mehr im Landesinneren nach einheimischen Lokalen Ausschau hält. Die meisten Klettergebieten verfügen über nahe gelegene Picknickplätze, was für Familien sehr praktisch ist, die den Familienurlaub mit Sportklettern oder Bouldern verbinden wollen. Sogar mit Kleinkindern lohnt sich ein Besuch.

Jingo Wobbly Topo-Führer sind alles andere als normale Kletterführer. Wir geben Gebietsführer für Kletterer heraus, die für eine ganze Region den ausführlichsten und genauesten Führer wollen. Unsere Bücher sind für all diejenigen besonders wertvoll, die keine Topkletterer sind und von den Informationen erfahrener Kletterer profitieren wollen. Verglichen mit billig zusammenkopierten Topoführern mag unsere Reihe teuer erscheinen aber wir setzen alles daran verlockende Führer mit hunderten von Farbfotos in bester Druckqualität und robuster Bindung herzustellen.

Das Wichtigste an einem Topo-Führer sind natürlich die eigentlichen Topos, doch wir hoffen mit unseren Führern ein gutes Stück weiter zu gehen. Unsere Reihe ist Gegenden gewidmet, in denen man ohnehin gerne Urlaub machen würde und daher dort auch längere Zeit verbringt. Deshalb nutzen wir allen zur Verfügung stehenden Raum in unseren Führern für Informationen über Aktivitäten für Ruhetage – oder für Tage, an denen es zu heiß zum Klettern ist. Wir möchten Eure Aufmerksamkeit auch auf schöne Landschaften lenken und die Fülle an Kultur und Erholungsmöglichkeiten näher bringen, die ein Kletterurlaub bieten kann. Wir können natürlich nicht so umfangreiche Informationen über Übernachtungsmöglichkeiten geben wie das örtliche Fremdenverkehrsamt, legen aber großen Wert darauf, möglichst viele der Campingplätze der jeweiligen Gegend vorzustellen. Wir versuchen alle Campingplätze selbst anzuschauen und ihre Vorzüge darzustellen. Die Ausstattung wird durch die Farbgebung des Campingsymbols verdeutlicht: von gelb für sehr einfach (wie bei den Schwierigkeitsgraden) – bis zu violett für einen Platz mit luxuriösem Swimming-Pool, üppig grünem Gras, gut geführter Gastronomie usw.. Preise anzugeben ist unserer Meinung nach sinnlos, da auf Campingplätzen in der Regel das Preis-Leistungsverhältnis stimmt.

Der Umgang mit unseren Führern ist sehr einfach. Auf der vorderen Umschlagseite befindet sich eine Karte der Klettergebiete und auf der hinteren eine vergleichende Felsübersicht. An den Seitenrändern sind die im Führer beschriebenen Klettergebiete dargestellt und das zu den jeweiligen Seiten gehörende Gebiet ist farblich hervorgehoben. Wir verwenden gelb für Felsen mit Morgensonne, rot für Abendsonne und blau für schattige Felsen. Auf diese Weise findet man sofort jeden Fels im Führer und weiß, ob man dort gegrillt oder vor Kälte zittern wird – besonders nützlich in Gebieten die man nicht gut kennt. Gebietsneulinge finden für jedes Klettergebiet eine Einführung auf Englisch und Portugiesisch. Es folgen 2 Karten; eine weist den Weg vom örtlichen Campingplatz zum Parkplatz des Klettergebiets und die andere zeigt den Zustieg zum Fels. Bitte parkt mit Bedacht und respektiert eventuell geltende Kletter- und Parkplatzregelungen.

Wir stellen jedes Klettergebiet von links nach rechts vor, ganz gleich von welcher Seite der Zugang erfolgt. Am Fuß jeden Topos sind auf einer Orientierungsleiste alle Sektoren des Gebiets dargestellt und der zum jeweiligen Topo gehörende Sektor ist in Gelb hinterlegt (in Rot bei Bouldergebieten). Das Topo enthält eine kurze Übersicht zur Felshöhe des Sektors, zur Zustiegszeit und welche Sektoren beiderseits angrenzen. Steht genügend Platz zur Verfügung, findet sich zudem eine kurze allgemeine Beschreibung des Felscharakters. Unsere Topos gehören zu den genauesten die es jemals gab. Für jede Route wird über Farben die Schwierigkeit dargestellt, die Position der Bohrhaken und ob am Ausstieg umgelenkt oder abgeseilt wird. Die zwei wichtigsten Symbole die wir im Führer verwenden sind der rote Jingo und der gelbe Wobbly. Sie signalisieren einen besonders schweren Zug. Jingo steht dabei für rohe Kraft und wenig Köpfchen, wenn es eben nur darum geht brachial durchzureißen. Wobbly dagegen taucht dann auf, wenn ein technisch anspruchsvoller Zug zu meistern ist oder eine Passage, in der rohe Kraft durch Bewegungsgeschick und Einfallsreichtum ausgeglichen werden kann. Ein symbolischer Reichweiten-Maßstab weist auf ausgeprägte Längenzüge hin. Manche Einstiege sind mit einem Warndreieck markiert, das vor einem hoch angebrachten ersten Haken warnt; 1 - Gefahr eines Handgelenkbruchs; 2 – Gefahr von Rippen- oder Wirbelsäulenbruch; 3 – möglicherweise fatal!

Unser Bewertungssystem macht zunächst einen komplizierten Eindruck ist aber für ortsfremde Kletterer sehr informativ und hilfreich. Über eine Farbskala wird zunächst die schwerste Einzelstelle jeder Route bewertet – in der hinteren Umschlagseite werden die entsprechenden Fontainebleau- und V-Bewertungen dargestellt. (Die Farben entsprechen denen der Fontainebleau-Parcours und dieselbe Rangfolge wird z.B. auch bei Skipisten verwendet). Jeder Boulderbewertung entspricht ein bestimmter Sportkletter-Schwierigkeitsgrad. Hat eine Route viele ungefähr gleichschwere Züge fällt die Sportkletterbewertung etwas höher aus – die Farbbewertung der Boulderschwierigkeit dagegen etwas leichter (obwohl es sich schwerer anführt weil man müde wird). Unserer Meinung nach mögen die meisten Kletterer diese Art der Kletterei, weil sie in der Regel eher durch ihre Maximalkraft als durch ihre Ausdauer limitiert sind. Der blaue Blitz kennzeichnet eine Route mit übersichtlicher Kletterei, die gut onsight zu klettern ist. Mit dem Rotpunkt-Symbol dagegen werden Routen mit versteckten Griffen oder komplizierter Kletterei markiert, die zunächst ausgecheckt werden müssen. Für jede Route listen wir den Namen auf, Sterne für die Schönheit, die Routenlänge, eine kurze Beschreibung und die Art des Kalksteins in dem sie sich befindet (Legende im Anhang). Über ein System an Symbolen beschreiben wir für jede Route die Art der Kletterei, die Steilheit der Wand und ob knallharte Einzelstellen lauern. Zudem wird die Flughöhe im Fall eines Sturzes angezeigt; Helikopter – kleiner Hopfer am Haken; Kampfflugzeug – ein 1-2 Meter Kurzflug ist möglich; 747 – ein transatlantischen 2-4 Meter Flug droht; die Rakete bedeutet, dass der Flug mit einer Reise ins Jenseits enden könnte. Häufig ist auch die Anzahl der Expressschlingen angegeben, die mit der Flugbewertung zusammenhängen sollte. Hat eine Route mehr Haken als angegeben, haben wir uns entweder vertan oder die Route wurde saniert. Da Kletterer ihre Tagesplanung sehr stark vom Sonnenstand abhängig machen, wird für (fast) jede Route die Zeit der Besonnung angegeben. Zudem zeigt ein Symbol, ob der Fels Morgen- oder Nachmittagssonne erhält; grüne Farbe bedeutet, dass man dort selbst im Sommer im Schatten klettert. Bei alledem sollte man jedoch nicht vergessen, dass Kletterführer Erfahrungen der Vergangenheit wiedergeben und sicher nicht zukünftige Entwicklungen vorhersagen können!

LA GRANDE 7c, Reguengo do Fétal; Ben Moon

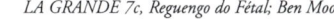

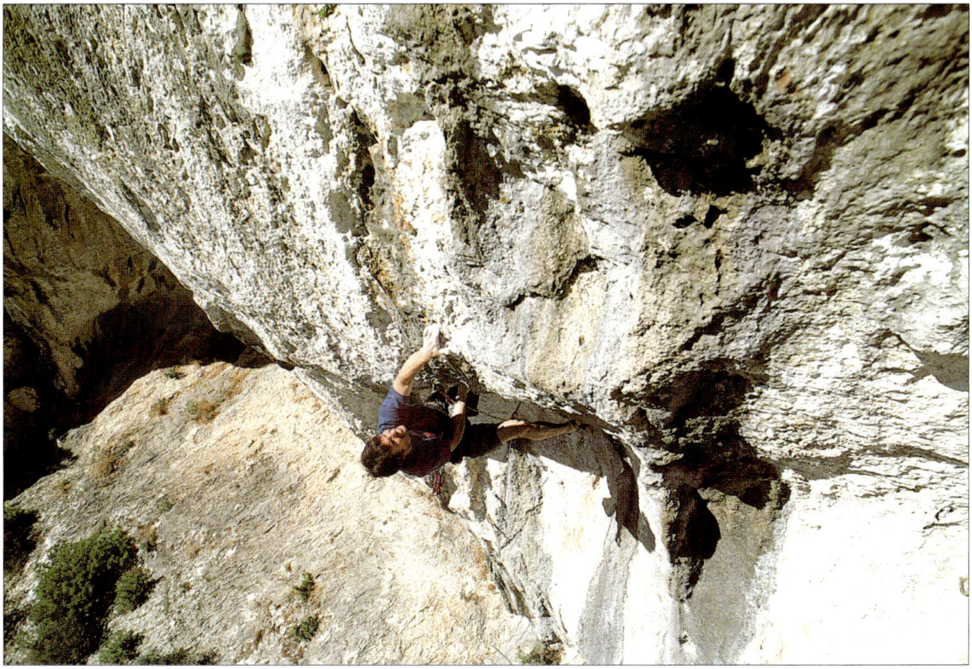

R. da PENA
SAGRES
FENDA-OUTAO
FAROL-GUIA
MEXILHOEIRO
SINTRA
CAPUCHOS
PENINHA
MALVEIRA-CAV
MONTEJUNTO
REGUENGO
REDINHA
POIOS
BURACAS
PEDRA-URSO
P. GARCIA

Vous êtes en possession du nouveau guide Jingo-Wobbly qui vous invite à découvrir les sites d'escalade du Portugal. C'est un pays qui n'offre pas de grandes montagnes ou de canyons gigantesques mais il a cependant une bonne sélection de petites falaises et des zones de blocs intéressantes. Tous les grimpeurs quel que soit leur niveau prendront du plaisir à grimper au Portugal puisque l'escalade y est très variée. Le Portugal n'est pas un pays qui offre des milliers et des milliers de voies mais c'est une des meilleures destinations d'Europe pour passer des vacances agréables. Les zones d'escalade sont superbes et sont situées très proches de plages magnifiques. Alors si vous souhaitez passer des vacances sympas avec votre famille ou vos amis et grimper sur de beaux sites, continuez votre lecture.

REGUENGO DO FÉTAL

Paysage et climat

Le Portugal est un pays vallonné et tout en longueur, avec quelques montagnes qui atteignent une altitude de 2000 mètres. Le temps y est très changeant et il est donc impossible de donner une tendance générale du climat. En un mot le temps est chaud mais jamais trop chaud et est largement influencé par l'Océan Atlantique. Tout front venant de l'Ouest apporte en général du mauvais temps. Cependant puisque le pays est largement ouvert sur l'Atlantique, le mauvais temps a tendance à passer rapidement et le soleil à revenir très vite. Le Portugal est situé très au sud ce qui lui permet de recevoir les rayons d'un soleil chaud qui sèchent tout rapidement. Il y a également beaucoup de vent ce qui aide le séchage après la pluie. Le temps change si souvent que vous pouvez voir la pluie de mousson un après-midi et un glorieux soleil avec des conditions d'escalade parfaites le matin suivant.

Falaises et escalade

Vous ne trouverez pas au Portugal de falaises gigantesques comme celles de Ceuse ou d'Ailfefroide, il y a cependant de nombreuses petites falaises de très bonne qualité. Tout au sud de l'Algarve il y a Rocha da Pena qui est une crête de calcaire avec environ 10 petits sites différents. Il y a seulement quelques voies sur chacun d'entre eux, mais ils sont situés dans un lieu idyllique et calme. Autour de Lisbonne, il y a une très bonne sélection de blocs de calcaire côtier et des petites falaises. Un peu plus haut dans les collines, vous trouverez le granite blanc de Sintra. Ici la falaise a une très bonne exposition et dans les bois il y a quelques blocs de granite qui sont excellents. Plus au centre du Portugal il y a les hautes crêtes de calcaire de Montejunto et Redinha, petites falaises avec des vues magnifiques et un emplacement idéal. Pour les grimpeurs de plus haut niveau les gorges de Reguengo, Pojos et Buracas offrent des voies abruptes sur un calcaire de très bonne qualité dans un cadre pittoresque. Il ne faut pas manquer bien sur la zone de blocs de Pedra do Urso, située au-dessus de la ville de Covilha dans les montagnes de Serra da Estrala. Le granite offre une bonne adhérence du fait des températures plus fraîches. Les blocs ont des formes superbes et offrent de nombreux problèmes - seulement une partie de cette zone est décrite dans ce guide. Il reste de nombreux problèmes non résolus comme le bloc au nom de Cannonball par exemple que vous devez absolument visiter et tester. Plus au nord de nombreuses zones sont en cours de développement et nous avons essayé de donner autant d'information que possible les concernant grâce à la FPME et aux clubsd'escalade locaux. Enfin au nord il y a quelques zones qui offrent un type d'escalade plus traditionnel etavec un peu d'exploration vous découvrirez encore plus de falaises et de blocs à grimper.

Voyage

Le plus facile est de voyager par avion à destination de Lisbonne, Porto ou Faro. Vous pouvez louer une voiture facilement depuis ces aéroports et les prix de location sont en général plutôt bons marchés. Le Portugal est un pays vallonné avec des routes assez anciennes et pleines de virage. Heureusement depuis les 15 dernières années un réseau d'autoroutes payantes a été construit ce qui permet de couvrir de longues distances rapidement et facilement. Les péages ne prennent pas les cartes de crédit alors assurez-vous d'avoir assez de liquide lorsque vous quittez l'aéroport. Si vous retournez a l'aéroport de Lisbonne à la fin de vos vacances prévoyez de partir très tôt. La circulation peut en effet être très dense et vous faire rater votre avion. Un conseil s'il y a un bouchon, prenez le périphérique A9 pour contourner la ville et trouvez une autre route pour l'aéroport. Pour ceux qui ne peuvent pas ou ne souhaitent pas louer de voiture, vous pouvez prendre le train pour aller à Cascais et les bus jusqu'au camping de Guincho pour la falaise de Farol da Guia, Les trains vont également à Sintra. Cependant faites attention, les montagnes peuvent attirer du mauvais temps et il n'estdonc pas conseillé de camper près d'elles.

Plages et surf

Le Portugal a une ligne côtière tres étendue qui est exposée aux ravages de l'Atlantique. L'Océan développe de grandes vagues et surfer le long des plages de sable doré est très en vogue. Faites attention l'Océan est dangereux, certaines vagues sont énormes et demandent un peu d'expérience. La mer est fraîche (froide selon moi) et une combinaison est de rigueur. Le vent souffle 364 jours de l'année et nous vous conseillons donc de le prendre en considération avant de placer votre tente. Si vous venez durant les grands vents de Pâques et d'octobre, n'oubliez pas d'apporter de quoi protéger votre tente. Si vous aimez pratiquer la planche à voile alors le Portugal est la meilleure destination d'Europe. Quelques-unes des plages les plus populaires sont gigantesques et ont des sentiers pédestres au-dessus du sable pour aller jusqu'à la mer. Vous trouverez à certains endroits des petites criques totalement désertes et donc tranquilles. La majorité des sites d'escalade sont situés à environ une demi-heure des plus belles plages (certains sont seulement à quelques minutes de distance).

Appréciez vos vacances

Il fait très chaud au Portugal durant le mois d'août et de nombreux touristes viennent en vacances à cette période. Il vous faut vous lever tôt pour ne pas griller sur le rocher à cette époque de l'année. Cependant il est possible de grimper sous la forêt dense de Sintra ou sur les hauteurs de Pedra do Urso. Septembre-octobre et mai-juin-juillet sont les meilleurs mois pour une visite puisque vous pouvez apprécier un temps chaud et de bonnes conditions d'escalade. Durant ces mois, il est également plus facile de trouver un hébergement et de la place aux terrains de camping. Durant les mois de mars et d'avril, il pleut beaucoup plus mais il y a également de belles périodes ensoleillées et de beau temps, c'est pourquoi c'est une destination à conseiller pour les vacances de Pâques. La période de novembre à février n'est pas conseillée puisqu'il pleut beaucoup. Vous trouverez en vente de nombreux guides de voyage sur le Portugal qui vous donneront toute l'information nécessaire concernant l'histoire du pays, la culture et les plats traditionnels. Les grandes villes ont beaucoup à offrir avec de nombreux monuments, musées, concerts et des bars très animés. La majorité des restaurants touristiques sont somptueux et ont souvent de superbes vues sur la mer. Cependant recherchez les restaurants locaux à l'intérieur du pays et vous serez récompensé. Les falaises ont en général des aires de pique-nique qui sont idéales pour une famille souhaitant faire des voies et du bloc, et même avec des tous petits, vous pouvez pleinement apprécier votre visite.

MEXILHOEIRO

Les topo-guides Jingo Wobbly ne sont pas des guides d'escalade ordinaires. Nous produisons des guides pour les grimpeurs qui désirent avoir le plus d'information possible pour un pays ou une zone d'escalade précise. Ces guides peuvent être d'une aide inestimable lors d'une première visite. Ils peuvent peut-être paraître chers comparés à certains topos, mais nous sommes engagés à produire des guides attrayants avec des centaines de photos couleur, une excellente qualité d'impression et une reliure solide.

Les guides d'escalade offrent en général d'excellents topos cependant nous espérons aller un peu plus loin avec nos livres en offrant une information plus détaillée. Notre série de guides est dédiée à des zones d'escalade qui sont également touristiques. Ainsi nous donnons de nombreux renseignements sur les choses à faire où à visiter durant les jours de repos ou lorsqu'il fait trop chaud pour grimper. Concernant l'hébergement, nous ne pouvons pas reproduire l'ampleur de l'information donnée par les syndicats d'initiative ou les offices du tourisme. Cependant nous essayons de donner autant de détails que possible sur les endroits où camper. Nous visitons nous-mêmes chaque camping et indiquons leurs points forts. Les icônes ont des couleurs différentes : du jaune pour les campings les plus simples jusqu'au violet pour les campings les plus luxueux avec piscine, restaurant, etc. Les prix sont académiques puisqu'en général le niveau de confort équivaut au prix que vous payez.

Naviguer autour du guide est très simple, il y a une carte indiquant tous les lieux d'escalade à l'intérieur de la couverture avant et un tableau comparant les falaises à l'intérieur de la couverture arrière. Tout le long du bord du livre sont indiquées les différentes zones incluses dans le guide et sur les pages appropriées ces zones sont en couleur. Nous utilisons le jaune pour indiquer la présence du soleil le matin, le rouge pour le soleil l'après-midi et le bleu s'il n'y a pas de soleil. Vous pouvez ainsi trouver une falaise dans le guide et savoir immédiatement si vous aurez chaud ou froid - d'autant plus pratique si vous ne connaissez pas très bien la zone d'escalade. Chaque falaise a une introduction en anglais et en portugais. Vous trouverez également 2 cartes : la première montre le parking depuis le camping pour la falaise indiquée, la seconde permet de localiser la falaise. S'il vous plait garez votre voiture avec considération et respectez les notices et les restrictions de parking et d'escalade qui sont en place.

Chaque falaise est présentée de la gauche vers la roite quelle que soit la marche d'approche. En bas de haque topo il y a une barre de navigation qui indique ous les secteurs de la falaise et le topo approprié st indiqué en jaune (en rouge pour l'escalade à loc). Le topo donne également une indication de la auteur de la falaise pour chaque secteur et le temps 'approche pour aller au parking et aux autres ecteurs. Si nous avons suffisamment de place nous onnons une brève introduction pour chaque topo. os topos sont probablement les plus détaillés de tous les guides l'escalade. Chaque voie est numérotée, la difficulté est illustrée en couleur et le positionnement des goujons et des relais en fin de voie est également indiqué. Les deux icônes les plus importants utilisés dans le guide sont le Jingo en rouge et le Wobbly en jaune. Ils sont placés là où les mouvements sont les plus difficiles. Jingo illustre l'utilisation de la force et non du cerveau. Wobbly est utilisé pour illustrer un mouvement d'une grande difficulté technique ou une section où l'adresse et l'ingéniosité peuvent remplacer la force. Nous utilisons également une règle pour indiquer si une prise est difficile à atteindre. Vous trouverez souvent en bas de page un triangle d'avertissement vous indiquant d'être prudent en début de voie du fait du haut placement du premier goujon (en cas de chute) : 1-vous risquez de casser un poignet ; 2-vous risquez de casser des côtes ; 3-danger de mort !

Notre système de cotation paraît au premier abord omplexe, mais il est informatif et pratique pour la ajorité des grimpeurs. Toutes les voies sont cotées out d'abord par couleur afin de montrer le mouvement e plus difficile - il y a un index à l'intérieur du olet qui montre la cotation correspondante selon les ystèmes de Fontainebleau et V (les couleurs sont galement les mêmes que celles que vous trouvez sur es circuits de Fontainebleau et vont en ordre roissant en suivant les couleurs utilisées pour les istes de ski). Chaque cotation de bloc a une cotation quivalente d'escalade sportive. Si la voie a de ombreux mouvements difficiles du même type alors elle ura probablement une plus haute cotation mais btiendra la couleur de base pour le mouvement le plus ur. Nous savons par expérience que de nombreux rimpeurs apprécient ce système car en général ils ont plutôt limités par la force et la puissance lutôt que par l'endurance. Nous utilisons un éclair leu si la voie a des mouvements qui sont faciles à eviner et qu'elle peut se faire a vu. Nous utilisons ne icône avec un point rouge si la voie a des prises achées ou des mouvements difficiles qui doivent être travaillés. Nous donnons à chaque voie son nom, des étoiles pour la qualité, sa longueur, une brève description et le type de calcaire (c. f. annexe a la fin du livre). Nous utilisons un système d'icônes pour représenter le style d'escalade pour chaque voie, l'angle et les mouvements très difficiles voir impossibles. Nous donnons également une indication du vol en cas de chute : hélicoptère-chute au niveau du goujon ; avion de chasse-chute rapide d'un ou deux mètres ; 747-vol transatlantique de deux ou quatre mètres ; fusée-vol qui peut vous emmener en voyage galactique. Nous essayons également d'indiquer le nombre de dégaines nécessaires. Si vous découvrez qu'il vous en faut plus que ce qui est indiqué, alors c'est que nous avons fait une erreur ou que la voie a été de nouveau équipée depuis notre visite. Nous donnons une indication de l'ensoleillement pour chaque voie et l'heure à laquelle le soleil est sur la voie. Nous avons des indicateurs pour le soleil le matin et le soleil l'après-midi et si ceux-ci ont du vert cela signifie que vous serez à l'ombre en été. Enfin rappelez-vous toujours que les guides d'escalade donnent une représentation de l'expérience que leurs auteurs ont eue mais ne donnent jamais une prédiction des conditions futures des voies

LE BLOC TRÉS SIMPLE - Font 7c, Cavalo; André Neres

Bienvenido a éste libro sobre escalada en Portugal. Usted debe de ser alguien estimulado por la curiosidad - afortunadamente, porque Portugal no es famoso por ningunos Alpes o desfiladeros gigantes y profundos. Sin embargo, tiene con certeza algunos riscos pequeños y áreas de búlder que valen la pena. Estos han dado mucha diversión y escaladas muy placenteras para mucha gente. La forma más apropiada de conseguir conocer un área dada, es mirarla en la perspectiva correcta para uno mismo, y apreciar en cuanto será amplia y útil para usted. Portugal no es un destino de escalada "pleno", en donde se tiene kilómetros y kilómetros de vías. Simplemente no tiene el maquillaje geográfico necesario para producir tales riscos. Portugal por otro lado, es uno de los mejores destinos de vacaciones de toda Europa, con algunas áreas de escalada muy respetables, distando un paso de playas magníficas y locales de "surf". Si usted quiere ir de vacaciones, pasar un buen rato con sus amigos, familia, etc., y también hacer unas escaladas de maravilla, entonces siga leyendo.

Paisaje y clima

Portugal es un país estrecho de suelo accidentado, con una cadena de "montes" hasta casi los 2000 metros. Tiene una gran variedad de padrones meteorológicos, y no se puede dar una evaluación climática general. En pocas palabras, es caliente, pero aparentemente nunca demasiado, y es muy influenciado por el Océano Atlántico. Cualquier frente que se origine en el viento oeste dominante va a despejar en Portugal. Sin embargo, porque está muy abierto al Atlántico, el mal tiempo tiene la tendencia a pasar muy pronto y volver el sol enseguida. Usted esta también muy a sur por lo que el sol es fuerte y lo seca todo espléndidamente rápido. También es un lugar ventoso, en donde uno puede tener lluvia de monzones por la tarde y un sol glorioso y condiciones de escalada perfectas en la mañana siguiente.

Riscos y escaladas

No hay ningunos riscos gigantes en Portugal como en Céuse o Ailefroide, pero si hay pequeños riscos de muy alta calidad, y sectores que no quedarían muy fuera del lugar, en cualquiera de esos grandes riscos. Usted tendrá un saco completamente mezclado de localizaciones y alturas. En él extremo sur del Algarve está la Rocha da Pena, que es una encantadora cresta de caliza con cerca de 10 pequeños contra fuertes distintos. Sólo con una mano llena de vías en cada uno, pero con una localización preciosa que está suficientemente lejos de los centros turísticos de vacaciones muy abarrotados para quedarse en una quietud rural completa. Alrededor de Lisboa, hay una magnifica variedad de búlderes costeros de caliza y pequeños riscos junto al mar; muy cerca, en las colinas, está el granito blanco de Sintra. Aquí el risco ha sido recompensado con una exposición asombrosa, mientras ocultos en la cubierta de la floresta existen muchos búlderes de granito excelente. En la parte más central de Portugal, están las crestas altas de caliza de Montejunto y Redinha, riscos cortos con vistas bonitas y localizaciones preciosas. Para los escaladores más duros y agresivos, las pequeñas gargantas de Reguengo, Poios y Buracas, ofrecen vías muy empinadas en caliza de gran calidad, y mucho más en el aspecto escénico. A no perder naturalmente es el área salvaje de búlder de la Pedra do Urso, bien arriba de la ciudad de Covilha en las montañas de la Serra da Estrela. La temperatura es más fresca, y el granito tiene una adherencia excelente. La forma de los bloques es muy bonita y solo incluimos una de las muchas áreas en esta guía. Quedan muchos problemas por resolver, tales como el búlder Cannonball, venga usted e intente su suerte en él. La voluntad estará allí y sólo su piel le impedirá escalar sin parar por una semana. Más para Norte hay muchas otras áreas en desarrollo, y hemos incluido tanta información cuanta posible, que nos ha sido facilitada por FPME y por los clubes de escalada portugueses locales. También existen áreas de escalada clásica tradicional en el Norte del país; lleve usted sus exploraciones más lejos y descubra aún riscos y búlderes para escalar.

Viaje

Mucha gente decidirá volar para Portugal y utilizar los aeropuertos de las ciudades mayores de Lisboa, Porto y Faro. Puede alquilar un coche muy fácilmente en todos estos aeropuertos y el precio se compara muy favorablemente con el de los países más caros como Francia. Portugal es un país de colinas, y hay muchas carreteras viejas serpenteando sin parar. Afortunadamente, durante los últimos 15 años, una magnifica red de auto-vías con peaje han sido construidas, permitiendo la cobertura fácil de largas distancias. Los peajes no aceptan tarjetas de crédito, por eso asegúrese que esta cargado con euros en moneda, para escaparse pronto del aeropuerto. El tráfico en las auto-vías, para volver al aeropuerto de Lisboa, puede ser muy intenso, por eso cuente con bastante tiempo. Consejo: si hay un atasco, considere utilizar la auto-vía circular exterior A9, para coger otra carretera alrededor de la ciudad. Para quienes no pueda alquilar un coche, hay trenes para Cascais y buses locales para el camping de Guincho, más allá del risco del Farol da Guia. También hay trenes para Sintra, pero la montaña puede atraer tiempo dudoso, y por eso no es el mejor lugar base.

Playas y surf

Portugal tiene una enorme extensión de costa que se expone a la acción destructiva del Atlántico, y no es nada como el Mediterráneo. Tiene olas muy grandes y el surf es muy popular en las largas y doradas playas de arena. Mire a su guía de surf porque algunas de estas olas son demasiado grandes para llevar. El mar es frío (helado para mí), y los trajes secos están en la orden del día. ¡El viento sopla, si sopla- 364 días al año! Le aconsejamos para montar su tienda respetando el viento, y se viene durante los vendavales de la Pascua o Octubre, traiga una significativa "erección" a prueba de vendaval. Si esta en una de Windsurf o Kitesurf, es este lugar numero uno de toda Europa. Algunas de las playas más populares son muy grandes y tienen pasillos sobre arena para llegar al mar. En otras áreas, usted podrá encontrar pequeñas calas, completamente desiertas. Casi todas las áreas de escalada están a una media hora de excelentes playas (algunas solamente algunos minutos).

Disfrutando sus vacaciones

Portugal es muy caliente en el principal mes de vacaciones de Agosto, y es muy abarrotado. Tiene que levantarse muy temprano para no asarse en la roca en esta época del año. Pero, así mismo por debajo de la cubierta de la floresta de Sintra o en las alturas de Pedra do Urso, usted puede aún disfrutar de su actividad de verano. Septiembre-Octubre y Mayo-Julio son los mejores meses para visitar y tener una buena combinación de tiempo caliente y buenos días de escalada. Durante esta época, descubrirá que es muy fácil reservar alojamiento, y los campings estarán "agradablemente" abarrotados. Durante Marzo y Abril tendrá por supuesto mucho más lluvia pero también tendrá algunos periodos de buen tiempo, por eso es un destino práctico para la Pascua. De Noviembre hasta Febrero no se recomienda - estará realmente mojado (sin embargo puede ser que no en Algarve). No hay falta de excelentes guías de viaje, que le ayudarán a apreciar la maravillosa comida, tradiciones y cultura histórica de Portugal. Las ciudades grandes tienen mucho que ver, museos para visitar, conciertos y bares animados. Muchos restaurantes turísticos son espléndidos, y tienen muchas veces vista sobre el mar; pero busque algunos más para el interior, y será fabulosamente recompensado. Muchos de los riscos tienen áreas de comida en el campo muy cerca, y son bastante prácticos para una familia que quiera hacer un poco de deporte de escalada y búlder. Mismo con niños muy pequeños, podrá llevarse mucho de una visita aquí.

CHAMINÉ 6a, Farol da Guia; Miguel Suarez

IMPRÓPRIO PARA CONSUMO 6c, Pedra do Urso; Ben Moon

Las topo-guías Jingo Wobbly son seguramente las guías de escalada fuera de lo normal. Producimos topo-guías para escaladores que quieren la guía más detallada y específica para la totalidad de una región. Pueden ser más que inestimables si no escala grados elevados y tuviera que confiar en la información de los escaladores más experimentados. Nuestros libros pueden parecer caros si los comparan con topos ordinarias, fotocopiadas, pero estamos totalmente empeñados en producir guías atrayentes, con centenas de fotografías en color y nos esforzamos por conseguir una calidad superior de reproducción, impresión y encuadernación.

El corazón de cualquier topo-guía reside obviamente en los propios topos en ella contenidos, pero tenemos esperanzas de ir mucho más lejos con estas guías. Nuestra serie esta dedicada a las áreas en donde normalmente se va de vacaciones y donde se pasa un periodo de tiempo razonable. Es por eso que llenamos cualquier espacio adicional que exista en las guías, con informaciones relevantes para ocupar sus días de descanso o pasar el tiempo cuando tuviera demasiado calor para escalar. También podemos picotear a su atención para todas aquellas cosas típicas y encantadoras que cualquier área tiene para ofrecer, e ilustrar la dimensión cultural y recreativa de que se pueden revestir unas vacaciones de escalada. Nunca podremos reproducir la riqueza de información sobre alojamientos suministrada por un puesto de turismo local, pero intentamos hacerlo para todos los parques de camping disponibles en un área dada. Intentamos visitar cada uno de ellos y presentar sus puntos fuertes. Atribuimos colores diferentes a nuestros símbolos de acampada desde el amarillo que es más simple, (como el grado de las vías de escalada), hasta al púrpura que caracteriza un área de acampada con piscina asombrosa, césped exuberante, restaurante gastronómico, etc. Nos parece que los precios son meramente teóricos, una vez que casi siempre se tiene lo que uno se dispone a pagar.

La navegación a través de la topo-guía es simple. En el reverso de la portada, hay un mapa con todas las escuelas y en la contraportada un cuadro comparativo de las mismas. Descendiendo al largo de la frente del libro están indicadas todas las escuelas en él incluidas y en la página respectiva está marcada la exposición al sol con el color correspondiente: amarillo para indicar sol por la mañana, rojo para sol por la tarde, y azul para zonas sin sol. De esta manera podrá encontrar fácilmente cualquier escuela en la topo-guía, saber inmediatamente si se va asar o quedar helado – lo que es particularmente útil si no conoce bien el área. Cada escuela tiene una introducción en ingles y en portugués, dirigida a quienes la visita por primera vez. Habitualmente ofrecemos dos mapas: uno para lo conducir desde el camping local hasta el aparcamiento de la escuela – otro para localizar la escuela en si. Por favor aparque su coche con civismo, respetando siempre las restricciones eventuales al aparcamiento y a la escalada. Las paredes son presentadas siempre de la izquierda a la derecha, independiente del lado donde se hace la aproximación. En el rodapié de cada sector existe una barra de navegación conteniendo todos los sectores de la zona, presentándose el sector corriente destacado en amarillo (o rojo en caso de búlder). Para cada sector indicamos también la altura de la pared bien como el tiempo de aproximación desde el aparcamiento y de los sectores adyacentes. Cuando el espacio disponible lo permita, hacemos un pequeño resume a título de introducción de carácter general.

Nuestras topo-guías son de las más detalladas en la historia de escalada. Cada vía esta numerada, su dificultad señalada en colores, incluye también la localización de las protecciones y del tope. Los dos símbolos más importantes que utilizamos en la topo-guía son el Jingo rojo y un Wobbly amarillo, colocados en donde exista un paso particularmente duro. El Jingo señala un paso de fuerza pura en que los sesos tienen poco efecto y solo es necesaria habilidad para darle a la manivela. El Wobbly es usado para ilustrar un paso técnico de gran dificultad, o una sección donde la pericia y la creatividad pueden sustituir fácilmente la fuerza. También usamos una regla de alcance para indicar si un paso exige un lanzamiento largo. Frecuentemente se usa un triangulo de advertencia para la altura de la primera protección:1- Se puede partir una muñeca; 2- Se puede partir las costillas o la espalda; 3- ¡Probablemente se puede morir!

Nuestro sistema de clasificación al inicio parece complejo, pero es de lejos más informativo y útil para los escaladores visitantes. Todas las vías están clasificadas en primer lugar con un color que señala el paso más duro de bloque – en la haba trasera interior ha sido incluida una tabla de correspondencia para los sistemas de graduación Fontainebleau y V. (Los colores son también los de los circuitos de Fontainebleau, y suben de acuerdo con los mismos esquemas de colores que se usan en él esquí). Cada graduación de bloque tiene una graduación deportiva correspondiente. Se una vía dada tuviera muchos pasos duros del mismo nivel, tendrá probablemente un grado superior deportivo – más mantendrá el color inferior del paso de bloque más duro (a pesar de parecer aún más duro debido al cansancio). Acreditamos que a la mayoría de los escaladores les gusta este sistema, porque, frecuentemente, la fuerza y la potencia necesarias para ejecutar un movimiento los limita más que la continuidad. Utilizamos además un rayo azul adicional para señalar las vías con movimientos de lectura fácil, presumiblemente agradables para escalar "a vista". Usamos un punto rojo si la vía tuviera presas escondidas o movimientos muy intricados que exijan ensayo previo. Para cada vía indicamos su nombre, la calidad (con estrellas), el largo, una breve descripción y el tipo de caliza que la constituye (la tabla de correspondencia haz parte del apéndice y se encuentra al final del libro). Usamos un sistema de símbolos para representar el estilo de escalada, el ángulo de la vía, y los pasos individuales de bloque más violentos. Indicamos igualmente el tipo de vuelo en la eventualidad de una caída: Helicóptero- suspenso por la protección; caza- vuelo rápido de 1-2 metros; 747- vuelo transatlántico de 2-4 metros; y Cohete- vuelo que lo puede transportar en un viaje intergaláctico. También le mostramos con frecuencia el número de cintas que deberían estar relacionadas con el indicador de vuelo. Si hubiera más, o nos engañamos o la vía ha sido re-equipada. Porque los escaladores necesitan planificar la escalada en términos de sol o sombra, incluimos un indicador de exposición solar (casi) para cada vía, mostrando a que hora el sol golpea; también han sido incluidos otros más pequeños para informar si una vía queda al sol por la mañana o por la tarde- si estuvieran verdes significa que podrá quedar en la sombra en el verano. Sin embargo, acuérdese siempre de que todas las guías de escalada representan una experiencia pasada y no una previsión de las condiciones futuras en que las vías se pondrán encontrar.

PÊRA DOCE 7a, Rocha da Pena; Antonio Gonzales Gonzales

The Southern end of Portugal is known as the Algarve, and is very nicely described as a land of contrasts. The coastline has exceptional variations in theme; from lovely sandy beaches in a quiet glimmering setting, to high rise holiday flats designed by prison architects – accompanied by restaurants that pride themselves with limited menus in giant lettering, need I say more! The excellent motorway along the Algarve is completely essential to travel any distance, at any appreciable speed; and separates the modern developments from the rural countryside. If you approach Rocha da Pena from the local major town of Loulé, your spirits will lift within minutes, as you thankfully exit the fume infested urban sprawl, for glorious olive groves and open quiet roads. You have to pass some 20km over a complete range of hills to reach the quiet village of Salir, and then onto Rocha da Pena, hidden away in the Serra do Caldeirão. This is its saving grace from too much popularity. The local area around Pena has been nationally designated as a protected area, which is fantastic, and the whole area has marked footpaths and a host of wildlife to observe. Climbing is allowed but I must express the intense wishes of everyone, to keep the area spotlessly clean and tidy.

Rocha da Pena itself, is a long ridge of some 2-3 kilometres with some 20 different separated rock buttresses, rising out of trees and small (but sharp pronged) undergrowth. I can recommend that you do the approach walk for the further away cliffs – with long thick trousers for sure. The limestone is really varied, and includes the typical Spanish red rock (that polishes quickly), smaller pockets like Finale and Buoux, and more classical provence style of long cracks. The whole ridge faces south and gets the full blast of the sun – which in summer is intense. Cliffs at the left end however do stay in the shade until midday, and some of the others start to get shade after 3pm – so there is some hope. Also because the cliffs are set up quite high, they often do attract any wind that is around, and make it almost bearable. Not all of the areas have been developed and there are a lot of very new routes at the cliff, so expect some very sharp and painful holds, along with some more new climbs in the future. It's not a giant cliff, but the short routes are very impressive and worthwhile, and pack a lot of climbing into their length; making a short visit here really worthwhile.

A região Sul de Portugal é conhecida por Algarve e muito bem descrita como uma terra de contrastes. Toda a costa se caracteriza por uma variação extraordinária de temas, desde lindíssimas praias de areia branca num cenário bruxuleante e tranquilo, a enormes apartamentos para férias desenhados por arquitectos de prisões – acompanhados por restaurantes que se orgulham de apresentar menus limitados em letras gigantes… e não é preciso dizer mais nada! A esplêndida auto-estrada ao longo do Algarve é essencial para se poder transpor qualquer distância a uma velocidade apreciável e faz a separação entre urbanizações modernas e zona rural. Se se aproximar da Rocha da Pena por Loulé, a cidade local mais importante, o seu estado de espírito vai melhorar rapidamente, ao trocar agradecido a vasta zona urbana carregada de fumo, por olivais magníficos e estradas amplas e tranquilas. Tem de atravessar uma cadeia de montes com cerca de 20km até chegar à pacata aldeia de Salir, e seguir então para a Rocha da Pena, escondida na Serra do Caldeirão – uma bênção que a protege da popularidade excessiva. A zona em redor da Rocha da Pena foi classificada como área protegida, o que é fantástico, dispõe de percursos marcados e de uma imensa vida selvagem para observar. É permitido escalar no local, mas tenho de pedir a todos que o mantenham imaculadamente limpo e bem arranjado.

 A Rocha da Pena propriamente dita, é uma crista comprida com cerca de 2-3 quilómetros e mais ou menos 20 contrafortes de rocha separados, erguendo-se sobre as árvores e a vegetação rasteira (mas com picos afiados). Recomendo que faça a marcha de aproximação pelas paredes mais afastadas – e está claro, com calças compridas e grossas. O calcário é de facto muito variado, e vai desde a típica rocha vermelha espanhola (que fica "lavada" rapidamente), aos buracos pequenos como em Finale e Buoux, ou ainda ao estilo mais clássico de fendas compridas como na Provença. Toda a encosta está virada a Sul, por isso recebe o sol em cheio – que no Verão é muito intenso. No entanto, as paredes do extremo

Rocha da Pena

Rocha da Pena (Salir-Loulé)

Camping Albufeira***
Estrada des Ferreiras, 8200-555 Albufeira
Tel: 289 587 629   Fax: 289 587 633
www.roteiro-campista.pt/faro/albufeira.htm
Notes: This is a giant campsite by any standards.
Open: (01/01-31/12) - 1000 places; 19 hectares;
Bungalows for hire.

Bar- Rocha, Alcaria, Salir   Shop- Alcaria, Salir (Post office-Salir)
Petrol Station- Salir   Supermarket- Loulé   Climbing Shop-Faro

Gite: Casa de Mae, Ameijoafora, Salir (289 489 179)
Hotel: Pensao A Tia Bia, Barranco do Velho (289 846 425)
Tourist Info: Salir;
Alté; Casa Memória d'Alte, Estrada da Ponte, n.17

Rocha da Pena

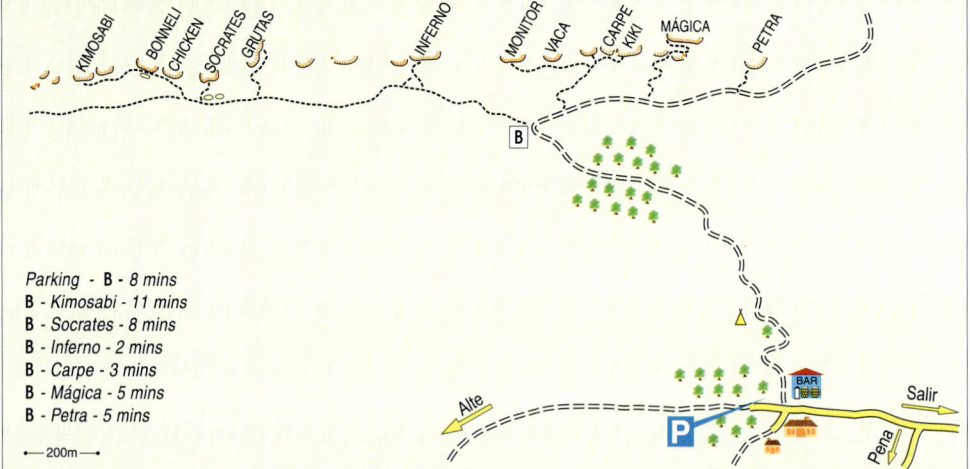

Parking - **B** - 8 mins
B - Kimosabi - 11 mins
B - Socrates - 8 mins
B - Inferno - 2 mins
B - Carpe - 3 mins
B - Mágica - 5 mins
B - Petra - 5 mins

ROCHA DA PENA

The village of Pena is down in the valley below, whilst Rocha is higher up and has a solitary 'Bar das Grutas.' One of those really quiet places to get away from it all. There is also a lovely old water fountain opposite - but that's about it. The land around is owned by the Bar das Grutas, so if you do want to camp on the hill - you must ask for permission first.

esquerdo ficam à sombra até ao meio-dia, e algumas das outras começam a ter sombra por volta das 3 da tarde – por isso há sempre alguma esperança. Por outro lado, como as paredes estão bastante altas atraem frequentemente algum vento que por lá ande, pelo que se torna quase suportável. Nem todas as áreas estão equipadas e há muitas vias extremamente recentes nesta escola, por este motivo conte com algumas presas afiadas e dolorosas bem como algumas novidades no futuro. Não é uma escola gigantesca, mas as vias curtas são muito impressionantes, valem a pena, e têm muito que se lhes diga ao longo do seu percurso; uma visita curta tornar-se-á realmente proveitosa.

BOULDERING, CRAGGING,

Whatever aspect of
CLIMBING
You're into......
WE'VE GOT THE KIT

PEGLERS
THE MOUNTAIN SHOP

www.peglers.co.uk
UK-tel: 01903 - 884 684
I/nat-tel: 0044 1903 884 684

The BIGGEST range in the U.K. probably....

69 Tarrant St, Arundel, Sussex BN18 9DN

SPORT, INDOOR, HIGH ALTITUDE,

BIGWALLING, ALPINE, CHALK

SCOTTISH WINTER, ICE FALL

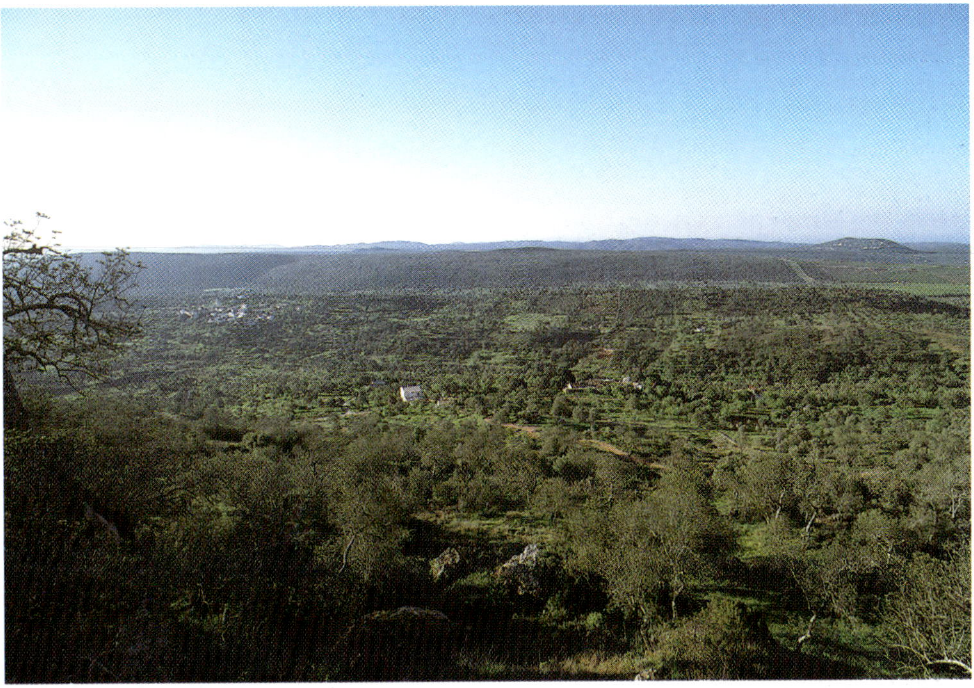

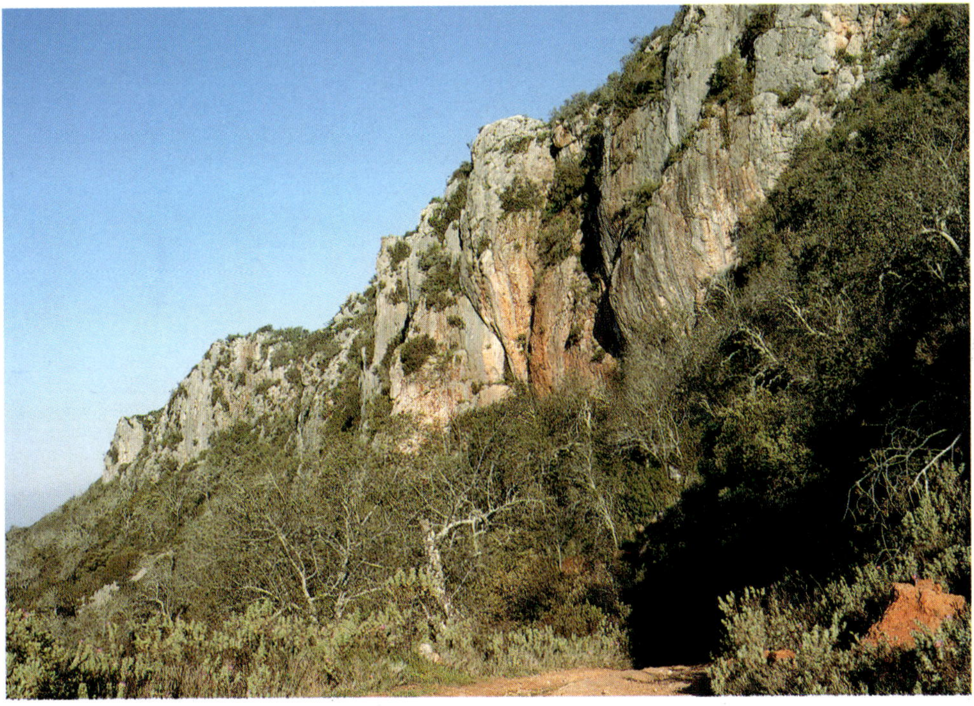

ROCHA DA PENA

① **7b** ● Chill Out*
15m. A very difficult boulder problem start, long clip stick essential; gets easier but still no doddle. (Cal: J, C)

② **7a+** ● Kimosabi**
15m. What a lovely start and a great airy finish; it's the in between bit that is either unobviously technical, or obviously hard. Often climbed at 7b+ for the un-technical - no clues given. (Cal: B, J, F)

③ **6b+** ● Flash**
13m. Lots of pockets to begin with, then it goes all pear shaped for those with fat fingers. Taped up fingers bump up the grade to 6c bloc, mostly knowing the numbers., (Cal: B, K)

④ **6a** ⚡ Estrunfina**
19m. A lovely route with a fabulous view, enjoyable moves and plenty of friction on the rock. (Cal: F, C)

⑤ **5b** ⚡ Quebra Nozes
19m. A bit overgrown & very sharp rock, could do with traffic and bolting. (Cal: C, F)

Résumé. A very nice small sector which is generally quiet - being the furthest from the car park. Some excellent climbs on lovely rock. Stays cool for a while in the morning - worth going to early on.

Kimosabi - Bonneli - Chicken - Sócrates - Grutas - Inferno - Monitor - Vaca - Águia - Carpe Diem - Májica - Kiki - Petra

KIMOSABI 7a+, Rocha da Pena; Jingo

Rocha Da Pena

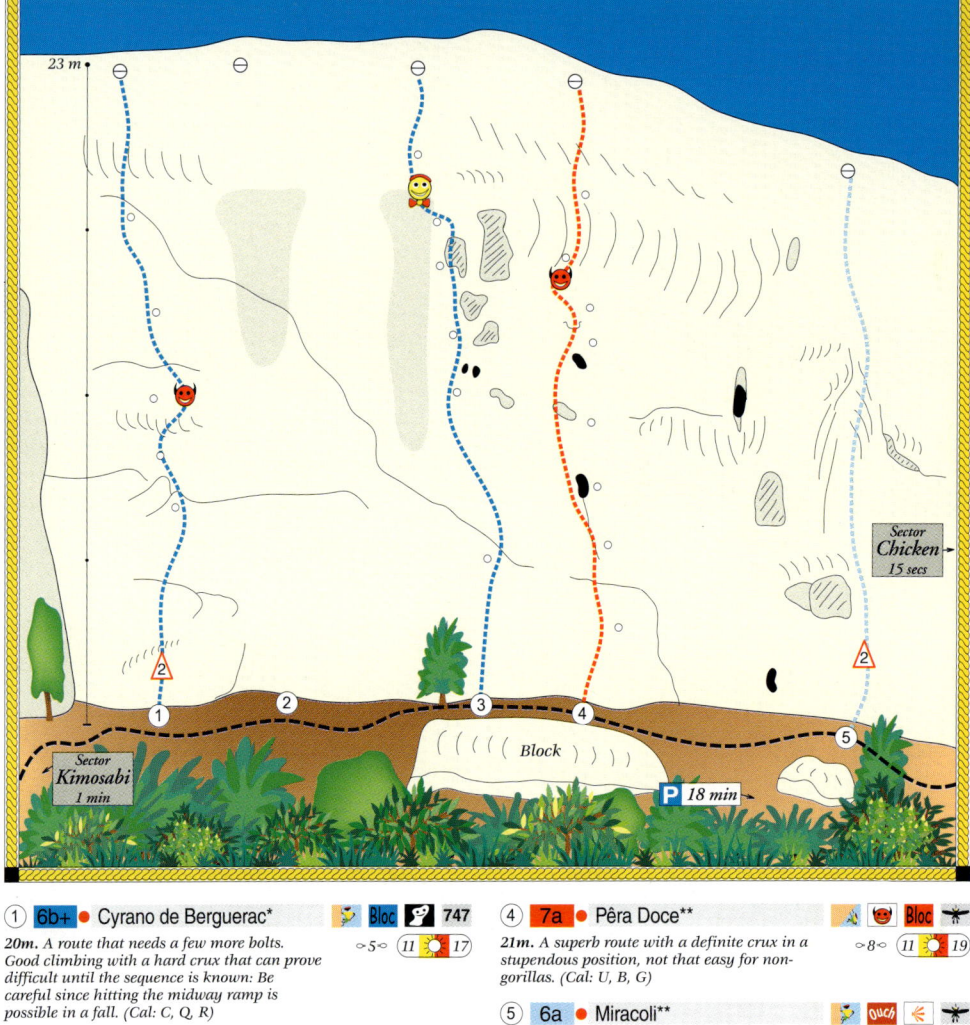

① **6b+** ● Cyrano de Berguerac*

20m. A route that needs a few more bolts. Good climbing with a hard crux that can prove difficult until the sequence is known: Be careful since hitting the midway ramp is possible in a fall. (Cal: C, Q, R)

② ***

20m. No climb yet, but looks quite hard. (Cal: D)

③ **6b** ⚡ Bonneli Express**

22m. An absolute classic that will polish really nicely due to the fine grained type of rock. A wonderful route that keeps threatening a hard move, but never arrives. Don't miss the hands off headlock; a good cruise in an outrageous position. (Cal: E, B, K, T)

④ **7a** ● Pêra Doce**

21m. A superb route with a definite crux in a stupendous position, not that easy for non-gorillas. (Cal: U, B, G)

⑤ **6a** ● Miracoli**

19m. The first wall goes well - if somewhat apprehensively to the first clip. Confronting the bulge is overcome by reach - as are most of the clips. Sustained and fab views. (Cal: C, C)

Résumé. A newly developed sector with some very sharp pockets, especially in top sections of the routes. Plenty of scope here for further desperates. Could have oversized birds nesting that would eat you! A nice big pillar to belay well in shade, gets any breeze that is going.

Kimosabi - Bonneli - Chicken - Sócrates - Grutas - Inferno - Monitor - Vaca - Águia - Carpe Diem - Májica Kiki - Petra

BONELLI EXPRESS 6b+, Rocha da Pena; Antonio Gonzales Gonzales

Sector Chicken, Rocha da Pena

ROCHA DA PENA

① **5c+** ● Portugueisha**
13m. Nice pockets - but wow! are they sharp. Crux leaves those short of reach with a few problems. (Cal: C, J)

② **6b+** ● Chicken George*
13m. The climb has a typical power bloc move that seems easy when you know how. (Cal: J, C)

③ **6c** ● Finger Linking**
13m. The start, middle and top of this route provides fingertip nasty territory. A good suggestion would be to take pain killers before starting this one. (Cal: J, C)

④ **7a+** ● Vertigem Parcial**
12m. A real jolly mixture of leg locks, reaches and sequency moves; all to end up in a dead end alley. Tricky onsight. (Cal: J, C)

⑤ **7a** ⚡ Finger Party**
12m. All seems to be going so well, until your left arm either locks off - or doesn't. Nasty on the finger joints. (Cal: J, C)

⑥ **6a+** ⚡ Shortcut**
23m. A good intensive 1st half, with lots of painful holds, needs to get polished, fab view on the top half. (Cal: C, C, C)

Résumé. A superb sector but needs a lot of traffic since it is exceptionally sharp and disgustingly painful. Here you dream of polished rock - believe it or not! Good belay shade with nice views, and a comfortable picnic base.

Kimosabi - Bonneli - **Chicken** - Sócrates - Grutas - Inferno - Monitor - Vaca - Águia - Carpe Diem - Kiki - Petra - Májica

ROCHA DA PENA

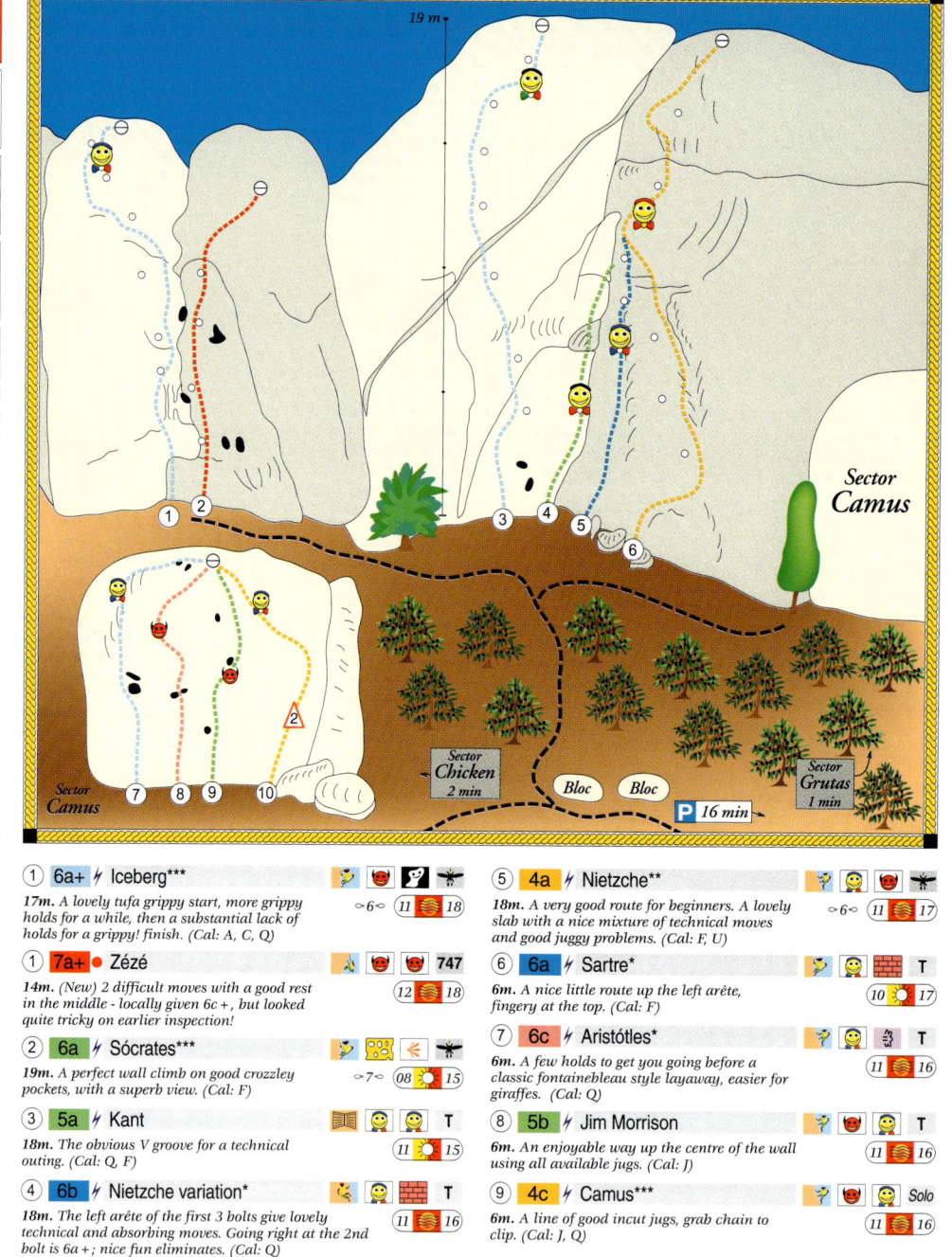

① **6a+** ⚡ Iceberg***

17m. *A lovely tufa grippy start, more grippy holds for a while, then a substantial lack of holds for a grippy! finish. (Cal: A, C, Q)*

① **7a+** ● Zézé

14m. *(New) 2 difficult moves with a good rest in the middle - locally given 6c+, but looked quite tricky on earlier inspection!*

② **6a** ⚡ Sócrates***

19m. *A perfect wall climb on good crozzley pockets, with a superb view. (Cal: F)*

③ **5a** ⚡ Kant

18m. *The obvious V groove for a technical outing. (Cal: Q, F)*

④ **6b** ⚡ Nietzche variation*

18m. *The left arête of the first 3 bolts give lovely technical and absorbing moves. Going right at the 2nd bolt is 6a+; nice fun eliminates. (Cal: Q)*

⑤ **4a** ⚡ Nietzche**

18m. *A very good route for beginners. A lovely slab with a nice mixture of technical moves and good juggy problems. (Cal: F, U)*

⑥ **6a** ⚡ Sartre*

6m. *A nice little route up the left arête, fingery at the top. (Cal: F)*

⑦ **6c** ⚡ Aristótles*

6m. *A few holds to get you going before a classic fontainebleau style layaway, easier for giraffes. (Cal: Q)*

⑧ **5b** ⚡ Jim Morrison

6m. *An enjoyable way up the centre of the wall using all available jugs. (Cal: J)*

⑨ **4c** ⚡ Camus***

6m. *A line of good incut jugs, grab chain to clip. (Cal: J, Q)*

Résumé. *The* **'FILÓSOFOS'** *area with a good small slab to warm up on. Only a few routes, but superb quality climbing to be found. The slanting crack in the centre can be climbed traditionally, but always seems overgrown. On the way to this sector you will pass a couple of boulders with various problems, a bit scrappy unfortunately.*

Kimosabi - Bonneli - Chicken - **Sócrates** - Grutas - Inferno - Monitor - Vaca - Águia - Carpe Diem - Májica Kiki - Petra

SÓCRATES 6a, Rocha da Pena; Wobbly

BAR DAS GRUTAS 6a+, Rocha da Pena; Jingo

Rocha Da Pena

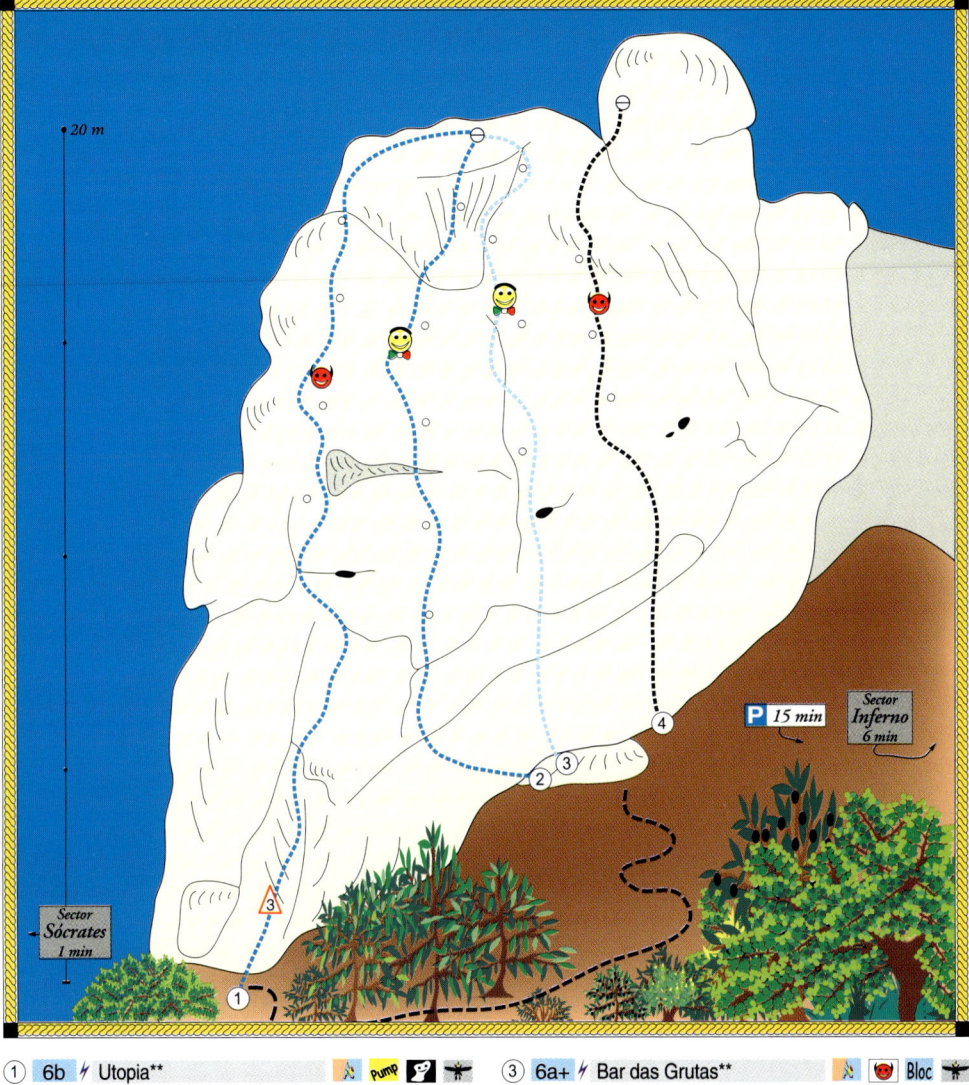

① **6b** ⚡ **Utopia****
19m. A superb climb in a wonderful position. The key is to keep an eye out for footholds. (Cal: F)

② **6a+** ⚡ **Besunta****
14m. A great little route that feels very airy indeed. Needs commitment. Taking the top overhang completely direct is 6b/c. (Cal: F)

Résumé. The first sector on the crag to get the sun - and the early afternoon shade - always worth a visit. High up and does catch a breeze - or even a gale. Great views but awkward to move around, not so comfortable for a picnic.

③ **6a+** ⚡ **Bar das Grutas****
13m. A superb route in an elevated position. Holds just run out unfortunately; make sure you swing out onto the top aréte for the full out there experience. (Cal: I, F)

④ **7b** ● **Amor e Psique**
14m. A two move route around Font 6c, and is not one you would want to solo onsight! (Cal: S, L)

Kimosabi - Bonneli - Chicken - Sócrates - *Grutas* - Inferno - Monitor - Vaca - Águia - Carpe Diem - Kiki - Májica - Petra

ROCHA DA PENA

① **4c** ⚡ Paradox***

20m. A great groove with some very interesting moves. Lovely views and position but quite run out, cams could easily supplement pro. (Cal: C)

② **5c+** ⚡ Ambivalent tearaway**

20m. A nice variation out right onto the wall, sharp and slowly getting worn in. (Cal: C)
Direct route to be bolted - 7a etc!

③ **6c** ● Petrus Durus Inhumanos*

21m. A mad start in the trees, preclip 1st runner from lowering off. Power climbing eventually leads to a razor bed of entertainment; Ok when you know how. (Cal: C)

④ **6b+** Busílis***

21m. Nice climbing on jugs all the way; however, they sometimes appear too far apart. Nice, flowing and technical - ouch! (Cal: C)

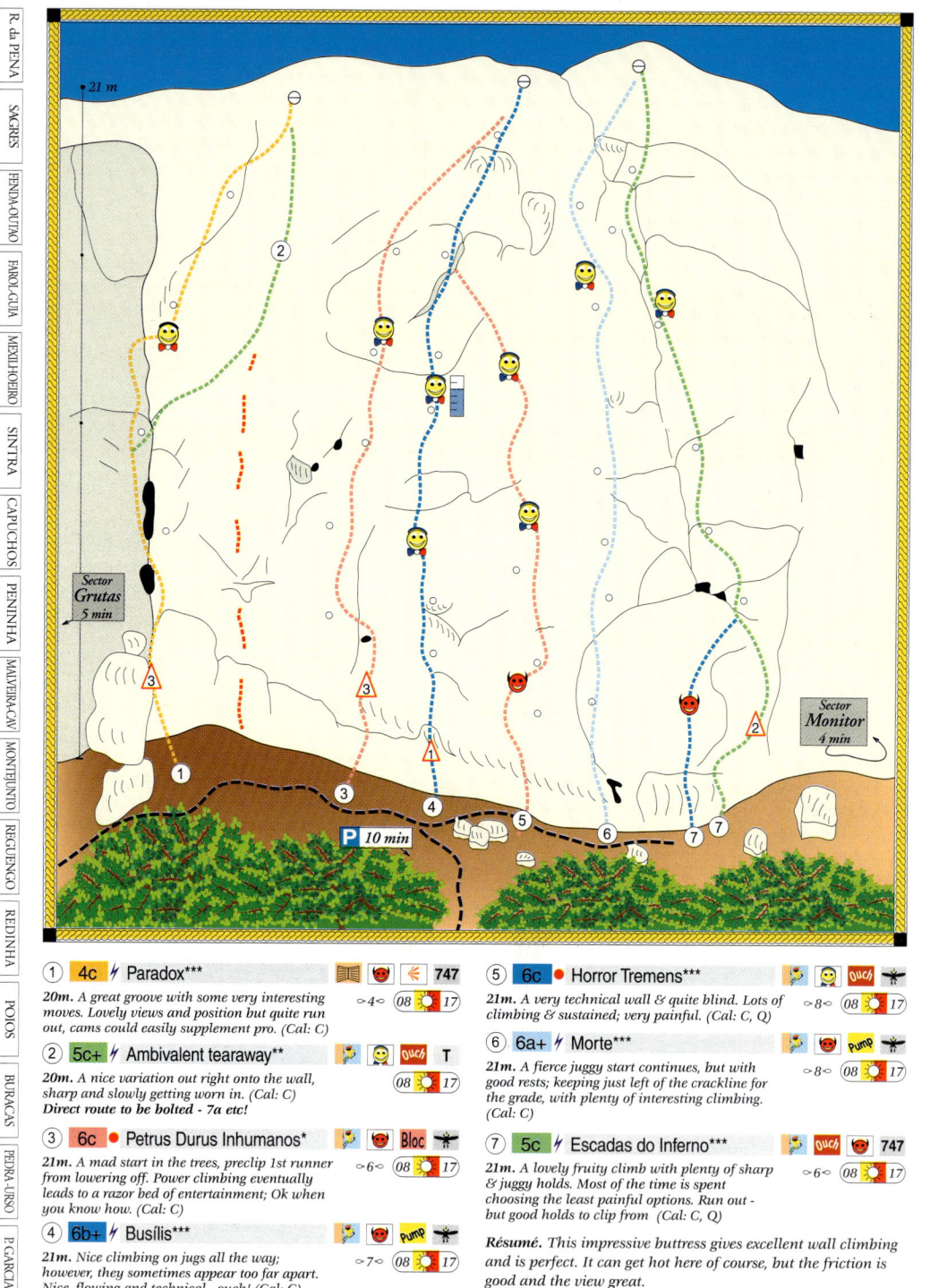

⑤ **6c** ● Horror Tremens***

21m. A very technical wall & quite blind. Lots of climbing & sustained; very painful. (Cal: C, Q)

⑥ **6a+** ⚡ Morte***

21m. A fierce juggy start continues, but with good rests; keeping just left of the crackline for the grade, with plenty of interesting climbing. (Cal: C)

⑦ **5c** ● Escadas do Inferno***

21m. A lovely fruity climb with plenty of sharp & juggy holds. Most of the time is spent choosing the least painful options. Run out - but good holds to clip from (Cal: C, Q)

Résumé. This impressive buttress gives excellent wall climbing and is perfect. It can get hot here of course, but the friction is good and the view great.

Kimosabi - Bonneli - Chicken - Sócrates - Grutas - Inferno - Monitor - Vaca - Águia - Carpe Diem - Kiki - Petra - Májica

RURAL ALGARVE - SALIR

SALIR CHURCH

SALIR is not somewhere you pick when you want the fast life - quite the opposite. The pace of life here is slow - like almost stopped! But that's the attraction; to read a book, drink some beers, and then go off climbing when it gets a bit cooler. The deepness of the blue skies here is staggering, as the heat can also be in high summer. Salir, has exactly what you need, but nothing else, perfect for a holiday, zzzz.

Há um castelo em Salir
Dizem ser o mais belo
Mesmo depois de cair
Não deixa de ser Castelo.

Joaquim de Barrada

SALIR

SALIR TOURIST OFFICE

SILENT COMETS 6a+, Rocha da Pena; Wobbly

ROCHA DA PENA

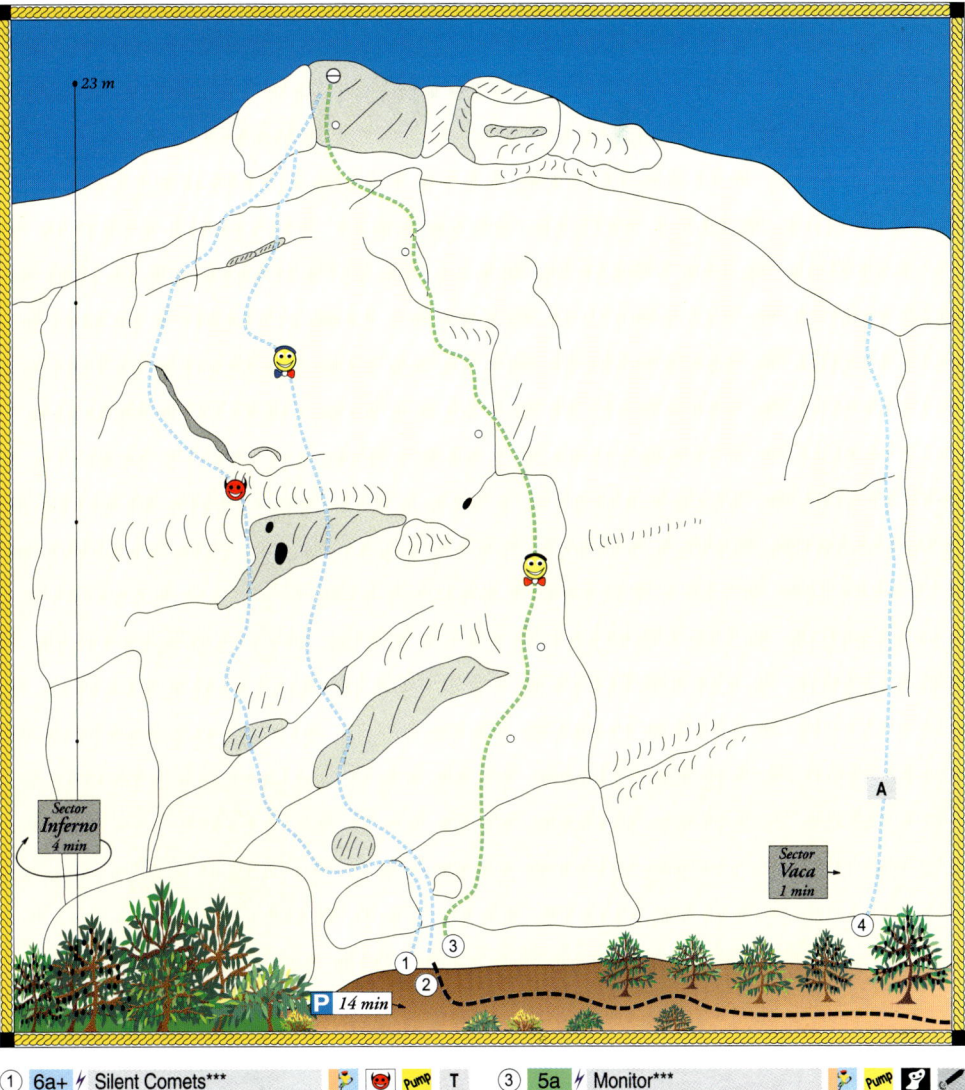

49

① **6a+** ⚡ **Silent Comets*****

23m. A superb wall climb. Have fun exiting the holes to the left and a wonderful rising hand traverse in a great position with superb holds. (Cal: U, G, I, C)

② **6a+** ⚡ **Moss Dieb*****

23m. A direct line up the flat shield at its flattest part. A good left hand layaway allows delicate climbing on tip toes - invigorating. (Cal: U, Q, C)

③ **5a** ⚡ **Monitor*****

23m. Widely spaced gear (and badly placed), makes this a serious undertaking for a beginner. Cams can solve your dilemma. A brilliant route, especially when the wall gets steep. (Cal: I, U, C)

④ **6a+** **Bill Me**

23m. An overgrown groove would make a good route. (Cal: X)

Résumé. *A very underdeveloped buttress and one of the best pieces of rock for the 6a climber in Southern Portugal. Excellent array of jugs, great views, belay in the shade or in the sun all day. Could easily get another 5 routes of 6a-6b +.*

Kimosabi · Bonneli · Chicken · Sócrates · Grutas · Inferno · **Monitor** · Vaca · Águia · Carpe Diem · Májica · Kiki · Petra

RURAL ALGARVE - SERRA DO CALDEIRÃO

ALTE

You have a wonderful rural side to the Algarve which is now catered for by the tourist board. You can pick up different fold out plans from the local tourist bureau points, which illustrate all the interesting things to do and visit. In the very close area to Rocha da Pena there is Alte with its lovely water springs and serene architectual brilliance. There are many churches to visit, and even a buddist temple up at Malhão in the foothills of the Serra do Caldeirão. To the East of Salir, you have a lovely tour that goes up past Barranco do Velho and the cork forests, and then up to Cacopo where there is a host of local craftwork artisans. Here also there are renovations of rural life through thousands of years in museums and a 'rural discovery centre' (Casas Baixas). If its raining, go south to Santa Catarina where you can visit an olive oil press and maybe to quote ' witness the distillation process of "medronho" firewater.' Várzea do Vinagre is apparently the place to get the wicked stuff. If you are willing to search out interesting antiquity, there is a lot to find here.

BARRANCO DO VELHO

ALTE

ROCHA DA PENA

51

① **6b** Boi*

20m. A very good wall with an insitu peg and some insitu natural slings. Apart from the move above the peg, it is pleasant 4a, unfortunately the crux is almost impossible without actually standing on the peg (Cal: J, C)

② **4a** PP***

31m. A superb wall climb that can be naturally protected - if you're that way inclined! A superb route and sustained for the grade. (Cal: C)

③ **3b** Vaca***

31m. Nice slab climbing with a well protected (Natural gear) top headwall. [Cam,2,3,Sling, Nut 3]. Bolt lower off at the top and a 60 metre rope if used cautiously is fine; you can climb back down the last few metres. (Cal: C, R)

Résumé. A very good buttress with amazing quality of rock, and no moves to worry you, or rip out your tendons. Superb views and position; perfect at 6pm after a hot day - when it goes into shade. Attracts a cool evening breeze. Natural gear that is generally in a straight line.

Májica

Kimosabi - Bonneli - Chicken - Sócrates - Grutas - Inferno - Monitor - Vaca - Águia - Carpe Diem - Kiki - Petra

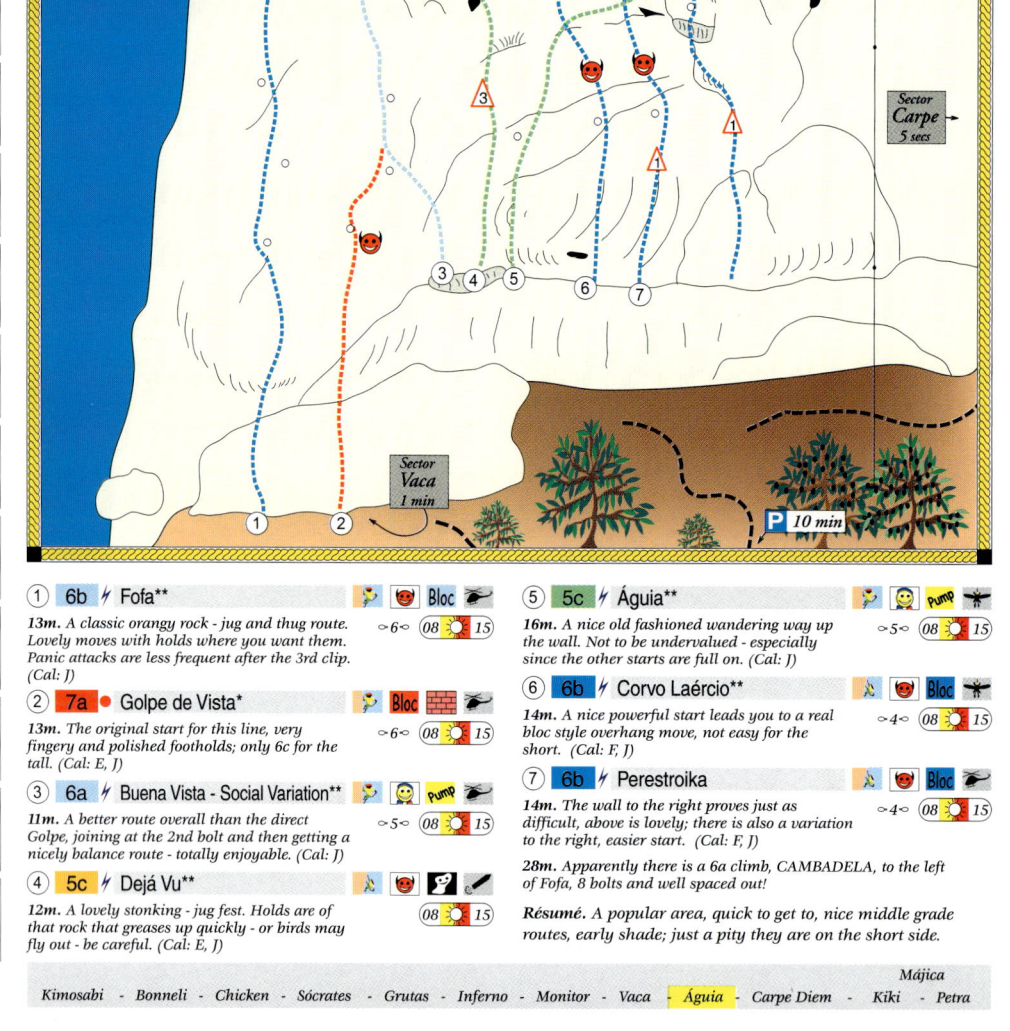

ROCHA DA PENA

① **6b** Fofa**
13m. A classic orangy rock - jug and thug route. Lovely moves with holds where you want them. Panic attacks are less frequent after the 3rd clip. (Cal: J)

② **7a** Golpe de Vista*
13m. The original start for this line, very fingery and polished footholds; only 6c for the tall. (Cal: E, J)

③ **6a** Buena Vista - Social Variation**
11m. A better route overall than the direct Golpe, joining at the 2nd bolt and then getting a nicely balance route - totally enjoyable. (Cal: J)

④ **5c** Dejá Vu**
12m. A lovely stonking - jug fest. Holds are of that rock that greases up quickly - or birds may fly out - be careful. (Cal: E, J)

⑤ **5c** Águia**
16m. A nice old fashioned wandering way up the wall. Not to be undervalued - especially since the other starts are full on. (Cal: J)

⑥ **6b** Corvo Laércio**
14m. A nice powerful start leads you to a real bloc style overhang move, not easy for the short. (Cal: F, J)

⑦ **6b** Perestroika
14m. The wall to the right proves just as difficult, above is lovely; there is also a variation to the right, easier start. (Cal: F, J)

28m. Apparently there is a 6a climb, CAMBADELA, to the left of Fofa, 8 bolts and well spaced out!

Résumé. A popular area, quick to get to, nice middle grade routes, early shade; just a pity they are on the short side.

Kimosabi - Bonneli - Chicken - Sócrates - Grutas - Inferno - Monitor - Vaca - Águia - Carpe Diem - Májica - Kiki - Petra

CORVO LAÉRCIO 6b, Rocha da Pena; Bruno Mendes

FIM DE PICADA 8a, Rocha da Pena; Antonio Gonzalez Gonzalez

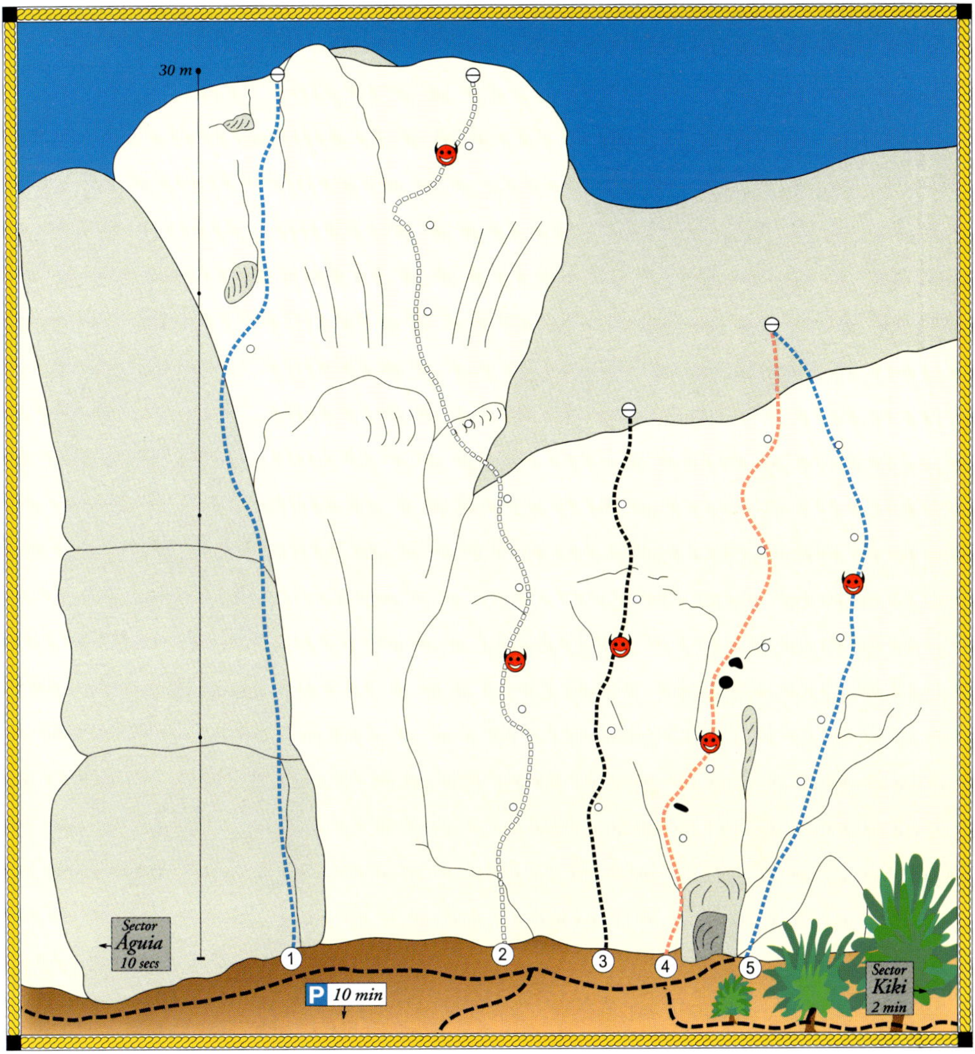

ROCHA DA PENA

① **6b** Nem todo o mel é doce

30m. *A simple groove leads to a challenging headwall - not equipped at present; currently occupied by bushes, wasps and no doubt snakes!! (Cal: U, C, J)*

② **8a** Fim da Picada**

30m. *A really technical and fingertip testing start. A complete rest before the daunting onslaught of the sustained headwall. (Cal: W, F, W)*

③ **7b** Prize of Patience*

12m. *There might be only one hard move on this climb, but it certainly is a move to stop you Recommended for those with strong fingers - Font 6b+. (Cal: H, W)*

④ **6c** Carpe Diem***

15m. *Quite a powerful start, which certainly warms you up for the delights to come. Good and punchy climbing on above average sized holds - superb. (Cal: H, J)*

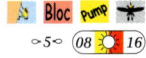

⑤ **6b** Elixir Afrodisíaco**

15m. *A very comfortable route that is perfect for a warm up on the harder routes in this sector. Good finger crimping fun. (Cal: W)*

Résumé. *A good and popular sector that gets early shade. Trees at the base give belayers a shady time too. Sector to the right may get developed - 7b-c by the look of it.*

Kimosabi - Bonneli - Chicken - Sócrates - Grutas - Inferno - Monitor - Vaca - Águia - **Carpe Diem** - Májica - Kiki - Petra

GOLPE DE VISTA (Font 6a+ bloc), Rocha da Pena; Rui 'Pop' Appolinari — *'Seriously overheating engine'*

'Precautionary water cooling'

Beach drifing at Quarteira - 30 mins from Rocha da Pena

ROCHA DA PENA

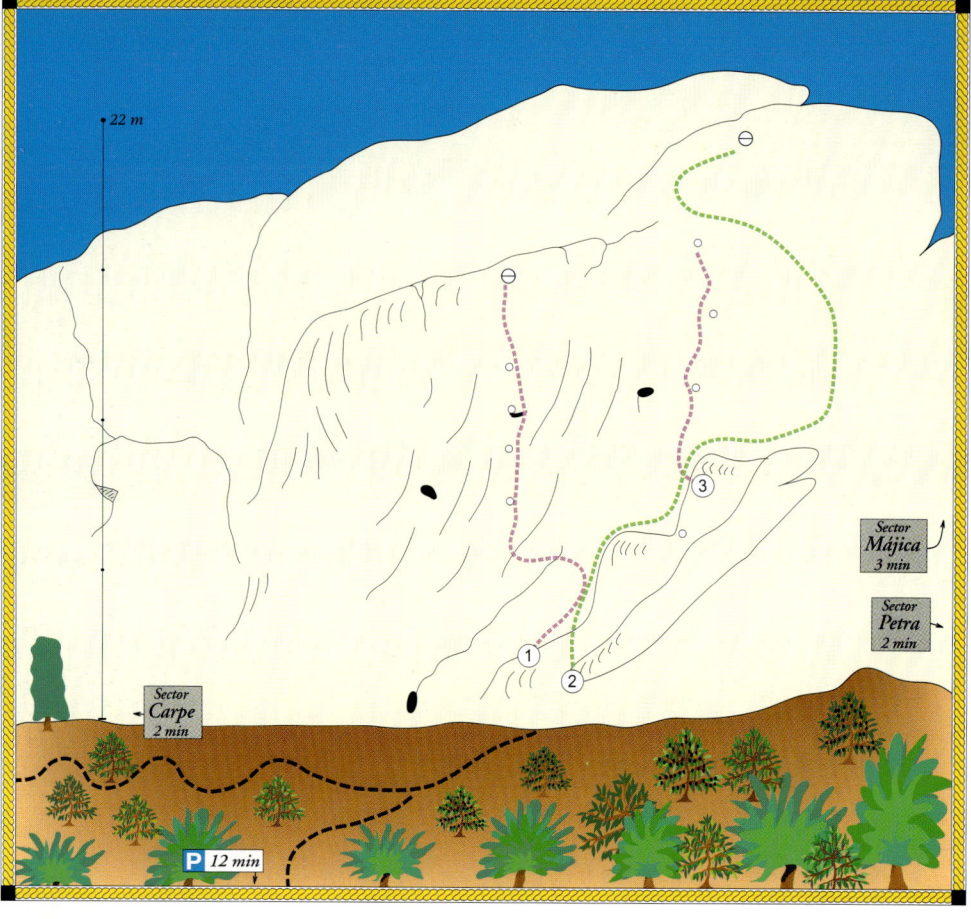

① **8b** ● Casa dos Espiritos**
17m. A big steep bulging wall, using occasional pockets. (Cal: B, F)

② **5c** ⚡ Kiki**
25m. A wandering route up this very impressive bit of rock - not yet bolted. (Cal: U)

③ **8?** ● ?
16m. An obvious challenge. (Cal: B)

Résumé. One of the first pieces of rock that catches your eye on the walk up. Too steep and devoid of holds for normal human beings.

BOREAL

Kimosabi - Bonneli - Chicken - Sócrates - Grutas - Inferno - Monitor - Vaca - Águia - Carpe Diem - Májica - Kiki - Petra

Sector Kiki, Rocha da Pena

ROCHA DA PENA

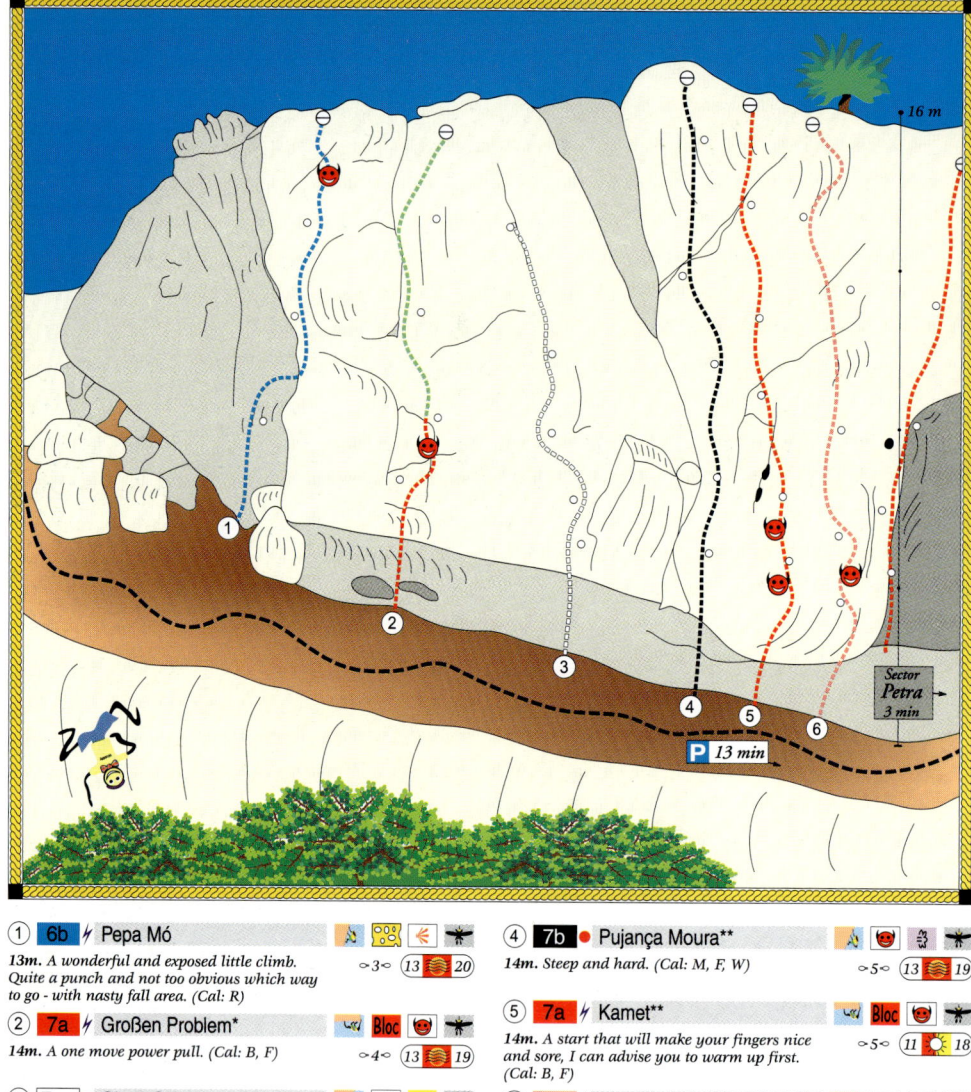

① **6b** ⚡ Pepa Mó
13m. A wonderful and exposed little climb. Quite a punch and not too obvious which way to go - with nasty fall area. (Cal: R)

② **7a** ⚡ Großen Problem*
14m. A one move power pull. (Cal: B, F)

③ **7c+** ● Ghost Shit
14m. A steep leaning pillar which gives a combination of fingery stamina. (Cal: H, W)

Résumé. *A lovely evening sector, it does get the sun until late, but attracts a breeze which keeps the humidity away from the cliff. Very undercut at the start and extremely powerful. A lovely terrace for sunbathing and looking over to the sea in the distance. (UK-Rock very similar to Upper Pen Trwyn).*
Note: *Approach is a bit of a scramble so have both hands free; could loose kids over the edge, but a great picnic spot.*

④ **7b** ● Pujança Moura**
14m. Steep and hard. (Cal: M, F, W)

⑤ **7a** ⚡ Kamet**
14m. A start that will make your fingers nice and sore, I can advise you to warm up first. (Cal: B, F)

⑧ **6c** ● Poção Mágica do Druida***
14m. A real power thumper of a start on good jugs - but someone has stolen all the footholds. Fabulous and sustained climbing to finish in an incredible position. (Cal: B, F, Q, C)

⑨ **7a+** ● Marafada
14m. A hard start, overhanging and pumpy to the top. (New climb)

Kimosabi - Bonneli - Chicken - Sócrates - Grutas - Inferno - Monitor - Vaca - Águia - Carpe Diem - Kiki - Petra

Májica

PEPA MÓ 6b, Rocha da Pena; Wobbly

TÉDIO 4a, Rocha da Pena; Jingo

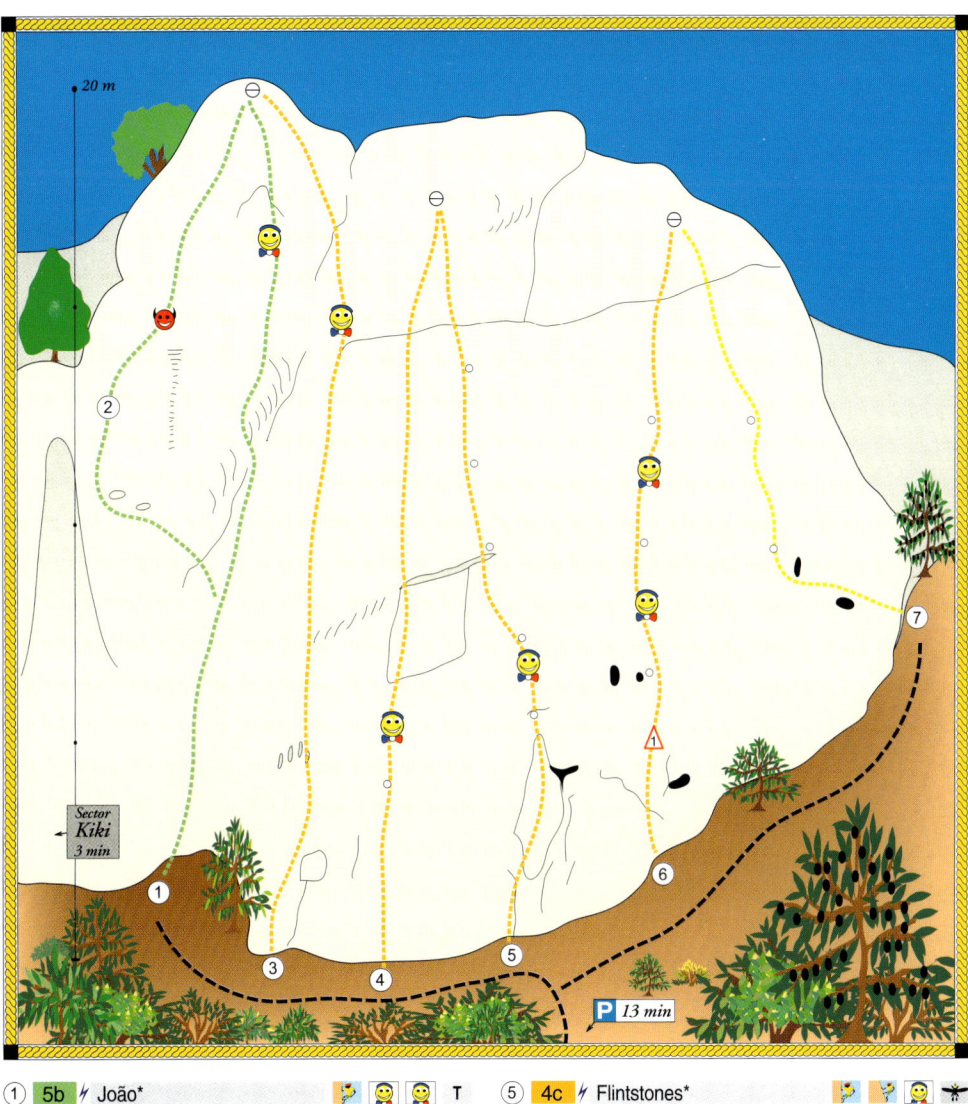

ROCHA DA PENA

① 5b ⚡ João*
18m. Fun pockets, then a lovely steep headwall; keep left of the groove for the most fun. (Cal: R, C, Q)

② 5c ● Ninja**
18m. A very good variation, following the big hand jugs then going straight up. (Cal: R, C, Q)

③ 4a ⚡ V2*
18m. A perfect wall climb on good crozzley pockets, with a superb view. (Cal: F)

④ 4c Nervos em Franja*
16m. Good moves up to the square impression, then nervous moves to enter the square - fun. (Cal: R, Q)

⑤ 4c ⚡ Flintstones*
16m. Graunch up the starting pillar, then lovely delicate climbing ensues for the central section. (Cal: R, Q)

⑥ 4a ⚡ Tédio*
14m. A good lead for a beginner, lovely position with views. (Cal: C)

⑦ 2a ⚡ Petra*
15m. A very easy way up to set up top rope belays. (Cal: C)

Résumé. A lovely sector for a first visit to the cliff, with beautiful views and a nice aspect. Very friendly fun routes. An immaculate small slab with rock that gives tiny edges; top rope belays allow endless eliminates.

Tonal Slabs on the West side of the FORTALEZA, Sagres

The southern coast of Portugal is blessed with superb sunshine and golden beaches; even wonderful fishing and boating; windy days good for windsurfing and surfing in general. Notice that I didn't even mention climbing! It can't be classified as a 'sensible' climber's destination, whatever anyone may tell you! There are huge expanses of cliffs that tower above the Atlantic Ocean, and well - drop into it, from time to time. You might well suffer the same fate should you decide to climb here. The whole of the coastline is a mixture of congealed mud and shells, which stands tall and vertical; and is effortlessly extracted with the well aimed foot. In places it is highly congealed sandy mud, which is really deceiving up until around 3 metres away, then the ghastly reality of the desiccating texture is appreciated. There is however, just one tiny bit of rock that is however superb. This is the lower half of the Ponta de Sagres, almost an island of limestone beneath the village of Sagres. Here, a small peninsular sticks out into the ocean for a very good reason, that it's really hard rock, long may it live. There are also strong rumours of other superb bits of rock to be found on the coastline; I haven't found them yet, but am open minded - watch out on our website.

There are problems however in climbing at the Ponta de Sagres. This little promontory was fortified hundreds of years ago and the battlements are still there, hence you do have to pay a small charge to gain access to the promontory. Also you must sign a complete disclaimer with the desk to say that you are responsible for your death, suicide etc, just like an indoor climbing wall. There are route diagrams and climbing logbook kept at the Andromeda bar in Sagres, and they are generally very helpful with information, weather forecasts etc. There is however a big conflict with the fishermen. They have fished from the top of the cliffs for hundreds of years and have no intention of giving up their fishing rights; and if you start climbing below them, expect a lot of trouble. There are areas you can get away from the fishymen, but unfortunately on any day worth climbing, there are usually 30 or so fishy dudes taking up the best parts of the cliff. In a practical sense, the cliffs are very daunting and are not solid everywhere, so you need to be well experienced in sea cliff dangers to come here safely. Very few of the routes have ledges at the bottom, and some of the big bays are very overhanging, so access is very awkward. All the routes are classic-trad style – and there are no bolts at all. You need a completely separate abseil rope, and you also need someone to stay at the top all the time to keep an eye on the abseil gear, helping to tell fishermen that you are down there. There are no rescue facilities, and the seas can be devastatingly terrifying. So if it is a complete nutty and crazy experience you are searching for, this is the place for you; otherwise get some cool surf man.

We have decided not to put the topo's of these cliffs in this guidebook. They are available for looking at in the bar of Sagres, and also should be on our website for a free download. We have done this for several reasons. Firstly, in that adventure climbing here is wild and is never going to be popular with the majority of climbers. Printing another section in the guidebook would be a waste of space and needless waste of paper (trees). The guidebook would have to be larger, more expensive, and of no great benefit to the majority of climbers. Secondly, is that the cliffs are very inaccessible, which makes carrying an A5 guidebook like this, stupid. This is the perfect time for a cheap piece of paper in your pocket, that way you can easily carry it with you on the climb. There is a lot to be gained we feel from this approach for the larger and more difficult cliffs. Thirdly (there's always a 3rd point isn't there), because this area is away from the major populations, it has not really had a great deal of development. There are always new climbs to be done, and other areas might well get development. There is also some willingness to open up new sport climbing zones here. By running this information on the web, it can easily be kept up to date, and is handy for the few people who would like to use it. We have included some nicely reproduced photos in our guidebook to give you a feel for the area.

Sagres

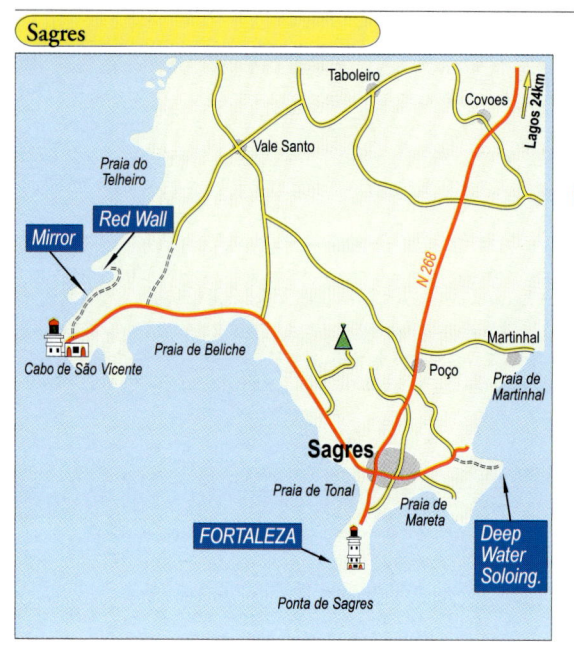

🔺 Camping Sagres*
Cerro das Moitas, 8659 Sagres
Tel: 282 624 371/441   Fax: 282 624 445
Open: (01/01-31/12)
medium size, shade, windy.

🛍 Bar: Sagres   Shop: Sagres (No credit cards)
Supermarket: Budens (N268,16km)
Climbing Shop: ?
Camping shop: Gaz, milk & cans.
Local climbing topos: All kept and up to date at
Bar DROMEDÁRIO on the main street in Sagres.
A good surfing bar, and excellent up to date
weather reports. Modern, clean and stylish.
Restaraunt & pizzeria (Bossa Nova)
Tel: 282 624 219

**TOPO - CROQUIS
WWW.JINGOWOBBLY.COM**

Lighthouse of Cabo de São Vicente

SAGRES - INTRODUÇÃO

A costa sul de Portugal foi abençoada com um sol soberbo e praias douradas; pescarias e passeios de barco igualmente maravilhosos; e ainda com dias ventosos, bons para windsurf e surf em geral. Note que eu nem sequer referi a escalada! Não se pode considerar um destino "sensato" para escaladores, independentemente do que lhe disserem! Há uma enorme extensão de falésias que se erguem sobre o Oceano Atlântico, e bom – que caem nele de tempos a tempos. Pode muito bem ter o mesmo destino se decidir escalar aqui. A totalidade da costa é uma mistura de lama compacta e conchas, que se eleva verticalmente e se desfaz sem esforço, com um pé bem dirigido. Em determinados lugares torna-se numa lama arenosa extremamente compacta, realmente enganadora numa extensão de mais ou menos 20 metros, onde se pode então apreciar a realidade terrível da textura dissecada. Contudo, há apenas um pedacinho de rocha realmente excelente. Trata-se da metade inferior da Ponta de Sagres, quase uma ilha de calcário abaixo da vila de Sagres. Aqui, uma pequena península projecta-se pelo oceano dentro por uma boa razão, é rocha realmente sólida; que assim se conserve por longos anos. Há também fortes rumores da existência de outros excelentes pedaços de rocha na orla costeira; ainda não os encontrei, mas estou alerta – estejam atentos ao nosso website.

Existem contudo alguns problemas para escalar na Ponta de Sagres. Este pequeno promontório foi fortificado há centenas de anos e as ameias ainda lá estão, por isso tem de pagar uma pequena quantia para lhe aceder. Tem também de assinar uma declaração à entrada, assumindo a responsabilidade pela sua morte, suicídio, etc. tal como num rocódromo. Existem topos das vias e um diário de escaladas guardados no bar Andrómeda, em Sagres, onde costumam ser muito prestáveis, fornecendo informações, previsões meteorológicas, etc. Há no entanto um pequeno conflito com os pescadores: sempre pescaram do cimo das falésias durante centenas de anos e não têm intenção de ceder os direitos de pesca; se começar a escalar por baixo deles, prepare-se para ter montes de problemas. Há áreas onde se pode ver livre de pescadores, mas infelizmente qualquer dia em que valha a pena escalar, tem cerca de 30 parceiros da pesca a ocupar as partes melhores da falésia. Sob o ponto de vista prático, as paredes são assustadoras e nem sempre sólidas, por isso para vir aqui com segurança deve ter bons conhecimentos sobre os perigos das falésias. Poucas vias têm plataformas por baixo, e algumas das baías grandes são muito extraprumadas pelo que o seu acesso é bastante complicado. Todas as vias são do estilo clássico tradicional e não têm chapas nenhumas. É necessária uma corda completamente separada para rapelar, bem como alguém para dar uma olhada pelo dispositivo de rapel e para informar os pescadores de que está lá em baixo. Não existem facilidades de resgate e o mar pode ser devastadoramente assustador. Por isso, se o que procura é uma experiência completamente louca e alucinante, este lugar é para si; caso contrário… respire um pouco da brisa fresca!

Decidimos não pôr os topos destas paredes no guia. Estão disponíveis para consulta no bar de Sagres, e estarão também no nosso site para download grátis. Fizemo-lo por várias razões. Em primeiro lugar, a escalada neste local é uma aventura selvagem e nunca será muito popular para a maioria dos escaladores. Imprimir outra secção no guia seria um desperdício de espaço e um gasto desnecessário de papel (árvores). O guia teria de ser maior e mais caro, sem grandes benefícios para a maior parte dos escaladores. Em segundo lugar, as falésias são bastante inacessíveis, o que faz com que o transporte dum guia de formato A5 como este seja uma coisa completamente estúpida. Esta é a ocasião ideal para levar no bolso um pedaço de papel barato, de forma a poder transportá-lo facilmente consigo durante a escalada. Pensamos que muito se pode ganhar com esta abordagem quando as paredes são maiores e mais difíceis. Terceiro, (há sempre um terceiro ponto, não há?), porque esta área está longe das povoações mais importantes e não tem evoluído muito. Haverá sempre novas escaladas para fazer, e podem também desenvolver-se outras áreas. Há ainda alguma boa-vontade para abrir novas zonas de escalada desportiva por aqui. Disponibilizando esta informação na web, pode manter-se actualizada, e ficar sempre à mão das poucas pessoas que gostariam de utilizá-la. Incluímos algumas belas reproduções de fotografias no nosso guia para lhe dar uma ideia da área.

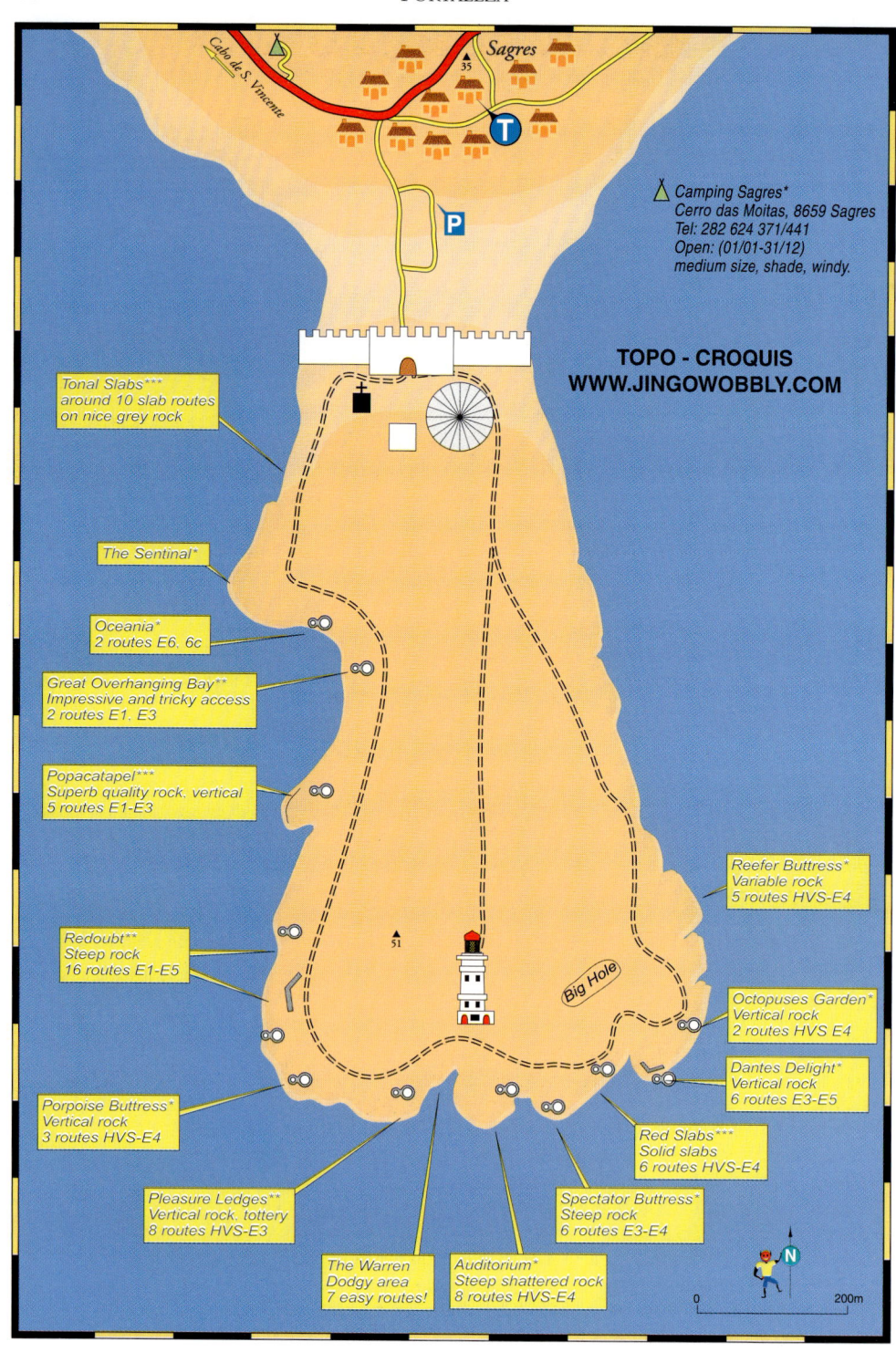

FORTALEZA

Camping Sagres*
Cerro das Moitas, 8659 Sagres
Tel: 282 624 371/441
Open: (01/01-31/12)
medium size, shade, windy.

TOPO - CROQUIS
WWW.JINGOWOBBLY.COM

Tonal Slabs***
around 10 slab routes
on nice grey rock

The Sentinal*

Oceania*
2 routes E6. 6c

Great Overhanging Bay**
Impressive and tricky access
2 routes E1. E3

Popacatapel***
Superb quality rock. vertical
5 routes E1-E3

Reefer Buttress*
Variable rock
5 routes HVS-E4

Redoubt**
Steep rock
16 routes E1-E5

Big Hole

Octopuses Garden*
Vertical rock
2 routes HVS E4

Dantes Delight*
Vertical rock
6 routes E3-E5

Porpoise Buttress*
Vertical rock
3 routes HVS-E4

Red Slabs***
Solid slabs
6 routes HVS-E4

Pleasure Ledges**
Vertical rock. tottery
8 routes HVS-E3

Spectator Buttress*
Steep rock
6 routes E3-E4

The Warren
Dodgy area
7 easy routes!

Auditorium*
Steep shattered rock
8 routes HVS-E4

0   200m

Tab labels (left margin): R. da PENA | SAGRES | FENDOULTAO | FAROLGUIA | MEXILHOEIRO | SINTRA | CAPUCHOS | PENINHA | MALVEIRA-CAV | MONTEJUNTO | REGUENGO | REDINHA | POIOS | BURACAS | PEDRA-URSO | P.GARCIA

Great Overhanging bay area

Fisherman at the top of BILLY FRANGO E1, Auditorium; taken from Pleasure L.

Robbie Warke on a new route E2, Cabo de São Vicente

MIRROR; a 70m high cliff. (Page 69 lower, 70,71 photos, Andy Reid)

WEST FACE - CABO DE SÃO VICENTE

(Forgotten the name) E4 6a, 6a, West Face; Andy Reid

Setúbal

Setúbal - is pronounced Stu-bal, and is a lovely busy town that gets a huge amount of sunshine. The old historic part is well worth checking out - once a busy port, and as a result, has narrow streets with lots of different shops, selling everything that you don't find in shopping mall's. There's also a great variety of good seafood restaurants, which are wonderful.

Serra Da Arrábida

The hills of the Serra da Arrábida, stretch between Sesimbra and Setúbal - about 30 mins drive south of Lisboa. The beaches are lovely and it is just the place to go and relax. Even being this close to Lisboa, it still remains very quiet, especially outside the main 6 week summer holiday period. The Atlantic sea is still a bit chilly, but the whole ambience is something quite special. The whole area features well in travel books for info. Don't miss the José Maria de Fonseca winery at Azeitão - daily tours; also the Costa Azul wine trail house in Palmela (Non-Sat), essential imbibing.

The bay of Portinho da Arrábida, with the cliffs in the background. *Top: Beach near Outáu.*

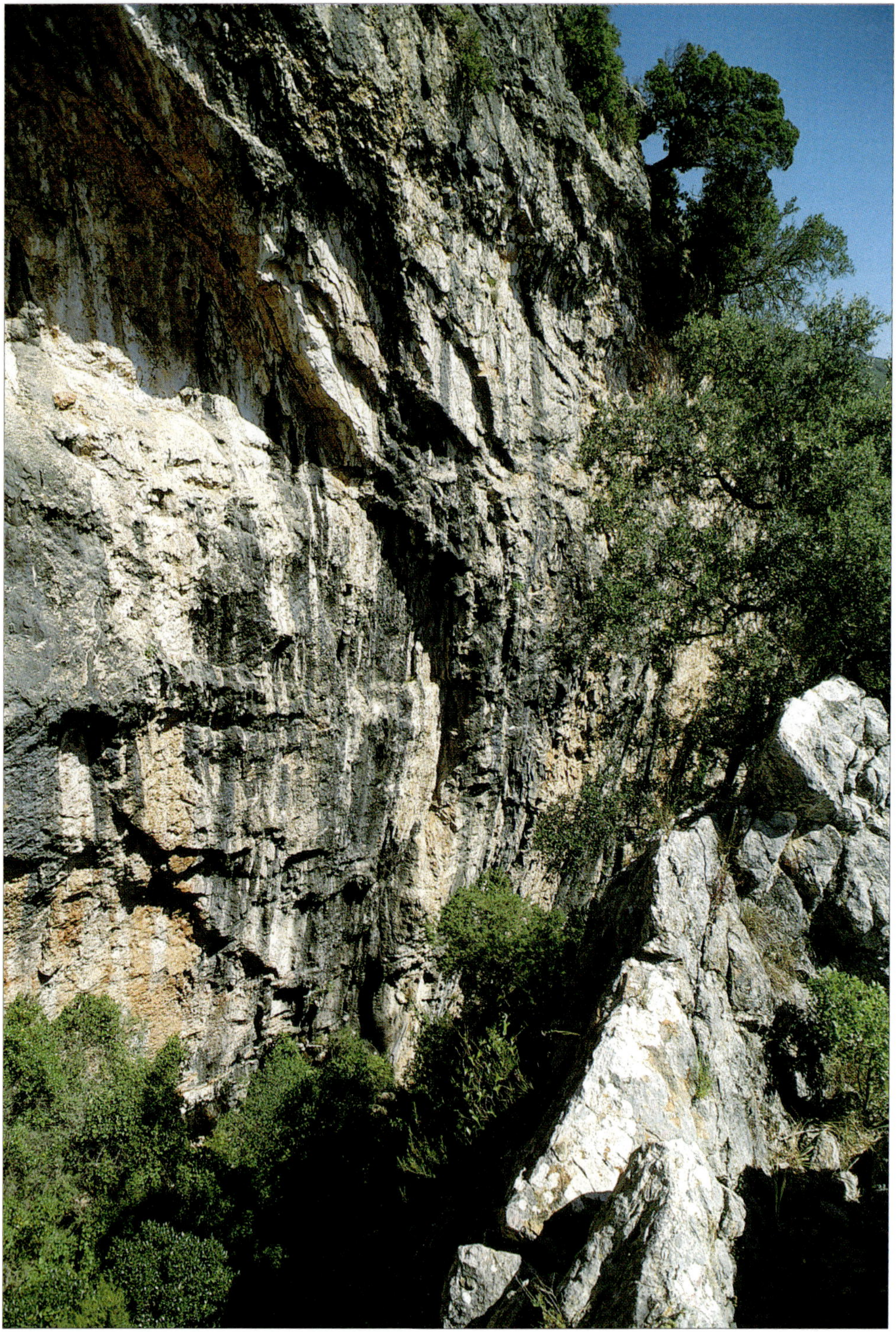

The cliffs of Fenda are situated in the lovely Arrábida nature park, about 30 mins drive south of the Lisbon bridges. There are some rare native flora specimens to be found here, and are fully protected by the three absolute reserves of ; Mata do Solitário, the Mata do Vidal and the Mata Coberta. Access to these areas is forbidden, and the whole issue of access in the area is of great concern, and is to be understood with important consideration. There are the lovely cliffs of Fojo, near to Sesimbra; but climbers here appreciate the importance of the nature reserve and do not climb here at all, in agreement. The cliffs of Fenda on the other hand, overlook the commercial beach area of Portinho da Arrábida, and are encircled by the 2 roads that lead down to the rocky cove. They have also been historically climbed on for many years now. There are issues of access here to protect the natural environment of this particular area. The position of access is unclear and you should obey any notices restricting climbing to particular periods etc. The most important consideration is to really care for the landscape, not to leave any litter at all, and look after it as a very special and beautiful spot. The authorities seem to have a sympathetic view to a handful of climbers visiting this area from time to time, because they are small in number and look after the area. It also has to be said that all the climbs are so hard, that it will be of use to only 1% of climbers anyway. The base of the cliff is also deep in the ground, and there isn't any view; so if you want a nice day, please don't risk upsetting the access issue, and have a great time down below on the lovely, golden sandy beach.

The climbing at Fenda is characteristically hard. Steep and impending walls of good quality limestone. Some of the routes are real stamina tests, and others have block moves from hell. On the Crododillo sector you have a slab directly behind the routes, which you can stand on to place all the quick draws by clip stick. You also have to be a bit careful, not to hit it – if/when you fall off. The central sector is tall and impressive and has some super long routes that pump the forerms right up. The crag is made up of lots of different walls and is accessed by a labyrinth of pathways below. It feels like a giant gash in the ground, and although it faces south, the temperature is often not too bad. In the rain it can stay dry, but after a few days of heavy rain, it begins to seep - and stay very humid. It is a great place to visit and climb, and at least if there is an access issue and you cannot climb, there is the lovely beach with some good cafés and restaraunts.

A falésia da Fenda situa-se no encantador Parque Natural da Arrábida, cerca de 30 minutos de carro a Sul de Lisboa, por qualquer das pontes. Existem aqui algumas espécies de plantas endémicas, protegidas pelas 3 reservas integrais: Mata do Solitário, Mata do Vidal e Mata Coberta. O acesso a estas áreas é proibido. Toda a questão dos acessos naquela área é bastante preocupante, e deverá ser seriamente considerada. Existem as fabulosas falésias do Fojo, mais próximas de Sesimbra, que actualmente não são frequentadas, de acordo com as normas do Parque e em consideração pelos valores naturais ali existentes. Já a falésia da Fenda, debruçada sobre a frequentada praia do Portinho da Arrábida, encontra-se entre duas estradas que levam, uma à praia e a outra a Setúbal. Escala-se neste local há várias décadas, mas também aqui se discute a possibilidade de restringir o seu acesso. Como a questão não está totalmente esclarecida, os escaladores deverão obedecer a qualquer sinal informativo sobre possíveis restrições. Em qualquer caso, é imperativo que se tenha um cuidado muito particular em preservar este local, não deixando qualquer lixo nem marcas de presença. Aparentemente é aceitável que os escaladores o visitem, com uma frequência moderada, enquanto forem em pequenos grupos e cuidem bem da área. De qualquer forma a dificuldade média das vias é tão elevada que apenas interessará a uma pequena percentagem dos escaladores. A base das vias é um carreiro enterrado entre rochedos de onde não se avista paisagem, por isso se procura um dia agradável, prefira abster-se de discutir a questão dos acessos e dirija-se antes à praia doirada e solarenga lá em baixo.

A escalada na Fenda é tipicamente dura. As vias decorrem em placas verticais ou extraprumadas de calcário de excelente qualidade. Algumas são verdadeiros testes de continuidade, outras têm movimentos de bloco que não lembram ao diabo. No sector Rampa dos Crocodilos existe uma placa tombada, mesmo encostada às vias – bastante extraprumadas – que facilita a utilização de um clip stick para colocar previamente as protecções. Muito cuidado nas quedas para não atingir esta placa. O sector central é alto e impressionante, com vias tão longas que vos deixarão os antebraços inchados antes do topo. A fenda é constituída por inúmeras paredes, cujo acesso se faz por baixo e é um verdadeiro labirinto. Dá a sensação de ser um gigantesco golpe no solo e, embora a parede seja virada a Sul, a temperatura nunca é muito elevada. Pode manter-se seca mesmo que chova, mas após vários dias de chuva intensa, acaba por encharcar-se. É um local fantástico para visitar e, se entretanto houver restrições de acesso, tem sempre a belíssima praia do Portinho onde há bons cafés e restaurantes.

WAY DOWN - EAST SIDE: Here there is no definite landmark to get your bearings on. Set your kilometer measure in the car as you pass the buildings at Figueirinha; after 2.4k you get the first turn down to the beach - reset - then at 0.7km you will see these blocks and a path leading down. You must find this correct path since the whole hillside is covered with caverns and gorges, and is impassable. The track is well worn. Eventually it twists and turns and ends up at the bottom of the gorge. It takes around 15-20 mins to walk the length of the cliff at the bottom because it is incredibly blocky and up and down. (6 mins down - 9 mins up)

WAY DOWN - WEST SIDE: At least on this side you have a good and definite marker as the 26km post, which is also 0.9km from the turning down to Portinho da Arrábida. Just near here there is a small parking spot for a couple of cars. The path down however is back towards the km marker and drops down from the other side of the wall by the leg marker. This is a steep path and you need the insitu rope for this descent. You certainly need the rope for ascent in the rain. This takes you to the Crocodilo sector, and is best used for the first 3 sectors. (4 mins down, 8 mins up)

WAY UP - FROM BEACH: At least you can see the cliff from this direction, and have the car in a more protected area. Take the track along the beach past a building and some islands at 70 metres; continue for another 70 metres and just before some huts and the track opens up onto the big beach; a path leads off left and up the hill. After 80 metres the path heads to the left and up the barren steep slope to the cliff - arriving at Paparrazzi sector. (10 -15 mins) Note: Road to Portinho is single width, and can easily get gridlocked - Chaos; go back to the bar for yet another!

Pedreiras - Fenda - Outão

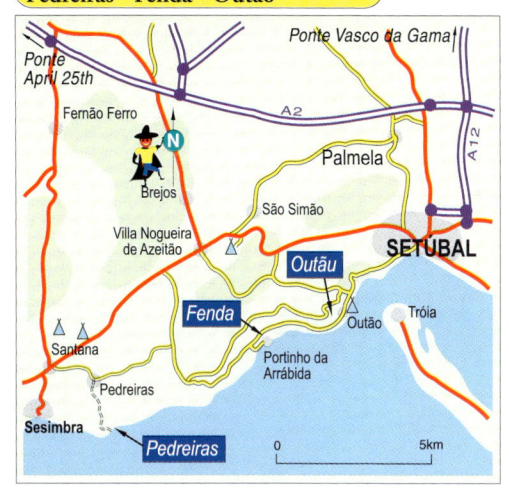

Fenda

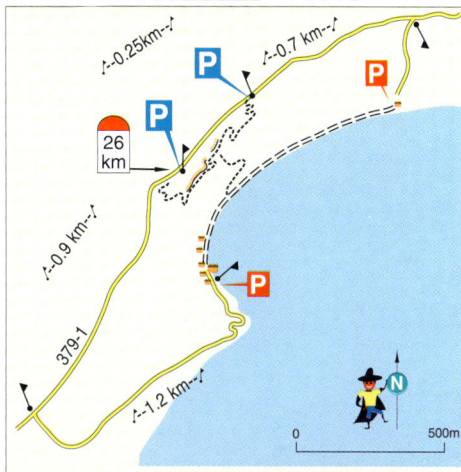

Camping Outão***
Estrada da Figueirina, 2900-182 Setúbal
Tel: 265 238 318   Fax: 265 228 098
www.roteiro-campista.pt/Setubal/outao.htm
Notes: A small campsite, right on the sea and only 4km from Setúbal. Stoney ground.
Open: (01/01-31/12) - medium size; 3.6 hectares;

Bars - Portinho, Setúbal, Sesimbra
Shop - Setúbal, Azeitão
Petrol Station - Setúbal
Supermarket - Setúbal
Climbing Shop - Lisboa

Fenda Access problem

Local Info: This whole area is known as the Costa Azul, and much of it is a national park; also - some parts of it are completely forbidden to enter. It is however a definite place to visit on the tourist map and the beaches are superb. At present there is climbing in some areas, but this is always under review. Do not use these cliffs as a climbing holiday destination, and restrict your visits to a rare, and single day.

Fenda Access agreement

To climb at Fenda, you must register with the National Park;
Parque Natural da Arrábida,
Praça da República, 2900-587 SETÚBAL
Fax: (351) 265 541 155

Pedreiras - Fenda - Outão

BRANCA DE NEVE 7b, Fenda; Miguel 'Mikey' Loureiro

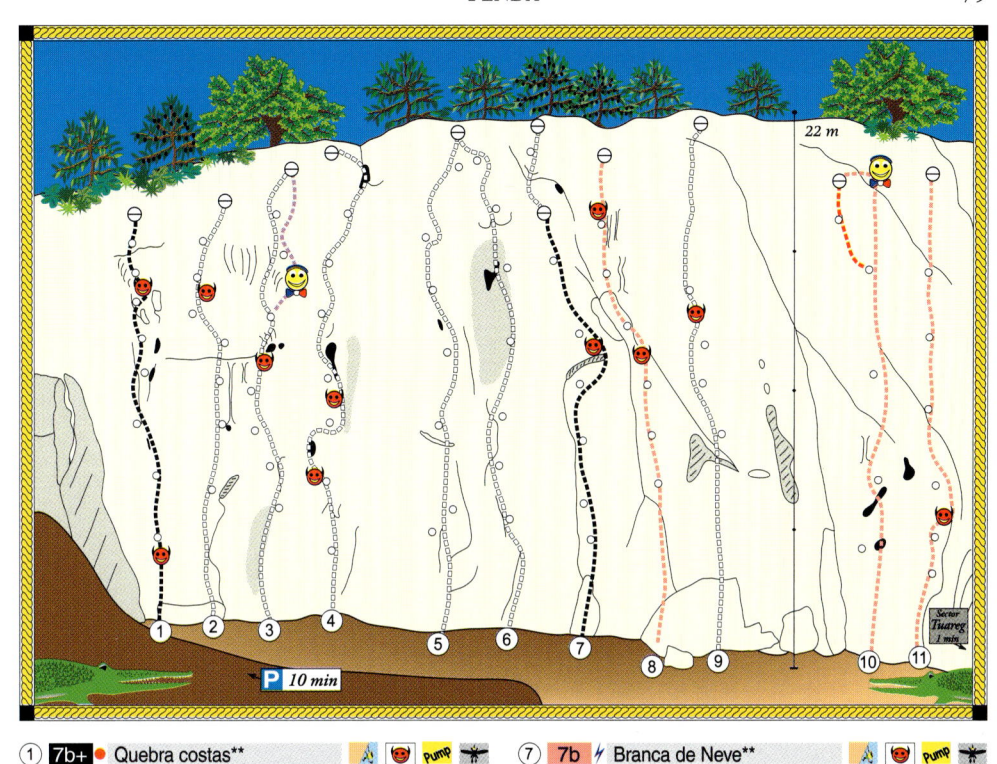

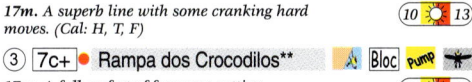

FENDA

① **7b+** ● Quebra costas**
17m. The first of the overhanging terrors. Deep in the dark, shady corner. (Cal: H, T, F)

② **7c+** ● Tona***
17m. A superb line with some cranking hard moves. (Cal: H, T, F)

③ **7c+** ● Rampa dos Crocodilos**
17m. A full on fest of forearms getting chomped through. Hard variation finish to the right. (Cal: H, T, F)

④ **7c** ⚡ O meu nome é Tó-Tó***
17m. A superb overhanging stamina fest. No hard moves, except the finish feels like font 8a. (Cal: H, T, F)

⑤ **7c+** ● A Canalha**
17m. Start with the first 2 bolts pre-clipped, and keep on in there. (Cal: H, T, F)

⑥ **7c** ● O rei manda***
17m. Energy sapping and steep. (Cal: H, T, F)

⑦ **7b** ⚡ Branca de Neve**
16m. A steep groove that offers plenty of holds, but is a bit polished, so care in belaying for sudden falls. (Cal: E, H, B)

⑧ **6c** ● Canja Laranja***
18m. The big groove line in the centre of the sector. (Cal: E, H, B)

⑨ **7c+** ● Fungágá da bicharada**
19m. Technical. (Cal: H, C, M)

⑩ **6c+** ⚡ Bad Boy***
13m. An excellent climb which has an action packed finish. There are 2 finishes offering either crimps or slopers. (Cal: H, B, T)

⑪ **6c** ● Speedy Gonzalez**
14m. A sequency start that works better as a dyno. Long route on good holds, last move is not hard, but definitely the crux for the 6c climber.. (Cal: H,X, B, A,T)

Résumé. This is the first sector that you arrive at and is easily recognised by a giant diagonal slit in the ground. The whole sector overhangs a lot, and stays dry in the rain; but seeps quite badly after a few days of heavy rain. You can virtually clip up most of the hard routes from the slab opposite. You also must clip all of the bolts quite quickly, or else if you fall, you may smash your back on the slab. A demanding sector but perfect for those on stamina training. There is also a good 8a traverse along the base of this sector. It does get sun on the top of the routes, but the lower halfs are deep in a trench so get quite a lot of shade.

Crocodilos - Tuareg - Jardim - Limpopo - Paparazzi - Carallon - Putos

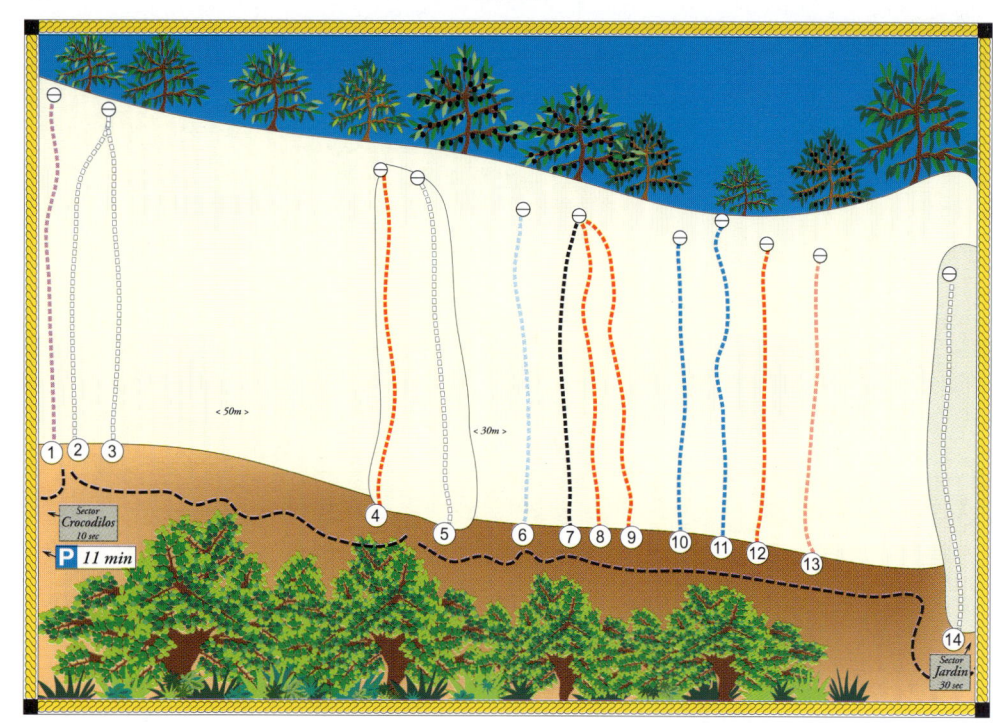

FENDA

#	Grade	Name
1	8b	Quáquá come kiki

19m.

#	Grade	Name
2	7c+	Oitava Comédia
3	7c	Chuva de Estrelas
4	7a+	Cara de Mau
5	7c+	Olho de Vidro

Résumé. *This area is a bit spread out, but does offer some very good climbing.*

#	Grade	Name
6	6a	Abre as Pernas
7	7b	Pata de Elefante
8	7a	Terra à Vista
9	7a	Dança da Pança
10	6b+	Berber
11	6b	Tuareg
12		O Ultimo Shamã
13	6c	Galeão Negro
14	7c	Torre do Tombo

Crocodilos - **Tuareg** - Jardim - Limpopo - Paparazzi - Carallon - Putos

Fenda

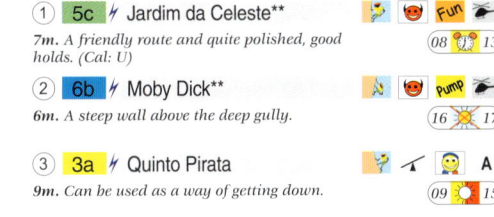

① **5c** Jardim da Celeste**
7m. *A friendly route and quite polished, good holds. (Cal: U)*

② **6b** Moby Dick**
6m. *A steep wall above the deep gully.*

③ **3a** Quinto Pirata
9m. *Can be used as a way of getting down.*

④ **6b** Terror na Autovia
11m.

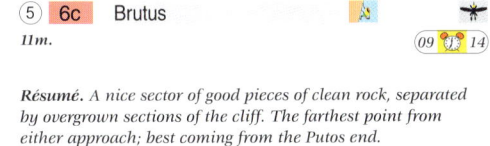

⑤ **6c** Brutus
11m.

⑥ **7b** Já Enganei Mais Um
16m.

⑦ **7b+** Chapa3
16m.

⑧ **7a+** Aldeia dos Macacos
14m.

⑨ **6c** B-a-ba
13m.

⑩

⑪ **8a** Tira Teimas
13m.

Résumé. A nice sector of good pieces of clean rock, separated by overgrown sections of the cliff. The farthest point from either approach; best coming from the Putos end.

Crocodilos - Tuareg - **Jardim** - Limpopo - Paparazzi - Carallon - Putos

FENDA

① **6c** ⚡ Maricão**
24m. *The best 6c in the area with a punchy start over an amazing chasm!. (Cal: A, T, C)*

② **7c** ● Dói-Dói**
26m.

③ **7c** ● Tripas à Moda do Portinho**
28m. *A superb wall climb, with a bit of loose rock.*

④ **8a+** Bambi
28m.

⑤ **7c+** Osga Pitosga
30m.

⑥ **7b+** Bodas de Muxacho
30m.

⑦ **7b+** O Gato da Bruxa
25m.

⑧ **7b+** Meia Suja
27m.

⑨ **7a+** Limpó-pó
24m.

⑩ **7b** Capitão Hadock
24m.

⑪ **7b+** Gugudádá
24m.

⑫ **7b+** Cabra Cega
20m.

⑬ **8a+** A Terceira Visão
30m.

⑭ **7b+** Fita Métrica
30m.

⑮ **7a** Uma ns Moita
30m.

Résumé. *This is a very impressive sector with some of the best climbs at Fenda. It is also a nice open sector with a bit of a view. You do have to scramble around in the big blocks to find the routes over on the left.*

Crocodilos - Tuareg - Jardim - **Limpó-pó** - Paparazzi - Carallon - Putos

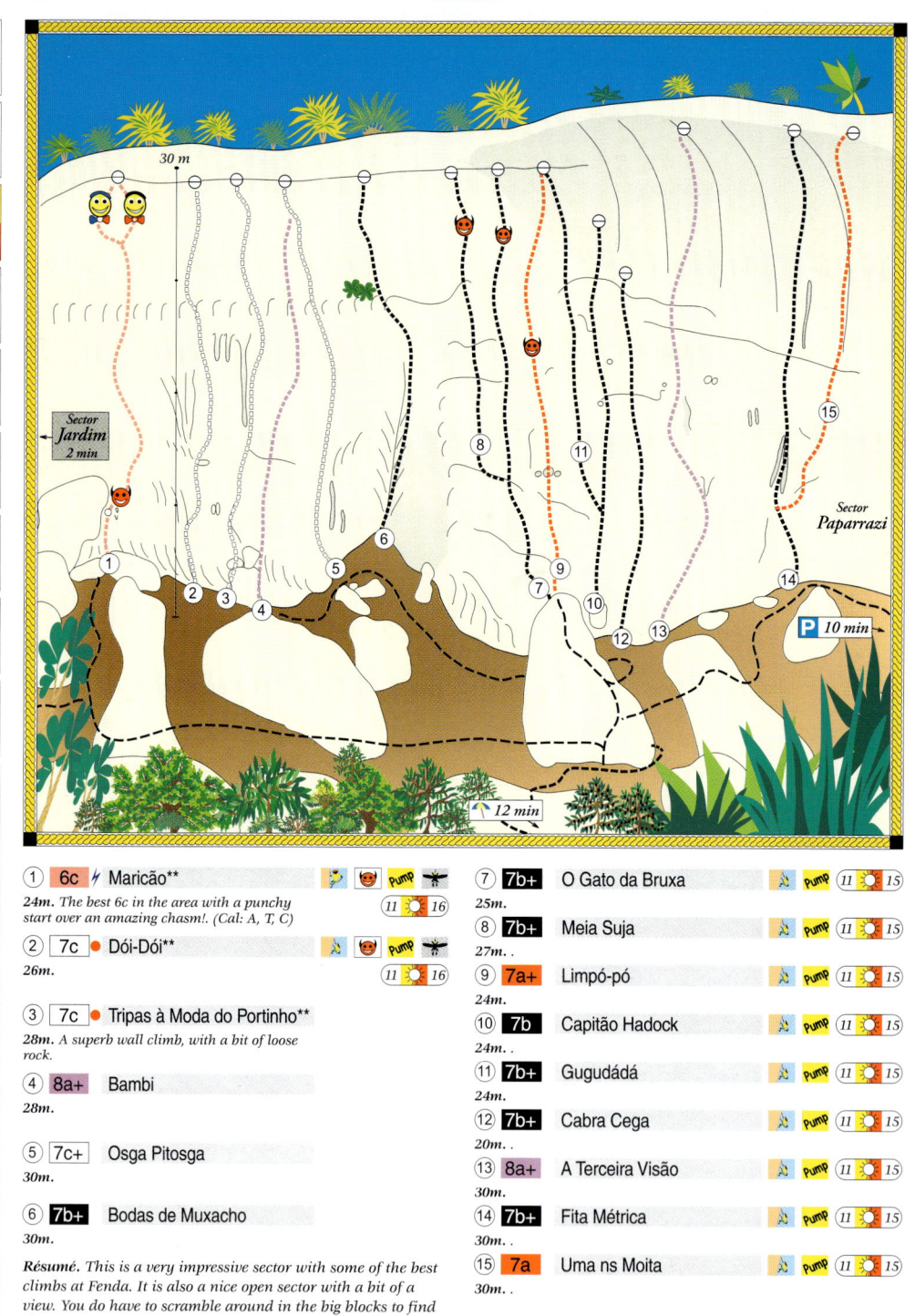

LIMPÓ-PÓ 7a+, Fenda; João Schiappa

PÃO DE NOZ 7c+, Fenda; Nuno Pinheiro

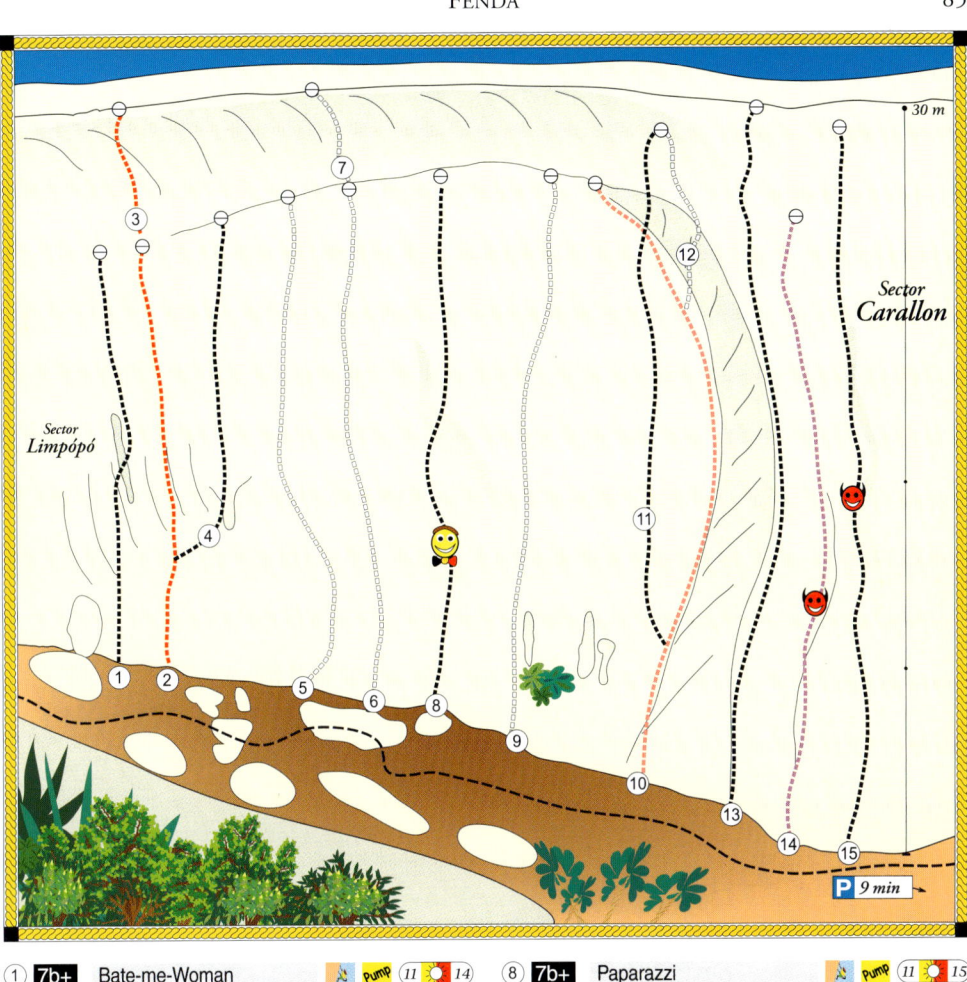

FENDA

Sector Limpópó

Sector Carallon

30 m

P 9 min

#	Grade	Name					#	Grade	Name				
1	7b+	Bate-me-Woman 24m.		Pump	11	14	8	7b+	Paparazzi		Pump	11	15
2	7a+	Um-dó-li-tá		Pump	11	14	9	7c+	Rei da Sardinha		Pump	11	15
3	7a	Os Ilegais			11	14	10	6c+	Reforma Educativa		Pump	11	15
4	7b	Baba de Camelo		Pump	11	14	11	7b+	Nosferatu		Pump	11	15
5	7c+	Pão de Noz		Pump	11	14	12	7c	Clic e Cai		Pump	11	15
6	7c	Tiro e Queda			11	14	13	7b+	Ran-tan-plan		Pump	11	15
7	7c+	Intifada		Pump	11	14	14	8a	Marsupilami		Pump	11	15
							15	7b+	Unicórnio		Pump	11	15

Résumé. An area of big smooth walls that have plenty of sustained climbs.

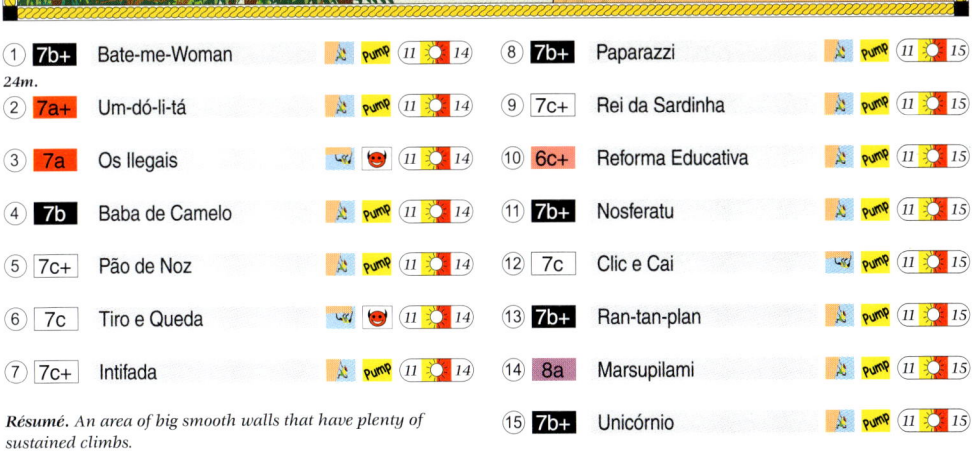

Crocodilos - Tuareg - Jardim - Limpó-pó - Paparazzi - Carallon - Putos

FENDA

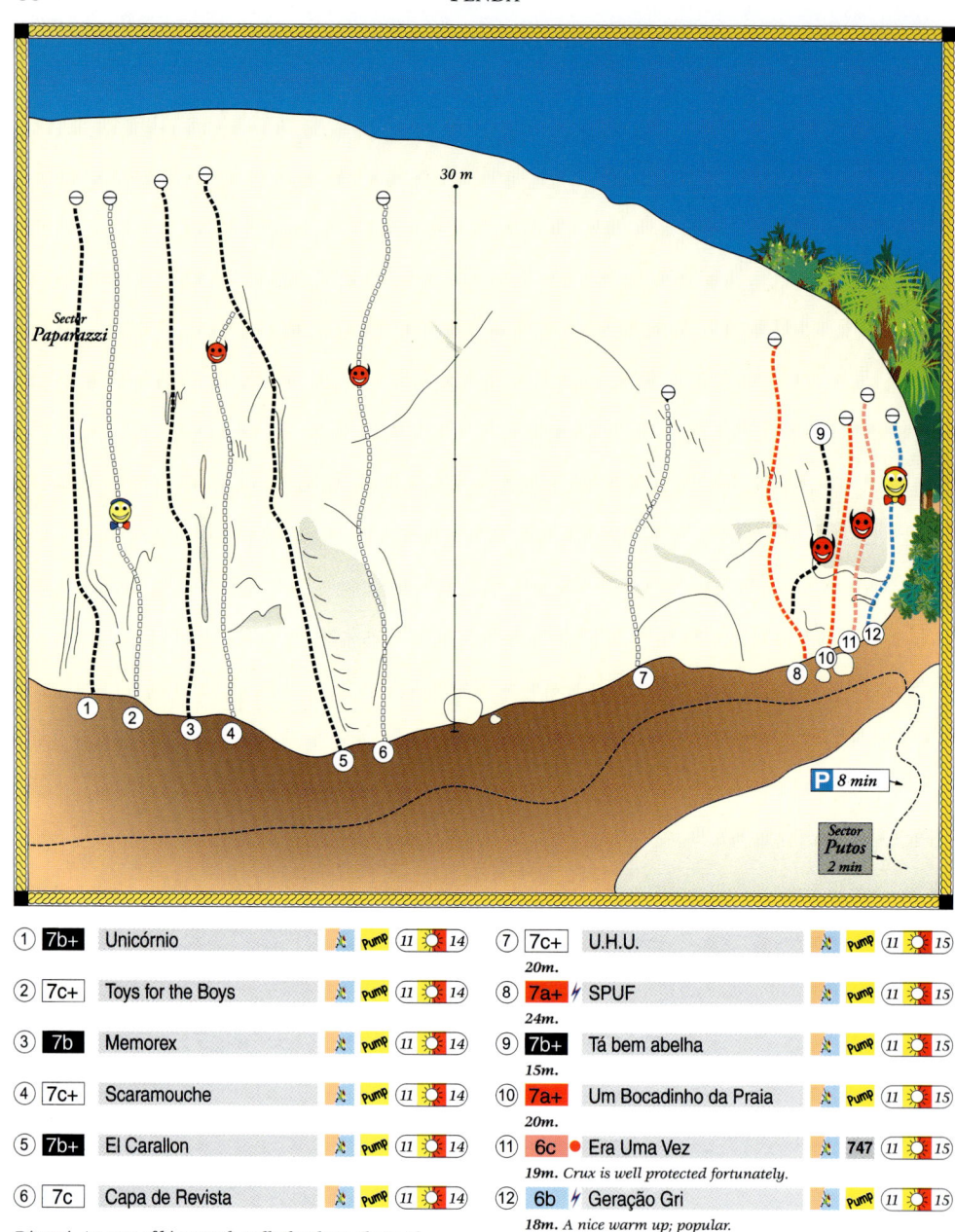

#	Grade	Name	Info
1	7b+	Unicórnio	Pump (11) 14
2	7c+	Toys for the Boys	Pump (11) 14
3	7b	Memorex	Pump (11) 14
4	7c+	Scaramouche	Pump (11) 14
5	7b+	El Carallon	Pump (11) 14
6	7c	Capa de Revista	Pump (11) 14
7	7c+	U.H.U. — 20m.	Pump (11) 15
8	7a+ ⚡	SPUF — 24m.	Pump (11) 15
9	7b+	Tá bem abelha — 15m.	Pump (11) 15
10	7a+	Um Bocadinho da Praia — 20m.	Pump (11) 15
11	6c ●	Era Uma Vez — 19m. Crux is well protected fortunately.	747 (11) 15
12	6b ⚡	Geração Gri — 18m. A nice warm up; popular.	Pump (11) 15

Résumé. An area of big smooth walls that have plenty of sustained climbs.

Sector Paparazzi

Sector Putos 2 min

P 8 min

Crocodilos - Tuareg - Jardim - Limpó-pó - Paparazzi - Carallon - Putos

EL CARALLON /7b+, Fenda; The Ledgendary; Francisco 'Chico' Ataíde

PUTOS IN THE GYM 6c, Fenda; Jingo

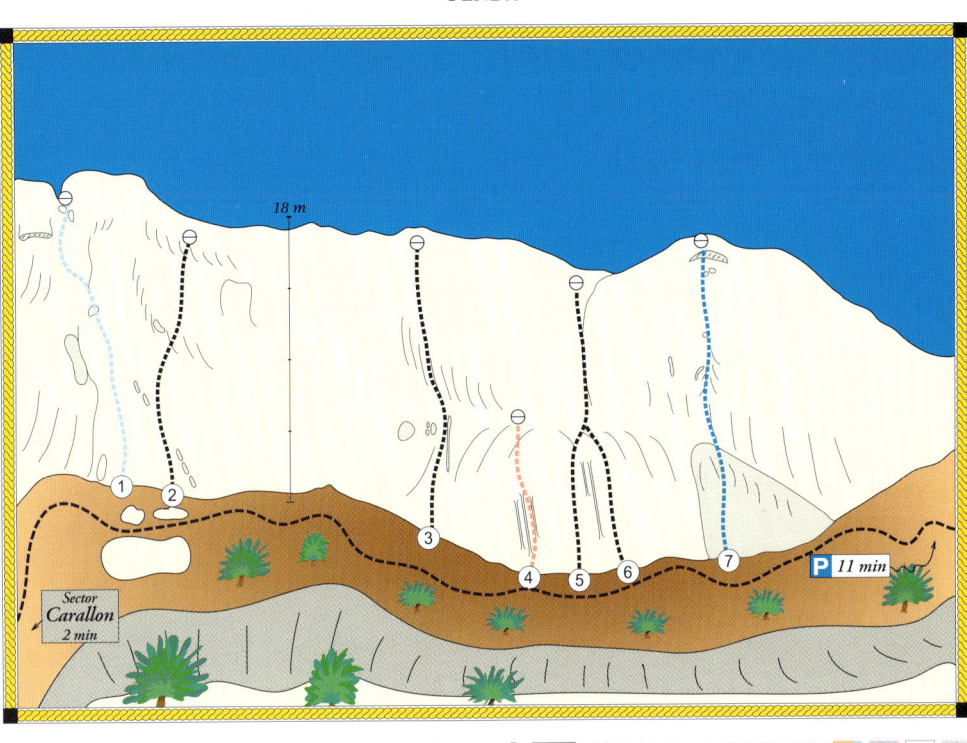

FENDA

① **6a** ⚡ Verde-código-verde**
18m. *A surprisingly good little route. (Cal: J, C, H, F)*

② **7b** Clã do Botanova
17m.

③ **7b** Papão com Manteiga
15m.

④ **6c** ⚡ Putos in the Gym
8m. *Short, sharp and full on power. Too steep also to ever get the sun.*

⑤ **7b** Bic
17m. *Friggin steep.*

⑥ **7b** Bosh
17m. *Friggin steep.*

⑦ **6a** Beija-flor

Résumé. *This sector forms a small gorge on your way down from the Eastern parking area. It can be overgrown and damp as hell after rain; but then it can be lovely and dry, and in the shade. Very steep and powerful, a complete contrast to the long stamina routes of the main sectors.*

Crocodilos - Tuareg - Jardim - Limpó-pó - Paparazzi - Carallon - **Putos**

Outão

① **5b** ⚡ Montanha***

34m. *A superb climb and very well situated. An easy climb for the grade and handy tree to belay in the shade. You can split the climb into 2 pitches easily. (If you pull the rope through from the top, it can easily get stuck in the trees to the right, directly above.) (Cal: U, C)*

∽13∽ (11) ☀ (17)

② **3b** ⚡ Little climb

8m. *A small little pillar that could be useful for kids. (Cal: Y, D)*

∽4∽ (10) ☀ (17)

Résumé. *A very nice cliff, only seconds away from the ugliest cement factory on the planet, which is completely out of sight thank goodness! Except when you peep over the top. Great views over the fortress and hospital and azure sea. The bedding plane of the rock here is coming up and out of the cliff, so big blocks of the cliff could always come away. Most parts do seem solid, but act with caution after rainy periods. The great central wall has still to be developed. There is room for another 20 routes here of excellent quality.*

Central Wall

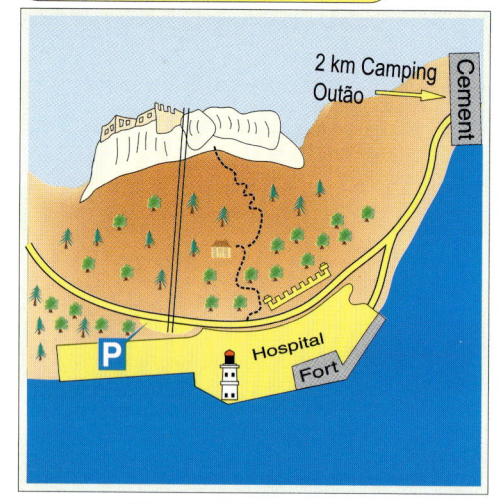

MONTANHA 5b, Outão; Wobbly

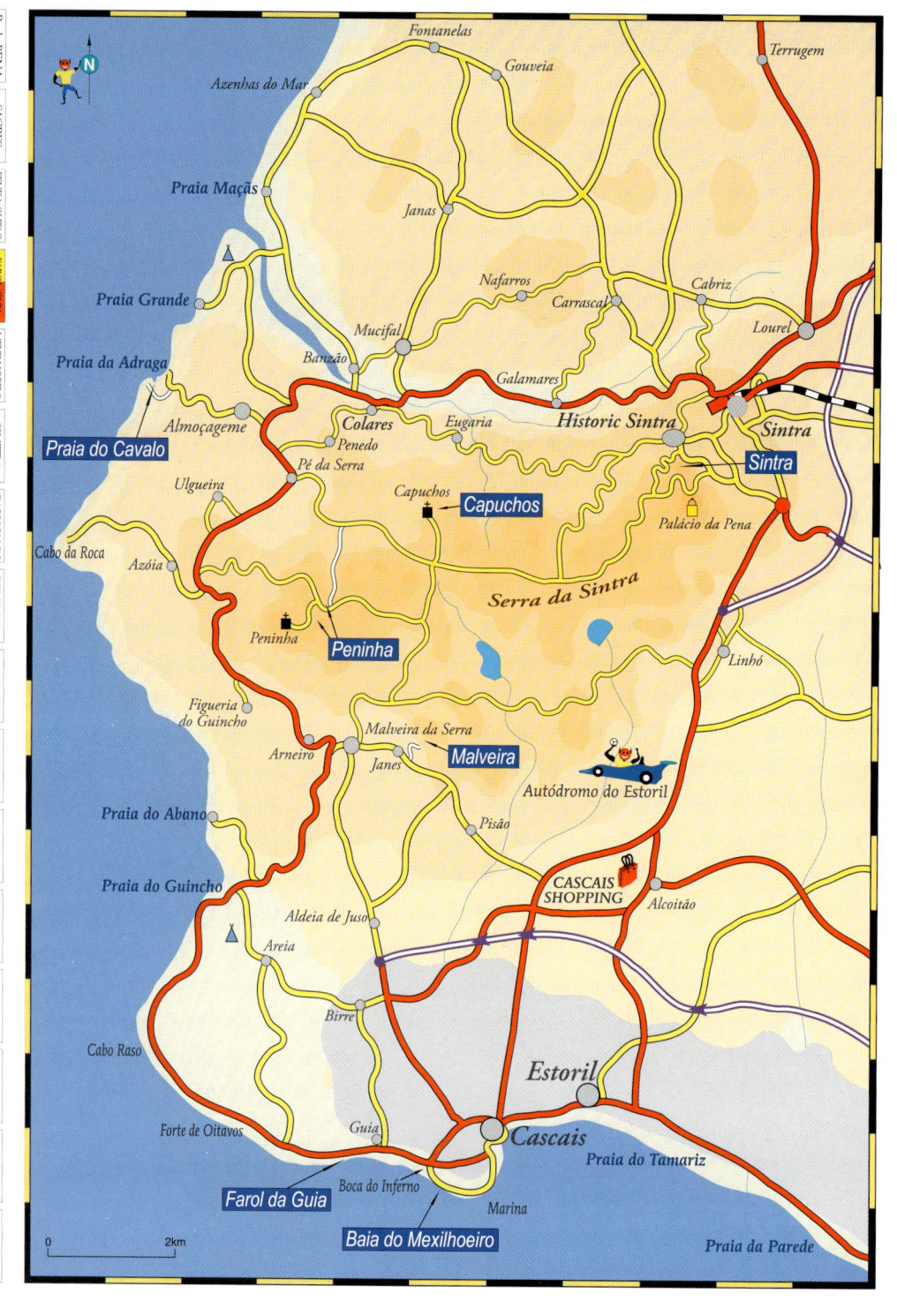

Farol Da Guia

OVOMALTINE 6a+, Farol da Guia; Jingo

TAXI 6c, Farol da Guia; Juan Manuel Perez

Introduction - Introdução

The coastline to the west of Lisbon is known as the Costa do Estoril, and fortunately is nothing like the usual, uncharismatic, hideous, touriod ridden Costas, you may have seen in pleby travel brochures. This is an upmarket Costa for a start, but happily we are in Portugal and you don't get the off the scale wealth that, inhabits Monaco. Also the Atlantic Ocean tends to be a bit too bumpy for the gin and tonic brigade; and pointedly, you actually have to be a damm competent sailor, to venture out of the ports on this coastline and return alive on a regular basis. The town of Estoril is fine enough, with its Casino and superb Palácio hotel. The perfect residence to get through stacks of wedge at an alarming rate. Happily, further on down the coast is the beautiful town of Cascais. This was once a quaint old fishing village, which nestled behind a powerful citadel style fort, which commanded the headland ahead of Lisbon. Today, it is a bustling little town, however, still with lovely character and fine, ritzy little boutiques. There are plenty of good restaurants, modern sleek bars, and traditional seafood restaurants. There are open piazzas, sandy beaches, and exotic gardens. There is a very proactive Centro Cultural de Cascais, which has a series of concerts and other cultural attractions. Cascais is a lovely place to visit and either stay at, or somewhere close by. It has perhaps undergone a bit too much development, but still remains charming and a very relaxing place to chill out.

As you drive out of town to the west, the landscape changes immediately to a very rugged, wind blown Atlantic. You will very quickly come to Farol da Guia – lighthouse of the hamlet of Guia. This light has been used to alert thousands of ships about the impending doom, if they attempt to scale the vertical 15-20 metres of limestone below. It also acts as the beacon, leading us to the lovely climbing that the cliffs offer. Almost opposite the petrol station, there is a banner above a footway, 'Escola de Escalada da Guia.' This leads directly to a little picnic area with a view of the sea, and where proper steps lead down to the platforms at the base of the cliff. Most of the climbs are vertical and on very good quality limestone. Some of the more popular routes are a slightly polished, but the rock in general stays pretty rough. All the routes are equipped with stainless bolts, and are for the most, sympathetically bolted. It can get a bit hot down at Guia when the sun is fully out. But if you are out of season, it can be a lovely sun trap that allows you to climb in a T-shirt and shorts, when those up at the top of the cliff, are togged up in duffle coats. You can climb here at all states of the tide, but not in a rough sea!

O litoral a Oeste de Lisboa é conhecido por Costa do Estoril; por sorte não é nada semelhante às habituais Costas invadidas por turistas, medonhas e pouco cativantes, que pode ter visto nos panfletos de viagens económicas. Para começar é uma zona de luxo, mas felizmente estamos em Portugal, onde não se atingem os extremos da opulência que caracterizam por exemplo, o Mónaco; por outro lado, o oceano Atlântico é demasiado batido para a brigada do gim tónico e claro, é preciso ser um marinheiro extremamente competente para se aventurar a sair regularmente dos portos desta costa e voltar vivo. O Estoril é bastante agradável com o seu Casino e o magnífico hotel Palácio. Um lugar perfeito para se ficar sem cheta a um ritmo assustador. Felizmente, um pouco mais adiante, fica a bonita cidade de Cascais. Foi em tempos uma aldeia piscatória, antiga e engraçada, escondida atrás duma poderosa fortaleza que dominava o promontório à entrada de Lisboa. Actualmente é uma cidadezinha animada, mantendo contudo o carácter encantador e pequenas boutiques elegantes e requintadas. Tem muitos restaurantes excelentes, bares modernos e atraentes, bem como marisqueiras tradicionais. Tem ainda praças abertas, praias cheias de areia e jardins exóticos. O Centro Cultural de Cascais é muito dinâmico por isso apresenta sempre uma série de concertos e outras iniciativas culturais. Cascais é um lugar encantador para visitar e para ficar lá ou nas redondezas. Talvez se tenha desenvolvido um pouquinho demais, mas continua a ser fascinante e um local muito tranquilo para descontrair.

 Saindo da cidade em direcção a Oeste, a paisagem torna-se imediatamente num Atlântico muito agitado e ventoso. Chega-se rapidamente ao Farol da Guia – farol do lugarejo da Guia. Este farol foi usado para alertar milhares de navios para o perigo iminente, se tentassem aproximar-se dos 15-20 metros de calcário que lhe ficam por baixo. Também serve de sinal para nos conduzir ao lugar de escalada encantador que as falésias oferecem. Quase em frente da estação de serviço, há um letreiro por cima duma passagem calcetada onde pode ler-se "Escola de Escalada da Guia". Esta conduz directamente a um pequeno local para piquenique, com vista para o mar, onde existe uma escada que dá acesso às plataformas na base da falésia. A maior parte das vias são verticais e de calcário de muito boa qualidade. Algumas mais populares estão um pouco patinadas, mas a rocha dum modo geral mantém-se bastante aderente. Todas as vias estão equipadas com tiges de inox e, para a maior parte das pessoas, simpaticamente distribuídas. Com o Sol a pino, a parte inferior da Guia pode ficar um pouco quente, mas fora da época torna-se numa espécie de estufa agradável que lhe permite escalar de calções e T-shirt, enquanto quem estiver no cimo da falésia terá de vestir casaco de lã. Pode escalar aqui com qualquer maré, mas não com o mar encrespado!

The coastline around Guincho can be spectacular in any weather. The winds are nearly always from the West, as all the bent and twisted trees will illustrate. There is a constant battering from the sea, yet no sooner is the wind gains its strength, than it dies away to leave dazzling golden beaches and great sunbathing weather.

GUINCHO itself, is a mixture of bays, with rocks and flat beaches. There are some great waves for surfing, and you often get around 2-300 people out surfing every day at weekends. There is a nice trendy beach bar, and some restaraunts all along the coast. It's world famous, yet is still very unspoilt - it cannot be tamed!

Cascais old harbour and beach.

Museu Condes Castro Guimarães, Cascais

EXPEDIÇÃO
Loja Técnica de Aventura

Qual é a tua próxima via?

*What's your next route?

HAGLÖFS

EDELRID

KONG

Rua João Saraiva 34 A/B
Alvalade 1700-250 Lx

Telf: 218 435 580
Fax: 218 462 834

expedicao@cipreia.pt

FAROL DA GUIA

Cascais

Cascais - Guincho - Accommodation

Guincho: Approach Directions:
In this area there are plenty of different accommodation styles to suit any taste. The whole area is quite up-market, so the hotels are definitely in the medium price category. The Palacio hotel in Estoril is off the scale and lovely to stay at, but will cost you as much as central London or Paris! There are many reasonable hotels and it is best to contact the tourist board in Cascais.

There are a few campsites to the west of Lisboa, but the most convenient by far is the pleasant site at Guincho. This is under 1km from the beach, and has a bus stop outside. From here you can very easily reach most of the cliffs in the area. For Sintra-Traffic in the area can be a problem near the autodromo-motor circuit, so a route via Malveria is well worth considering. The wind in Portugal can blow hard, so pick a camping spot that is sheltered from the prevailing westerlies. A robust tent in Easter gales is essential, and one that stays up without pegs!

Camping Orbitur Guincho***
Areia, Guincho, 2750-053 Cascais.
Tel: 214 870 450
Fax: 214 872 167
Notes: Mixed site of camping and permanent caravans
Good shade with low pine trees; chalets to rent.
Small shop, bar and restaurant.
Open: (1/01-31/12)

Bar: Guincho beach, Marina Cascais
Shop: Birre & Camping
Petrol Station: Birre - near end of A5
Supermarket: Cascais shopping - giant centre
Jumbo-Cascais centre
Climbing shop: Vertical at Sintra

Farol da Guia: Approach Directions:
1). Autostrada: Follow signs from end of A5 to Cascais, then signs towards Guincho to end up on the roundabout at Guia. Here follow sign going west to Guincho. After 500 meters there is a petrol station on the right - with an artificial giant pine tree. On your left is the entrance down to the cliff. There is a sign above the path with 'Escola de Escalada da Guia.' The cliff is only 2 mins away, and with a nice picnic area at the top, which is also the best area for tiny kids.

Top Tip: Check out the Moinho D. Quixote bar at Azoia, for late night drinking in a stylish joint.

Farol da Guia

FANTAMAR 4c+, Farol da Guia; José Texiera

Farol Da Guia

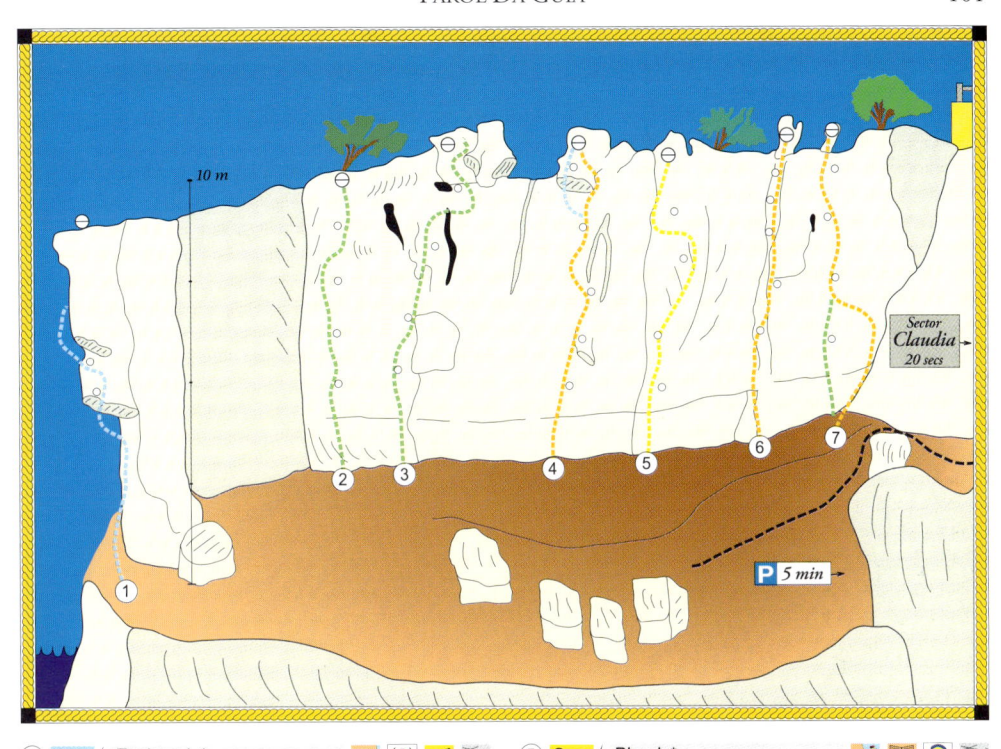

① **6a+** ⚡ **Esplanada***
9m. You get a wonderful feeling of the sea here on a rough day, it gets louder the higher you get. A physical excursion. (Cal: S, P, L)

② **5a** ⚡ **Cogumelos***
7m. A short wall that is certainly more technical than it looks, a good outing for a lower grade climber. (San)

③ **5a** ⚡ **Gália***
9m. Good juggy climbing to an awkward crux. Pulling on the top giant block is optionally scary! (San) Note: A bird often nests in the top break, so clip 4th bolt early.

④ **4c** ⚡ **Fantamar***
9m. A wall with fragile jugs, and a good thuggy finish. Going left at the last bolt around the overhang is a good 6a power reach. (San)

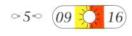

⑤ **3a+** ⚡ **Bloody***
9m. A nice delicate wall, followed by a difficult move for the shorter climber. (San)

⑥ **4a+** ⚡ **Crateras da Lua***
9m. A nice arête with a few sharp, but sandy holds. An excellent introduction route. (San)

⑦ **3c** ⚡ **Querubin***
8m. A flat wall with some different variations. Going right then left is the easiest. A direct line is possible at around 5c. (San)

Résumé. This is the far end of the cliff that can be reached easily by walking along the bottom. You can access the top quite easily, from the track to the right of the building on top of the cliff. The rock is really sandstone and quite soft. It does give a good sector for beginners, and with plenty of protection points. Short and sweet.

Esplanada - Claudia - Tubo - Ovomaltine - Astérix - Taxi - Solo - Metamorfose - Corta Unhas - Cantinho - Fred Astaire

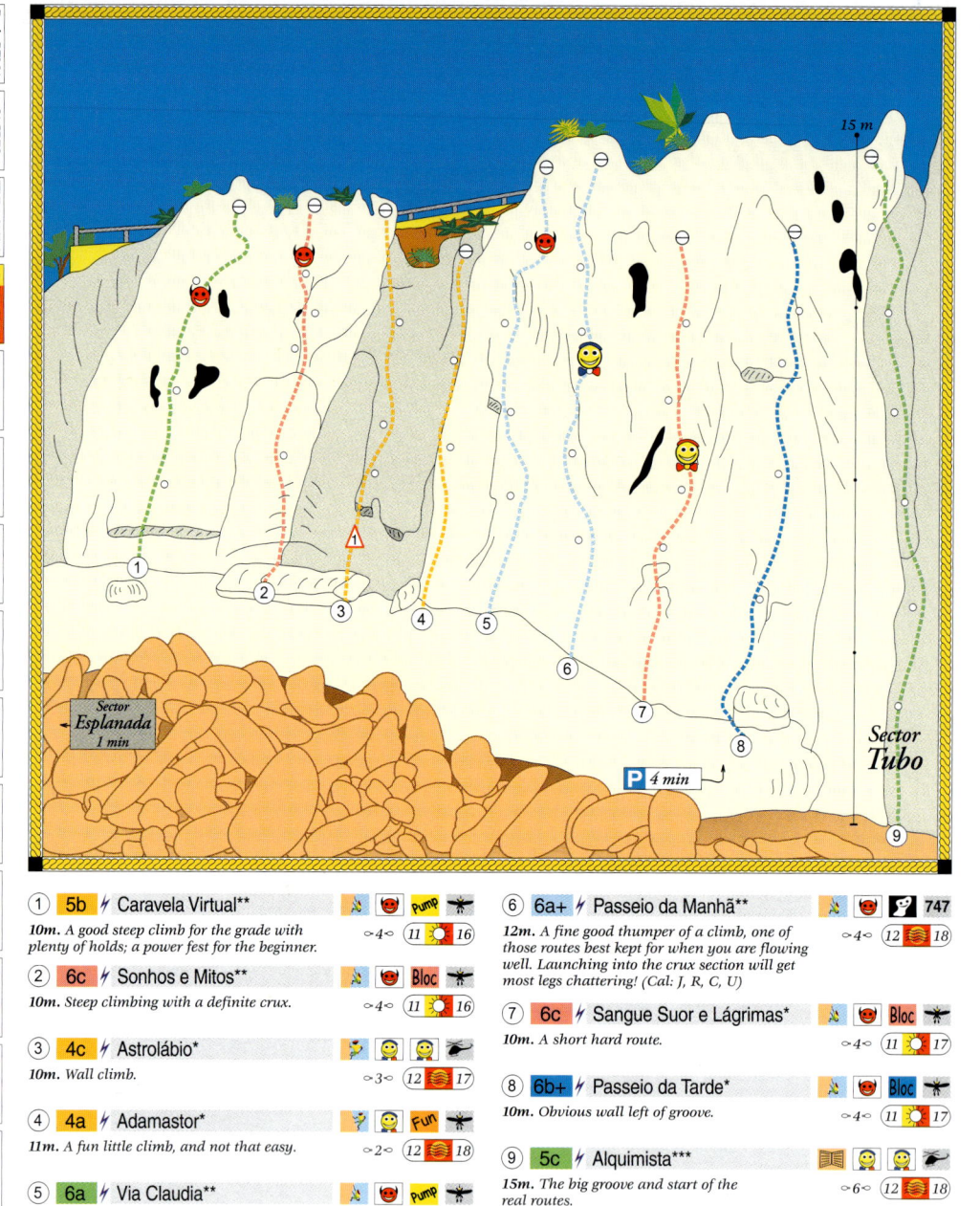

FAROL DA GUIA

① **5b** ⚡ Caravela Virtual**
10m. *A good steep climb for the grade with plenty of holds; a power fest for the beginner.*

② **6c** ⚡ Sonhos e Mitos**
10m. *Steep climbing with a definite crux.*

③ **4c** ⚡ Astrolábio*
10m. *Wall climb.*

④ **4a** ⚡ Adamastor*
11m. *A fun little climb, and not that easy.*

⑤ **6a** ⚡ Via Claudia**
11m. *A classic route and an old sandbag at grade 5! Don't finish directly up but step right 1 metre to belay. (Cal: C, L, I)*

⑥ **6a+** ⚡ Passeio da Manhã**
12m. *A fine good thumper of a climb, one of those routes best kept for when you are flowing well. Launching into the crux section will get most legs chattering! (Cal: J, R, C, U)*

⑦ **6c** ⚡ Sangue Suor e Lágrimas*
10m. *A short hard route.*

⑧ **6b+** ⚡ Passeio da Tarde*
10m. *Obvious wall left of groove.*

⑨ **5c** ⚡ Alquimista***
15m. *The big groove and start of the real routes.*

Résumé. *A good sector to begin at, if you are warming up or coming to the cliff for the first time. Short routes - but with good climbing on their entire length. Completely non-tidal.*

Esplanada - **Claudia** - Tubo - Ovomaltine - Astérix - Taxi - Solo - Metamorfose - Corta Unhas - Cantinho - Fred Astaire

ADAMASTOR 4a, Farol da Guia; Mariá Garcia Campos

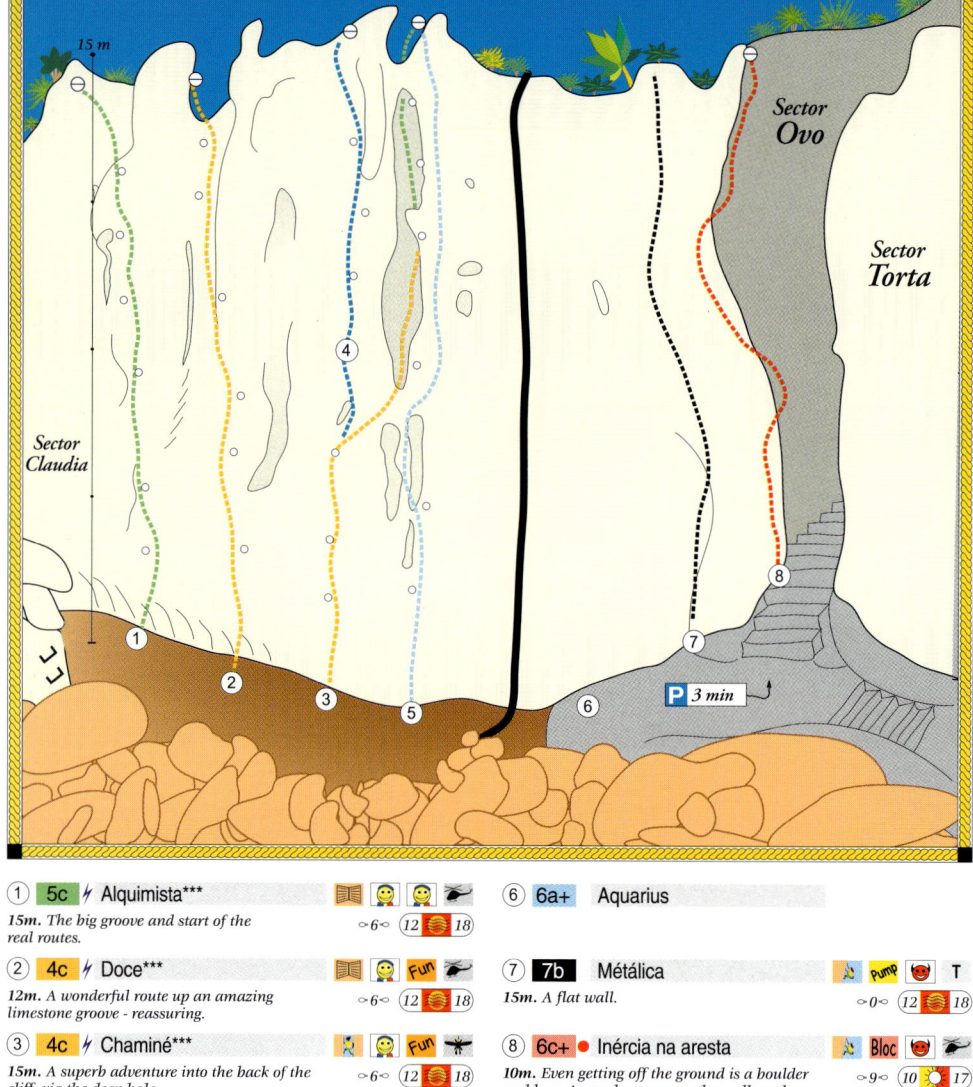

Farol Da Guia

① **5c** ⚡ Alquimista***
15m. The big groove and start of the real routes.

② **4c** ⚡ Doce***
12m. A wonderful route up an amazing limestone groove - reassuring.

③ **4c** ⚡ Chaminé***
15m. A superb adventure into the back of the cliff, via the deep hole.

④ **6b** ⚡ Assim Tá Bom***
15m. The wall directly up is quite tiring.

⑤ **6a** ⚡ Tubo**
11m. A slightly artificial line but a tremendous climb. Do not enter the groove on the whole top part and keep to the right, wonderfully sustained and out there.

⑥ **6a+** Aquarius

⑦ **7b** Métálica
15m. A flat wall.

⑧ **6c+** ● Inércia na aresta
10m. Even getting off the ground is a boulder problem. A sneaky move up the wall on the right is enough to crack the problem. Staying purely on the arête is 7a. (Cal: T, H, J)

Résumé. *An excellent sector with a lovely central formation of a giant chimney. You can actually climb up inside the cliff and get to the top. A bit slippery as you may imagine, but well protected and easy to wedge your body for resting. Routes on the outside wall have endless variations as there is a multitude of holds. Only the angle will defeat you.*

Esplanada - Claudia - Tubo - Ovomaltine - Astérix - Taxi - Solo - Metamorfose - Corta Unhas - Cantinho - Fred Astaire

DOCE 4C, Farol da Guia; Esther Zaragoza

Farol Da Guia

17 m

① **7a** ⚡ Inércia na aresta***
16m. A hard problem at the grade if you don't use any of the holds to the right, on Over the Top. Only 6c+ if you sneak the big r/h hold (Cal: T, J, H)

② **6c+** ⚡ Over the Top***
16m. Steep climbing that comes at you from the start. (Cal: J, H, U)

③ **6a+** ⚡ Ovomaltine**
16m. A fine wall climb that certainly proves to be trickier that you might think.

④ **6b** ⚡ Rapozinho**
16m. The dark cavernous start is nasty, then you enter the world and it all becomes easy.

⑤ **7a** ⚡ Via Latea***
17m. A route that certainly feels longer than it is. Great for the stamina merchants.

⑥ **7b+** ● Psico-Ritual***
17m. All line up for the on-sight attempt, not that straight forward.

⑦ **7c+** ● Kind of Magic**
16m. A short hard route with a powerful crux.

⑧ **7c+** ● Domínio dos Deuses**
15m. Steep.

⑨ **6c+** ⚡ Levitação**
15m. A steep wall that suddenly comes at you. By going left at the top you have to be prepared to go for it! But at least you tick a 7a this way.

Résumé. This is the first sector that you see coming down the steps to the cliff. A nicely impending wall that goes into afternoon shade. A very good selection of hard routes. Takes a while to dry after rain, and is quite a chilly place to belay.

Esplanada - Claudia - Tubo - Ovomaltine - Astérix - Taxi - Solo - Metamorfose - Corta Unhas - Cantinho - Fred Astaire

LEVITAÇÃO 6c+, Farol da Guia; Miguel Louiero

Farol Da Guia

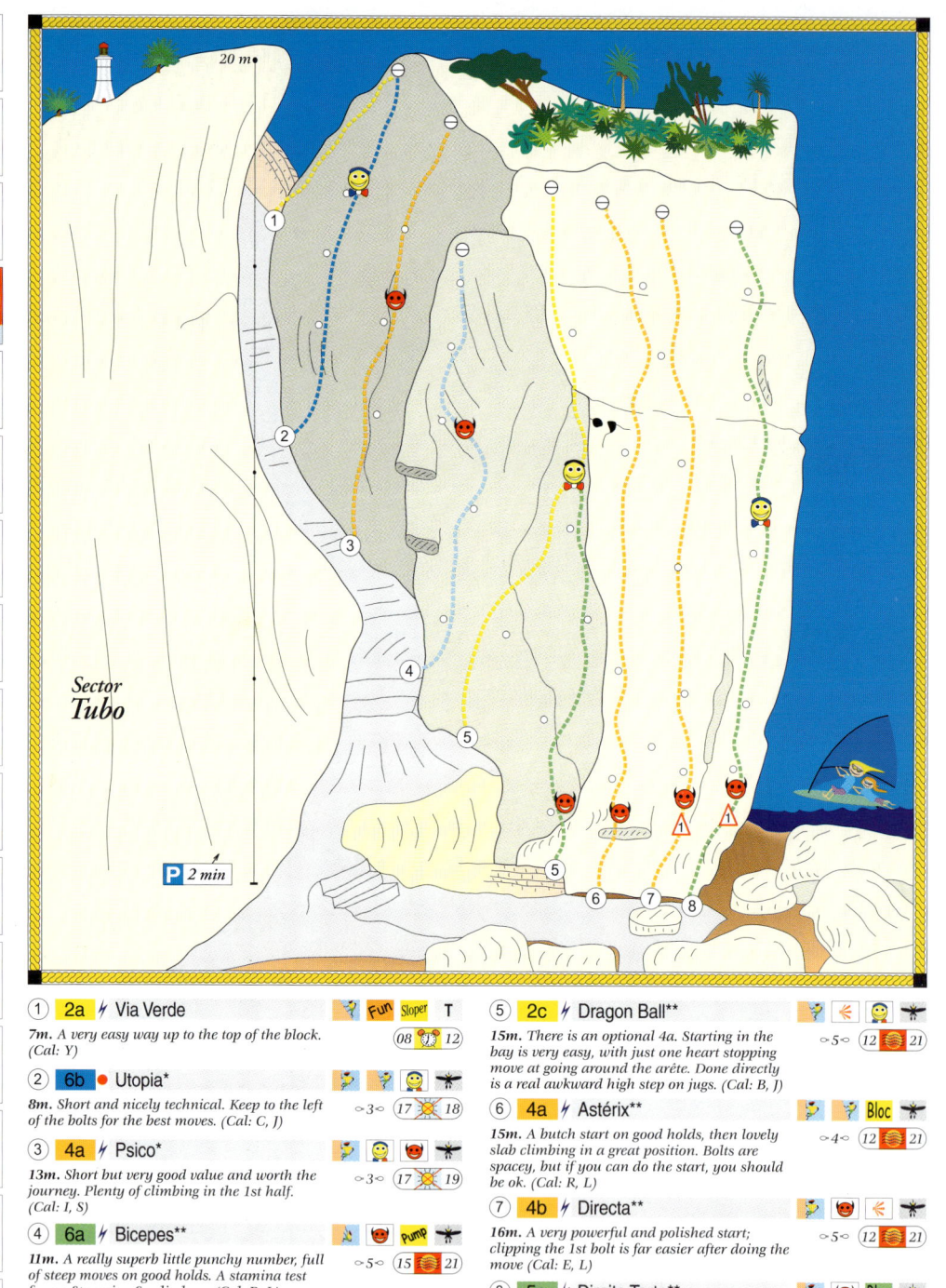

① **2a** ⚡ Via Verde
7m. A very easy way up to the top of the block. (Cal: Y)

② **6b** ● Utopia*
8m. Short and nicely technical. Keep to the left of the bolts for the best moves. (Cal: C, J)

③ **4a** ⚡ Psico*
13m. Short but very good value and worth the journey. Plenty of climbing in the 1st half. (Cal: I, S)

④ **6a** ⚡ Bicepes**
11m. A really superb little punchy number, full of steep moves on good holds. A stamina test for up & coming 6a climbers. (Cal: B, L)

Résumé. Always popular since this sector is at the base of the descent route to the cliff. A good selection of nice routes. No horrors here.

⑤ **2c** ⚡ Dragon Ball**
15m. There is an optional 4a. Starting in the bay is very easy, with just one heart stopping move at going around the arête. Done directly is a real awkward high step on jugs. (Cal: B, J)

⑥ **4a** ⚡ Astérix**
15m. A butch start on good holds, then lovely slab climbing in a great position. Bolts are spacey, but if you can do the start, you should be ok. (Cal: R, L)

⑦ **4b** ⚡ Directa**
16m. A very powerful and polished start; clipping the 1st bolt is far easier after doing the move (Cal: E, L)

⑧ **5a** ⚡ Direita Torta**
16m. Keep right of Direita for the full on 5a start. There are some lovely technical wall moves here in a great position. Looks run-out but isn't too bad. (Cal: L, R)

Esplanada - Claudia - Tubo - Ovomaltine - **Astérix** - Taxi - Solo - Metamorfose - Corta Unhas - Cantinho - Fred Astaire

DIRECTA 4b, Farol da Guia; Wobbly

PINÓQUIO, Farol da Guia; Luis Asensio

FAROL DA GUIA

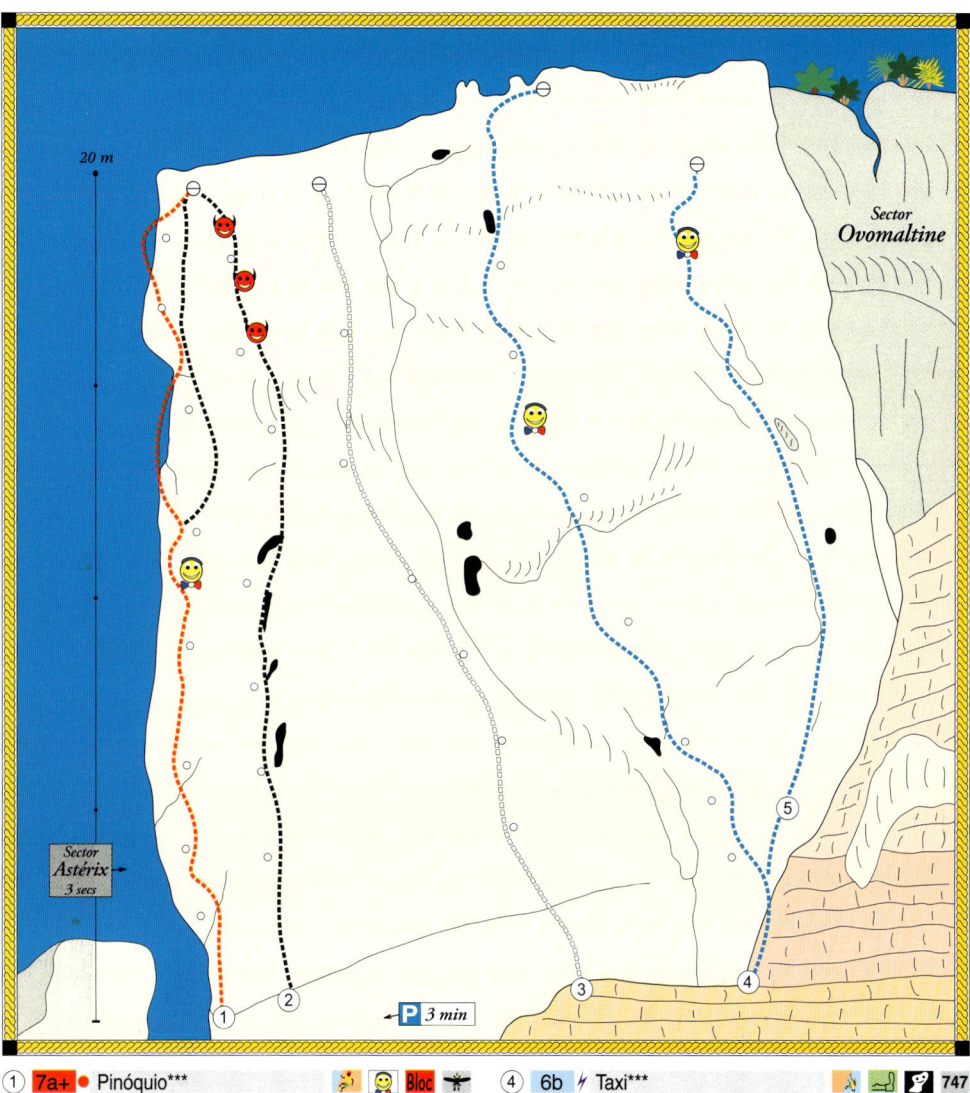

Sector Ovomaltine

Sector Astérix 3 secs

① 7a+ ● Pinóquio★★★
18m. A superb arête climb that is technically demanding, and even pumpy; with a rest before the final infuriating finish! Keeping on the right all the way pumps you up to 7b. (Cal: O, T, U)

② 7b ● Martine★★★
18m. A slightly unbalanced route with both easy and hard moves, a great position and superb. (Cal: D)

③ 7c ● Cristo★★
19m. A long and steep bugger. (Cal: K, B, O)

④ 6b ⚡ Taxi★★★
19m. A fantastic climb which warms you up and then wears you out. Lots of good climbing on rock that is actually more solid than it looks! Almost like conglomerate. (Cal: B, X-Cong)

⑤ 6b+ ● Quebra ossos★
17m. A weird route that gets progressively harder as you go up. Not equipped and still the odd loose hold. Getting to the belay is demanding, since the footholds are unobvious. (Cal-Conglomerate)

Résumé. One of the best sectors of Farol da Guia. Steep and intimidating routes that offer a energetic outing for most climbers. Note: There is a sea cave beneath the boulders where you belay; so when you pull your rope through, it can go down into the drink and get soaked if your not careful.

ENTRE PRISES Climbing Walls

Esplanada - Claudia - Tubo - Ovomaltine - Astérix - Taxi - Solo - Metamorfose - Corta Unhas - Cantinho - Fred Astaire

Belaying at the bottom of Pinóquio and Taxi, looks a bit wet!

Life at Guia, on a nice day.

Fred Astaire sector on the East side of Farol da Guia

DESCANSO DOS GUERREIROS 6c, Farol da Guia; Miguel Loureiro

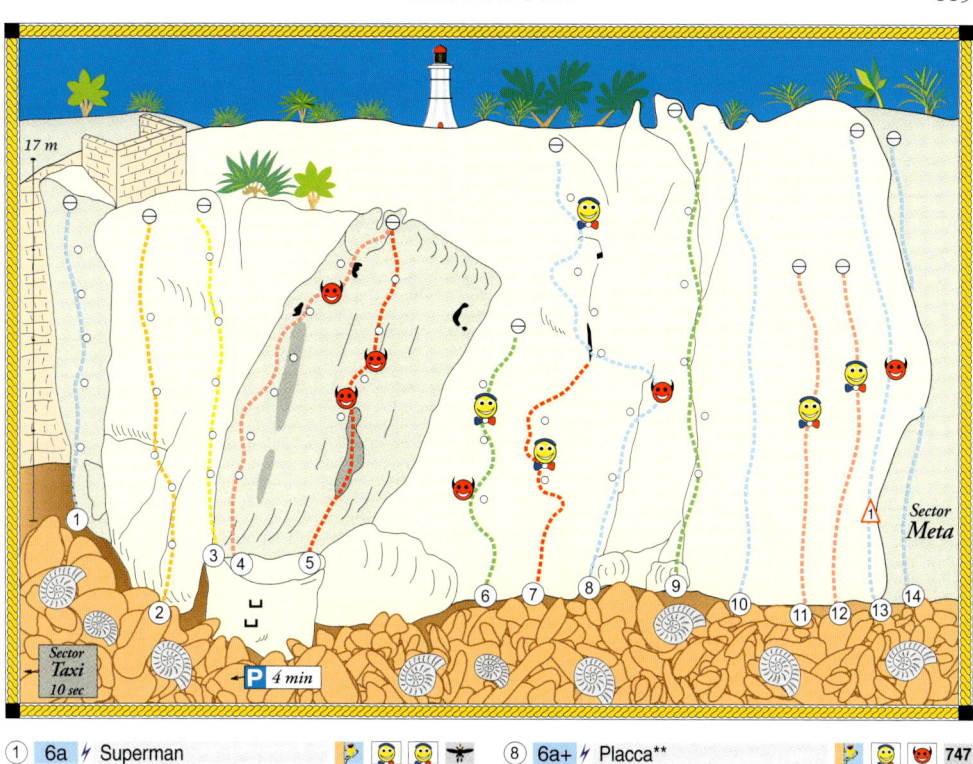

Farol Da Guia

① **6a** ⚡ Superman
17m. Wall right of block wall.

② **4c** ⚡ Zen
17m.

③ **3a** ⚡ Solo**
13m. A lovely route to begin with. (Cal: R)

④ **6c** ⚡ Decanso dos Guerreiros**
15m. A fine looking, overhanging arête, powerful and very exhilarating. (Cal: C, K)

⑤ **7a+** ⚡ Striptease**
14m. The odd hard move. Does stay wet often so may not be dry in the morning. (Cal: H, J, K)

⑥ **5b** ⚡ Fissura
8m. Short but quite technical and a good slab. Ignoring the crack completely - raises the grade to a nice and comfortable 6a. (Cal: O)

⑦ **7a** ● Nestum com Grelos
15m. The first 5 metres are the obvious difficult moves; If you can do this route completely static, pull your finger out and get on something much harder you wimp. (Cal: W, L)

⑧ **6a+** ⚡ Placca**
15m. A nice fine route. The old bolt placements were better positioned! (Cal: E, I, T, S)

⑨ **5c** ⚡ Alcatifa**
15m. A real classic that now has a horrible polished start. Any grade 5 climber is excused for falling off this one. Top part is lovely. (Cal: E, I, O)

⑩ **6a+** ● Equilíbrio**
16m. A good route. (Cal: O)

⑪ **6c** ● Septomania**
10m. A fine thin crack offers 2 routes. On the left is a nice pure 6c, and on the right it starts to get quite a bit harder. Many versions and eliminates available - short and sharp. (Cal: O, E)

⑫ **6c** ● Cornucópia**
16m. Lovely technical climbing that offers a good climb, low in the grade. No really powerful moves, but thin and technical. (Cal: I, R, B)

⑬ **6a** ● Sumol Directa**
14m. An awkward little bugger this one, nice climbing all the same. The overhang can be taken on the right at 6a+ version. (Cal: H)

⑬ **6a** ⚡ Sumol**
14m. The obvious groove. (Cal: I)

Résumé. *A very good area that is very popular at weekends. All the routes start from a platform of boulders well above high tide, and most dry out very quickly after rain. Very sheltered, and a good spot to visit.*

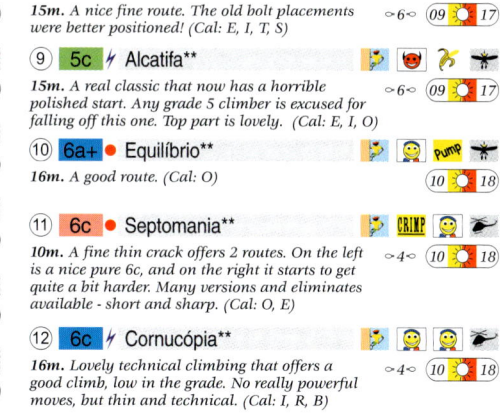

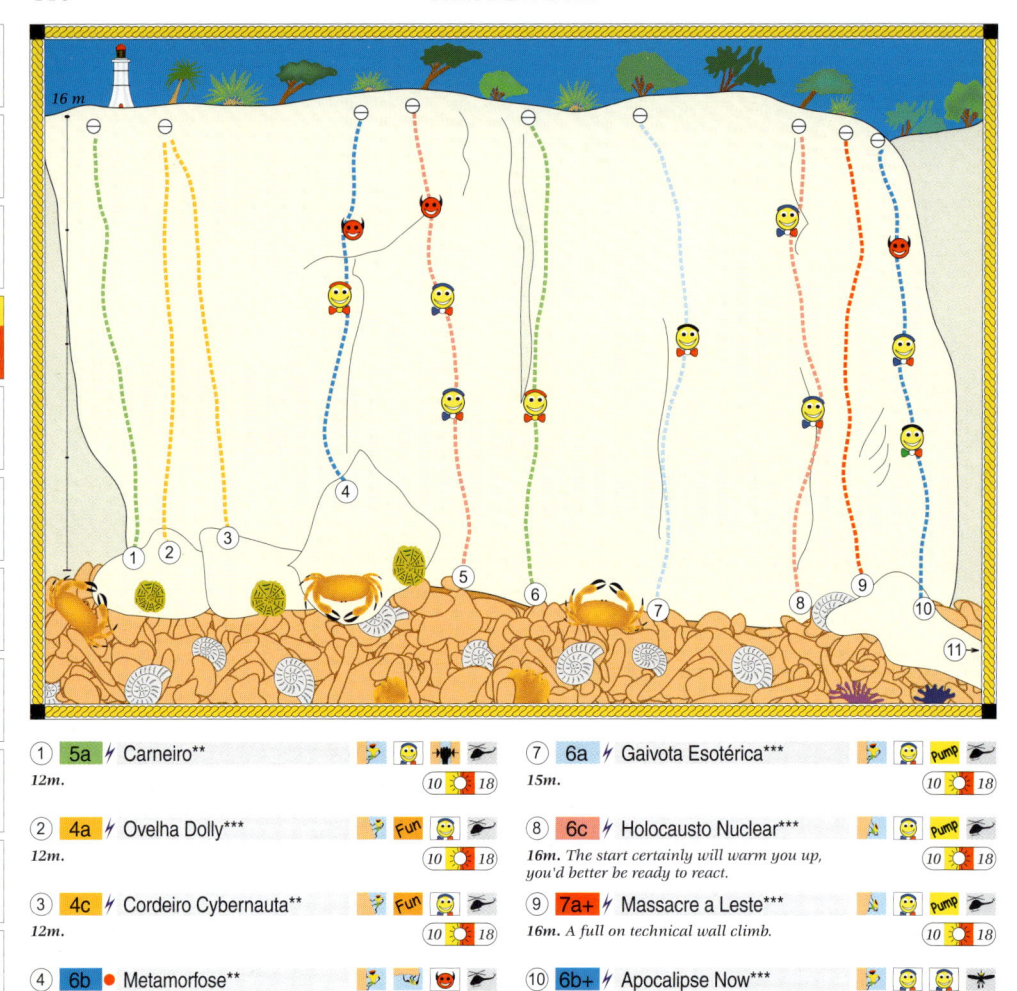

FAROL DA GUIA

① **5a** ⚡ Carneiro**
12m.

② **4a** ⚡ Ovelha Dolly***
12m.

③ **4c** ⚡ Cordeiro Cybernauta**
12m.

④ **6b** ● Metamorfose**
13m. *A very nice technical wall that is surprisingly good, then take pot luck with the overhang. (Cal: H, U)*

⑤ **6c** ⚡ Intuição Primária***
14m. *A very good wall climb.*

⑥ **5c** ⚡ Fénix***
14m. *A nice short wall climb.*

⑦ **6a** ⚡ Gaivota Esotérica***
15m.

⑧ **6c** ⚡ Holocausto Nuclear***
16m. *The start certainly will warm you up, you'd better be ready to react.*

⑨ **7a+** ⚡ Massacre a Leste***
16m. *A full on technical wall climb.*

⑩ **6b+** ⚡ Apocalipse Now***
16m.

⑪ **6b** ⚡ Osso**
16m. *The groove line about 6 metres to the right - midway to the large corner of Inde.*

Résumé. *A nice section, with a reasonable boulder beach that is well above the high tide and still flat enough to sunbathe. Mainly vertical wall routes.*

Esplanada - Claudia - Tubo - Ovomaltine - Astérix - Taxi - Solo - Metamorfose - Corta Unhas - Cantinho - Fred Astaire

HOLOCAUSTO NUCLEAR 6c, Farol da Guia; Miguel Loureiro

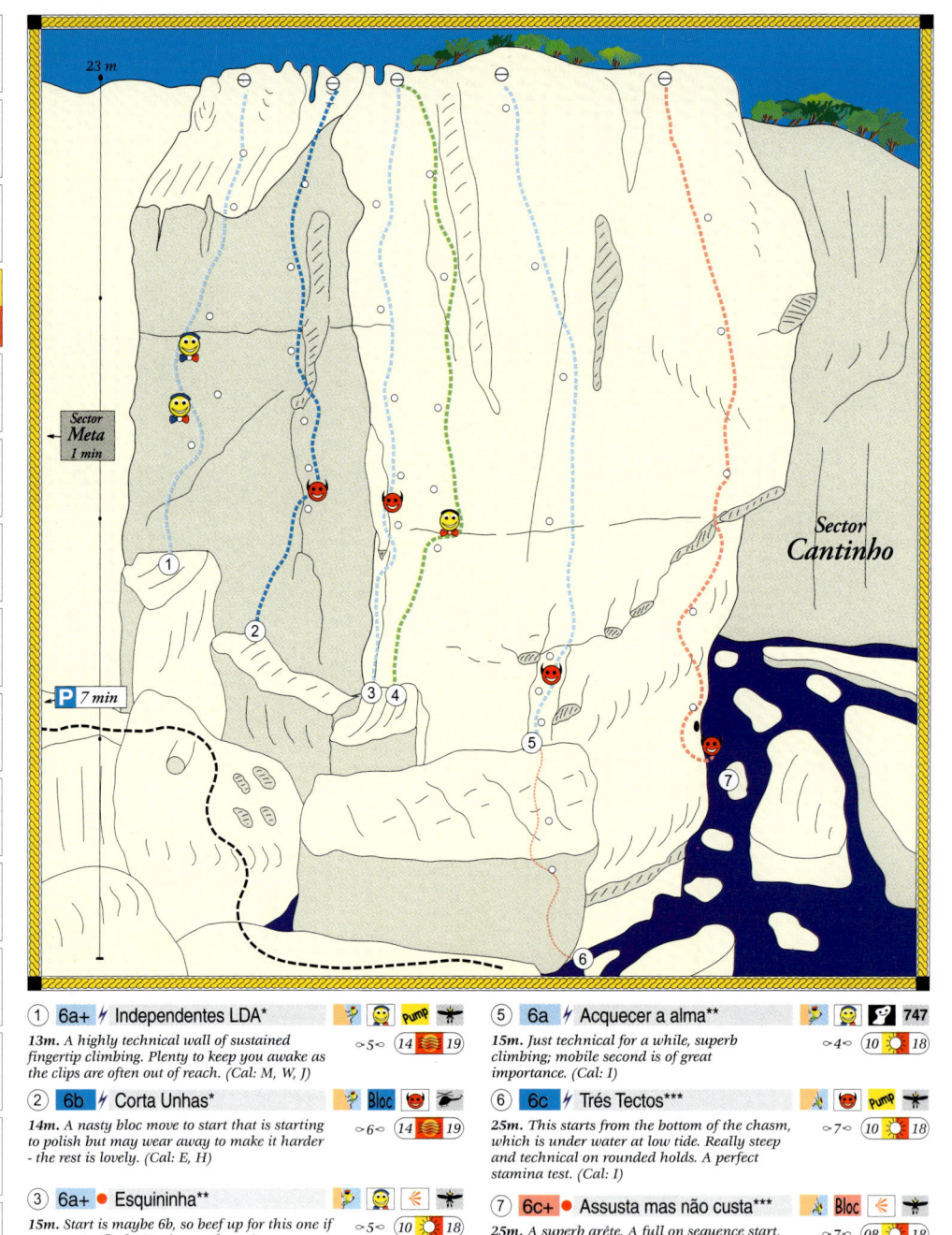

FAROL DA GUIA

① **6a+** ⚡ Independentes LDA*
13m. A highly technical wall of sustained fingertip climbing. Plenty to keep you awake as the clips are often out of reach. (Cal: M, W, J)

② **6b** ⚡ Corta Unhas*
14m. A nasty bloc move to start that is starting to polish but may wear away to make it harder - the rest is lovely. (Cal: E, H)

③ **6a+** • Esquininha**
15m. Start is maybe 6b, so beef up for this one if you want a flash. Staying on the arête proves worthwhile for the fabulous position. (Cal: O, L)

④ **5b** ⚡ Tatum***
15m. Technique unlocks this one, superb position and wonderful climbing. The start is 6a for the shorties. (Cal: O, B)

⑤ **6a** ⚡ Acquecer a alma**
15m. Just technical for a while, superb climbing; mobile second is of great importance. (Cal: I)

⑥ **6c** ⚡ Trés Tectos***
25m. This starts from the bottom of the chasm, which is under water at low tide. Really steep and technical on rounded holds. A perfect stamina test. (Cal: I)

⑦ **6c+** • Assusta mas não custa***
25m. A superb arête. A full on sequence start, then enjoyable plain sailing. (Cal: X, O)

Résumé. One of the most impressive parts of the cliff and well worth the scramble along the boulders to get to it. You need a calm sea and low tide for the last routes, and you often get a booming sea sound. Very atmospheric - and in a storm it's wild!

Esplanada - Claudia - Tubo - Ovomaltine - Astérix - Taxi - Solo - Metamorfose - Corta Unhas - Cantinho - Fred Astaire

TRÊS TECTOS 6c, Farol da Guia; Jingo

ASSUSTA MAS NÃO CUSTA 6c+, Farol da Guia;

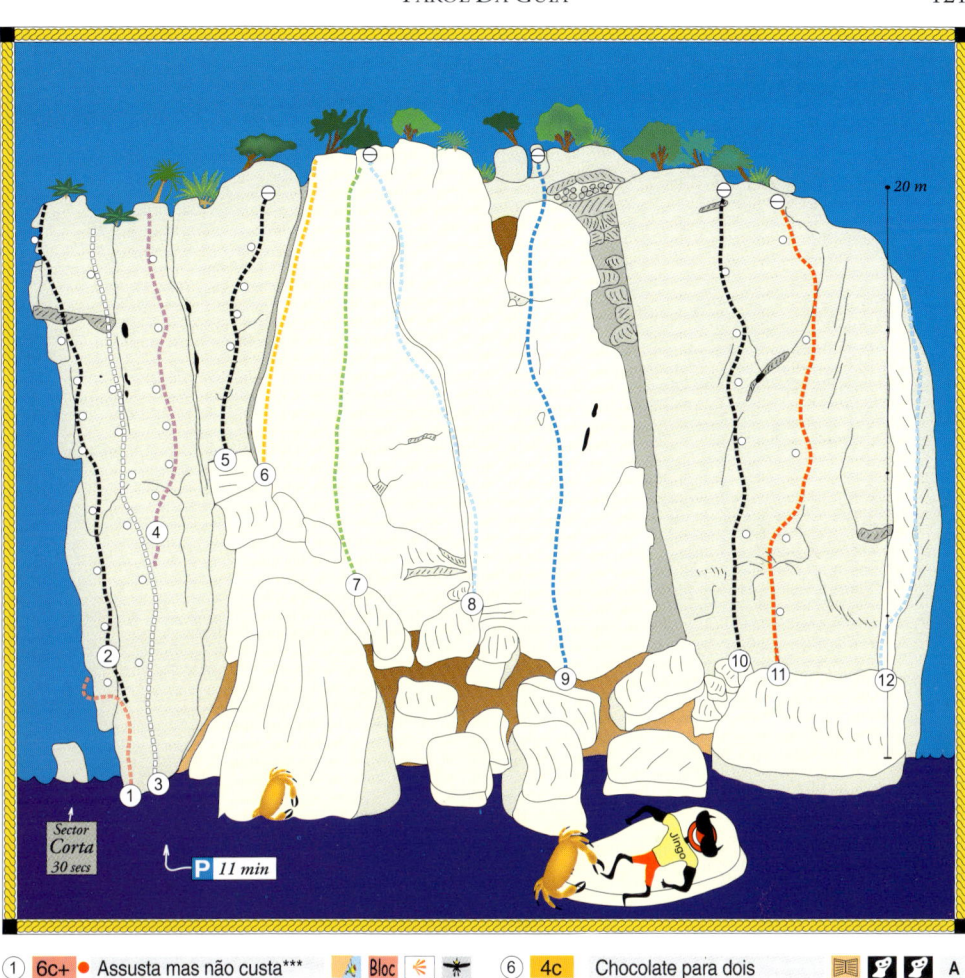

Farol Da Guia

① **6c+** ● Assusta mas não custa***
25m. A superb arête. A full on sequence start, then enjoyable plain sailing. (Cal: X, O)

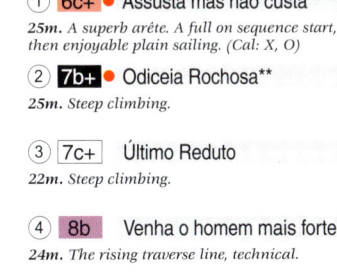

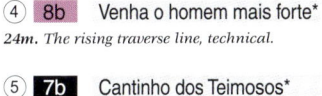

② **7b+** ● Odiceia Rochosa**
25m. Steep climbing.

③ **7c+** Último Reduto
22m. Steep climbing.

④ **8b** Venha o homem mais forte*
24m. The rising traverse line, technical.

⑤ **7b** Cantinho dos Teimosos*
9m. The angle is too hot to handle for most climbers to get the onsight. (Cal: C, H, J)

Résumé. *An area with 3 different sectors. You need low tide for the longer routes, and the Cantinho wall, will definitely stay wet for sometime after rain. The back wall is a bit dubious, but the right wall offers the best, excellent climbing in the evening sun. Forget this area if the sea is rough, you get spray and all sorts. You can easily check the cove by walking to the top, and you can also set up top ropes.*

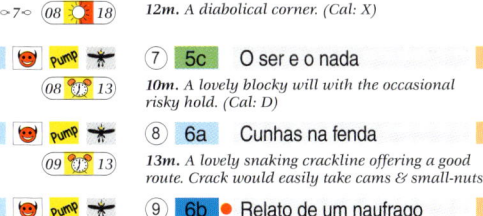

⑥ **4c** Chocolate para dois
12m. A diabolical corner. (Cal: X)

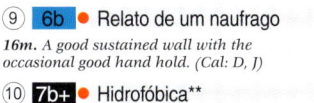

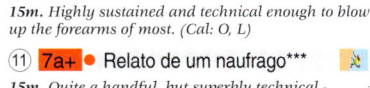

⑦ **5c** O ser e o nada
10m. A lovely blocky will with the occasional risky hold. (Cal: D)

⑧ **6a** Cunhas na fenda
13m. A lovely snaking crackline offering a good route. Crack would easily take cams & small-nuts

⑨ **6b** ● Relato de um naufrago
16m. A good sustained wall with the occasional good hand hold. (Cal: D, J)

⑩ **7b+** ● Hidrofóbica**
15m. Highly sustained and technical enough to blow up the forearms of most. (Cal: O, L)

⑪ **7a+** ● Relato de um naufrago***
15m. Quite a handful, but superbly technical - useful to have chalked up. (Cal: W, J)

⑫ **6a** A fenda e o mar
16m. The next line along

Esplanada · Claudia · Tubo · Ovomaltine · Astérix · Taxi · Solo · Metamorfose · Corta Unhas · **Cantinho** · Fred Astaire

Farol Da Guia

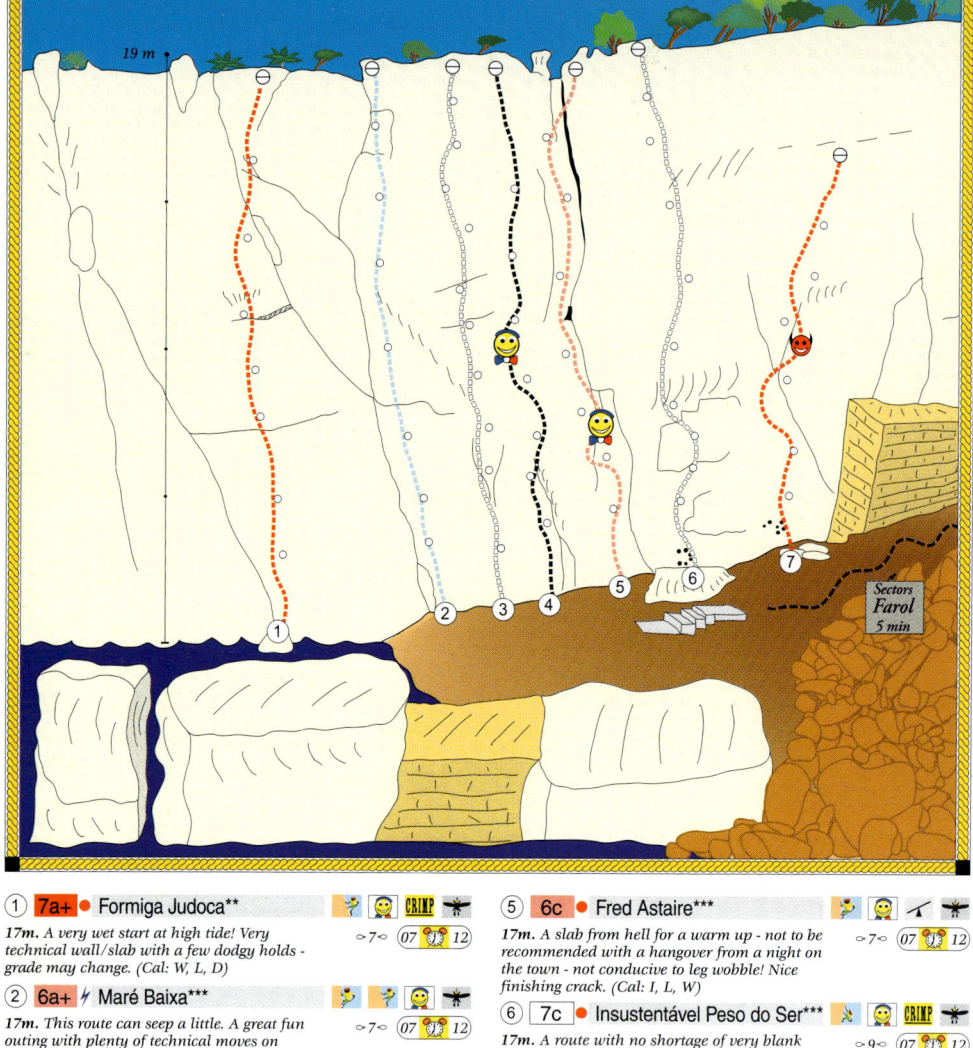

① **7a+** ● Formiga Judoca**
17m. A very wet start at high tide! Very technical wall/slab with a few dodgy holds - grade may change. (Cal: W, L, D)

② **6a+** ⚡ Maré Baixa***
17m. This route can seep a little. A great fun outing with plenty of technical moves on awkward holds.

③ **7c** ● Quebra Pressas**
17m. Wall climb with nasty small crimps.

④ **7b+** ● Bacalhau com Grelos***
17m. A superb wall climb that is nice and technical, quite a lot to work out though, even the top slab. (Cal: H, T, W)

⑤ **6c** ● Fred Astaire***
17m. A slab from hell for a warm up - not to be recommended with a hangover from a night on the town - not conducive to leg wobble! Nice finishing crack. (Cal: I, L, W)

⑥ **7c** ● Insustentável Peso do Ser***
17m. A route with no shortage of very blank sections - crimp at will. (Cal: W)

⑦ **7a+** ⚡ Kamikaze*
12m. A surprisingly technical climb that looks covered with holds; but proves a real handful in the first half (Cal: D)

Résumé. A very good sector for those climbers who are not suited to giant overhangs. Climbing here is technical and very fingery. Plenty of shade in the afternoon and generally very quiet.

Esplanada - Claudia - Tubo - Ovomaltine - Astérix - Taxi - Solo - Metamorfose - Corta Unhas - Cantinho - **Fred Astaire**

BACALHAU COM GRELOS 7b+, Farol da Guia; Miguel Loureiro

TRAVESSIA 7a, Farol da Guia; Miguel Loureiro

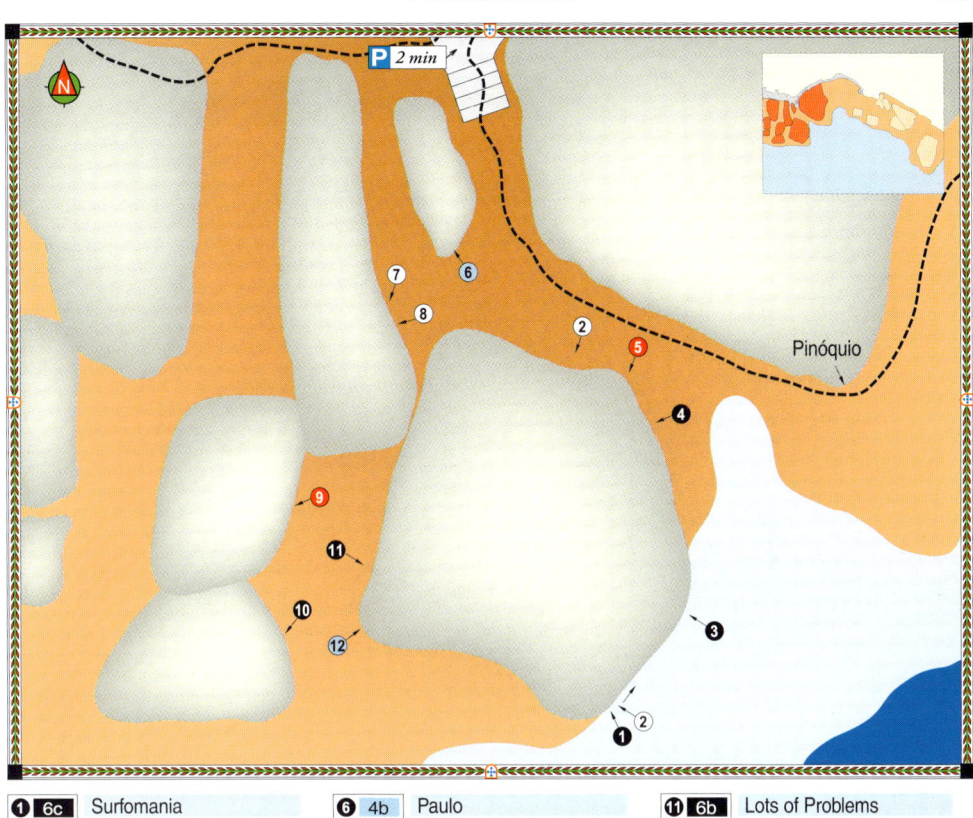

Farol Da Guia

❶ 6c Surfomania
Sloper
Start as the traverse, but then go up to the big sloper on the wall.

❷ 7a Travessia
Pump
The good low traverse, keeping feet under lip and then finishing up the wall rt of Q-costas.

❸ 6b+ Kafkicana
Traverse to start Anticristo

❹ 6b+ Anticristo
Straight up from undercut wall.

❺ 6a+ Quebracostas
From underneath the overhang, grab the good holds, then move up onto the arête and up

❻ 4b Paulo
The nose of the overhanging arête.

❼ 7a Talkual
CRIMP
Going straight up on the crimp.

❽ 7a Kual
CRIMP
Going left then right.

❾ 6a Viagra
?

❿ 6b Sei La
?

⓫ 6b Lots of Problems
This small wall offers many problems, all around 6b - 6b+. Good landings.

⓬ 4b Tainha
A nice fun overhang.

Résumé. A handy bouldering area with some nice problems, not a major location but still worth a visit. The classic traverse does need a couple of pads, especially at the end for your back.

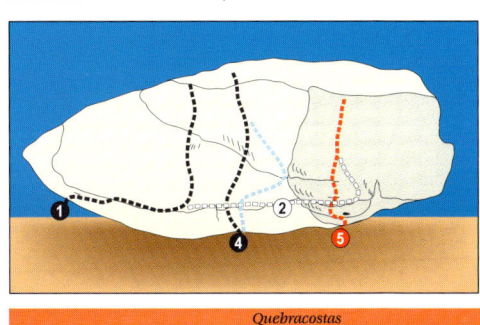

Quebracostas

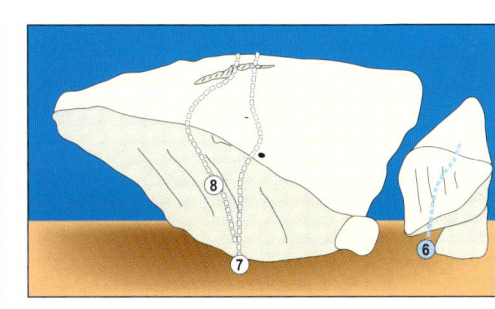

Sexolina

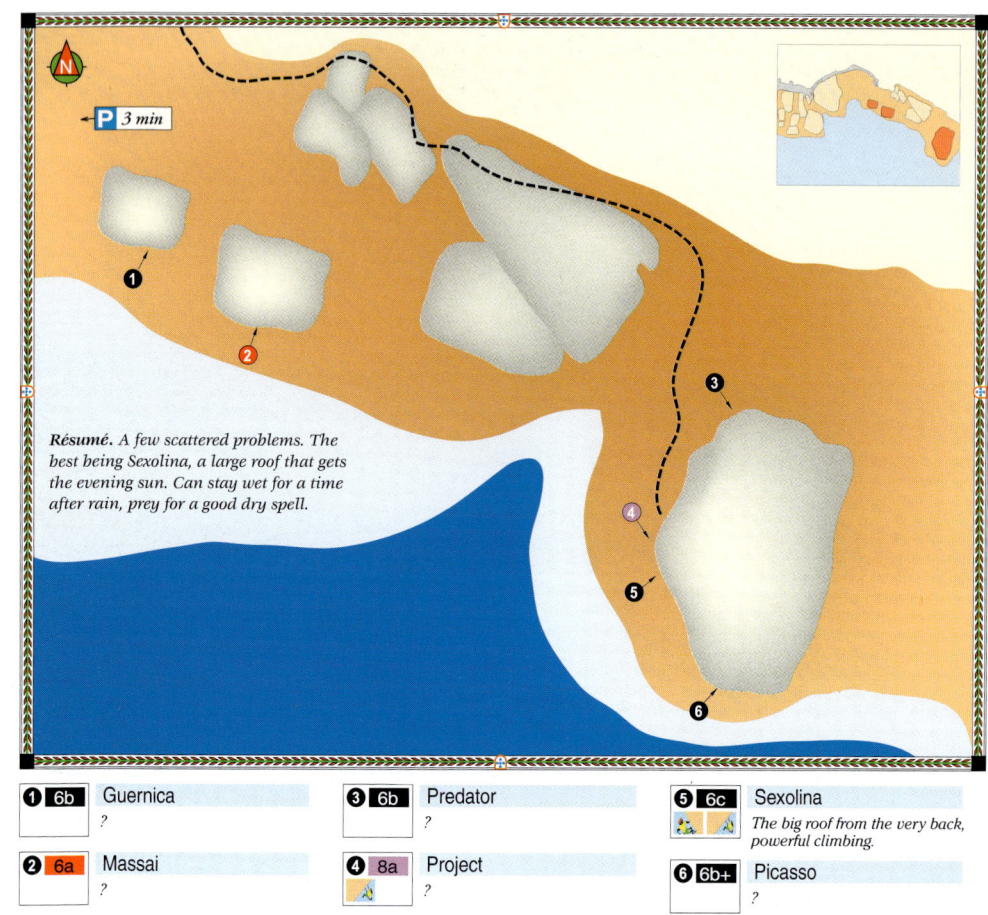

FAROL DA GUIA

P 3 min

Résumé. A few scattered problems. The best being Sexolina, a large roof that gets the evening sun. Can stay wet for a time after rain, prey for a good dry spell.

❶ 6b	Guernica
	?

❷ 6a	Massai
	?

❸ 6b	Predator
	?

❹ 8a	Project
	?

❺ 6c	Sexolina
	The big roof from the very back, powerful climbing.

❻ 6b+	Picasso
	?

BOULDERING FUN, Farol da Guia; Wobbly

Quebracostas — Sexolina

SEXOLINA 6c, Farol da Guia; André Neres

Jingo going surfing from the start of Sexolina

I've always regarded Fontainebleau as the most perfect bouldering venue on the planet, and by a very long shot indeed. It has superb rock forms, the most perfect rock texture and interesting problems; not forgetting the enchanting forests, and a wealth of good restaurants. How could you want any more! Well, just wait until you discover Baía do Mexilhoeiro. To say that one of the sectors is called Bikini, is simple enough. Here there is a selection of boulders that are small, big and big-big! There are also invariably a selection of bronzed bodies, of varying shapes and forms. It is a truly tidal and seawashed area, with wonderfully clear rock pools, and there is a lovely low rocky platform, which makes going swimming in the sea, nice and fun. And of course there are some superb seafood restaurants around the corner in Cascais. It's not got the perfection of Fontainebleau, but it certainly has an excellent feeling to it, and as a location, it is one of the finest.

For those people not deft with Portuguese, then pronouncing the words is going to be the most difficult problem you are likely to encounter. It translates as Bay of Mussels, which is quite fun, since you need an ample supply of 'muscles.' Maybe a useful name to use on the interim until you have perfected Portuguese is Mussel Beach. Parking the car only an instant away is simply a delight, and there is even a good set of steps takes you down to the sea. It's a bit tricky with a pram, but at least when you are down there, you are well out of the way of any rocks falling from above. The whole area is a jumble of limestone blocks, set upon a nearly horizontal platform. There are many little potholes, which are real ankle breakers, but with the use of a bouldering pad, you can have superb landings and easy spotting ground. The whole array of boulders is nice and extensive to give problems that face all directions. Whilst there is plenty of climbing in the non-tidal areas, it is the tide that makes this place really special. Some of the big boulders at the far end are very tidal, and offer really good sport. You can be really trying to get a problem, just 'one more last go' style; but the tide is coming in fast, and your crash pad is starting to float – can you get the tick in time? The worst time to visit is when it is warm and muggy, overcast and having rained earlier, and of course - just past high tide. The humidity can be off the scale at these times, so you are best off going surfing. The best time to visit is in the morning, when you get cool rock from a star studded night, but warm muscle relaxing sunshine. It's a great place to chill out in spring or autumn, and to enjoy the fabulous light which comes from the low sun at this time of year, reflecting off the sea onto the boulders. The other great time to visit, is on really hot evenings, when the setting sun blasts an orange glow across the whole bay, and when you invariably stay cool with a fresh breeze, courtesy of the Atlantic.

Sempre considerei Fontainebleau como a zona de bloco mais perfeita do Planeta, e em larga medida assim é. Tem formas de rocha majestosas, com a textura mais perfeita e os problemas mais interessantes, sem esquecer as florestas encantadoras e a profusão de bons restaurantes. O que é se pode querer mais?! Bem, espere até descobrir a Baía do Mexilhoeiro. Dizer que um dos sectores se chama Bikini, é suficiente. Há uma grande variedade de blocos pequenos, grandes e grandes a valer! Também aqui existe invariavelmente uma diversidade de corpos bronzeados, com as mais variadas formas e feitios. É sem duvida uma zona paradisíaca, onde se formam múltiplas piscinas de água cristalina espalhadas por uma vasta plataforma rochosa mais baixa, que nos permite entrar na água para nadar de uma forma agradável e divertida. E claro, não poderia deixar de mencionar as diversas e espectaculares Marisqueiras situadas em Cascais, mesmo ao virar da esquina. Não tem a perfeição de Fontainebleau, mas tem sem dúvida uma atmosfera vagamente parecida, e como local é dos mais aprazíveis.

A pronúncia das palavras, se não for particularmente dotado para Português, vai ser o seu maior problema. Traduz-se por "Bay of Mussels" o que é bastante divertido pois vai precisar de uma ampla reserva de "muscles" (músculos). "Mussel Beach" talvez seja um nome recomendável enquanto não aperfeiçoar o Português. Estacionar o carro "à porta" é simplesmente uma delícia, e há mesmo uma série de degraus que o levam até ao mar. Pode ser um pouco complicado descer com um carrinho de bebé,

BANGING THE BACK DOORS IN 6a+, Mexilhoerio; Miguel Loureiro

mas pelo menos quando lá estiver em baixo tem a garantia de ficar fora do trajecto de quaisquer pedras que possam cair do topo da falésia. A área inteira é uma salgalhada de blocos de calcário, assentes numa plataforma quase horizontal. Há muitos buracos pequenos que são verdadeiros quebra tornozelos, mas com o uso de um crash pad, pode fazer aterragens excelentes e dispor de uma base fácil para fazer segurança. O conjunto de blocos é bonito e vasto, originando problemas em todas as direcções. Apesar de se escalar muito em zonas completamente secas, é sem dúvida a maré que torna este lugar tão especial. Alguns dos blocos maiores mesmo ao fundo da Baía, sofrem uma forte influência da maré e oferecem um bom passatempo. Pode estar a tentar resolver um problema difícil, do estilo "só mais um tiro", mas a maré continua a subir rapidamente e o crash pad começa a boiar – será que vai conseguir a tempo? A pior ocasião para aqui vir é quando está quente e abafado, o céu encoberto depois de ter chovido, e está claro – a seguir à maré-cheia. Nestas alturas a humidade pode rebentar a escala, por isso o melhor é ir fazer surf. A melhor altura para visitar a escola é durante a manhã, enquanto a rocha está fria após uma noite estrelada, o sol aquece e relaxa os músculos. Um lugar fantástico para espantar o frio na Primavera ou no Outono e para disfrutar da luz fabulosa desta época do ano, enquanto o sol está baixo e o mar se reflecte nas paredes dos blocos. Outra ocasião excelente para uma visita é em tardes verdadeiramente quentes, quando o sol poente explode e enche a baía de tons laranja, ao mesmo tempo que se mantém fresco com a brisa suave, cortesia do Atlântico.

Baía Do Mexilhoeiro

Cascais

Baía do Mexilhoeiro

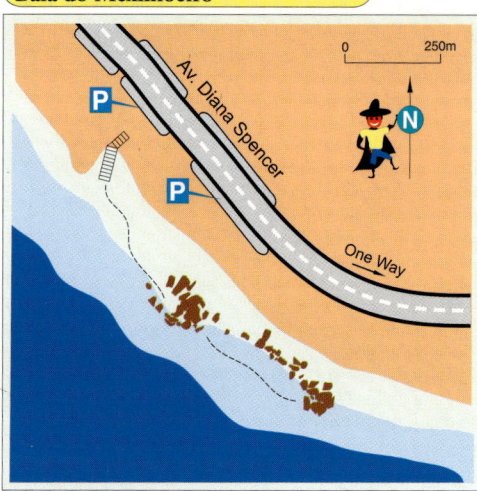

Baía do Mexilhoeiro Approach Directions:
1). Autostrada: Follow signs from end of A5 to Cascais, then signs towards Guincho to end up on the roundabout at Guia. Here follow sign to Boca do Inferno. The road will split to the right and the steps to the cliff are 300 metres from this turning. Steps lead down to rock platforms which are dry at all times. The area is tidal, but only just. You will get climbing at any time, but after low tide you will get the best conditions.

Camping Orbitur Guincho***
Areia, Guincho, 2750-053 Cascais.
Tel: 214 870 450
Fax: 214 872 167
Notes: Mixed site of camping and permanent caravans Good shade with low pine trees; chalets to rent.
Small shop, bar and restaurant.
Open: (1/01-31/12)

Camping Orbitur Guincho; a nice quiet campsite out of school holidays, with nice shade.

DOGGY STYLE 7a, Baía do Mexilhoeiro; André Neres

BAÍA DO MEXILHOEIRO

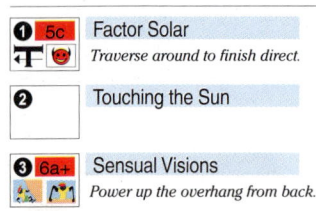

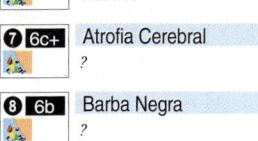

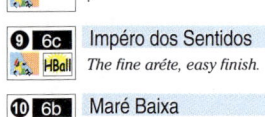

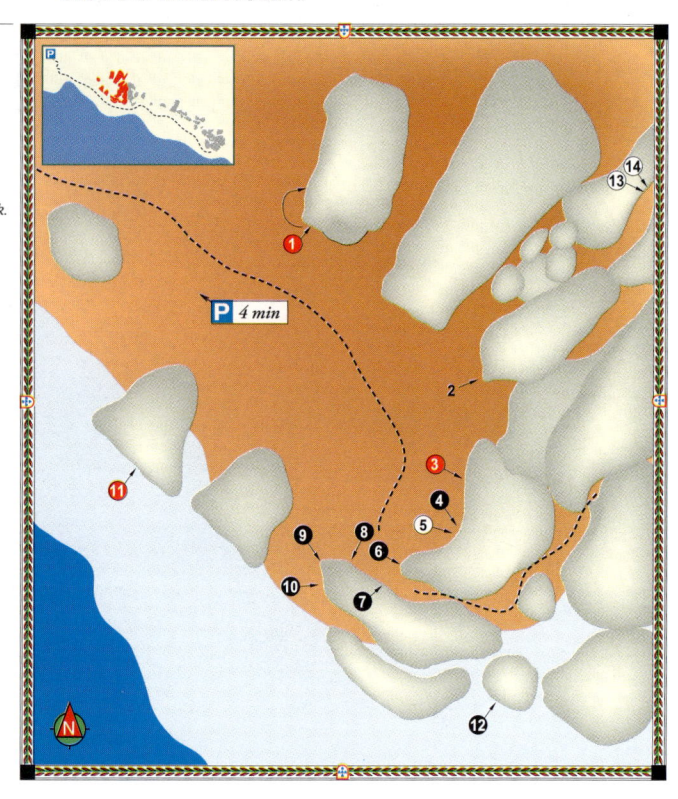

1 `5c` **Factor Solar**
Traverse around to finish direct.

2 **Touching the Sun**

3 `6a+` **Sensual Visions**
Power up the overhang from back.

4 `6b` **Bikini**
Follow the crackline-finsh left.

5 `7a+` **Trikini**
Going right through the roof.

6 `6b+` **Transatlàntico**
Traverse

7 `6c+` **Atrofia Cerebral**
?

8 `6b` **Barba Negra**
?

9 `6c` **Impéro dos Sentidos**
The fine arête, easy finish.

10 `6b` **Maré Baixa**
All in the start.

11 `6a+` **Travessia Maravilla**
?

12 `6b` **Maré Viva**
?

13 `7a` **Quebra Coco***
Steep wall going left.

14 `7a+` **Quebra Coco Direct***
Direct straight up.

FACTOR SOLAR 5c, Bikini - Mexilhoeiro; Ben Moon & Jerry Moffatt

Bikini - Endomorfismo - Flying Pig - Atlantica

Sector Endomorfismo - Mexilhoeiro

IMPÉRO DOS SENTIDOS 6c, Bikini - Mexilhoeiro; Mário Albuquerque

AMERICA NOIDE 7c, Endomorfismo - Mexilhoeiro; André Neres

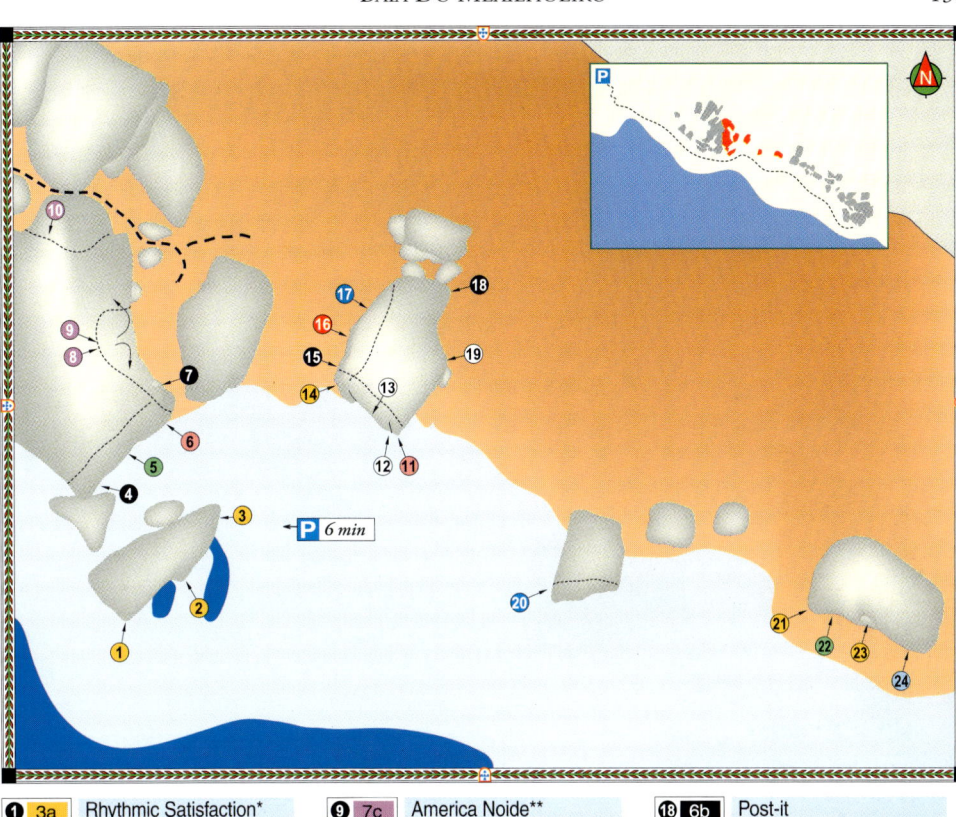

BAÍA DO MEXILHOEIRO

❶ 3a — Rhythmic Satisfaction*
Fun | HBall
Left arête.

❷ 3a — Tide Rising Fast*
Fun | HBall
Groove in the centre.

❸ 3c — Bachallu Express*
Fun arête.

❹ 6b — Roads to Freedom**
Pump
Start in corner over hole, hang loose! Long wild reach right, across to slopers on arête, then up slanting gangway. 13 metres.

❺ 4a — Jug Fest**
HBall
Big jugs beneath hole, go up trending left, awkward landing but top is nice and easy.

❻ 5b — Show Trip*
HBall
Very awkward step up, then juggy past birds nest hole. Good landing.

❼ 6b — Eclipse Solar**
CRIMP
1 metre R of arête, taking the sloping ramp. Low r/h crimp 60cm up; crimp l/h. Cross over left and go up ramp to red hole.

❽ 7b — Endomorfismo**
Sloper
Start 1.5m in cave, 2 hand u/cut. l/h up to jug on lip, match on big sloper on left, then up left crux) slapping for the gangway.

❾ 7c — America Noide**
Sloper | HBall
Start for Endo, r/h pinch-crimp L, lay off the big sloping ramp L/H; slap up rt to crimp on sloper, dyno left with spotters.

❿ 7c — Trailer Park Girl*
Big o/hang wall in back of cave.

⓫ 5c — Solid Wast
Sloper
Many ways up sloping jugs.

⓬ 7a — Travessia
Low traverse of wall, finish on A.

⓭ 7a — Doggy Style*
CRIMP
Waist crimps, single or D-Dyno.

⓮ 3c — Fio Dental
Fun arête. SS - 6b. **6b**

⓯ 6b — Travessuras**
Pump
Low traverse, keeping body low, good holds, swing around to finish up arête on left.

⓰ 6a — Borbulha Fina*
Power overhang in centre.

⓱ 4c — Chunky*
Fun overhang on jugs.

⓲ 6b — Post-it
Technical arête and power start.

⓳ 6b — Crise Digestiva
Undercut crimp at waist, r/h slap to poor hold, l/h layaway. Short.

⓴ 5a — Mad Monk of Mafra*
Pump | Fun
The lovely looking overhang gives some good, strong, traversing.

㉑ 3c — ?
Left arête

㉒ 4a — ?
Centre wall.

㉓ 3c — ?
Central groove.

㉔ 4b — ?
Right wall.

Bikini — Endomorfismo — Flying Pig — Atlantica

135

BAÍA DO MEXILHOEIRO

① 6c · Dragon Balls
Fierce wall.

② 7b · Doors Closing
SS on the left wall, finishing left of the little niche.

③ 6b+ · Mind the Gap
Take the flat wall to finish up the niche.

④ 6c · Flight Simulator
Nice arête straight up.

⑤ 4c · Meia Lua*
A nice traverse with plenty of jugs on top..

⑥ 7b · Obesidade Morbida
This is the lower traverse and definitely technical.

⑦ 6a+ · Space Woman
Left.

⑧ 6a+ · Space Boy
Centre.

⑨ 6a+ · Space Invaders
Right.

⑩ 7a+ · Buraco Negro*
A very good steep overhang with good technicality, a spotter here is essential - boulder edge is close.

⑪ 7b · Flying Pig**
A superbly tricky wall/arête. Heel hooking is the key to the start, the crux is holding the top r/h.

⑫ 4b · Anti Pasta*
3m; A lovely steep and juggy arête.

⑬ 6a+ · Just for the Record*
A good traverse, awkward but keep hands and body below long crack line, go around arête and finish straight up.

⑭ 5a · Sex Appeal
R. arête on good holds to mantle.

⑮ 6a · Quasar
Traverse across the rhomboid wall on crimps, carry on at will.

⑯ 6a+ · Regretting the Reglettes
Going up and left is easier than to the right - both are fun though.

⑰ 6b+ · Fat Detector
Start on pockets at the back of the small cave, go straight up.

Bikini - Endomorfismo - **Flying Pig** - Atlantica

FLYING PIG 7b- Mexilhoeiro; André Neres

9 am - Mexilhoeiro

12 pm - Mexilhoeiro - SPANISH INQUISITON 6c; Miguel Loureiro (tide coming in fast!)

BAÍA DO MEXILHOEIRO

2 pm - Mexilhoeiro - TRAVESSIA 7a; André Neres

8 pm - Mexilhoeiro - ANTI PASTA 4b; Ricardo 'Macau' Alves

Baía Do Mexilhoeiro

#	Grade	Name	Description
1	3a	Errectus***	The arête is started on the right, and is covered with fabulous holds, highball but good pad area.
2	5b	Jacques Cousteau***	7m, a fun arête with a watery landing, start on left but go over to hang on right side all the way up.
3	6b+	Pata na Poça	3m. A definite root to do, start by getting R foot over, then pump.
4	7a	Mass Deleter**	5m; A fantastic line on a big wall, a full team of spotters is essential.
5	6c+	Filigrama	6m; L side of overhanging wall, nasty landing and steep.
6	6a+	Ice Scream	6m; Centre of wall with a terrible landing, sharp jugs on top though.
7	6b	Underground*	Super steep roof on flat slopers. Pulling onto top is wild!
8	7a	Preto e Branco	Obvious black wall with fingertip slopers, vertical and technical.
9	6a+	Banging the Back Doors In***	8m. Superb wall, starting bottom left and finishing up centre - dyno slap high up. (Flat landing)
10		***	6m. Direct up wall. (Flat landing)
11	6a	Naked Girl**	6m; Thin crack, 1m left of arête.
12	6a		Arête with crossly wall to right.
13	4a	Freerider**	6m; Arête - juggy and out there.
14	4a	Atlantica***	Easiest line up big wall.
15	4a	Cascais**	6m; Arête - juggy and fun.
16	6c	Spanish Inquisition***	15m. Traverse right low down, to then join up with Banging.....
17	6a		Short groove.
18	7b	Impulso Cardiaco	Undercuts to obvious paw (pinch) hold, then humungous pull.
19	5a	Lumination	A hard pull into the giant scoop, keep your body out & stay on the face, steep with nasty landing.
20	5a		Overhanging arête.
21	5b	Magico	Go up trending right, steep juggy.
21	7c	Hipertensão**	9m; Big route trending up right.
21	7a	Monofobia*	Finishing crack of H.

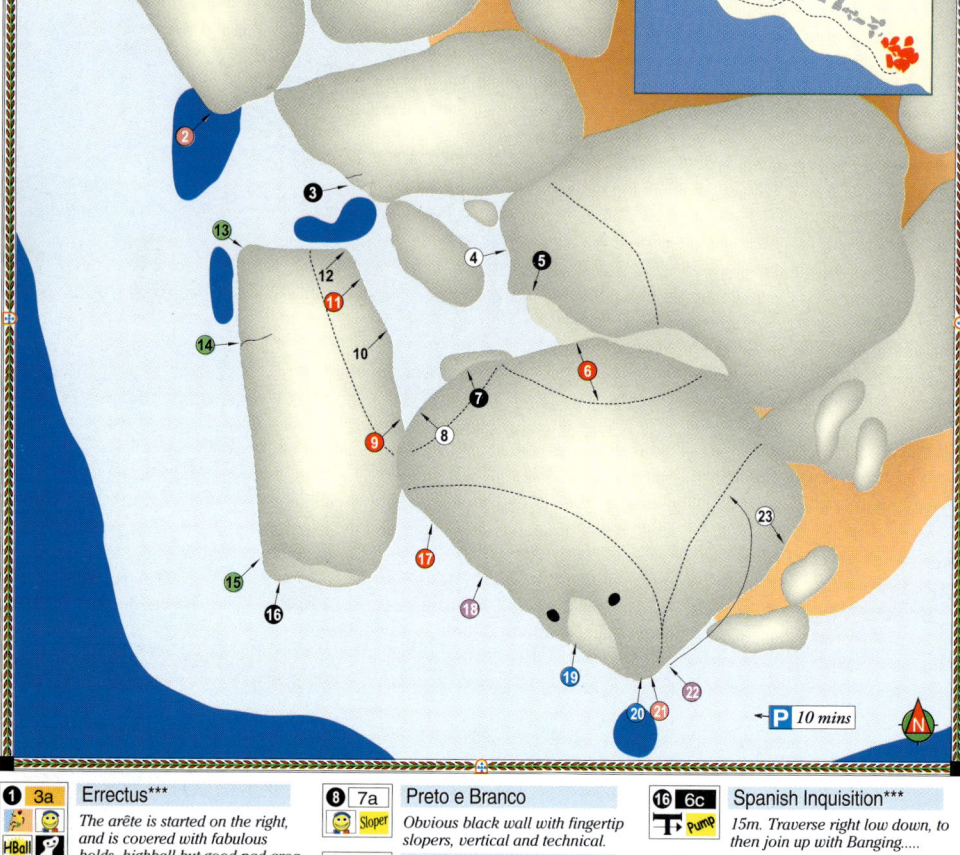

Bikini - Endomorfismo - Flying Pig - Atlantica

JACQUES COUSTEAU 5b, Atlanta - Mexilhoeiro; Miguel Loureiro

Top of the Tecto slabs, with Palácio da Pena in the far distance.

Sintra - Introduction

There are two separate towns of Sintra – new and old. The new version is a good, functional little town that is quite lively and has all the normal shops that you are likely to need in a pedestrian area. For wet days, there is the large Museum of Modern Art, with a small climbing shop Vertical – just around the corner. The new town allows the whole of Old, historic Sintra, to be left available for tourism. It is a beautiful old town, set on a steep hillside with bars and cafés. It is a bit touristy, but it still is a lovely place to visit. The other general tourist attractions of Sintra are stupendous. You should not miss a visit to the Palácio Nacional de Sintra, at the heart of the old town and recognised by the pair of conical chimneys. This is an old Moorish castle, but more of a lavish house with over 10 centuries of history and architectural development. Inside are quite lovely and ancient rooms, with staggering mozaics. But for true one upmanship, you should not miss out on a visit up to the Palácio da Pena. This is spotted on the top of the mountain as the yellow tower with the dome on top. This is not only stunning from the outside but majestic and opulent on the inside, with wonderful interior decoration and lavish furniture.

From the Palácio da Pena, you get a very good view of the big cliff of Sintra, which is known as Penedo da Amizade. You get a wonderfully proportional view of the cliff, hewn in a beautiful hillside of trees, set amongst private, grand historic houses; overlooking the lower hills and down to the sea. The cliff faces west and is of smooth, pure white, Granite. There are certain uneasy elements! It is dark and cold in the morning, and you approach through a mystic, errie, jungle. The rock will be cold to the touch, and you may make the mistake of choosing something, a bit too tricky to start on. You don't get too many holds on the routes here, and a lot of the moves are not very obvious. You soon get above the trees and the exposure suddenly hits you, with the lower valleys being 1000 foot below. Your calves start to ache on the tiny granite crystals. It can be a truly frightening warm up! By the second climb, the sun has come around onto the face and you are warm and flowing, you have got the feel of the friction, and now understand how to read the moves in the rock. The whole experience turns into ecstasy, and you thrive on the exposure and magnificent views. My advice is not to get sucked into climbing too late; the sun suddenly dips off the bottom of the cliff and leaves the belayer in the shade, they shiver ever more as you take your time on a desperate slab. Have a heart and quit to the bar at the right time, where you can enjoy the proper coolness, of a good beer.

Pode dizer-se que Sintra são duas vilas – a nova e a velha. A versão nova é uma povoação pequena e funcional onde apetece viver, e tem uma área pedonal onde se encontram todas as lojas necessárias. Para os dias de chuva, existe o Museu de Arte Moderna e uma loja de equipamento de escalada – a Vertical – mesmo ali ao lado. A vila nova deixa à Sintra antiga e histórica o papel de estar disponível para o turismo. Esta é uma bonita e antiga vila, distribuída por uma encosta íngreme repleta de bares e cafés. Um local bastante turístico, mas ainda assim encantador para visitar. As restantes atracções turísticas de Sintra são fabulosas. Não deve perder a visita ao Palácio Nacional de Sintra, no coração da Vila Velha, característico pelas suas colossais chaminés cónicas. Trata-se dum antigo edifício Mouro, que se tornou num exuberante palácio, com mais de 10 séculos de história e desenvolvimentos arquitectónicos. No interior encontram-se belas divisões bastante antigas e painéis de mosaico maravilhosos. Mas, como objectivo supremo, não deve perder a subida ao Palácio da Pena para visitá-lo. É o palácio que se vê lá no alto da Serra, com a torre amarela de topo abobadado. Para além de fantástico visto do exterior, é majestoso e opulento no interior, com a sua belíssima decoração e sumptuosa mobília.

Do próprio Palácio da Pena pode avistar o penedo de escalada de Sintra, conhecido por Penedo da Amizade. Uma bela visão da falésia e das suas proporções, emoldurada pelas árvores da encosta, no meio dos palacetes e quintas, de frente para o vale aberto até ao mar. A falésia está virada a Oeste e é constituída pelo mais branco e liso granito. Há alguns aspectos mais complicados! É escura e fria de manhã, e a aproximação decorre através de uma densa e mística vegetação. A rocha estará fria ao toque, e pode cometer o erro de escolher algo delicado para começar. Não encontra muitas presas

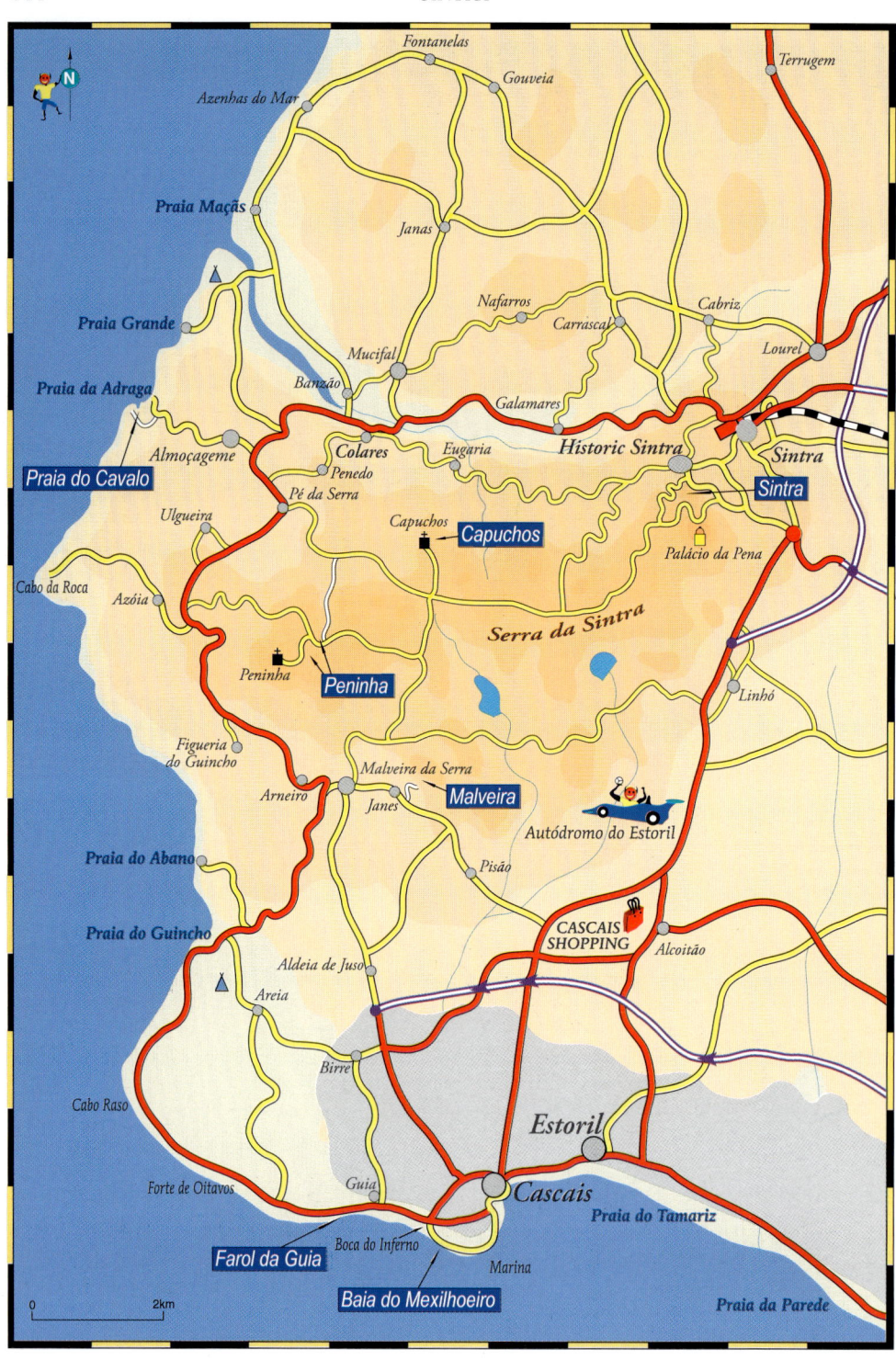

SINTRA

144

Museu de Arte Moderna, Sintra; Photo Mário Carvalho

Plaça de República, Historic Sintra; Photo M.C.

Palácio Nacional de Sintra, Historic Sintra; Photo M.C.

na maioria destas vias, e muitos movimentos não são exactamente óbvios. Mas depressa ultrapassará as copas das árvores, passando para a zona ensolarada das vias, de onde se vêm os vales quase 300m mais em baixo. Cedo começará a sentir dores nas pontas dos dedos por força da dureza dos pequenos cristais de granito. O aquecimento pode ser uma experiência assustadora! À segunda via já o Sol banhará toda a parede e já estará mais quente e solto, terá compreendido o significado da aderência e saberá ler melhor os movimentos. A experiência transforma-se em êxtase e acabará por ficar emocionado com a exposição das vias e com a vista magnífica. O meu conselho é que não se deixe apanhar na escalada pelo fim do dia; o Sol esconde-se rapidamente, deixando na sombra quem está no chão. Este gelará tanto mais quanto mais demorar a resolver um passo desesperante. Tenha dó e troque a falésia pelo café no momento certo, quando ainda pode saborear com gosto a frescura de uma boa cerveja.

Sintra - Penedo da Amizade

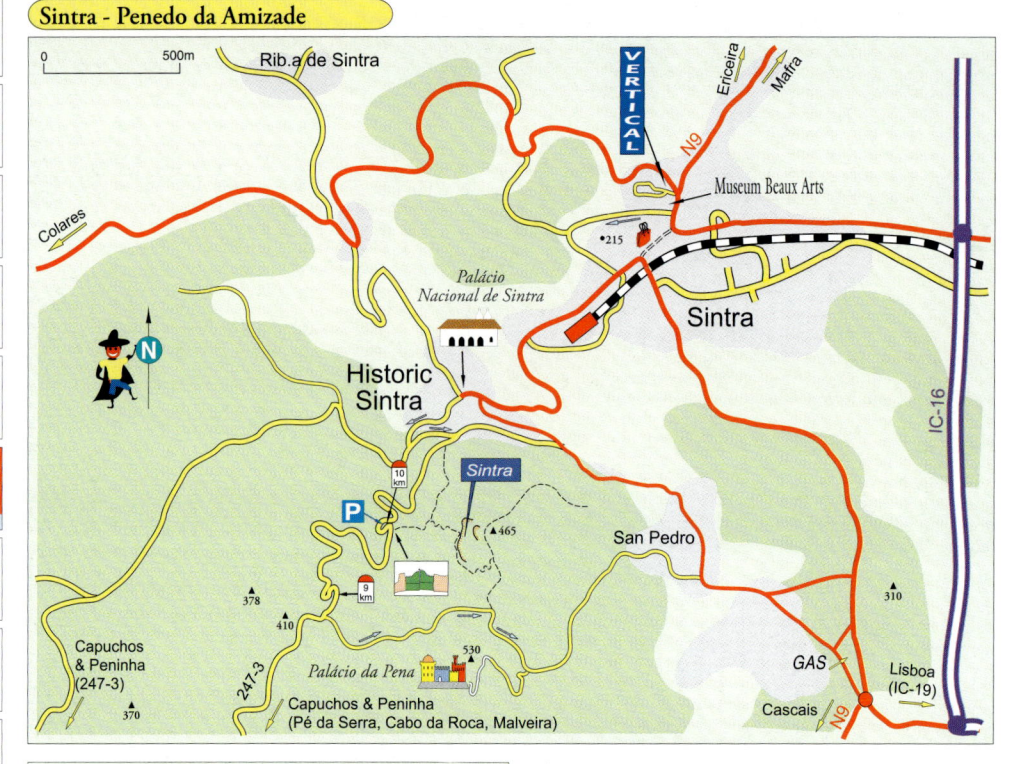

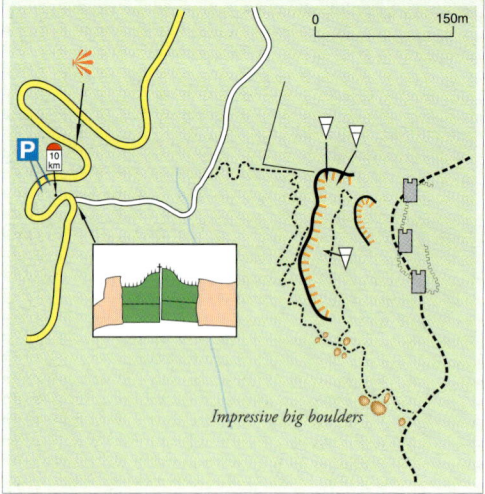

Sintra: Approach Directions:

1). Lisboa; The A5 (IC-19) takes you to Sintra, but be sure to follow signs for Historic Sintra, otherwise you get caught in a mess of a one way system and pedestrian precinct (Unless you need to visit the climbing shop). As you enter Historic Sintra, you need to look for a road on the left which will be signposted to Palácio da Pena and Parque. This road winds up the hill in the dense trees. Coming along the road, you will get a very quick view of the cliff, then the parking is soon close.

2) Cascais; as for Lisboa but beware, the N9 from Cascais to Sintra is often terrible for traffic and you are often quicker to go over the top of the hills.

3) Camping Guincho; easiest to go via Malveria and then over the top of Serra de Sintra. Only the small road past the Palácio da Pena is one way, so you can get down the narrow road to Sintra. A windy route, and not so good for a hangover victim. The main coastal road around via Colares may look quick, but is very windy, and has lots of old goats driving slowly.

Sintra Cliff: Approach Directions:

Go through the green gates and follow the level track that contours the hill, pass over a stream ravine, then 50 metres on, a track on the right leads up. Steep path up; very soon you have a wall on your left. Cliff is reached in 10 mins. To get to the main sector keep right and you arrive at the centre - New Wave.
TOP Sectors: A sneaky path leads back across the top of the cliff and with some very airy steps. Then you can make a short abseil; to get down to the main abseil of the AMIZADE sector. Many routes end at the top of the cliff (50m), walk down is just bearable in rock shoes, (worth taking lizard shoes though).

Bar: Old Sintra
Café: Vertical Shop, Old Sintra
Shop: Gift shops in Old Sintra, Shops-Sintra
Petrol Station: Main roundabout (N9 - IC-19)
Supermarket: Sintra
Climbing shop: Vertical at Sintra
(13-20; Mon-Fri; 10-20, Sat: closed sun)

www.vertical-outdoor.com

Rua General Alves Roçadas, Nº 10, Loja 5
2710 SINTRA
Tel. (+351) 219 243 885 / Email. vertical@sapo.pt

Sintra

① **7b** Voando Sobre um Ninho de Cucos
16m. –.

② **7c+** Ana-Franc
16m. –.

③ **7a+** Deus do Vento
25m. –.

④ **7c** ● Moura Maldita
25m. –.

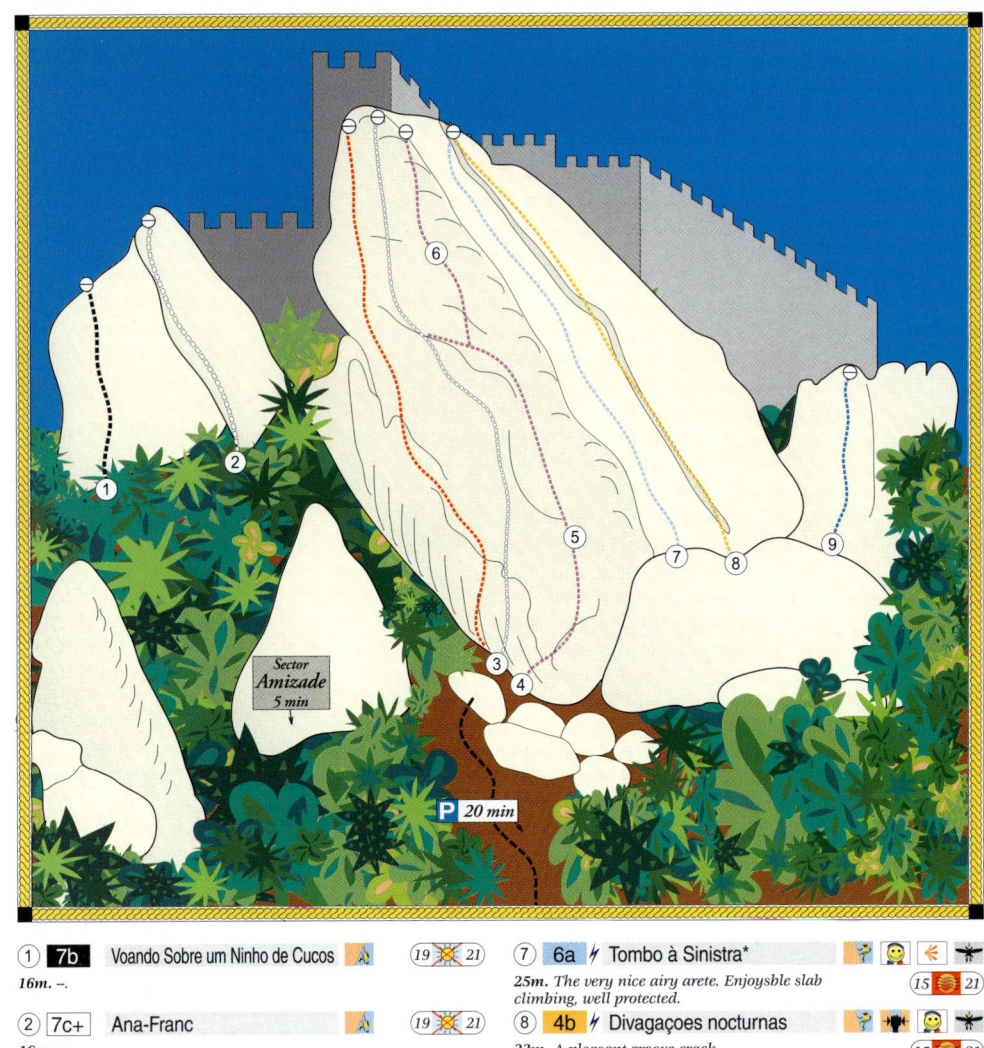

⑤ **8b+** ● Depende
25m. –.

⑥ **8b+** ● Tudo Depende
25m. –.

⑦ **6a** Tombo à Sinistra*
25m. The very nice airy arete. Enjoysble slab climbing, well protected.

⑧ **4b** Divagaçoes nocturnas
23m. A pleasant groove-crack.

⑨ **6b** Planet a fumo
12m. A short and technical wall.

Résumé. Situated high above the main cliff are these giant boulders of clean, white granite. They give a good selection of hard climbs which are in the shade during the afternoon. The view from here is stunning, and it is nearly always quiet.

Tombo - Amizade - Buraco - Gigante - New Wave - Solar

Penedo da Amizade; Photo Mário Carvalho

Palácio Nacional de Sintra, Historic Sintra; Photo Mário Carvalho

Approaching BÉBÉ 6a+, from the top abseil; José Teixeira

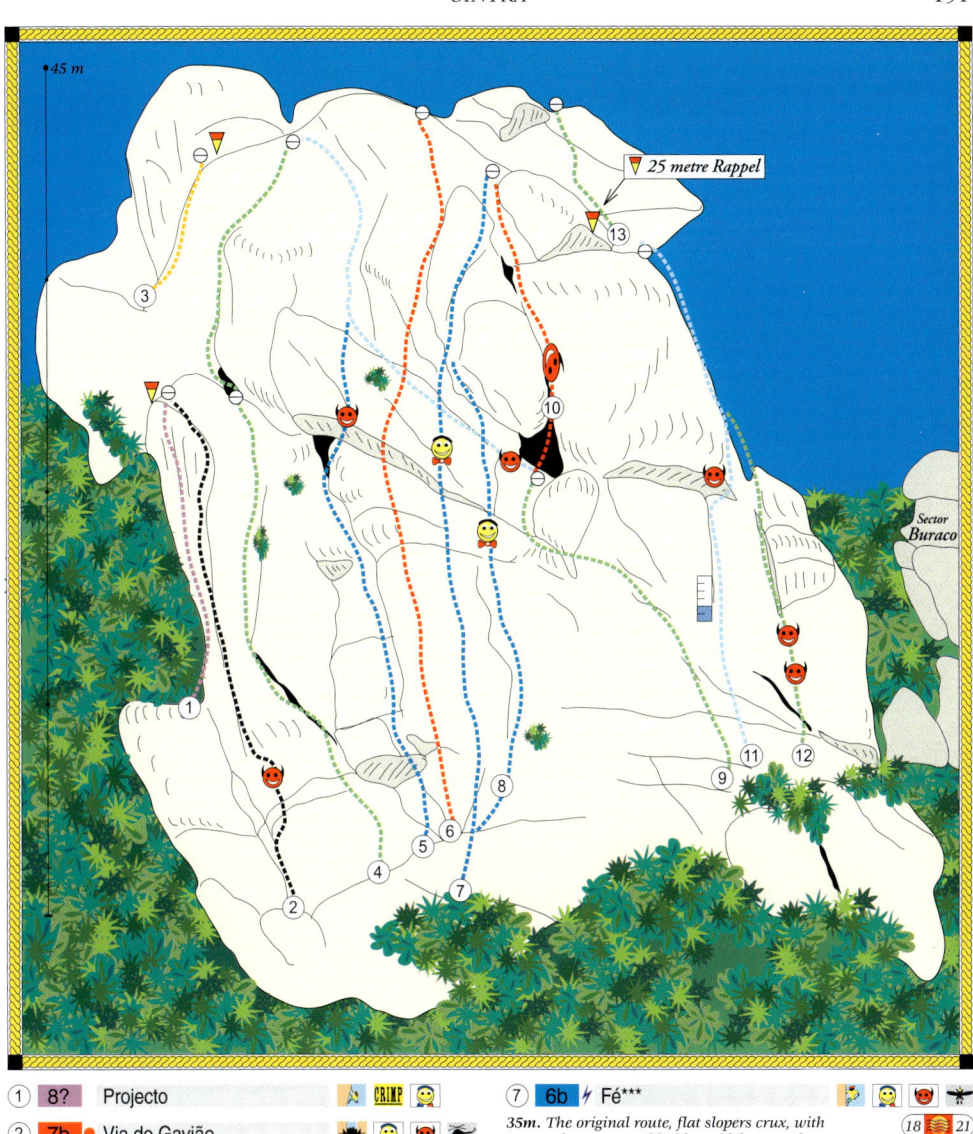

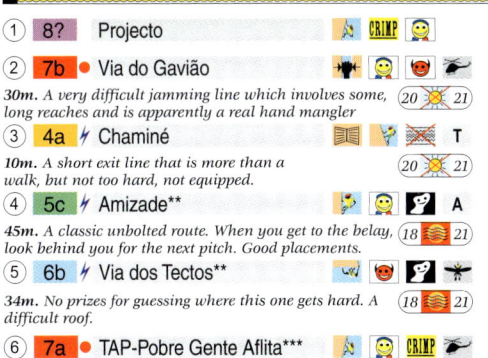

SINTRA

① **8?** Projecto

② **7b** ● Via do Gavião
30m. *A very difficult jamming line which involves some, long reaches and is apparently a real hand mangler*

③ **4a** Chaminé
10m. *A short exit line that is more than a walk, but not too hard, not equipped.*

④ **5c** Amizade**
45m. *A classic unbolted route. When you get to the belay, look behind you for the next pitch. Good placements.*

⑤ **6b** Via dos Tectos**
34m. *No prizes for guessing where this one gets hard. A difficult roof.*

⑥ **7a** ● TAP-Pobre Gente Aflita***
34m. *This line takes the wall comfortably, then gets nasty on the top wall. PGA is the 6b vatiation, finishing to the right up Fé.*

⑦ **6b** Fé***
35m. *The original route, flat slopers crux, with top overhang on good holds - widely spaced.*

⑧ **6b+** Dose Dupla de A derencia***
35m. *A trickier version of Fé.*

⑨ **5c** Via da Gruta**
18m,22m. *A two pitch classic, nuts needed.*

⑩ **7a+** Ritual Vertical
16m. *Classic offwidth - you need big cams.*

⑪ **6a+** Bébé***
22m. *Roof is good fun, and really exposed.*

⑫ **5b** Crista***
22m. *A great route on good holds. Use both sides of the crack, the route goes to the right of the bolts.*

Résumé. *A superb big sector, abseil in from the top.*

Tombo - **Amizade** - Buraco - Gigante - New Wave - Solar

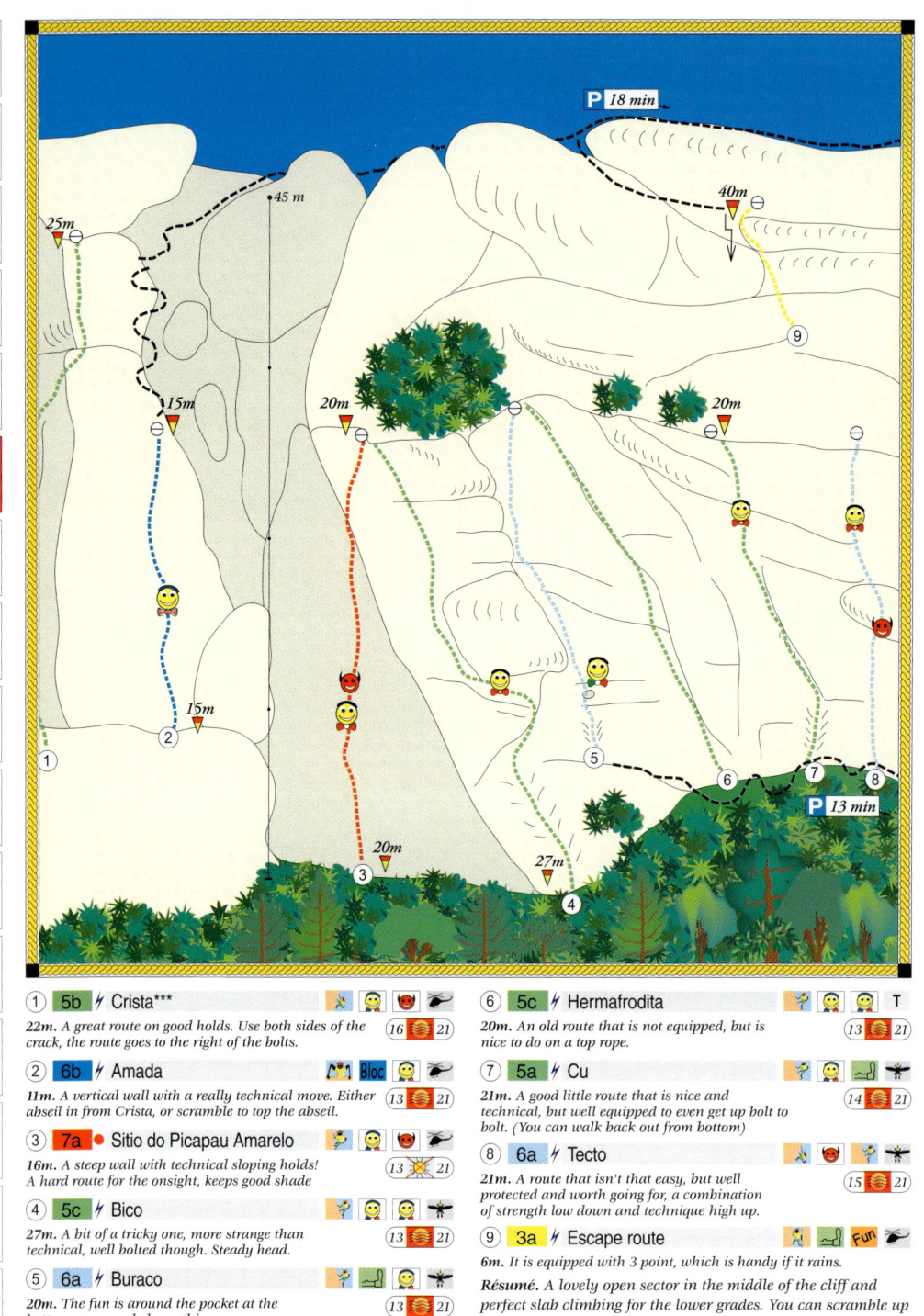

SINTRA

① **5b** ⚡ Crista★★★

22m. A great route on good holds. Use both sides of the crack, the route goes to the right of the bolts.

② **6b** ⚡ Amada

11m. A vertical wall with a really technical move. Either abseil in from Crista, or scramble to top the abseil.

③ **7a** ● Sitio do Picapau Amarelo

16m. A steep wall with technical sloping holds! A hard route for the onsight, keeps good shade.

④ **5c** ⚡ Bico

27m. A bit of a tricky one, more strange than technical, well bolted though. Steady head.

⑤ **6a** ⚡ Buraco

20m. The fun is around the pocket at the bottom, sorry no help on this one.

Rappel-abseil. Routes 1-4 are reached by abseil only.

⑥ **5c** ⚡ Hermafrodita

20m. An old route that is not equipped, but is nice to do on a top rope.

⑦ **5a** ⚡ Cu

21m. A good little route that is nice and technical, but well equipped to even get up bolt to bolt. (You can walk back out from bottom).

⑧ **6a** ⚡ Tecto

21m. A route that isn't that easy, but well protected and worth going for, a combination of strength low down and technique high up.

⑨ **3a** ⚡ Escape route

6m. It is equipped with 3 point, which is handy if it rains.

Résumé. A lovely open sector in the middle of the cliff and perfect slab climbing for the lower grades. You can scramble up an awkward path, or abseil in from the top where there are nice picnic views, and often a cool breeze.

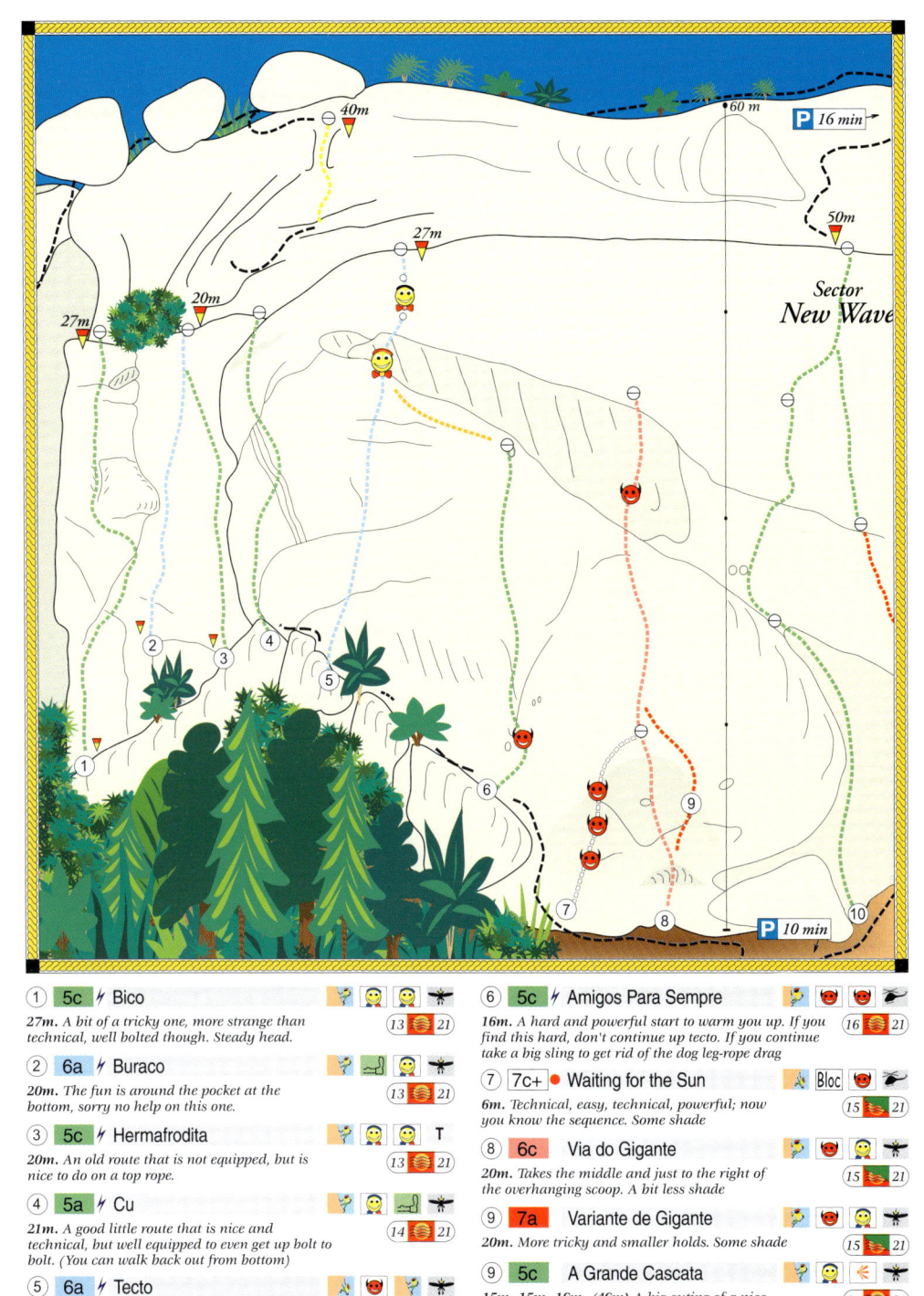

SINTRA

① 5c ⚡ Bico
27m. A bit of a tricky one, more strange than technical, well bolted though. Steady head.

② 6a ⚡ Buraco
20m. The fun is around the pocket at the bottom, sorry no help on this one.

③ 5c ⚡ Hermafrodita
20m. An old route that is not equipped, but is nice to do on a top rope.

④ 5a ⚡ Cu
21m. A good little route that is nice and technical, but well equipped to even get up bolt to bolt. (You can walk back out from bottom)

⑤ 6a ⚡ Tecto
21m. A route that isn't that easy, but well protected and worth going for, a combination of strength low down and technique high up.

⑥ 5c ⚡ Amigos Para Sempre
16m. A hard and powerful start to warm you up. If you find this hard, don't continue up tecto. If you continue take a big sling to get rid of the dog leg-rope drag

⑦ 7c+ ● Waiting for the Sun
6m. Technical, easy, technical, powerful; now you know the sequence. Some shade

⑧ 6c Via do Gigante
20m. Takes the middle and just to the right of the overhanging scoop. A bit less shade

⑨ 7a Variante de Gigante
20m. More tricky and smaller holds. Some shade

⑨ 5c A Grande Cascata
15m; 15m; 16m. (46m) A big outing of a nice 3 pitch route.

Résumé. A blocky scramble leads to routes 4-6.

Tombo - Amizade - Crista/Tecto - **Gigante** - New Wave - Solar

NEW WAVE 6a, Sintra; José Texiera

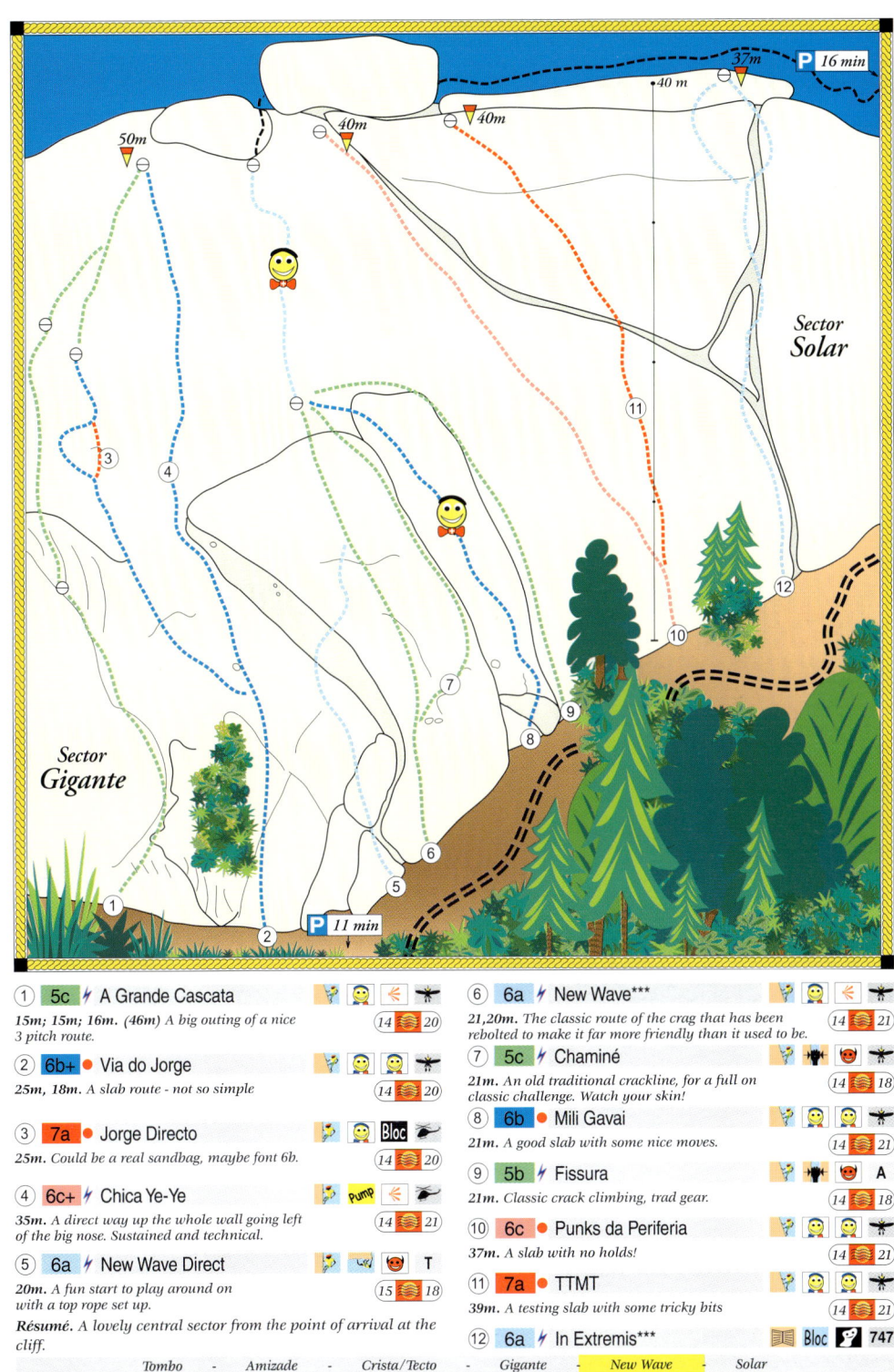

SINTRA

Sector Solar

Sector Gigante

① **5c** ⚡ **A Grande Cascata**
15m; 15m; 16m. (46m) A big outing of a nice 3 pitch route.

② **6b+** ● **Via do Jorge**
25m, 18m. A slab route - not so simple

③ **7a** ● **Jorge Directo**
25m. Could be a real sandbag, maybe font 6b.

④ **6c+** ⚡ **Chica Ye-Ye**
35m. A direct way up the whole wall going left of the big nose. Sustained and technical.

⑤ **6a** ⚡ **New Wave Direct**
20m. A fun start to play around on with a top rope set up.

Résumé. A lovely central sector from the point of arrival at the cliff.

⑥ **6a** ⚡ **New Wave***
21,20m. The classic route of the crag that has been rebolted to make it far more friendly than it used to be.

⑦ **5c** ⚡ **Chaminé**
21m. An old traditional crackline, for a full on classic challenge. Watch your skin!

⑧ **6b** ● **Mili Gavai**
21m. A good slab with some nice moves.

⑨ **5b** ⚡ **Fissura**
21m. Classic crack climbing, trad gear.

⑩ **6c** ● **Punks da Periferia**
37m. A slab with no holds!

⑪ **7a** ● **TTMT**
39m. A testing slab with some tricky bits

⑫ **6a** ⚡ **In Extremis***

Tombo - Amizade - Crista/Tecto - Gigante - **New Wave** - Solar

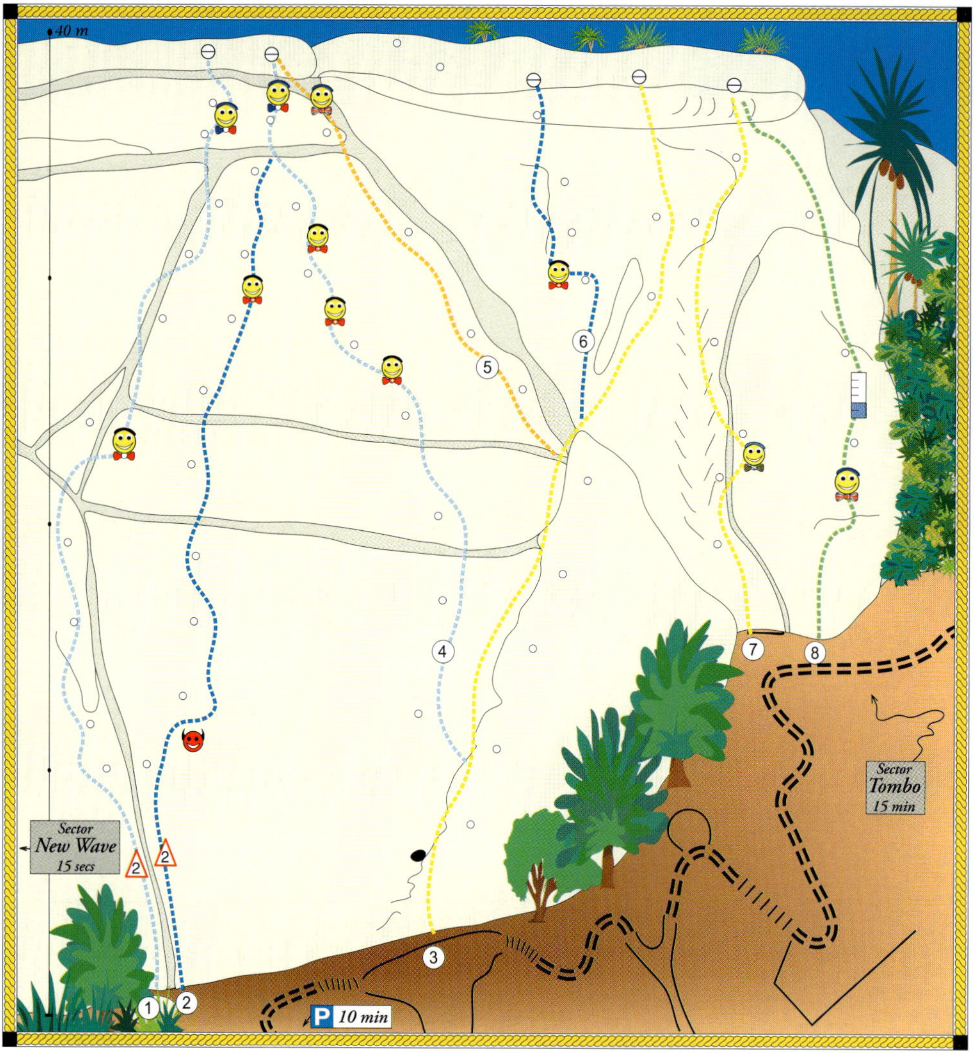

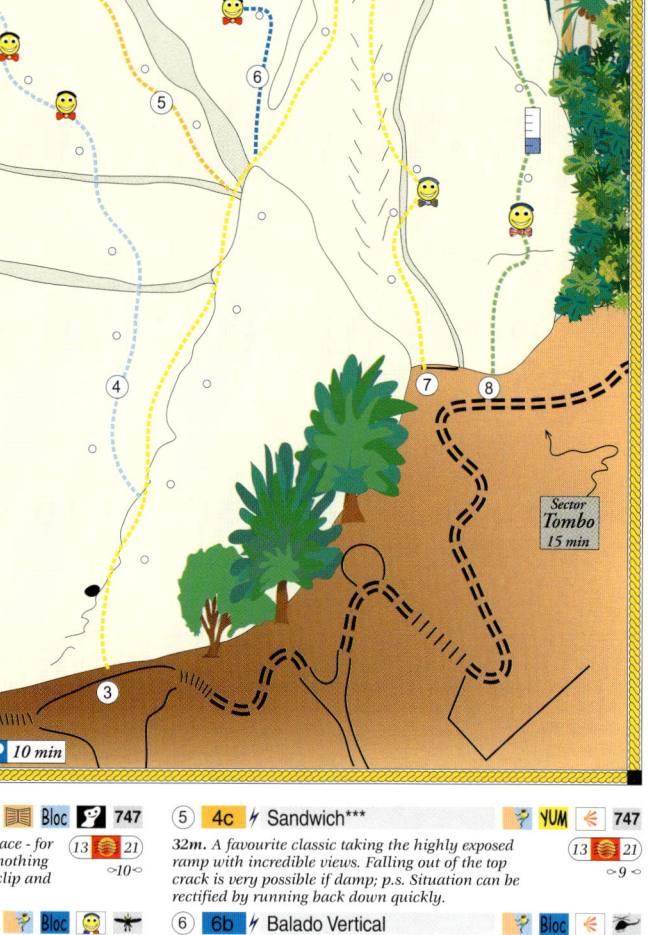

SINTRA

① **6a** ⚡ **In Extremis***** Bloc 747
37m. A wonderfully awkward adventure into space - for some. Nothing too testing on the one hand, but nothing too easy either. Cracks do not take cams, so it's clip and fly. (Rope stretch on a 70m gets you down)

② **6b** ● **Holendezas***** Bloc
37m. A start to make you feel like you got out the wrong side of the bed today. Really worth taking time to figure out the moves and not fluff the onsight - sneaky moves.

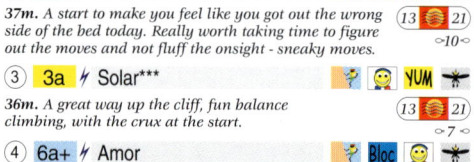

③ **3a** ⚡ **Solar***** YUM
36m. A great way up the cliff, fun balance climbing, with the crux at the start.

④ **6a+** ⚡ **Amor** Bloc
32m. If you can't climb slabs; expect good air time on this one. Slippery slab climbing on nicely rounded friction holds. Keeping to the right of the last 3 bolts is really worth it - for pure slab climbing.

Résumé. Superb, the most popular sector.

⑤ **4c** ⚡ **Sandwich***** YUM 747
32m. A favourite classic taking the highly exposed ramp with incredible views. Falling out of the top crack is very possible if damp; p.s. Situation can be rectified by running back down quickly.

⑥ **6b** ⚡ **Balado Vertical** Bloc
27m. A nice route with a real one move stopper. No strength needed, just pure technique for the feet. Low in the grade; but you certainly wouldn't be very happy without a rope! (Grade is for - onsight only)

⑦ **3b** ⚡ **Jardin Escola** Fun
17m. A nice easy groove that provides good fun for beginners and useful for those who aren't quite ready for the exposure on the big slab.

⑧ **5c** ⚡ **Via da Tania** Bloc
17m. A couple of moves to wake you up certainly, may be more problematic for the shorter climber.

Tombo - Amizade - Crista/Tecto - Gigante - New Wave - Solar

BALADO VERTICAL 6b, Sintra; Paulo Alves

ALUCINDA PELA ESQUINA 6b, Capuchos; André Neres

The Serra de Sintra are the hills that form the coastal, mini mountain range, which overlook Cascais and Estoril to the South, and stare at Mafra to the North. If you fly into Lisbon, you will get a very clear picture of them out to the west of the city. They are only 1780 ft high, but it is lofty enough to provide a completely different weather pattern at the top, to that of the coastal sandy beaches, only a couple of kilometres away. You can have a superb 25 degrees on the beach, and sun that makes it feel like 35 degrees. Yet up on the top of Peninha, it can be 17 degrees, and under a dense tree canopy with a cold wind, that makes it feel the same as 7 degrees. It is completely remarkable, how different it can be. To the hard boulderer, this can save the day. You might be sweltering down on Mexilhoeiro, yet up at either Capuchos or Peninha, you will have the most perfect friction conditions possible. The only – big – disadvantage with the forests of the Serra de Sintra, is that you are very close to the Atlantic. Sure, the wind can whip through the trees and dry the boulders superbly quickly, and on hot days, it's like an excellent air-con effect. But it can simple attract cloud like bees to a honey pot. Many a time I have flown into Lisbon, with blue skies everywhere – and the Serra de Sintra with its very own, private cloud, engulfing the top of the mountain. Peninha is at the west end of the ridge, and for some reason gets marginally better weather than the big cliff of Sintra, but there are times when you just cannot climb anywhere in the hills for several days.

The forest itself is magical, and is one of those luscious rainforests, with as many types of moss as the Amazon basin. We all know the old saying, a rolling stone gathers no moss. Well, since most of these boulders haven't moved for a thousand years, there's a frig of a lot of moss on them. There are granite boulders all over the whole mountain range, but in two venues they are close to the road, and are enough in number to give a good selection of climbs. The boulders are of all shapes and sizes, and give good boulder problems on medium to high quality granite. The popularity of the boulders has left all the problems nice and clean of moss, but the area is a national park and heritage site, so climbers are very careful to protect the local environment. This means no cutting down of trees, you! And leave only practical, small footpaths through the forest. The landings for the boulders in the forest are good, and even though a crash pad is always preferable – you should always use one to prevent all possible erosion. The forest canopy is thick and keeps many of the areas dark and broody. Occasionally sunlight creeps through to give a magnificent orange slash across a boulder, these are the magic moments. The coarseness of the rock will test your skin to the end. You have to try your hardest, but be contained with your dynos and slapping. You have to climb within your sloping limit here, or your skin won't even last a day. Both areas have some fine, highball lines. They are climbs which require both skill, and a good head. There are picnic areas in the woods, but if its good climbing conditions, you are better advised to go somewhere warmer to spend a relaxing hour or two.

A Serra de Sintra, é o conjunto de elevações que constitui uma mini cadeia costeira, separando Cascais e o Estoril a Sul, de Mafra a Norte. Se chegar a Lisboa de avião, pode vê-las claramente no quadrante Oeste da cidade. A sua altitude não ultrapassa os 540 metros, mas é suficiente para dar origem a condições meteorológicas completamente diferentes no cimo e nas praias que se situam apenas a alguns quilómetros de distância. Podem estar uns magníficos 25 graus na praia, com um sol que lhe dê a sensação de 35, enquanto no cimo da Peninha podem estar 17 graus, mas sob uma cúpula florestal tão densa e um vento tão frio, que mais pareçam 7 graus. É verdadeiramente extraordinária a diferença que pode existir – salvando o dia aos fanáticos do bloco. Pode sufocar-se lá em baixo no Mexilhoeiro, enquanto nos Capuchos ou na Peninha se encontram condições de aderência ideais. A única grande desvantagem das matas da Serra de Sintra é a de ficarem tão próximo do Atlântico. Sem dúvida que o vento pode infiltrar-se e secar tudo muito rapidamente, mantendo-se fresco mesmo nos dias mais quentes, mas também pode atrair as nuvens como abelhas a um pote de mel. Muitas vezes voei para Lisboa com céu limpo por toda a parte, mas a Serra de Sintra lá tinha a sua característica nuvem privada, cobrindo completamente o cume. A Peninha está situada na parte mais ocidental da crista montanhosa, e por alguma estranha razão tem sempre muito melhor clima do que o resto da Serra, no entanto, há ocasiões em que não se pode escalar durante vários dias, seja em que zona for.

Capuchos

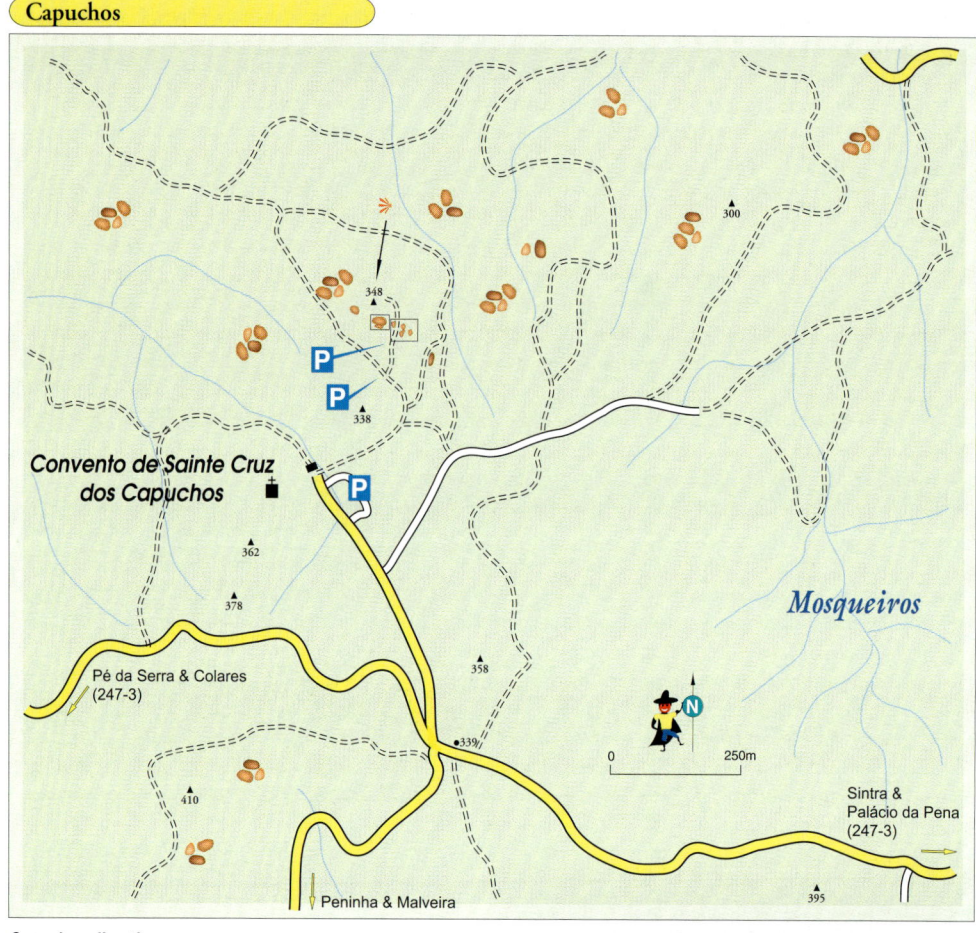

Capuchos directions:
See the map at the start of the Sintra section to locate the crossroads in the centre of the forest; a remote part of the Serra de Sintra. There are rarely any signposts at this crossroads, but Capuchos is usually marked, and is downhill. Follow to the end and the large parking area for the Convento. If you are happy to take your car off road, follow the track on the right to a T junction in about 150 metres. Here, turn left and continue for around 50 metres, to some parking on the left. You can park nearer the boulders, but the track becomes more exploratory for the underneath sump of 'ya moater.' The Forest authorities allow climbers to park here at the moment, but obviously respect the local environment.

Local knowledge:
This is a very beautiful spot, but is often spoiled by louts leaving cans and rubbish. Please tidy up if possible. In the trees and stays damp after rain, but is relatively quick drying as the wind can get, not too dense forest. There is a lovely viewpoint at the end of the track - to see the sea. There are lots of boulders in this forest, waiting to be explored, but the rock is often orange and a bit crumbly, or very blank. If you need a beer, then Malveira is most probably the closest.

Mushrooms enjoying the moist undergrowth of the rain forest.

BOREAL

A floresta propriamente dita é mágica, fazendo lembrar uma deliciosa floresta tropical, com tantos tipos de musgo quanto os da bacia do Amazonas. Todos conhecem o velho ditado: "Pedra que rola não ganha musgo". Pois bem, uma vez que estes blocos não se movem há milhares de anos, têm uma quantidade tramada de musgo em cima deles. Existem blocos de granito espalhados por toda a Serra, mas há duas zonas onde se encontram perto da estrada, em número suficiente para permitir uma ampla escolha de problemas. Os blocos são de todas as formas e tamanhos, num granito de média e alta qualidade. Devido à sua popularidade estão todos limpos de musgo, no entanto a área é considerada Parque e Património Nacionais, por isso os escaladores têm de ter muito cuidado para proteger o ambiente circundante. Quer dizer por exemplo: nada de partir as arvores! Deixe apenas pequenos trilhos na mata e só os indispensáveis. As aterragens são boas, mas mesmo assim o crash pad é sempre recomendável – deve usar sempre um para evitar qualquer tipo de erosão no terreno. As copas das árvores são bastante densas, fazendo com que muitas áreas sejam escuras e melancólicas. Esporadicamente, o sol espreita e espalha um magnífico tom alaranjado sobre os blocos, criando sem dúvida momentos mágicos. A aspereza da rocha testará a pele das suas mãos até ao osso. Vai ter de dar o seu melhor, mas conter-se nos lançamentos e palmadas; deve escalar dentro dos seus limites de inclinação ou a pele não durará nem um dia. Ambas as áreas têm linhas bonitas e altas, permitindo uma escalada agradável que requer qualidades tanto técnicas quanto mentais. Há locais próprios para fazer piqueniques na mata, mas se as condições para escalar forem boas, é aconselhável ir para um sítio mais quente e relaxar durante um par de horas.

RACHA LA RACHA 4c, Capuchos; Leopoldo Faria

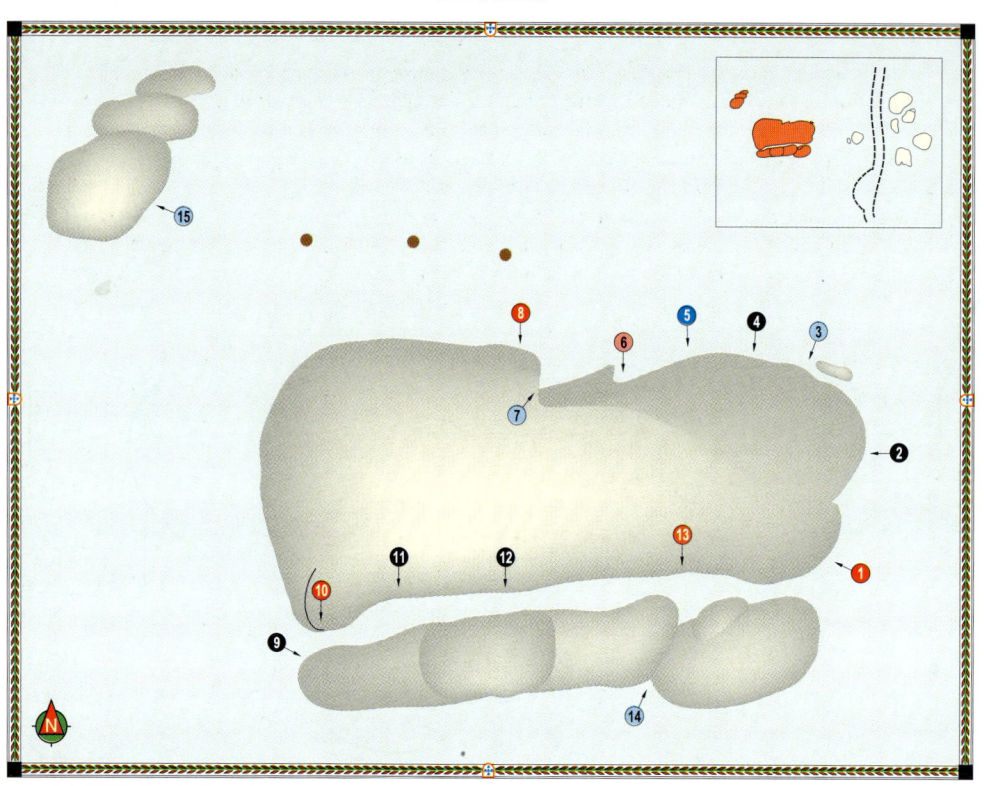

CAPUCHOS

162

#	Grade	Name	Description
1	6a	Tarantula*	3m; Very technical rounded bulge problem, foot & leg flexibility.
2	6c+	Mega Grip**	3m; Start on big undercut, feet on lower break; then up to jug n break; R on rounded slopers.
3	4b	Popeye*	3m; Easy way up left end of wall onto L foot rockover.
4	6c	Banana Milkshake*	3m; Start 3m left of groove. Start with LH in horizontal crack and go straight up.
5	5a	?	Wall left of shallow overlap.
6	5b	Strawberry Juice*	Not that hard, but you must have confidence & good footwork.
7	4c	Cleavage***	6.5m A highly technical groove.
8	6a	Tight Skirt*	Wall and thin seam right of cleavage, can be climbed easiest with the LH on the arête.
9	6b+	Lift Off	2.5m; Good crimps at shoulder height, R foot up and slap.
10	6a	Alucinda pela Esquina***	A superb arête on sloping and rounded holds - technical.
11	6c+	Jumping Jack Flash***	5m: The very vertical wall at its highest point, technical & small holds. Easier for tall, especially going to the curving-finger u/cut.
12	6b+	?***	A fine wall - fingertips.
13	5c	?**	Start 3m from the end of the wall. A good wall, graded for those who are tall enough to reach the holds.
14	4b	Mind Games*	A small low arête and slab. Using left edge to lay away on..
15	4c	Racha la Racha*	Thin crack on the front right of the boulder. Start R and go up L to rounded finish.

Jumping Jack Flash — Ovo

HAGLÖFS

JUMPING JACK FLASH 6c+, Capuchos; André Neres

Capuchos

#	Grade	Name	Description
1	5a	Ovo*	Obvious slanting crack R-L then rockover.
2	3a	Ovo Rachado*	Sloping crack in the middle of the wall. (6a-Sitting start.)
3	6a	Ovo Mexido*	Right arête climbed on ; feet on slab then slap up right.
4	6c+	Ovo Estrelado*	Start R of the arête, squeeze for the top.
5		Project	Small project slab.
6	6a	Ovo Escalfado*	High one finger pocket and friction.
7	5b	?	2m: Rock over.
8	5c	?	2m: Rock over.
9	5a	Fanta	
10	2b	Agua Mineral	
11		?	Small rounded wall.
12	6b+	Obstetra	
13	6c+	Guiccoligista	
14	6b+	Tecto**	4m: A good roof on layaways.
15	5c	Lavatório*	
16	4c	?	2m: Small rounded wall, rockover.

Jumping Jack Flash   Ovo

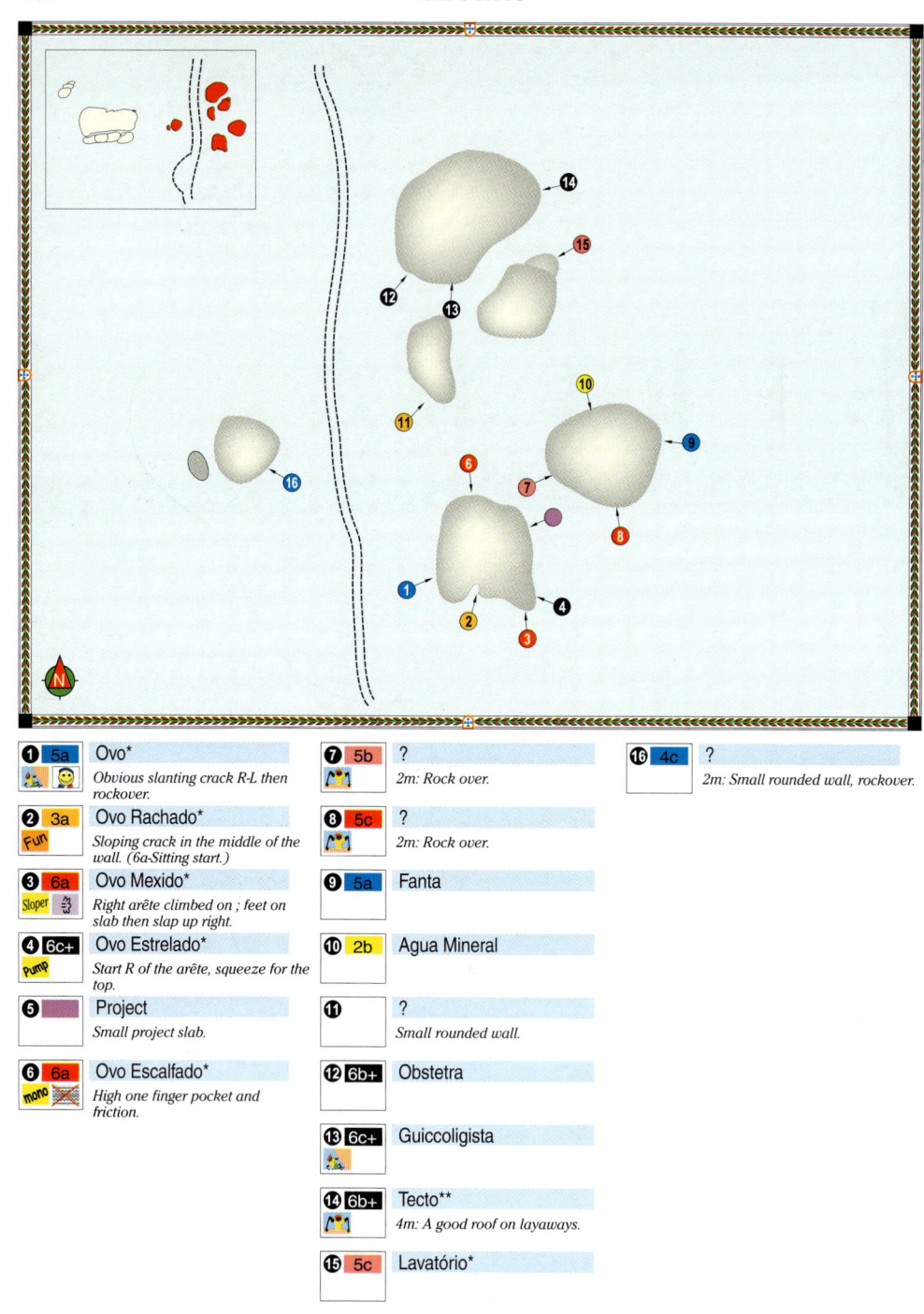

TECTO 6b+, Capuchos; André Neres

Peninha

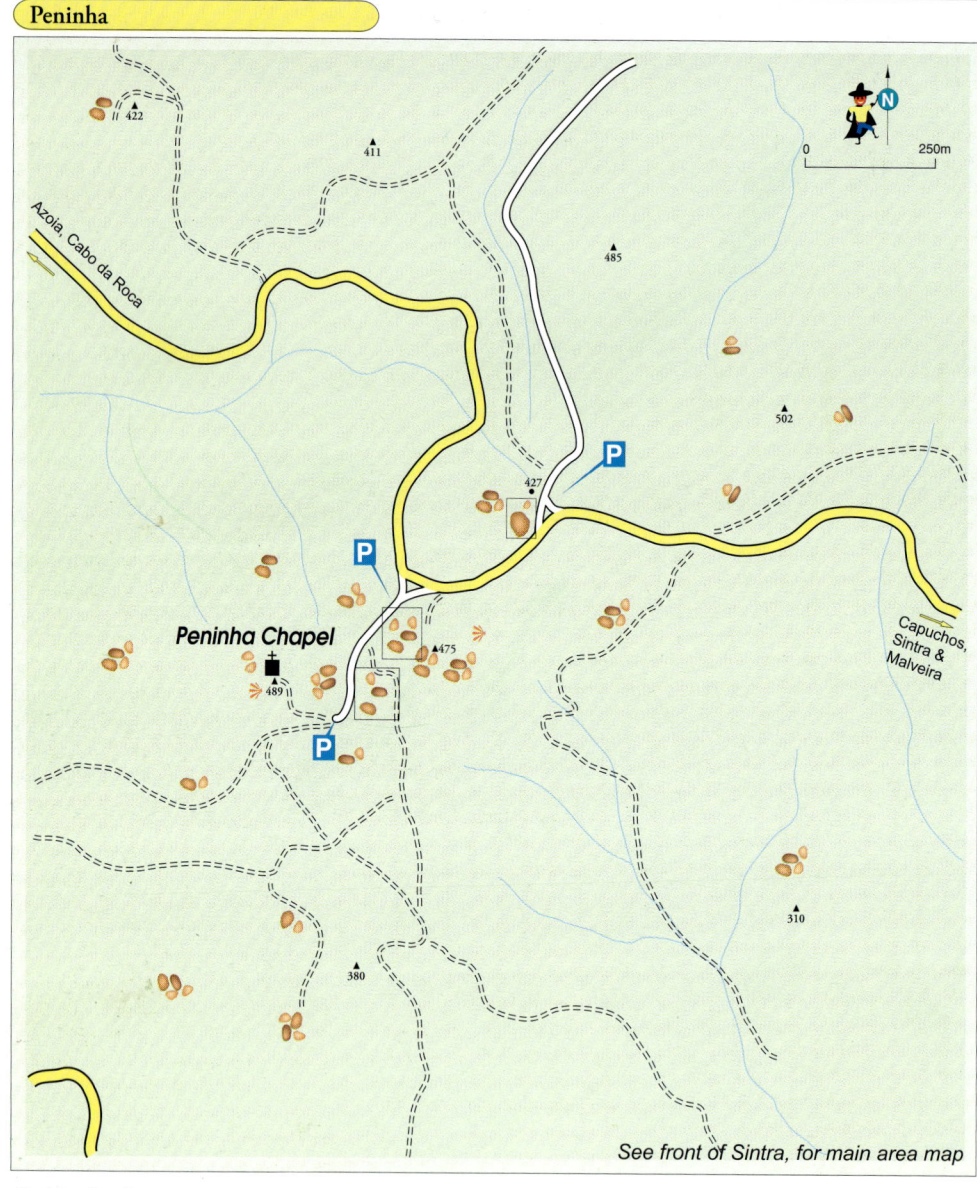

Peninha directions:
The surest way to find this spot (from Guincho), is to take the coast road to the Azoia turning, then just past it take the small steep road up to the right. The road is narrow and winds up the mountain for quite a while. You will easily recognise the Kalashnikov boulder on your left with the picnic tables.

Local knowledge:
A popular pic-nic spot, and a lot cooler than the coast, a lovely spot. Lots of fun problems on peak 475, nasty landings though. Plenty of boulders in the area to discover, very high quality granite

MASSA EXPANSIVA 7b, Peninha; Jerry Moffatt

PENINHA

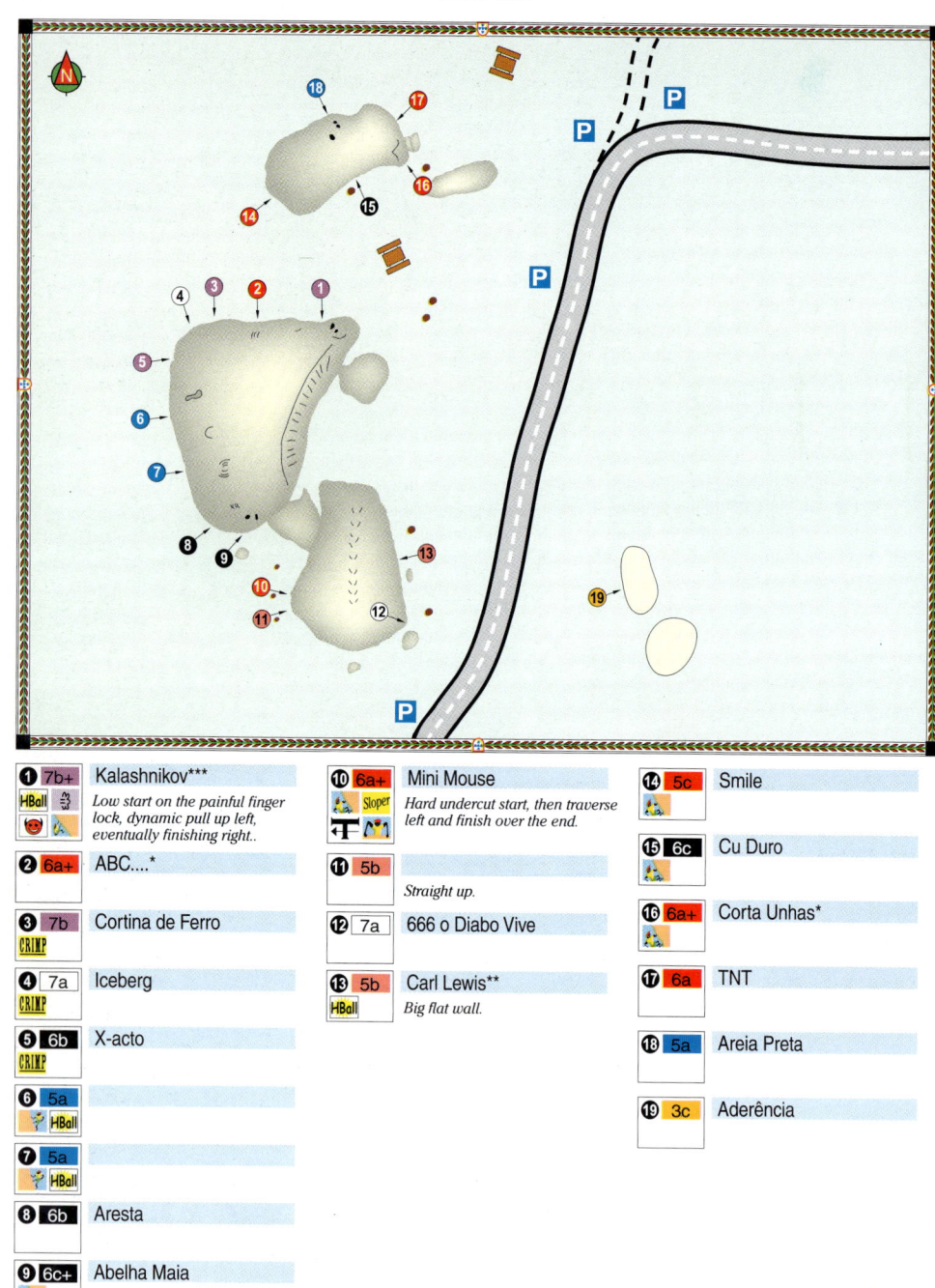

#	Grade	Name	Description
1	7b+	Kalashnikov***	Low start on the painful finger lock, dynamic pull up left, eventually finishing right..
2	6a+	ABC....*	
3	7b	Cortina de Ferro	
4	7a	Iceberg	
5	6b	X-acto	
6	5a		
7	5a		
8	6b	Aresta	
9	6c+	Abelha Maia	
10	6a+	Mini Mouse	Hard undercut start, then traverse left and finish over the end.
11	5b		Straight up.
12	7a	666 o Diabo Vive	
13	5b	Carl Lewis**	Big flat wall.
14	5c	Smile	
15	6c	Cu Duro	
16	6a+	Corta Unhas*	
17	6a	TNT	
18	5a	Areia Preta	
19	3c	Aderência	

www.vertical-outdoor.com

Kalashnikov — Metro — Bleuziana

KALASHNIKOV 7c, Peninha; Jerry Moffatt

PENINHA

#	Grade	Name	Description
1	6b	Metro	3m: Obvious crimps going L.
2	6b+	Quebra Ossos	3m: Crimp the R arête, run up with a nice mantle to finish.
3	6a	Tonelada	3m: Start 1m R of arête on a fine sloper, search for a mono hole.
4	4a		A problem from hell for short, high jug and step up.
5	3a	Nightingale	Kids problem off the stone by tree.
6	6a+	Travesseiro*	Big ledge needs outside edge, R foot step up with difficulty to gain niche; high jug - awkward.
7	7a	Karma de Serra*	Match on shoulder level hold, crimp up high and rock over.
8	7b	Moonshine**	SS on the L, then go right and finish up Karma de Serra.
9	6b	Equilibrium	A fine little steep wall on crimps.
10	5c	White Zombie	A classic rounded arête that gets some nice sunshine.
11	6c	Afromen	
12	6b	Spiritus Inquietus	
13	6c	Gripping in the Wind	
14	6c+	Hard Rock	
15	5c	Vai e Volta	
16	5a		
17	6a+	Caracol	
18	7c+	Moon Arête***	6m: The striking arête, just keep slapping up. Top is nice and easy.
19	6c+	Big Baldo	Incomplete, finish standing on crimp.
20	6c	Nautilus*	RH crimp, LH sloper in scoop, heel hook up to top on slopers, great low problem.
21	3b	Oceano Pacifico	Bridge to start. 4a if you traverse L to mantle in the centre.
22	5b	Clockwork	Somehow, mantleshelf into the depression.
23	7a	Anti-grip-in	
24	6c	Boomerang	Obvious mouth at back of the bay, using block 6c, without 7b.
25	6a	Green Arête	A little overhanging arête, jump onto foothold, ungradeable.
26	6a+	Ben's Move*	Stay on right, heel hooking over arête to finish with a mantle.
27	4c	Pé Descalço	6a – A nice mantle, rock over onto R foot, flexibility helps.
28	7b	Massa Expansiva**	From big sitting jug, slap up R, pocket L, up for RH sloper, then high LH sloper.
29	5b	Cogumelo Mágico*	The mantle will get harder as the ground wears away.
30	4a	Passeio de Domingo	

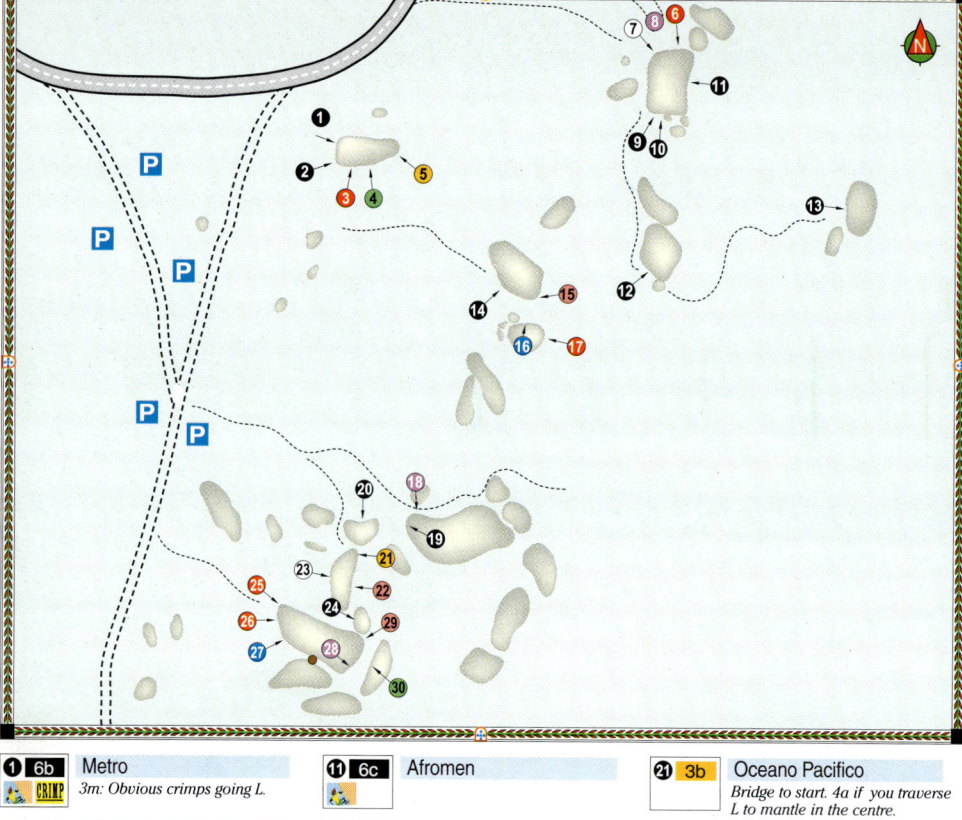

Kalashnikov — Metro — Bleuziana

MOON ARÊTE 7c+, Peninha; Ben Moon

FLY BABY FLY 6a, Peninha; Fred Silva

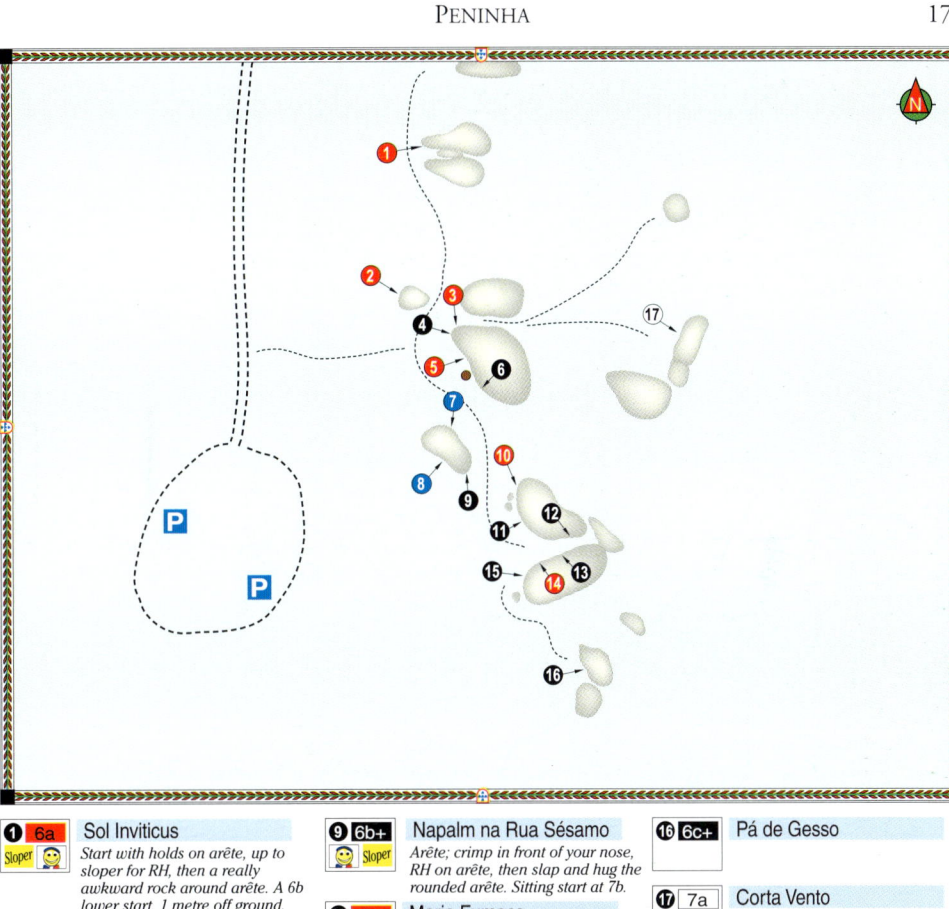

PENINHA

❶ 6a — Sol Inviticus
Start with holds on arête, up to sloper for RH, then a really awkward rock around arête. A 6b lower start, 1 metre off ground.

❷ 6a+ — Bleuziana

❸ 6a+ — Verde Canto

❹ 6b+ — Pulso Branco
Start on arête, RH to hole-pocket, cross over to top then rock on up.

❺ 6a+ — Halebop*
Start with RH on crimp, throw up into jug, easy finish. Can be 7a starting with hands low down.

❻ 6b+ — Com Tacto*
A hand traverse, R - L on slopers with foot hooking all the way; an awkward mantle to finish.

❼ 5a — Tobogan
Difficulty in reaching the pocket.

❽ 4c — Regent Street
Wall can be climbed, start using obvious foothold.

❾ 6b+ — Napalm na Rua Sésamo
Arête; crimp in front of your nose, RH on arête, then slap and hug the rounded arête. Sitting start at 7b.

❿ 5c — Maria Fumaça
Most have to jump for the hole (keep sweatshirt on to protect forearms).

⓫ 6c — Travessia a la Gardene
Seeps a lot. Start just R of boulder by big hole in undercut face. All the way to end - 7 metres.

⓬ 6c+ — Espanholada
St, at back L of cave; LH 2 finger pocket, RH sloping incut, jugs going up o-hang wall, jump down.

⓭ 6b+ — Tango ou Frango
St, opposite 12; Traverse R and go up faint groove.

⓮ 6a — Fly Baby, Fly
Right side of groove, on line with faint line of groove.

⓯ 6b+ — Soul Instinct
A crack of hell; climbed on the right as layaways the whole way.

⓰ 6c+ — Pá de Gesso

⓱ 7a — Corta Vento

Kalashnikov - Metro - Bleuziana

The most western point of Europe is Cabo da Roca, and is one hell of a wild place to be in a storm. It simply oozes bleak hardship, in anything but good weather. Giant cliffs run down to the ocean and are battered by waves. There is classic style climbing on most of this part of the coastline, but the rock is not the best around, and it is for the very adventurous and experienced climber – who requires a full, climbing experience! Just to the north of here there is the lovely fertile valley that comes down from Sintra to Colares, a superb vine growing and wine producing village. Here the coastline offers some good beaches. Secretly tucked away behind Praia da Adraga, is Praia do Cavalo. You have to scuttle down a steep ravine to reach the sand, which can vary in level according to sea swells from month to month. Here the waves are big, and also break short and powerfully. Tucked away though is a short overhanging wall above the sand. It can often stay wet from seepage, but it does dry out from time to time, and gives a great place to work away quietly on anything from Font 7c upwards.

Between Cabo da Roca and Guincho is the town of Malveira da Serra. The hills above here are strictly speaking, the Serra de Sintra. However the boulders that are of interest to climbers are just behind the village of Janes, and are so low down that they get a tropical, sunny aspect. They are a full-on, winter location. At all other times, they are like a furnace of orange granite that cooks in the midday sun. Here the bouldering is mainly short but powerful, and in two separate areas, and. The whole area is still getting opened up and developed, but will surely be popular as the rock dries very quickly, and the position is very nice too.

O ponto mais ocidental da Europa é o Cabo da Roca, um local verdadeiramente selvagem em dia de temporal; simplesmente transpira desolação e desgraça, se não estiver bom tempo. Penhascos gigantescos afundam-se no oceano e são castigados pelas ondas. Nesta parte da costa pratica-se escalada clássica, mas a rocha não é das melhores; trata-se dum local para escaladores aventureiros e com muita prática, que exigem ter sempre uma experiência de escalada total. A Norte daqui existe um vale fértil e encantador que desce de Sintra para Colares, uma zona de cultivo e excelente produção vinícola. A costa oferece muitas praias de boa qualidade. Secretamente escondida por detrás da Praia da Adraga, encontra-se a Praia do Cavalo. É necessário descer uma ravina muito íngreme para chegar à areia cujo nível, pode variar de mês para mês, ao sabor das marés. As ondas são grandes, curtas e extremamente poderosas. No entanto, há uma parede pequena e extraprumada escavada na rocha, que se eleva sobre a areia. Pode manter-se molhada devido às infiltrações, mas de vez em quando seca e dá um óptimo lugar para trabalhar sossegadamente em qualquer coisa de 7c para cima.

Entre o Cabo da Roca e o Guincho, encontra-se a povoação da Malveira da Serra. Os montes acima dela são, rigorosamente falando, a Serra de Sintra. Contudo, os blocos que mais interessam aos escaladores situam-se exactamente atrás da aldeia de Janes, e estão a uma altitude tão baixa que o sol mais parece tropical. Constituem um local exclusivo para a época de Inverno. Em qualquer outra altura, parecem mais um forno de granito laranja a cozinhar ao sol do meio-dia. Estes blocos são na sua maioria pequenos mas poderosos, distribuindo-se por duas áreas distintas. Toda esta zona ainda está a ser explorada e desenvolvida, mas vai ser com certeza um local bastante concorrido, já que a rocha seca muito rapidamente e a localização é também muito agradável.

STEAK HOUSE 7b+, Malveira; Macau - Ricardo Alves

Malveira

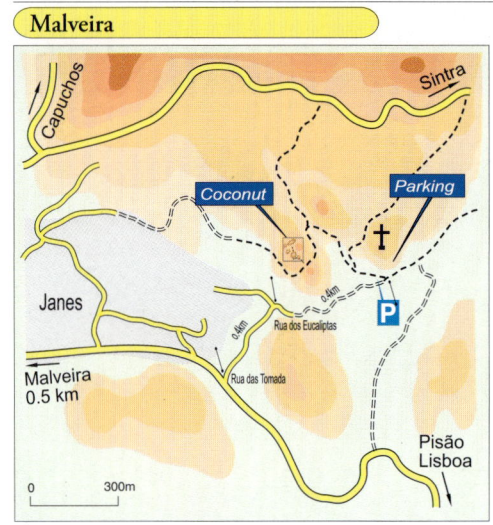

Local info:
Finding this bouldering area is not completely straightforward, but on the other hand, if you are keen and keep looking, you will find the boulders OK. You take the road going out of the East side of Janes, then after the town signpost, look for a road on the left - Rua das Tomada. Take this and then go right onto the Rua dos Eucaliptas, this goes down a steep gravel road for a bit - quite bumpy. After a while the track levels out to some big trees where there is parking for 8-10 cars.

Sector Parking:
This is up and to the South West of the big cross on the hill. There are lots of problems here and it is very quick drying - no problems in this guide. (2 mins)

Sector Coconut:
This is more complicated to find. Take the good track going back as a zigzag up the small valley. You soon (100m) pass some old buildings on your left, then branch right up the hill a bit and to the end of the wadi, here a footpath comes from the left. Cut back on this and follow it around to a small col. Here you can see boulders to the right. Seek and ye shall finde. (10 mins)

TRAVERSE 6a, Malveira; Sandra Albuquerque

MALVEIRA

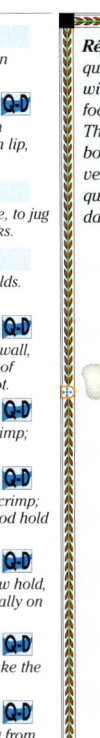

Résumé. The area is quite spread out, and with small problems that focus on short difficulty. There are many easier boulders here too. It is very open and dries quickly. Good for colder days since it gets full sun.

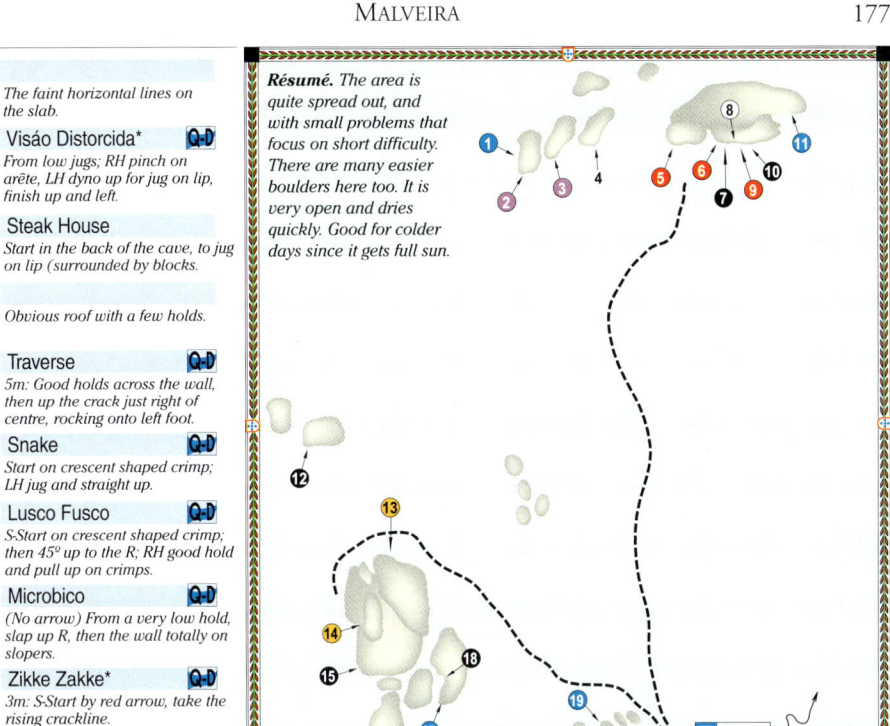

❶ 5a
The faint horizontal lines on the slab.

❷ 7b — Visáo Distorcida* Q-D
From low jugs; RH pinch on arête, LH dyno up for jug on lip, finish up and left.

❸ 7b+ — Steak House
Start in the back of the cave, to jug on lip (surrounded by blocks).

❹
Obvious roof with a few holds.

❺ 6a — Traverse Q-D
5m: Good holds across the wall, then up the crack just right of centre, rocking onto left foot.

❻ 6a — Snake Q-D
Start on crescent shaped crimp; LH jug and straight up.

❼ 6b+ — Lusco Fusco Q-D
S-Start on crescent shaped crimp; then 45º up to the R; RH good hold and pull up on crimps.

❽ 7a+ — Microbico
(No arrow) From a very low hold, slap up R, then the wall totally on slopers.

❾ 6a+ — Zikke Zakke* Q-D
3m: S-Start by red arrow, take the rising crackline.

❿ 6b+ — Slow Train Coming* Q-D
Full rising traverse, starting from the bottom left of the wall and finishing up Zikke Zakke.

⓫ 4c — Coconut Groove* Q-D
It's a wall - not a groove! Lovely wall on good clean holds, tricky top. Use pads to get first hold.

⓬ 6c
S-Start on the R, crossovers going L, the up and around the arête.

⓭ 3b — Science Friction*
4m: The lovely looking slab is not too hard, but does offer quite a lot of moves.

⓮ 3c — The Groove*
Getting into the groove is a bit awkward, exit up and right with a good head.

⓯ 6c+ — Laranja Mecanica
S-Start, LH pinch, Traverse up and right to holds, then up rounded arête.

⓰ 4a — Arête
Climbs the right arête.

⓱ 4c — Arête
Climbs the right arête

⓲ 6b — Centurion
3m: The groove in the centre.

⓳ 5a — Left Arête (2m) Q-D
⓴ 6b — SS-Left Arête (2m) Q-D
㉑ 4b — Nose on Right (2m) Q-D

COCONUT GROOVE 4c, Malveira: Jerry Moffatt

Coconut — Parking

Praia do Cavalo

Local info:
There is a popular beach of Praia da Adraga that has a good small parking area, and a bar with food, and set in a lovely location. The beach here is fun for the family, even though - the waves can be a bit tough at times. The beach of Cavalo is just to the West, but cannot be reached at sea level at all. The sea is also a bit powerful around here so don't even think of swimming around to the cove! The land approach is better, but still quite hazardous and hardly inviting. You have to scramble down a slope! then a loose gully from hell and a rope in place to clatter down to the bottom - which feels like the jaws of the earth.

Beach height:
Because this cove is highly battered by the waves, the seabound edge where the overhanging wall is situated, is very variable in sand height - 2-3 metres of change.

Conditions:
The wall is very steep, overhanging at 45º and gets a lot of sea spray coming in. It also seeps a lot after rain. If the beach is dry you can clean the holds, if it's low - you're stuffed. Morning sun, afternoon and evening shade, and generally a cool place even at sea level.

Classic Trad:
The whole wall of the West side of the cove has been climbed with trad routes and there are old rusty pegs in place. If access were better, it would be more popular. The headland of Ponta da Batureira are high limestone cliffs with slabbly possiblitites, very little protection though.

The sea here at Praia do Cavalo may look calm, photo's deceive!

Leo Faria - 'in bulk' on one of the many 7c problems at Cavalo

Sunset, drink, suntan, holiday etc, etc, etc,

Montejunto

 Parque de Campsimo; Montejunto
00 351 262 777 888
www.cadaval.org/campismo2/
Situation: A long way up a very big hill!
Open: 01/05-30/09. (Other times, book 3
3 days in advance: 01/10-31/04)

Local info:
Two limestone cliffs that offer quite different styles of climbing. **Velho** is medium high and technical. Lovely views and a great position. Climbing ban during bird season. **Novo** is much smaller and compact, north facing for those hot summer days. Both cliffs have a very short walk in.

Montejunto Novo sector

When you visit part of a country that is a natural reserve or a protected area, you certainly do appreciate the wildness and beauty that our natural world can offer. Just to the north of Lisbon is an area called Oeste (West) which includes the historic towns of Óbidos, Alenquer and Torres Vedras. Oeste also contains some of the most superb and beautiful natural reserves of Portugal. The archipelago of Berlenga near Peniche is home, to a superb wealth of flora, and substantial bird colonies. A substantial effort today, has gone into toursim-integration for these areas, so people can benefit from visiting them, without wreaking the natural environment. Another such natural reserve is the Serra de Montjunto, where the hills of Montejunto are an integrate part of the 'Maciço Calcário Estremenho.' This high area rises up to 666 metres, with a beautiful rounded limestone mountain, that is home to an identified 115 species of different birds. The whole area is benefit to its own micro climate, known locally as a dew ecosystem, and is subject to both continental and seaside weather patterns. The whole area has a mixture of anything from pine trees to wild chestnut and oak groves; a complete contrast to the sweeping eucalyptus forests that occupy the lower landscapes.

Just near the summit of Montejunto, there are several good limestone cliffs, which give around 50 routes of all different standards. There are two distinct sectors that offer completely different styles of climbing, and by orientation, are suitable for climbing at different times of the year. Both are at around 600 metres altitude and are substantially cooler than the coastline cliffs. The Novo sector faces north and is short, hard and boulder style. It is however, a very useful place to know about in summer, when in the afternoons and evenings you can both have a lovely picnic and climb. The views also from here are stunning. The other cliff of Velho, is only a short distance away, but is a popular breeding ground for birds and there is a total climbing ban during nesting season. This is from 1st February until 31st July. It is larger and offers lovely climbs in the medium to harder grades. The rock here is quite pocketed, and can feel quite sharp on the finger joints. The routes are vertical to overhanging, and even though they are relatively short – they certainly feel quite long enough for the forearm department. The whole area is beautiful, and must be carefully looked after – especially by climbers, to ensure that everyone who visits this protected landscape, respects it's fragile environment.

Quando visitamos as reservas naturais ou áreas protegidas de um país, apreciamos certamente o estado selvagem e a beleza que o nosso mundo físico pode oferecer. Mesmo a Norte de Lisboa fica a zona litoral do Oeste, que abrange as cidades históricas de Óbidos, Alenquer e Torres Vedras. Nela existem também algumas das mais belas reservas naturais do país. O arquipélago das Berlengas, perto de Peniche, alberga uma flora rica e variada, bem como importantes colónias de aves. Está a ser feito um grande esforço para integrar estas áreas em roteiros turísticos, de forma a poderem ser visitadas sem danificar o ambiente. A Serra de Montejunto, outra dessas reservas naturais, é parte integrante do Maciço Calcário Estremenho. A sua zona mais alta, uma formosa elevação arredondada de calcário, atinge um máximo de 666 metros e abriga cerca de 115 espécies de aves já identificadas. Toda a área beneficia do seu próprio microclima, conhecido por ecossistema húmido, e está sujeita à influência dos padrões climáticos tanto continentais, como marítimos. A sua camada florestal é constituída por uma mistura de quase tudo, desde Pinheiros a Castanheiros bravos e bosques de Carvalhos; um contraste total com as extensas matas de Eucaliptos que ocupam as zonas mais baixas.

Perto do cume de Montejunto, existem várias falésias calcárias com boa qualidade, e cerca de 50 vias de todos os níveis. Há dois sectores distintos que oferecem estilos de escalada completamente diferentes e que, devido à sua orientação, se tornam mais adequados para escalar em diversas épocas do ano. Ambos estão a cerca de 600 metros de altitude, sendo substancialmente mais frescos do que as falésias costeiras. No sector Novo, orientado a Norte, predominam as vias curtas e duras, estilo Bloco. Contudo, é um lugar que convém conhecer, para durante as tardes de Verão se poder fazer

MONTEJUNTO

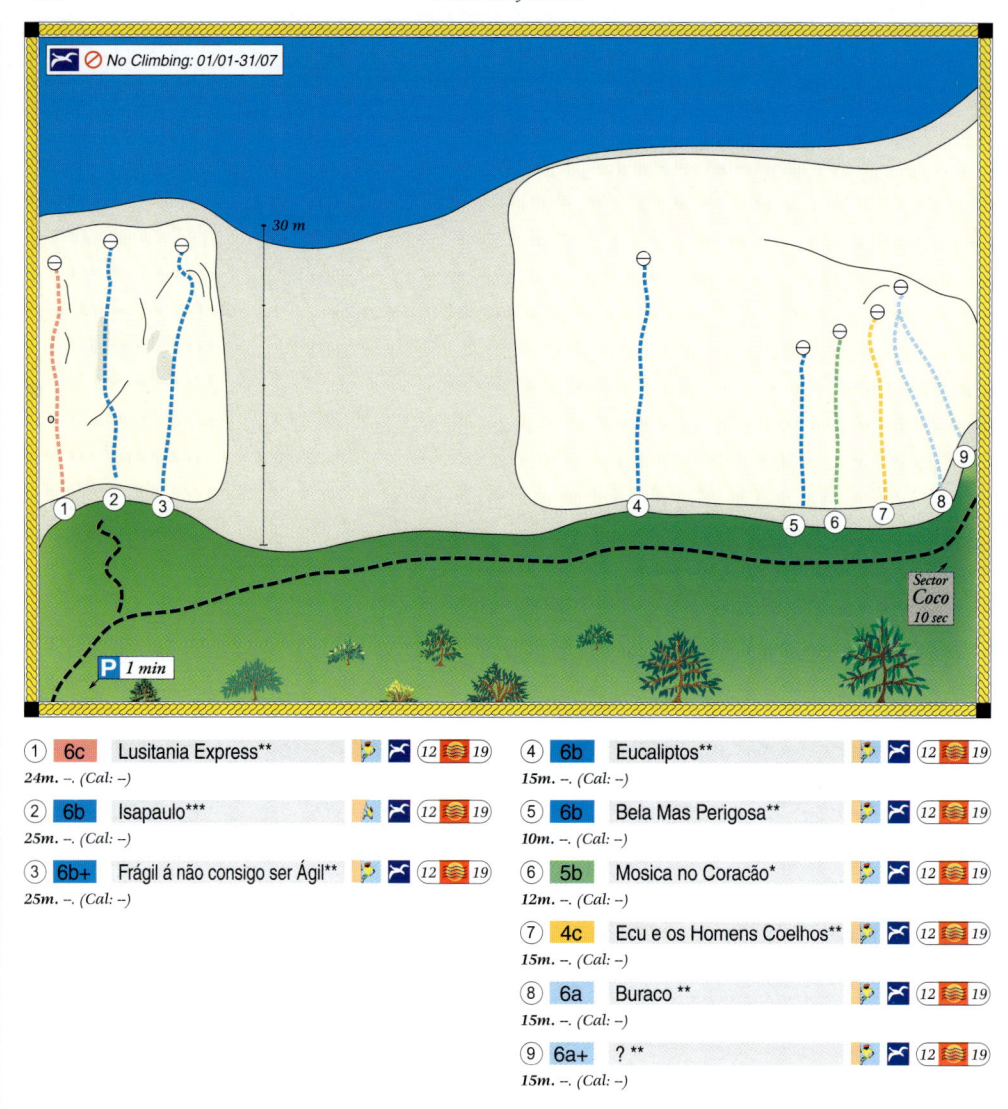

No Climbing: 01/01-31/07

30 m

Sector Coco 10 sec

P 1 min

① **6c** Lusitania Express** — 12 · 19
24m. –. (Cal: –)

② **6b** Isapaulo*** — 12 · 19
25m. –. (Cal: –)

③ **6b+** Frágil á não consigo ser Ágil** — 12 · 19
25m. –. (Cal: –)

④ **6b** Eucaliptos** — 12 · 19
15m. –. (Cal: –)

⑤ **6b** Bela Mas Perigosa** — 12 · 19
10m. –. (Cal: –)

⑥ **5b** Mosica no Coracão* — 12 · 19
12m. –. (Cal: –)

⑦ **4c** Ecu e os Homens Coelhos** — 12 · 19
15m. –. (Cal: –)

⑧ **6a** Buraco ** — 12 · 19
15m. –. (Cal: –)

⑨ **6a+** ?** — 12 · 19
15m. –. (Cal: –)

um belo piquenique e escalar. A vista é também deslumbrante. O sector Velho fica muito perto do primeiro mas, por ser um importante local de nidificação, está interdito à escalada entre 1 de Janeiro e 31 de Julho de cada ano. É maior e oferece vias encantadoras de nível médio a alto. A rocha tem bastantes buracos cujas arestas se podem fazer notar nas articulações dos dedos. As vias vão de verticais a extraprumadas e apesar de serem relativamente curtas, serão suficientemente compridas para se sentirem no departamento dos antebraços. Toda a área é bonita e tem de ser muito bem cuidada – especialmente pelos escaladores – para garantir que toda a gente que visite esta zona protegida, respeita o seu frágil ambiente.

Velho Eucaliptus - *Velho Coco* - *Novo Impotência* - *Novo Dementes*

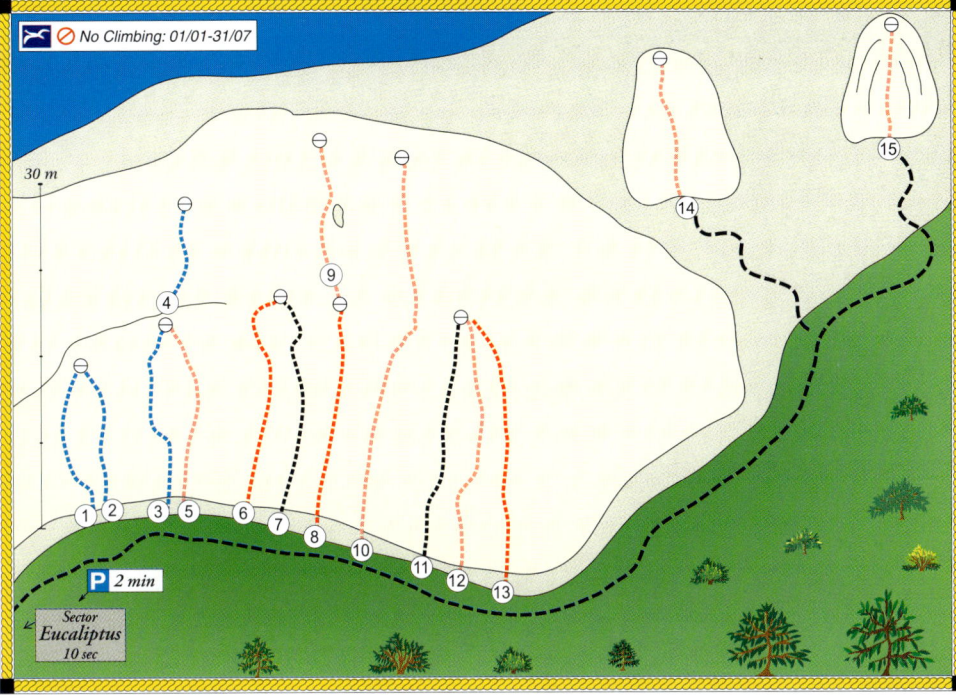

MONTEJUNTO

No Climbing: 01/01-31/07

Sector Eucaliptus 10 sec

#	Grade	Name	Length
①	6b	Greta e os Garbos**	7m. –. (Cal: –)
②	6b+	Porque Não**	7m. –. (Cal: –)
③	6b	Lobos Coco***	7m. –. (Cal: –)
④	6c	Os Bálcaros Voltam ao Ataque	12m. –. (Cal: –)
⑤	6c+	Coco Lobos***	7m. –. (Cal: –)
⑥	7a+	TecLuAn***	12m. –. (Cal: –)
⑦	7b	Nata Nifo***	12m. –. (Cal: –)
⑧	7a	Daniel Não Sejas Cruel**	12m. –. (Cal: –)
⑨	7a+	Missa (Daniel xtn)***	30m. –. (Cal: –)
⑩	6c	O Mistério dos Bálcaros***	25m. –. (Cal: –)
⑪	7b+	Manias e Tiranias**	15m. –. (Cal: –)
⑫	6c+	Bruxa***	15m. –. (Cal: –)
⑬	7a	West End Side***	15m. –. (Cal: –)
⑭	6c+	Impressões Digitais**	20m. –. (Cal: –)
⑮	6c	Cogumelo Mágico**	10m. –. (Cal: –)

Velho Eucaliptus - Velho Coco - Novo Impoténcia - Novo Dementes

MONTEJUNTO

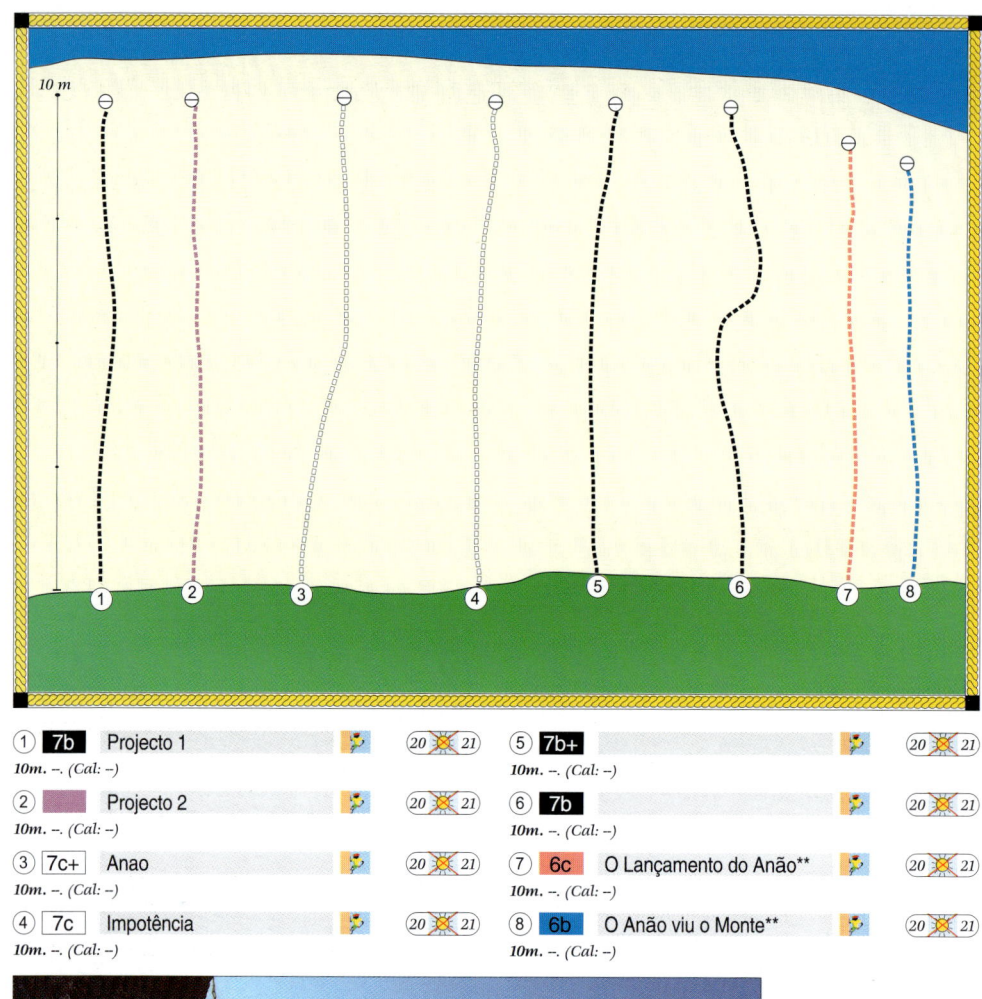

① **7b** Projecto 1	⑤ **7b+**
10m. –. (Cal: –)	*10m. –. (Cal: –)*
② Projecto 2	⑥ **7b**
10m. –. (Cal: –)	*10m. –. (Cal: –)*
③ **7c+** Anao	⑦ **6c** O Lançamento do Anão**
10m. –. (Cal: –)	*10m. –. (Cal: –)*
④ **7c** Impotência	⑧ **6b** O Anão viu o Monte**
10m. –. (Cal: –)	*10m. –. (Cal: –)*

View from Novo sector

Velho Eucaliptus - Velho Coco - **Novo Impotência** - Novo Dementes

One beautiful place on the tourist trail that is definitely worth a visit, is the old village of Obidos. It is only a few minutes from the main motorway that you take between Lisboa and Reguengo do Fétal, and just north of Montejunto. The whole village is set on a hill with impressive battlement walls encircling it. Lovely views and a nice place to stroll around when the heat makes it too unbearable to climb, or you need a rest day. Accommodation right in the town is a bit pricey, but locally there are many reasonable hotels and residencias.

MONTEJUNTO

#	Grade	Name		
①	6a+	Não Pisar o Musgo	7m. –. (Cal: –)	
②	5b	Quinto Esquerdo	7m. –. (Cal: –)	
③	4b	Quinto Frente	7m. –. (Cal: –)	
④	4a	Quinto Direito*	7m. –. (Cal: –)	
⑤	7b	**	7m. –. (Cal: –)	
⑥	6b+	Caraccol Desenfreado**	8m. –. (Cal: –)	
⑦	6b	***	8m. –. (Cal: –)	
⑧	6a+	Presa Livre**	8m. –. (Cal: –)	
⑨	7a	Pica Miolos**	10m. –. (Cal: –)	
⑩	7a+	Ultrapassagem Perigosa***	16m. –. (Cal: –)	
⑪	7b	Regresso dos Dementes***	12m. –. (Cal: –)	
⑫	8a	A Histérica e o Vibrador	12m. –. (Cal: –)	
⑬	7b+		10m. –. (Cal: –)	
⑭	7c	Ansiedade	10m. –. (Cal: –)	
⑮	7b	Emilio e os Detectives	9m. –. (Cal: –)	
⑯	6b	Só nós 2 é que sabemos	9m. –. (Cal: –)	
⑰	6a+	Lingua Viperina	8m. –. (Cal: –)	
⑱	6a+	Fissura Satânica	8m. –. (Cal: –)	

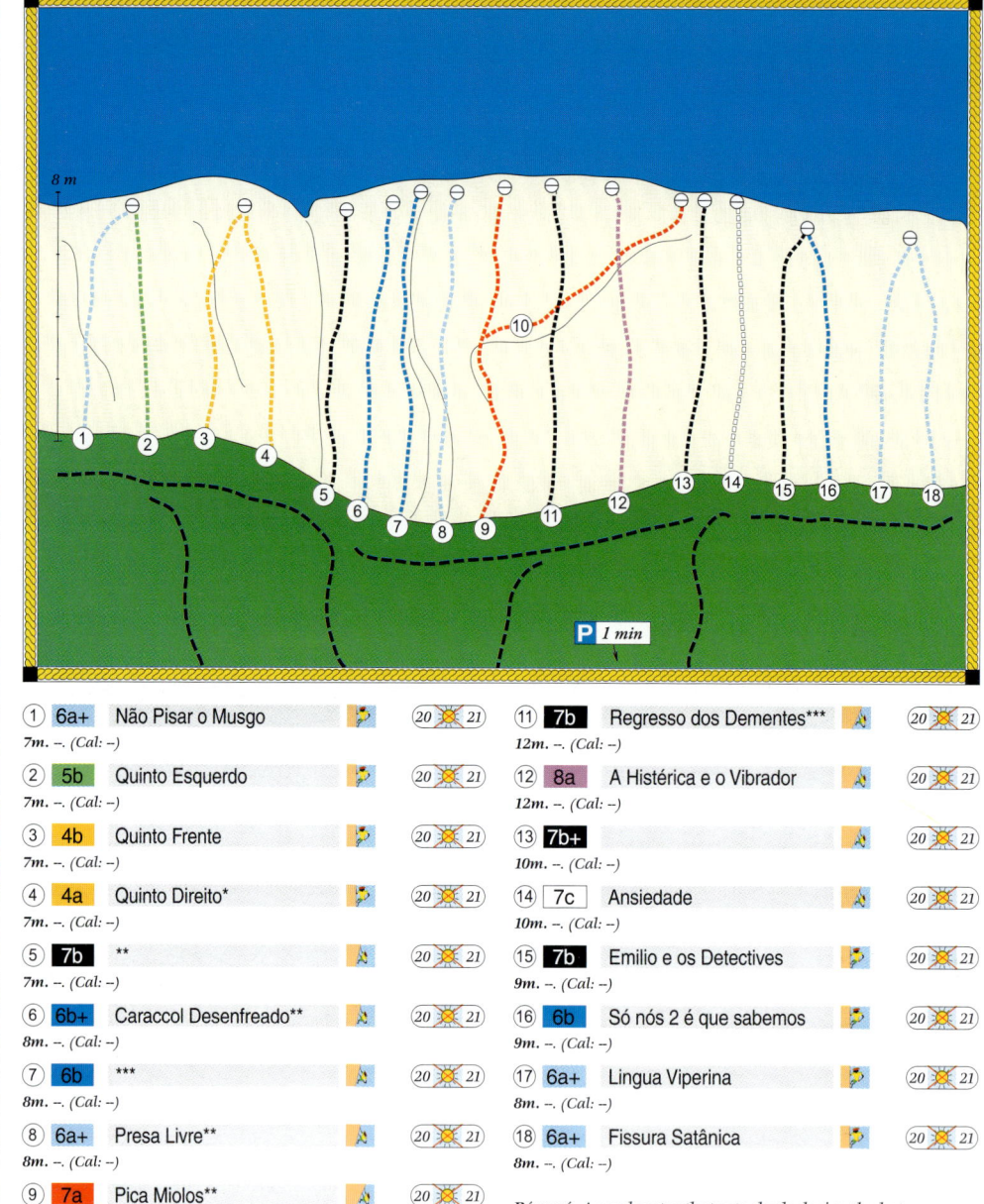

Résumé. *A good sector that gets shade during the hot summer months. Unfortunately - only a few easy routes, but they are nice. The hard routes are overgrown boulder problems, so expect a few hard moves. A lovely position with great views.*

Velho Eucaliptus - Velho Coco - Novo Impotência - Novo Dementes

REGRESSO DOS DEMENTES 7b, Montejunto Novo; Marío Santos

There are two popular travel destinations just south of the town Leiria: Fátima is the Portuguese capital of pilgrimage, on a par with Lourdes (France) or Santiago de Compostela (Spain). And at Batalha, you have the very popular tourist spectacle of the Dominican Abbey of Santa Maria, with its superb architectural, gothic splendour. Just about midway between these two famous attractions, is the tiny village of Reguengo do Fétal, and of course - a far more important national asset, since it is a really good climbing venue. How the masses just always get it wrong, thank goodness. The village itself is cute, and astoundingly quiet. It is fortunate that the geography of the centre, is tight and narrow and never going to attract the main road to go near it. Here there stands a photogenic lovely palm tree, which requires the widest angle of lens to capture it towering over the village square. There is a good little café, which is always nice to stop at before and after climbing, since they serve very good coffee. From here you can take either of two tiny roads up through the village, both are steep and narrow and wind their way up to the chapel at the top of the hill and into the gorge with the cliffs in.

The gorge itself is hardly spectacular in the world of climbing gorges, but does have a good selection of different cliffs, that all offer a very different style of climbing. What 'Reguengo' lacks in size, it makes up for in quality of moves, and pure rock texture. Besides which, if it were a lot bigger; then it would always be heaving with climbers and you would have to queue for routes. It's a small and quiet cliff, happy to be small and quiet, and best enjoyed by those climbers who appreciate this type of cliff. A lot of the routes are short, and have single boulder style moves, they are notorious for stopping most climbers in their tracks. Because of this we have relied on our bloc style grading colours to show how hard the climbs are here. We grade many 7a and 7b routes on a single move, which makes them easy for this level of climber. But then if you don't climb to this level – you won't move on them. So, it's an easy place to tick a few hard routes. On the other hand, there are still some lovely routes in the grade 6 category that will put you through your paces and get those forearms throbbing. There is a good selection of walls, giant roofs, pockets and even a few tufas to get to grips with. The cliffs are on both sides of the valley, therefore offering climbing that faces different ways, at all times of the day. This is of great benefit to climbers on a short visit, since you are likely to be able to climb whatever the weather. If it really does get too hot, then don't miss out on a visit to the Abbey at Batalha and make sure to see the stone masonry exhibition. But please don't get any creative ideas, we like the routes at Reguengo – just how they are, all with natural holds.

As viagens mais comuns a sul da cidade de Leiria têm dois destinos: Fátima, que é a capital portuguesa da peregrinação, tal como Lourdes (França) e Santiago de Compostela (Espanha); e Batalha, onde se localiza o turístico Mosteiro de Santa Maria da Vitória, com o seu imponente esplendor arquitectónico gótico. Mesmo a meio caminho entre estas duas famosas atracções, fica a pequena aldeia de Reguengo do Fetal e é claro, de longe património nacional muito mais importante, já que é uma excelente escola de escalada. Meu Deus, como as pessoas se enganam tanto! A aldeia em si, é engraçada e surpreendentemente sossegada. É uma sorte a geografia do seu centro ser tão estreita e acanhada, pois a estrada nacional nunca lá passará perto. Dominando a praça principal há uma encantadora e fotogénica palmeira que requer uma grande angular para ser fotografada. Há também uma pequena pastelaria, onde é sempre agradável parar antes e depois de escalar, uma vez que servem um café muito bom. Daqui pode seguir por qualquer das duas estraditas que sobem a aldeia, ambas estreitas e íngremes, que o conduzirão à capela no cimo do monte e daí até à garganta onde as vias se situam.

A garganta propriamente dita, dificilmente será espectacular no universo das gargantas de escalada, mas tem uma boa variedade de paredes e todas oferecem estilos de escalada diferentes. O que falta no Reguengo em tamanho, é compensado pela qualidade de movimentos e pela pureza da textura da rocha. Por outro lado, se fosse muito maior estaria sempre superlotada com escaladores e teria de entrar na fila para chegar às vias. É uma escola pequena e calma, feliz por ser pequena e calma, mas apreciada pelos escaladores que preferem este tipo de escolas. Muitas das vias são curtas, têm movimentos

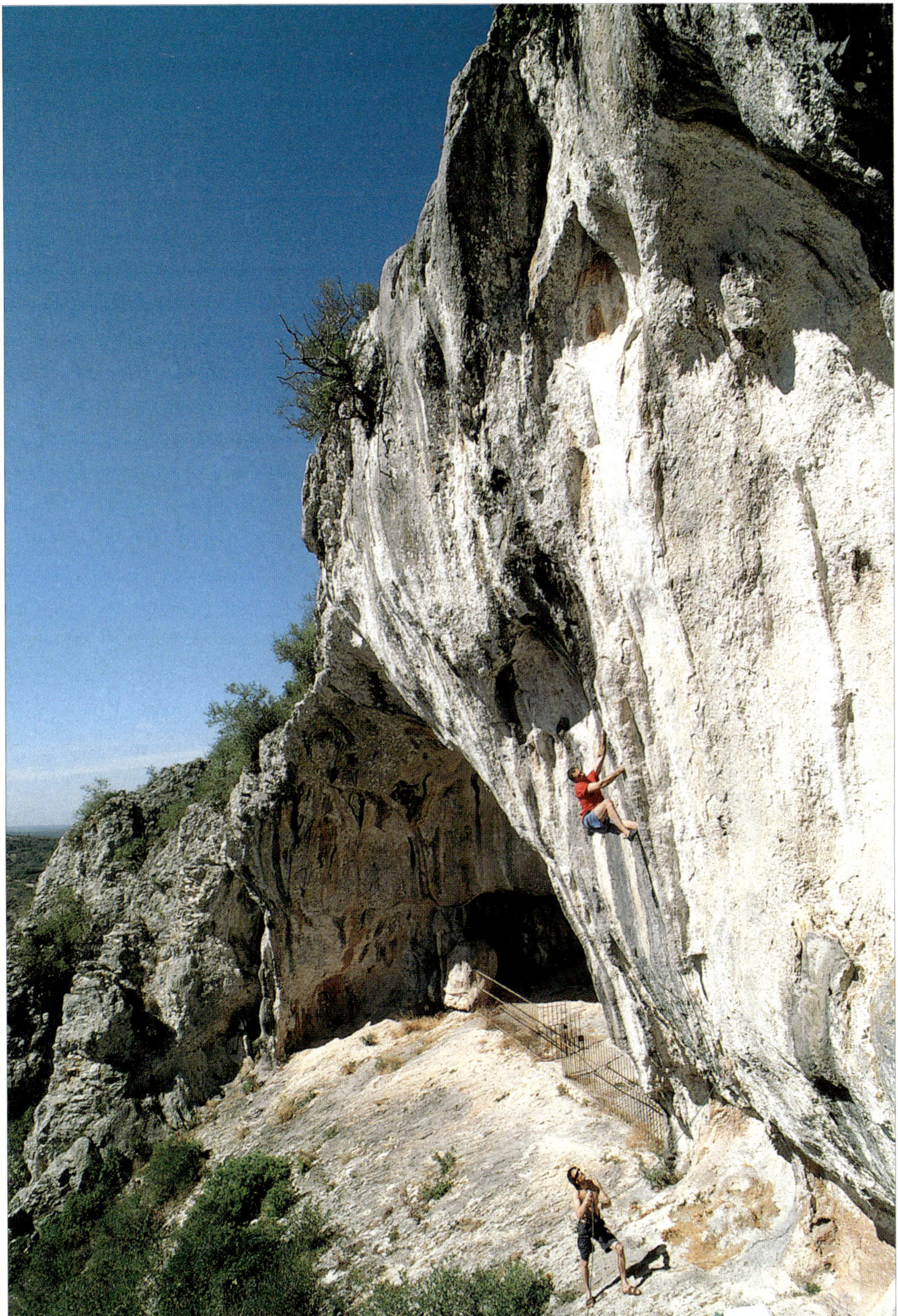

Reguengo do Fétal

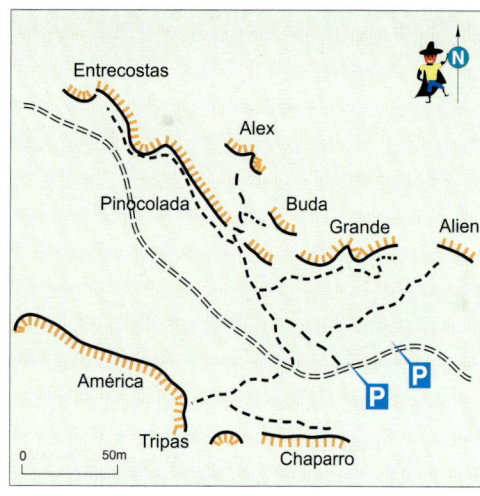

Camping Pedreiras
Largo Herióis do Ultramar
2480-109 Pedreiras
(4km SW of Porto de Mós, 10km SSW Batalha)
Tel: 244 471 522   Fax: 244 401 556
Situation: Access from IC2, just south of Pedreiras
Notes: Basic small site
Open: (01/06-30/10)

Local info:
There is no super campsite next to the cliff, and the local one is only seasonally open. Batalha is a nice town with a good selection of B & B (residnecias), that are quite reasonably priced. A reasonable distance away are the large coastal campsites of Nazaré. Here there are giant sunny beaches; and the location is good for the sheltered sandy bay of São Martinho do Porto; and the tourist spots of Alocbaça, Caldas da Rainha, Obidos, Peniche.

Vale Paraíso***
Estrada Nacional 242,   2450-138 Nazaré
(2km NW of Nazaré on North side of N242)
Tel: 262 561 800   Fax: 262 561 900
Situation: Access from N242
Notes: Large site, inland from sea.
Full selection of bungalows and caravans to rent
Open: (01/01-30/11) - (29/12-31/12)

Orbitur Nazaré***
Valado,   2450-148 Nazaré
(1km E of Nazaré on North side of N8)
Tel: 262 561 609   Fax: 262 561 137
Situation: Access from N8, main road from Alcobaça
Notes: Large site, inland from sea, full on amenities
Full selection of bungalows and caravans to rent
Open: (01/02-30/11)

Bar: Reguengo do Fétal
Shop: Reguengo do Fétal
Petrol Station: Reguengo do Fétal
Supermercado: Batalha   Nearest climbing shop: ?

isolados do estilo de bloco, e são conhecidas por fazerem parar muitos escaladores ao longo do seu percurso. Por este motivo, baseámo-nos nas cores da graduação do estilo de blocos para indicar a dificuldade destas vias. Graduámos muitas de 7a e 7b num só movimento, o que as torna mais fáceis para um escalador com este nível, mas se não o tiver, nem vai conseguir mexer-se nelas. Daí que seja um bom local, para despachar umas quantas vias duras. Por outro lado, existem ainda algumas bem bonitas na categoria do 6º grau, que lhe irão impor o ritmo e deixar-lhe os antebraços a latejar. Há uma boa variedade de paredes, tectos gigantes, buracos e até alguns tufos a que se poderá agarrar. As paredes elevam-se de ambos os lados do vale, pelo que oferecem vias orientadas em várias direcções a qualquer hora do dia. Isto é uma grande vantagem para escaladores que lhe façam uma visita curta, uma vez que é possível escalar, seja qual for o estado do tempo. Se na realidade estiver demasiado calor, então não perca a visita ao Mosteiro da Batalha e assegure-se de que vê a exposição de alvenaria. Mas por favor não tenha ideias criativas, nós gostamos das vias do Reguengo tal como são, todas com presas naturais.

ENTRE PRISES
International

LÍDER MUNDIAL EM
ESTRUTURAS ARTIFICIAIS DE ESCALADA
CERTIFICAÇÃO NP-EN 12572 E NF EN ISO 9001

DISTRIBUIDOR EXCLUSIVO EM PORTUGAL

TECNIaventura
PARQUES AVENTURA E ESTRUTURAS ARTIFICIAIS DE ESCALADA, LDA.

www.tecniaventura.pt
email - info@tecniaventura.pt
TLM: 917 54 85 82

www.entre-prises.com
PARCEIRO OFICIAL DA **F.F.M.E.**, **B.M.C.**, E DA **U.I.A.A.**

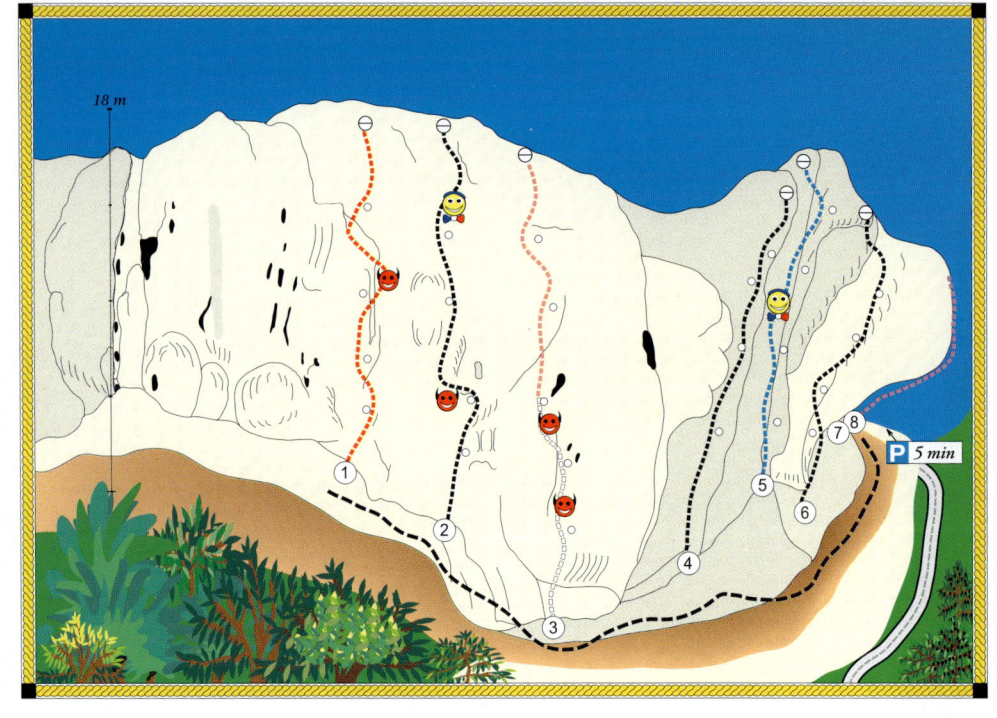

REGUENGO DO FÉTAL

① **7a** ⚡ Pinças ou Cais
11m. An easy tick for the grade, but a stamina blaster; you get to the crux when you are tired. Great tufa fun. (Cal: A, H, U)

② **7b** ● Arco da Velha
15m. The only easy part of the route is getting to the first clip. Both technical and demanding and a full value onsight; run out at the end but it's quite easy. (Cal: H, T, A)

③ **7c** ⚡ Pinças e Sais
14m. An easy tick for the lightweight. A beautiful array of good tufas and fantastic layaways. Quite steep and full on power, start is font 7a, so beef up. (Cal: A, T, B, U)

④ **7b+** ● Imagina Vagina
13m. This is a nasty little bugger. The angle is silly, and the lack of footholds gives good cause for alarm. (Cal: M, H)

⑤ **6b** ⚡ Entrecostas***
13m. A route that is equipped - for those who aren't likely to fall off! Daunting and quite awkward - but a wild experience. (Cal: J, T, H)

⑥ **7b+** ● Missao Impossível
17m. A full on stamina and power route, taking the easy wall on the side of the overhang.

⑦
17m. Roof climb

⑧
17m. Roof climb

Résumé. This is the first section above the road-track on the left. Easily recognised by the giant roof. The rock quality is very good, and the routes are top class. Useful morning shade and a nice place to get out of the wind usually. Access is best by a path from the central sector, and not by trying to go straight up from underneath.

Entrecostas - Pinacolada - Alex Cravo - Buda - La Grande - Di - Alien - Chaparro - Tripas - América

ARCO DA VELHA 7b, Reguengo do Fétal; Jingo

BURAQUINHOS 5a, Reguengo do Fétal; Wobbly

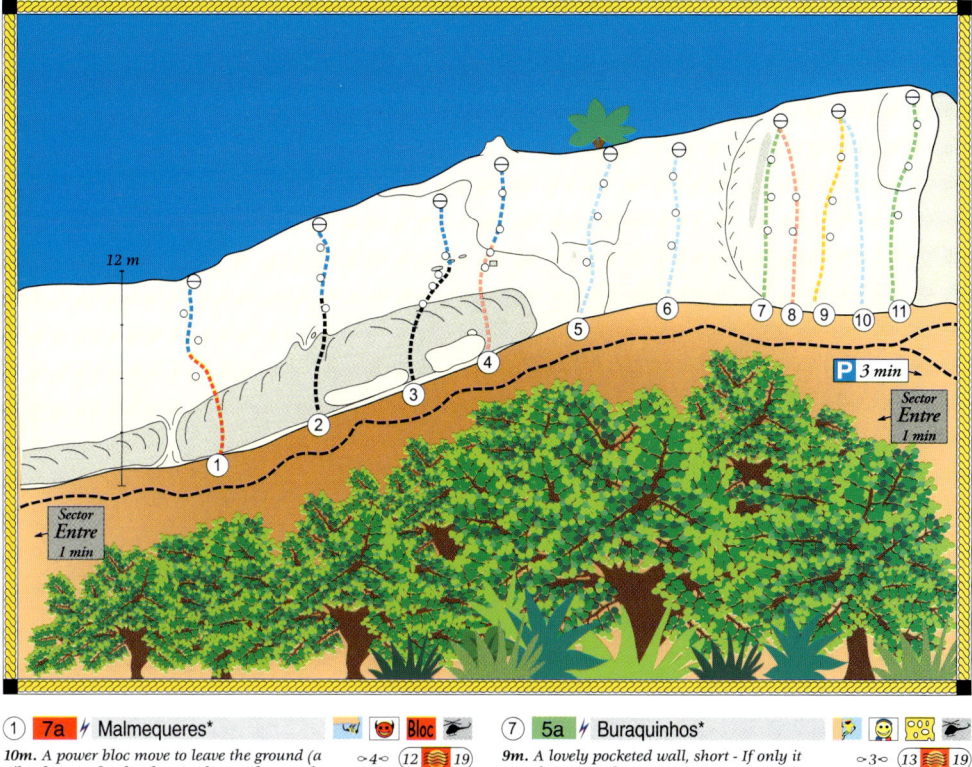

Reguengo Do Fétal

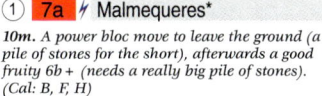

① **7a** ⚡ **Malmequeres***
10m. A power bloc move to leave the ground (a pile of stones for the short), afterwards a good fruity 6b+ (needs a really big pile of stones). *(Cal: B, F, H)*

② **7b** ⚡ **De Cavalo para burro**
9m. Start at the big hanging blob. A classic font 6b move to leave the ground. The rest of the climb is steep but quite containable. *(Cal: T, H F)*

③ **7b** ● **Cara da Morte***
11m. The really easy looking, slanting crackline - only joking. A real sandbag and incredibly powerful, for rampant gorilla's only. *(Cal: A, T, H, N)*

④ **6c** ⚡ **Calhau da Altura**
10m. Stepping off the big block (with an additional boulder), and grabbing the jug is easy; pulling up is another matter. Font 5b and painful too. After 2 moves the route is over. *(Cal: H, I)*

⑤ **6a** ⚡ **Salada de Grelos**
10m. A nice technical wall through the overlap. *(Cal: F, G)*

⑥ **6a+** ⚡ **Aderência**
10m. A nice wall with pockets. *(Cal: F, G)*

⑦ **5a** ⚡ **Buraquinhos***
9m. A lovely pocketed wall, short - If only it were longer. *(Cal: R, F)*

⑧ **6c** ⚡ **Via Láctea***
9m. Apart from the big jug to start, find your own eliminate line - without using any good handholds - of course. *(Cal: G)*

⑨ **4c** ⚡ **Pinacolada I**
7m. A nice little outing on very good, incut holds. *(Cal: U)*

⑩ **6a** ⚡ **Pinacolada II**
7m. Short and sharp - with a move entitled; spot the foothold! *(Cal: U, E)*

⑪ **5c** ⚡ **Porra, não consigo sair daqui**
8m. The little scoopy wall, fun! *(Cal: U, E)*

Résumé. There are 2 completely different styles of climbing in this sector. You have a very nice handful of routes in the middle grades, but they are quite short. You also have some very short and powerful routes that are really extended bouldering, and take the bouldering colours as the better example of the grades. It's a small area, but still offers good fun.

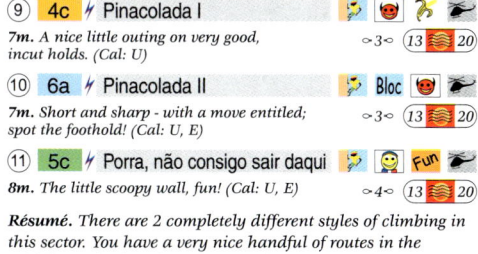

Reguengo Do Fétal

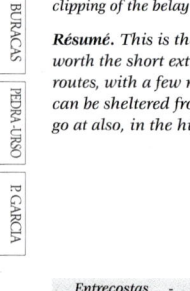

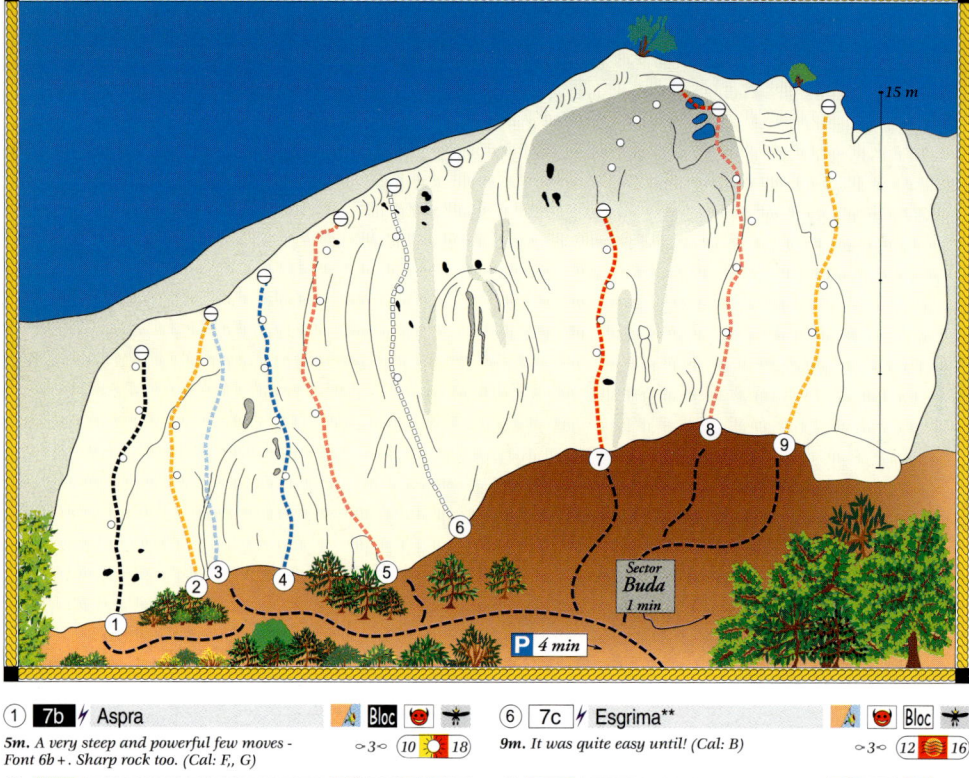

① **7b** ⚡ Aspra
5m. A very steep and powerful few moves - Font 6b+. Sharp rock too. (Cal: F,, G)

② **4c** ⚡ Pré-História 1*
6m. Going up the left side of the clips. Good sharp incuts to challenge the beginner, hurry or your arms will fade. (Cal: R, C)

③ **6a** ⚡ T Rex*
6m. A nice alternative; keeping right of the bolts all the way. Crisp and sharp pockets. (Cal: B, F, G)

④ **6b** ⚡ Pré-História 2**
8m. A climb that is absolutely packed with big holds, but is really sustained up until the end. Escaping left to rest is not allowed. This route proves that even short routes are not always easy. (Cal: B, E)

⑤ **6c+** ⚡ Alex Cravo**
9m. If you're looking for a Buoux or Céüse style climb - it's here. Pure fantastic moves which get steeper and harder as you go. Easy clipping of the belay needs ingenuity. (Cal: B)

⑥ **7c** ⚡ Esgrima**
9m. It was quite easy until! (Cal: B)

⑦ **7a+** ⚡ Indolor**
8m. A fine technical and pocketed wall to a belay before the overhanging nightmare. (Cal: F)

⑧ **6c** ⚡ Chaminé**
13m. A very nice wall which leads to a good power finish. A good intro to tufas for the 6b/c climber. Finishing up to hanging lower off on the left, a power undercut; Font 6a+/6b. (Cal: S,O,L)

⑨ **4a** ⚡ Maia
16m. Just like climbing in the Dolomites; flakey and solid rock - that may come off in your hand at any time. Interesting finish which is pleasantly exposed. (Cal: O, E)

Résumé. This is the high sector of the cliff that is certainly worth the short extra walk up to. A complete variation of routes, with a few real gems. Gets the full afternoon sun and can be sheltered from the wind at times. A few roof projects to go at also, in the higher grades. Superb quality rock.

ALEX CRAVO 6c+, Reguengo do Fétal; Wobbly

YOGASUTRE 6a+, Reguengo do Fétal; Jingo

Reguengo Do Fétal

① **6b** ⚡ Buda Sentado**

15m. A fabulous route, slightly harder than Yogurt, but still completely full of holds, and a superb position. Only stamina will prove a problem. *(Cal: F, G)*

② **6a+** ⚡ Yogasutre**

15m. Very nearly 3 stars, but only 15 metres long. Routes like this are fab. Good feast of fingertip dinner plates, giant run out at top but on good incuts. *(Cal: F)*

③ **7a** ● Nirvana**

15m. What a nastie! The natural line takes you left - oohps, sorry - you go straight up the groove to the hole, then sequence your way to the top - easily of course!!, *(Cal: T, B)*

④ **7a** ⚡ Pulso

6m. Power moves on pockets. *(Cal: F)*

⑤ **7b** ● Mijada

7m. A technical wall on small edges. *(Cal: F)*

⑥ **7b** ● Flash

7m. A very blank wall. *(Cal: F)*

Résumé. Two contrasting areas. You get to the bottom area first and it is soon very obvious that it is pure, desperate bouldering style routes. The routes on the top tier, are on the other hand, much easier and situated in a lovely position, they don't look so good from below, but they are really pleasant.

Entrecostas - Pinacolada - Alex Cravo - **Buda** - La Grande - Di - Alien - Chaparro - Tripas - América

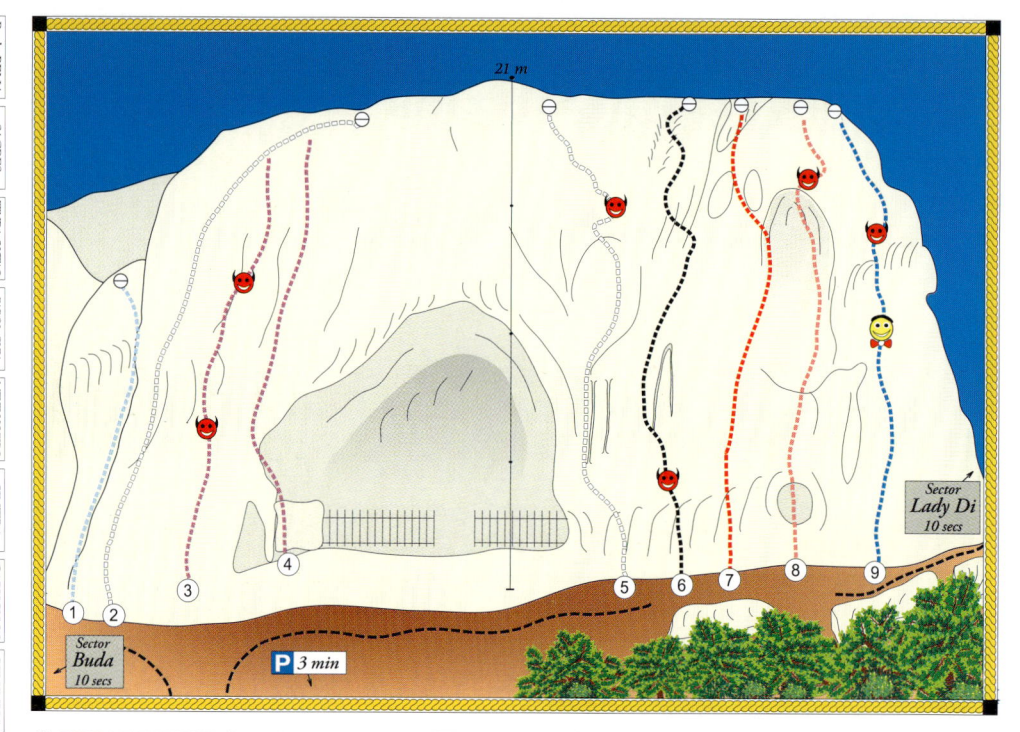

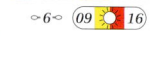

REGUENGO DO FÉTAL

① **6a+** ⚡ Insustentável Leveza do Ser

16m. 5a; A friendly short route and a popular warm up. (Cal: S, E)

② **7c** ● Sapão***

24m. A superb arc'ing line to the very high lower off. Energetic. (Cal: A, F, B)

③ **8a+** ● Cabra Branca, Cabra Preta**

23m. A few hard moves, as well as a stamina fest; stays in the shade under the roof. (Cal: A, F, B)

④ **8a** ● Buraco Negro**

23m. An easy way up the back wall of the cave. (Cal: H, B, W)

⑤ **7c** La Grande**

23m. A superb tufa pillar is a good warm up for the pinch grips. The bolt on the roof is clipped, then it all gets a bit tricky for about 2 metres. (Cal: W, H)

⑥ **7b** ⚡ Contra Tudo e Contra Todos***

22m. A superb line and climb. No really hard moves (apart from the start), but lots of energy sapping moves in a row. The route to onsight. (Cal: A, H, F)

⑦ **7a** ⚡ Uma Prova de Amor***

19m. The top pod is very reflective of hot sunshine, you can really get a sweat on here, working out the onsight. (Cal: F, B, M)

⑧ **6c** ⚡ Via Pública**

18m. Very nice and comfortable, until the overhang. Reach is useful here (Cal: H, M, U)

⑨ **6b** ⚡ Extérieure***

18m. A very nice technical wall that is quite sustained but low in the grade, The top suffers from loose rock so make sure your belayer is alert. (Cal: M, I, D)

Résumé. The centrepiece attraction at Reguengo; superbly sustained roof climbs for the real expert. Not a lot of these routes get very wet. There is seepage though at times, especially in the winter so keep your fingers crossed that your tick is dry. Faces south and can get hot, but main cave is pretty cool in the afternoon because it is so steep, it never gets warm from the sun.

LA GRANDE 7c, Reguengo do Fétal; Ben Moon

The very sleepy village centre of Reguengo do Fétal.

REGUENGO DO FÉTAL

① **6a** ⚡ Lady Di*
12m. A nice airy route in an exposed position. (Cal: D, U)

② **6a+** ⚡ Pilhas Alcalinas
11m. A couple of strong moves, but quite short. (Cal: D, U)

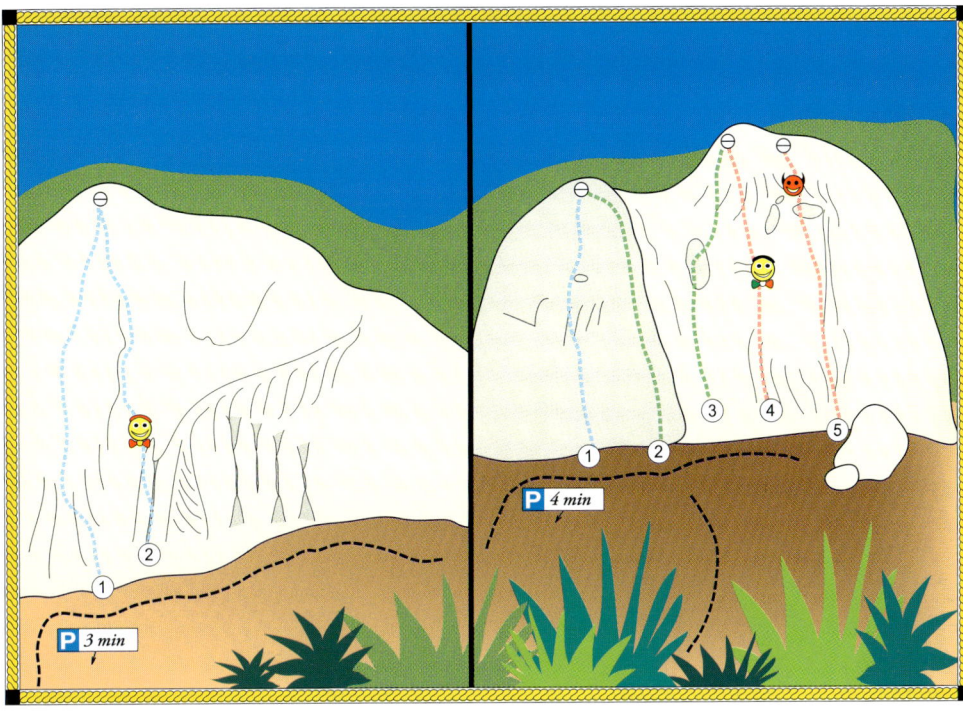

Résumé. A small little extension to the La Grande sector, which gets the early morning sun. The rock is a bit shattered, but the routes are nice.

① **6a** ⚡ Directa
6m. A short route! (Cal: Z)

② **5c** ⚡ A Minha primeira Vez
6m. A short route! (Cal: Z)

③ **5c** ⚡ Milenium*
7m. A nice little climb. (Cal: U)

④ **6c** ● X-Files*
8m. A right technical little bastard. (Cal: F, W)

⑤ **6c+** ● Alien*
8m. A good little power route up to the overhanging niche.. (Cal: H, U)

Résumé. This is the very tiny sector, high up on the right and looking almost inconsequential. There are some short and fun routes here, worth a little visit to warm up - perhaps.

HAGLÖFS

Entrecostas - Pinacolada - Alex Cravo - Buda - La Grande - Di - Alien - Chaparro - Tripas - América

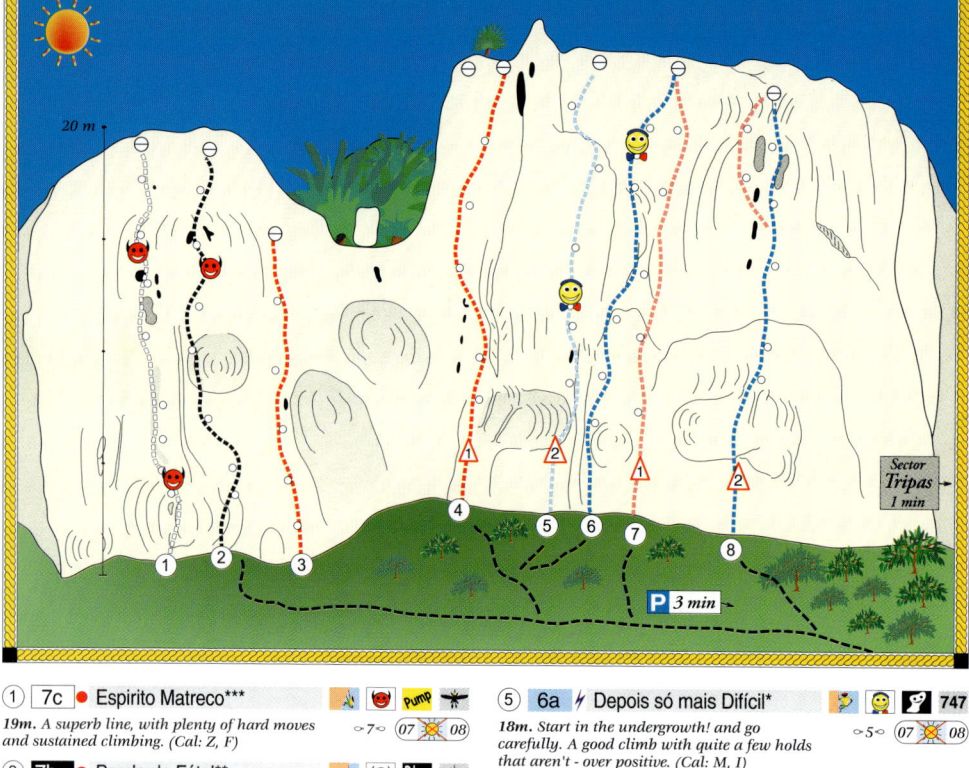

Reguengo do Fétal

① **7c** ● Espirito Matreco***
19m. A superb line, with plenty of hard moves and sustained climbing. (Cal: Z, F)

② **7b+** ● Perola do Fétal**
19m. A few hard sections, with very good rests in between. (Cal: Z, F)

③ **7a** ● **
17m. Quite a new climb.

④ **7a** ● Fétal 2000**
18m. A lonely lead, technical and tricky. (Cal: M)

Résumé. *A very good sector that is north facing and in the shade all day. The routes attract vegetation in the lower grades and may have some damp moss - just what you need eh! The harder routes can also seep. Great to have on scorching hot days though. Take care at the foot of the crag, maybe bring trousers as there are a few nettles (recent fire got rid of these). Please take a zig zag up to the cliff, to prevent landslip erosion.*

⑤ **6a** ⚡ Depois só mais Difícil*
18m. Start in the undergrowth! and go carefully. A good climb with quite a few holds that aren't - over positive. (Cal: M, I)

⑥ **6b** ⚡ Chaparro**
18m. A fair climb on steep and technical ground. Lots of slopers and holds that aren't quite good enough. (Cal: M)

⑦ **6c** ⚡ Galinheiro**
18m. No pushover! (Cal: M)

⑧ **6b+** ⚡ Entrada Maldita**
18m. A good piece of rock offering 2 finishes, both on well pocketed rock, if you are strong. Left finish (Manhosa) has another clip (6) but is harder. (Cal: F)

ESPIRITO MATRECO 7c, Reguengo do Fétal; Jerry Moffatt

TRIPAS Á MODO DO PORTO 6a, Reguengo do Fétal; Wobbly

REGUENGO DO FÉTAL

① **7a** ● Politica Industrial
7m. A technical short wall. (Cal: Z, W)

② **5c** ● Ninho do Charéu
7m. A technical short wall. (Cal: Z, W)

③ **6a** ⚡ Tripas á Moda do Porto
10m. A good in there start that will really test you, it's short - so keep going and give it your best. (Cal: Z, U, D)

④ **4a** ⚡ Penso Lodo Desisto
10m. A nice little climb; keep out of the groove and on the face to the left for the best moves and best climbing - no nasty surprises for once. (Cal: Z, U, D)

Résumé. Two small sectors that offer some fun routes, they are quite short, but can be used as warm ups for the better routes in the América sector.

⑤ **6b** ⚡ Acçào Indirecta
8m. Very low in the grade, but the clip placements and the technique involved, makes this a route you want to cruise. (Cal: K)

⑥ **6c** ⚡ Variante
8m. This variante may get harder with time, and even more polish on the foothold. (Cal: I, E)

⑦ **7b** ⚡ InforFur
14m. A newish climb with the odd problematic move, short but not that easy! (Cal: W)

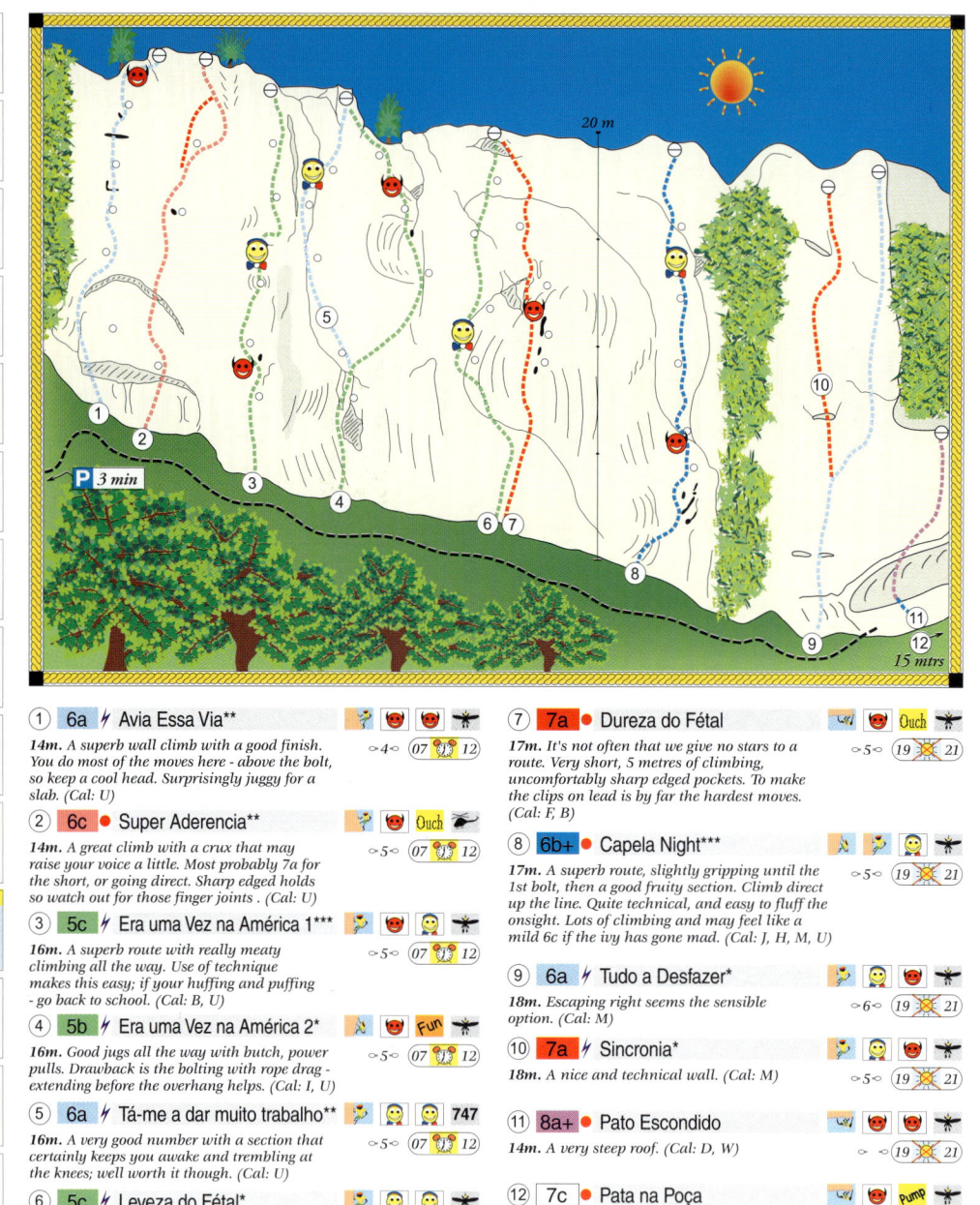

REGUENGO DO FÉTAL

① **6a** ⚡ Avia Essa Via**
14m. A superb wall climb with a good finish. You do most of the moves here - above the bolt, so keep a cool head. Surprisingly juggy for a slab. (Cal: U)

② **6c** ● Super Aderencia**
14m. A great climb with a crux that may raise your voice a little. Most probably 7a for the short, or going direct. Sharp edged holds so watch out for those finger joints. (Cal: U)

③ **5c** ⚡ Era uma Vez na América 1***
16m. A superb route with really meaty climbing all the way. Use of technique makes this easy; if your huffing and puffing - go back to school. (Cal: B, U)

④ **5b** ⚡ Era uma Vez na América 2*
16m. Good jugs all the way with butch, power pulls. Drawback is the bolting with rope drag - extending before the overhang helps. (Cal: I, U)

⑤ **6a** ⚡ Tá-me a dar muito trabalho**
16m. A very good number with a section that certainly keeps you awake and trembling at the knees; well worth it though. (Cal: U)

⑥ **5c** ⚡ Leveza do Fétal*
17m. A really enjoyable route of 2 halfs; nice and juggy and then quite airy. (Cal: U)

⑦ **7a** ● Dureza do Fétal
17m. It's not often that we give no stars to a route. Very short, 5 metres of climbing, uncomfortably sharp edged pockets. To make the clips on lead is by far the hardest moves. (Cal: F, B)

⑧ **6b+** ● Capela Night***
17m. A superb route, slightly gripping until the 1st bolt, then a good fruity section. Climb direct up the line. Quite technical, and easy to fluff the onsight. Lots of climbing and may feel like a mild 6c if the ivy has gone mad. (Cal: J, H, M, U)

⑨ **6a** ⚡ Tudo a Desfazer*
18m. Escaping right seems the sensible option. (Cal: M)

⑩ **7a** ⚡ Sincronia*
18m. A nice and technical wall. (Cal: M)

⑪ **8a+** ● Pato Escondido
14m. A very steep roof. (Cal: D, W)

⑫ **7c** ● Pata na Poça
19m. This is the very steep overhanging wall at the end of the overhanging terrace. A very airy position and quite wild, can be chilly to hang out here. (Cal: D, W)

Résumé. A mixed section of slabs and then very steep overhanging desperates. It does get the early morning sun, but always seems a very cool place to climb. Worth remembering in a real heat wave.

ERA UMA VEZ NA AMÉRICA 1, 5c, Reguengo do Fétal; Rui Rosado

The main road between Lisbon and Oporto is called the IC 2, and is one of those old traditional trunk roads that are hammered by lorries day and night. It carves a scything path through the endless miles of eucalyptus trees that inhabit the strip of land between the sea and the mountains. It's not a pretty road, for it is often edged with industrial estates, and an amazing multitude of outdoor barbecue manufacturers. The highlight is turning off the IC2. For safety reasons, you have to make sure that you don't have a juggernaught bulging in your rear view mirror, oblivious to the concept why anyone would slow down! for the turn off to the tiny village of Redinha. I promise, you can't make the bend doing 120kph. Within seconds, the rumbling madness is over and you tootle down into a quiet paradise of gentle rural life. You won't find Redinha in any tourist guidebooks, there's not much about it, but it's got a small shop, café and post office. It also has a curious hump back bridge over the river, with its set of functioning traffic lights – be warned, not all the locals seem to understand the full significance at the illumination of the red blob, and casually saunter at will. The road up to the hamlet of Poios deteriorates, but not beyond tarmac recognition – here too there is another café with varying opening hours, and a very tiny shop (good tomatoes). From here you can see the skyline ridge and the cliffs along it. The road out of the village does deteriorate as it cuts north up the hillside. It grinds up the vicious incline, which test the 1st gear of most cars, and then obliterates the underbelly with the smattering of stones thrown up by the spinning of front tyres. The result is however, to park your car almost on top of the skyline and step out onto the cliff.

There is a chapel 'Nossa Senora da Serra da Estrela,' which the cliff is often known by; but this can easily be confused with the mountains of the Serra da Estrela – which are nowhere near here! The cliff is far smaller that appearance would suggest from down below, but then again – the view is far better than could ever have been imagined. You can see the sea glinting in the distance, and hear the chiming church bells of nearby, Soure. It's handy for those wanting to picnic with small kids, and climb too. The rock is pretty good and offers superbly technical climbs, routes that will confuse those who are used to brightly coloured plastic holds from the gym. There are routes of all levels here, and it makes a worthwhile trip for anyone. You climb here not for the routes, but for the testing, individual climbing moves. In honesty, you mostly come for the lovely location and view, and to enjoy the openness of Portugal.

A estrada mais importante entre Lisboa e Porto denomina-se IC2, e nada mais é do que o exemplo típico das estradas principais batidas por camiões dia e noite. A IC2 abre caminho por entre quilómetros infindáveis de eucaliptos que habitam a faixa de terra que separa o mar, das serras. Não se pode dizer que seja uma estrada bonita, porque está ladeada por propriedades industriais e uma quantidade espantosa de fabricantes de grelhadores para exterior. O ponto culminante é a saída da IC2. Por razões de segurança, tem de certificar-se de que não há nenhum camião a crescer no seu espelho retrovisor, ignorando completamente as razões que podem levar alguém a abrandar no desvio para a pequena aldeia da Redinha! Garanto-lhe que não consegue fazer a curva a 120kms por hora. Subitamente acaba-se a loucura ruidosa da estrada principal, para dar lugar ao paraíso tranquilo da pacata vida rural. Não é possível encontrar a Redinha nos guias turísticos habituais, até porque não há de facto muito para ver, mas tem um minimercado, um café e um posto de correios. Tem também uma curiosa ponte corcunda sobre o rio, com os seus semáforos a funcionar – mas preste atenção, nem todos os indígenas parecem compreender o significado do sinal vermelho e passam quando lhes apetece. A estrada para a aldeola de Poios está muito deteriorada, mas ainda se consegue reconhecer o asfalto. Também lá existe um café, com um horário de abertura muito variado, e uma minúscula loja (com tomate muito bom). De Poios pode ver-se toda a crista montanhosa recortada no horizonte, e ao longo dela, as paredes. Saindo da aldeia a estrada piora bastante, subindo a encosta rumo a Norte. Começa por nos fazer vencer uma violenta ladeira, que obriga a testar a 1ª velocidade de muitos carros, e depois destrói-nos o cárter com a saraivada de pedras que a rotação das rodas da frente provoca. O resultado é, no entanto, poder estacionar o carro quase no topo e descer em cima das paredes.

FOTOGENICA 7a, Redinha; Jerry Moffatt

Existe uma capela a "Nossa Senhora da Serra da Estrela", nome pelo qual esta serra é frequentemente conhecida; mas pode confundir-se facilmente com a Serra da Estrela – e esta nem sequer fica perto! A escola é bastante mais pequena do que aparenta vista de baixo, mas mais uma vez a paisagem é muito melhor do que se poderia imaginar. Pode ver-se o mar a cintilar ao longe, e ouvir o som dos sinos das igrejas da vizinha Soure. Dá muito jeito para quem quiser fazer um piquenique com crianças pequenas, e escalar também. O tipo de rocha é muito bom e proporciona boas escaladas técnicas, mas as vias atrapalharão quem estiver habituado às presas de plástico dos ginásios, coloridas e brilhantes. Existem cá vias de todos os níveis de dificuldade, o que justifica a viagem, seja a quem for! Aqui escala-se não tanto pelas vias, mas para ensaiar passos isolados de escalada. Falando francamente, vem-se aqui pela beleza do local, pela vista encantadora e para disfrutar da vastidão de Portugal.

Camping O Tamanco

Village church, Redinha

REDINHA

Redinha - Poios - Buracas do Cagimil

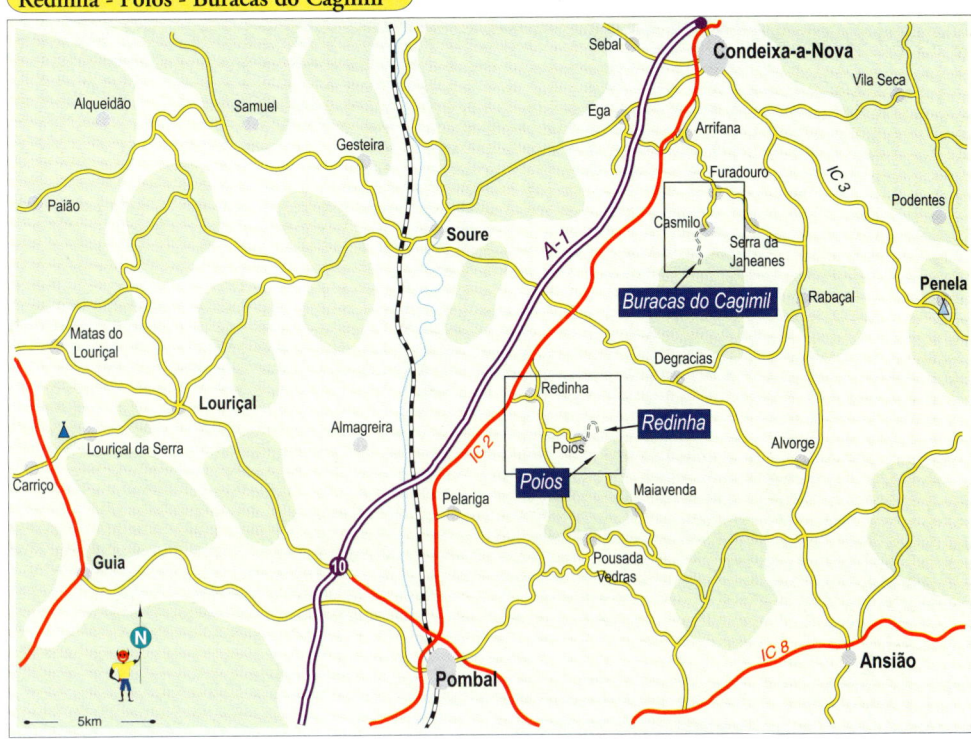

Parque de Campismo o Tamanco***
Casas Brancas 11, 3100-231 Louriçal
Tel & Fax: 351 236 952 551
E-mail: campismo.o.tamanco@mail.telepac.pt
www.campsimo-o-tamanco.com
Notes: Nice countryside site, run by a friendly Dutch couple, plenty of space and shade, fresh eggs, bar, restaraunt, good ambience with swimming pool and facilities.
2 Chalets to rent - sleep 4 each
Open: (01/02-31/10) - 100 places; 1.5 hectares

Camara Municipal de Penela**
Rua de Coimbra, 3230 Penela
Tel : 351 239 569 256 Fax: 239 569 400
www.roteiro-campista.pt/Coimbra/penela.htm
Notes: Municipal site, close to the village.
Open: (01/06-30/09) - 150 places

Bar: Poios (sometimes), Redinha
Shop: Tiny shop Poios, small shop Redinha
Petrol Station: 5km South on IC-2
Restaurant: Pombal, Soure, Louriçal, Camping.
Supermarket: Soure, Pombal

Redinha - Poios

Redinha

Redinha Approach Directions:
1). From the IC-2, turn off and go down into the village of Redinha. At the bottom of the town there is a small, hump back bridge with lights. Go over this and bear right (post office on left). Take the road along the valley floor for 1.2km. Then you will see a sign on the left for Poios and the viewpoint (Miradour) of the N. Senora Serra da Estrela. This is a chapel, high up on the ridge above Poios. Go through Poios and the road turns to a dirt track. Keep on this, and past the first steep turn (this bit is very steep). Then at the second turn, take this up the very steep hill (plenty of wheelspin here). The car can be driven to the bottom of the cliff.

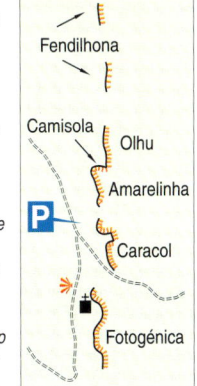

REDINHA

① **5a** ⚡ Não Nomeada**
12m. Wall climb. (Cal: M, R)

② **5c** ⚡ Bafo de Caracol**
15m. Wall climb. (Cal: M, R)

③ **7a** Derrocada*
12m. A powerful overhang.

④ **7b** Eu sou uma Lengenda***
12m. Steep overhang.

⑤ **7a** Fénix
12m.

⑥ **6c** Pega lá no Pau
12m. A powerful overhang.

⑦ **5c** Dáricá
12m. A technical wall.

⑧ **6b+** O Predador
10m. A technical wall.

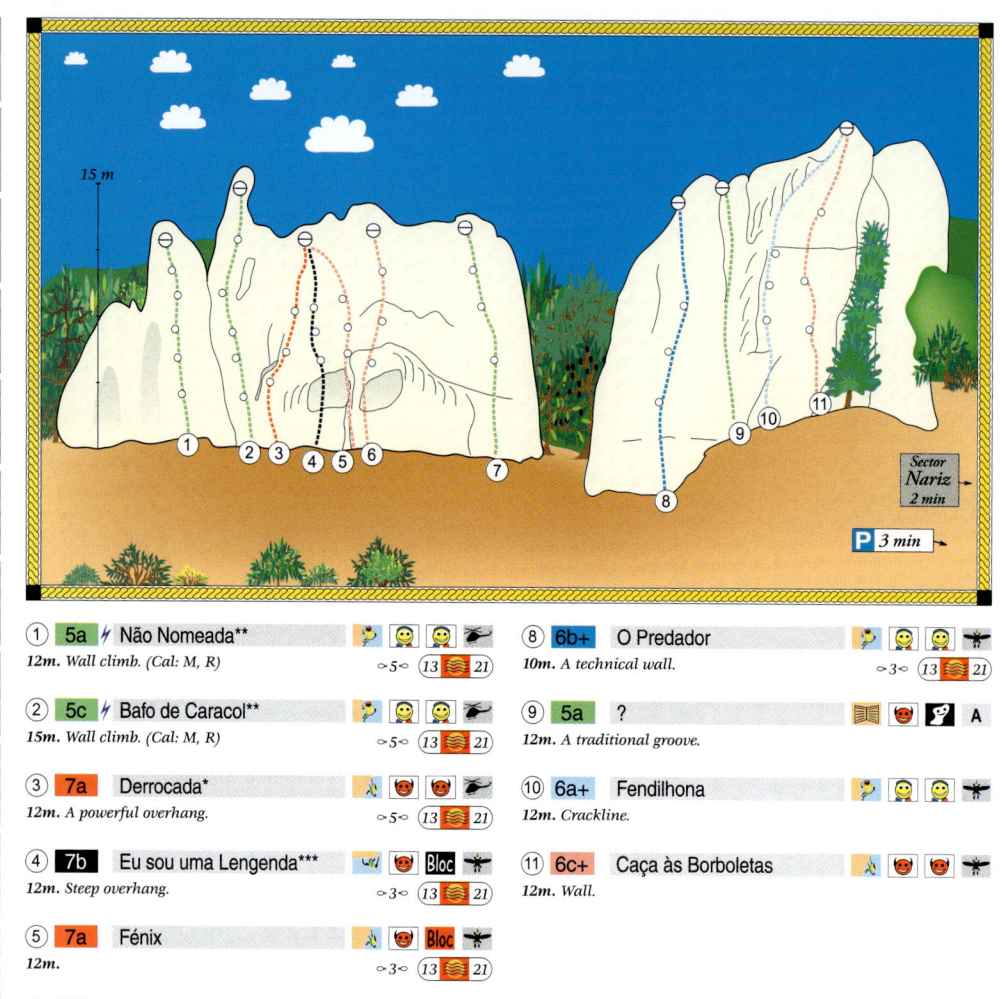

⑨ **5a** ?
12m. A traditional groove.

⑩ **6a+** Fendilhona
12m. Crackline.

⑪ **6c+** Caça às Borboletas
12m. Wall.

Résumé. *Two small sectors, the furthest from the car, but worth a look at for some good little routes.*

The views from Redinha are simply stunning as the weather blows in from the West.

Sector Olhu with sector Fendilhona in the distance

REDINHA

① **6a** Salsa**
8m. Technical wall.

② **6a+** Homo Tripadus**
8m. Powerful wall

③ **6a** É de caras*
8m. Technical.

④ **7a+** Babes in Babyland**
8m. Power dyno.

⑤ **7a+** Mónica

⑥ **7c** Rei dos Frangos
8m. Technical wall (7b+ perhaps?).

⑦ **6a** Olho
8m. Nice and airy arête, then a bit tricky.

⑧ **7c** Viste Sangue
12m. Going left is obviously tricky.

⑨ **6c** Nariz*
10m. Exit up from right of L-twin holes.

⑩ **7a+** Monstro das Bolhachas
10m. Powerful.

⑪ **6a** Orelha
9m. Technical.

⑫ **6b+** Trepa 89
8m.

⑬ **7a+** Passa por mim no Pinguim
9m. Powerful moves to the final wall.

⑭ **7a** Camisola Mágica
9m. Sharp fingery wall.

⑮ **7b** Electra
9m. Technical.

⑯ **7a+** Cometa na Valeta
9m. Technical.

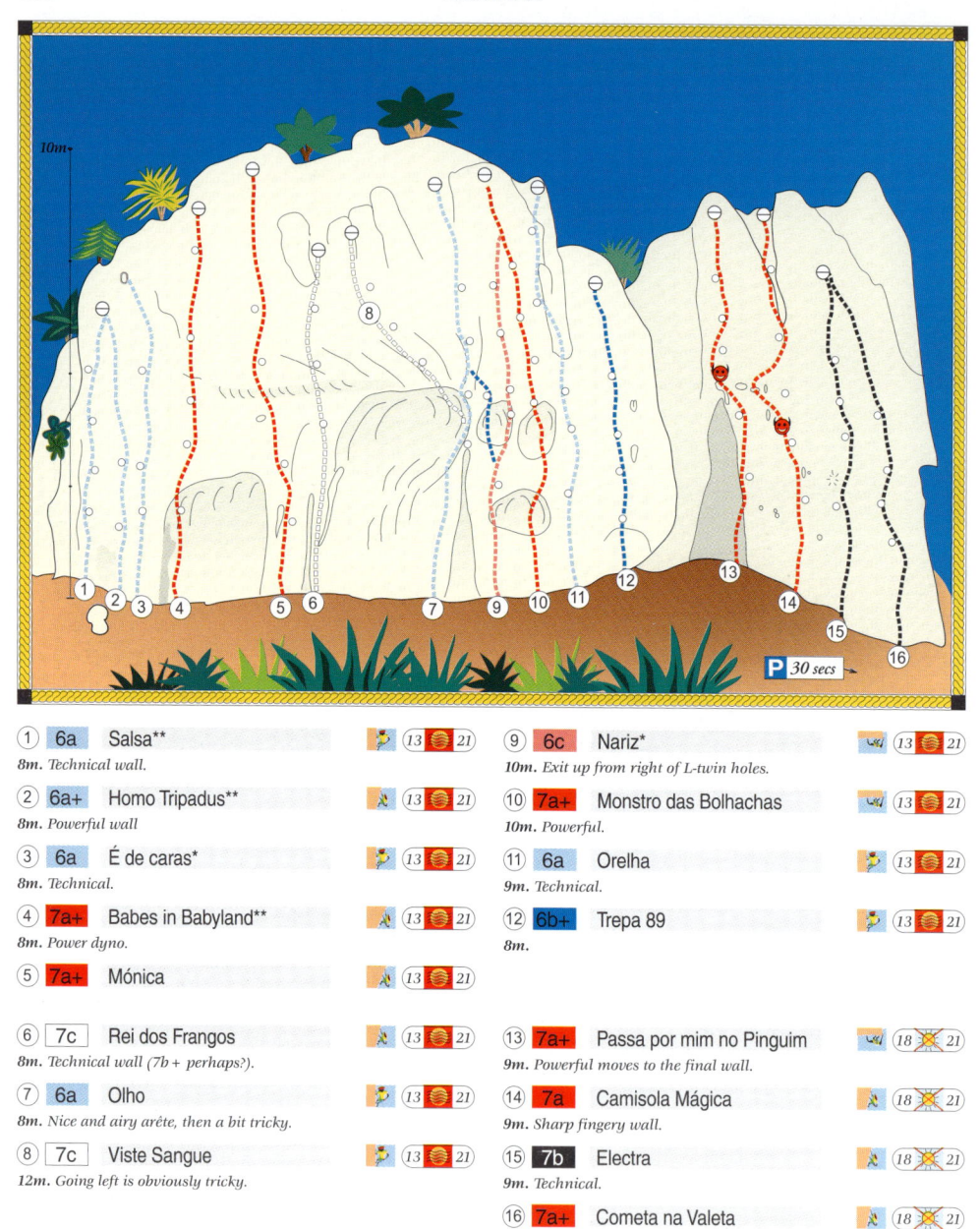

Résumé. Two sections with different characteristics;
Nariz; steep walls with undercut caves, powerful and sequency climbing.
Camisola; Slightly overhanging, fingertips and very technical - but very cool.

Fendilhona - Olho - Camisola - Amarelinha - Caracol - Fotogénica

BOREAL

CAMISOLA MÁGICA 7a, Redinha; Jerry Moffatt

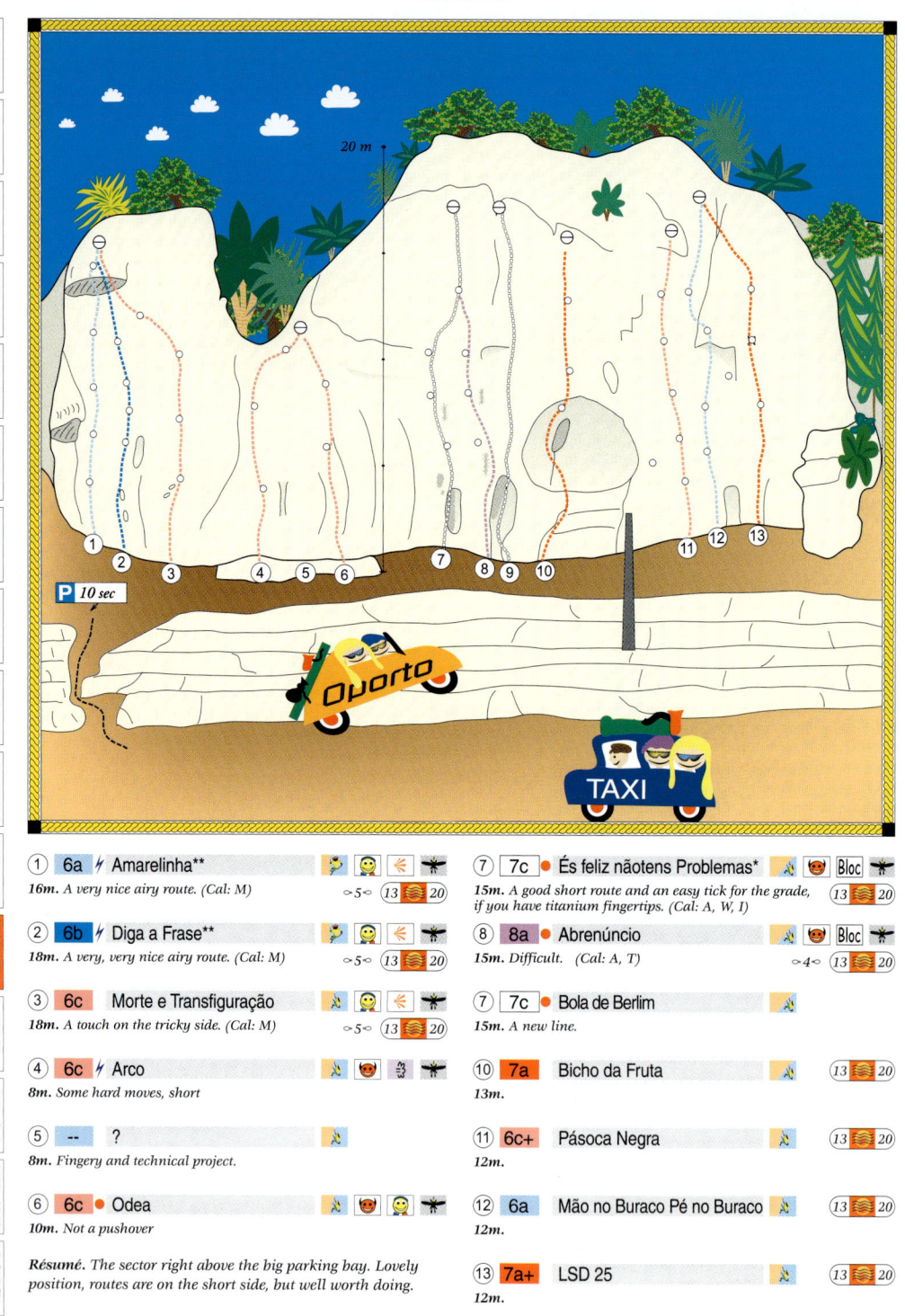

REDINHA

① **6a** ⚡ Amarelinha**
16m. A very nice airy route. (Cal: M)

② **6b** ⚡ Diga a Frase**
18m. A very, very nice airy route. (Cal: M)

③ **6c** Morte e Transfiguração
18m. A touch on the tricky side. (Cal: M)

④ **6c** ⚡ Arco
8m. Some hard moves, short

⑤ **--** ?
8m. Fingery and technical project.

⑥ **6c** ● Odea
10m. Not a pushover

Résumé. *The sector right above the big parking bay. Lovely position, routes are on the short side, but well worth doing.*

⑦ **7c** ● És feliz nãotens Problemas*
15m. A good short route and an easy tick for the grade, if you have titanium fingertips. (Cal: A, W, I)

⑧ **8a** ● Abrenúncio
15m. Difficult. (Cal: A, T)

⑦ **7c** ● Bola de Berlim
15m. A new line.

⑩ **7a** Bicho da Fruta
13m.

⑪ **6c+** Pásoca Negra
12m.

⑫ **6a** Mão no Buraco Pé no Buraco
12m.

⑬ **7a+** LSD 25
12m.

Fendilhona - Olho - Camisola - **Amarelinha** - Caracol - Fotogénica

ÉS FELIZ NÃOTENS PROBLEMAS 7c, Redinha; Ben Moon

BIVAQUE DO CARACOL 6a, Redinha; Nuno Neves

#	Grade	Name		
1	6a+	Urro do Vacão	13	20

13m.

2	7a	Estrebucho	13	20

13m.

3	6b	Diedro dos Físicos	13	20

13m.

4	6b+	7 Virtudes da Natacha	13	20

13m.

5	3a ⚡	Via Rápida	14	20

6m. A fun route as a first climb. (Cal: M, S)

6	3a ⚡	Portugalopitécus	14	20

6m. A small staircase. (Cal: M, S)

7	4a ⚡	La Cucaracha	14	20

7m. Steep but no hard moves. (Cal: M, S)

8	4c ⚡	Versos Satánicos	14	20

7m. A bit slippy in places. (Cal: M, S)

Résumé. The obvious section for beginners. Some of the classic routes such as Bivaque are very polished and demand strength for sure. Easy to arrange top ropes as well.

9	6a+	Cócó. Ranheta e Facada**	15	20

7m.

10	6b ⚡	Bivaque do Caracol**	15	20

8m. A desperate start that is well polished, the overhang has jugs, but take it to the left for the most fun. (exit right at 6a) (Cal: O, E)

11	6a ⚡	Força Marujo	15	20

12	6b	Redinha	13	20

9m.

13	6b+	A via - Netta	13	20

9m.

14	5	??	13	20

7m. The unequipped corner presents an obvious challenge.

15	6b	Bafo de Manteiga de Amendoim	13	20

7m.

Fendilhona - Olho - Camisola - Amarelinha - Caracol - Fotogénica

AZUL 6b, Redinha; Wobbly

REDINHA

① **5b** ⚡ Via de Capela
9m. *A short wall just left of the church. (Cal: F)*

② **8a+** ● A Ocasião faz o Ladrão
18m. *A complete roof - ceiling climb on flared pockets, tufa blobs and non-existant footholds. The crux would appear to be at the end moves where you play - spot the hold. (Cal: H, B, M, T) Some of the pockets need a dry spell.*

③ **7c+** ● Choque Futuro
22m. *A full on body route with a chimney squeeze rest. A completely weirdo route that is undescribable. Now continues to the top of the little cliff. (Cal: M, B, A)*

④ **7b+** ● Bugs Bunny**
20m. *A highly technical mixture of crimps to pump the forearms and calf's. A superb position with fantastic views; top sometimes has a wasps nest. (Cal: W)*

⑤ **7a** ⚡ Fotogénica**
18m. *Photogenic this is. A powerful big line. (Cal: S, L, C)*

⑥ **7a+** ⚡ Sanduìche**
18m. *Can be quite interesting. (Cal: S, L, C)*

⑦ **7a+** ● Vermelho
17m. *(Cal: S, F, U)*

⑧ **5c** ⚡ Branco**
17m. *A good little route with fine quality moves, keeping well out of the crack is great - if somewhat airy. (Cal: I, U)*

⑨ **6b** ⚡ Azul*
17m. *Lots of variations here, keeping to the right is best for the happy onsight. Two more variations are worth doing if you are here and find the other routes too hard. (Cal: M, U)*

Résumé. *This is the tallest sector of the whole cliff and gives a very exposed feeling. None of the routes are easy, and all are quite intimidating. Maybe get someone to pray for you at the chapel, so you flash all the routes.*

Chapel

Fendilhona - Olho - Camisola - Amarelinha - Caracol - **Fotogénica**

COM ESTA MÁQUINA É MEL 6c, Poios; Eduardo Costa

A climber once remarked to me that Poios was the most perfect cliff ever, except for the walk in. I disagree, because it is the 15 min walk, that makes Poios such a great cliff to visit, away from the crowds and any signs of modern mankind. The tiny hamlet of Poios is a mixture of a couple of new houses, set alongside old barns that dry the maize, and rusted out tractors, and with a smell that is most definitely very rural. The track leads up to a water hole that is home to hundreds of frogs, which leap for safety into the water as you arrive. Stay there for a while and they will gingerly edge there way back to the comfortable sunbathing positions on the dry clay rim. From here the path kicks right and through low olive groves, that illustrate a working countryside, if somewhat a hard living. Further on, a small cairn of rocks marks the climber's deviation to the left - from the main red and white footpath (easily missed). This path gently follows the hill around through somewhat more dense box trees, but never impeding the way, or discomforting the sun tanned legs. Then just at the point when you feel that you have walked far enough, you turn the corner to see the lovely valley of Poios with its selection of cliffs on both sides. It resembles a mini gorge, and if you have got it right, you are on the same level as the main cliff. If you've got it wrong, then the climb up to cliff will catch your breath, but only for a minute or so.

The main cliff is known as the 'microwave.' This is because you can burn and frizzle in a mere 90 seconds. Also because it is so steep that 'should' you fall off, you will end up in the air slowly spinning, cooking on all sides evenly, browning nicely all over. The whole valley has a selection of different cliffs. Some of these are small and a bit shattered, others are small and of good quality rock with a handful of routes. There will no doubt be more development in the forthcoming years of the surrounding rock, to give far more routes. The best and most impressive rock though, has been equipped and offers a fine selection of hard and desperate routes. There are also many contrasts of routes from technical vertical walls, to overhanging steep juggy routes, and finally include huge roof ceilings that wham out into space. The cliff gets the full blast of the afternoon sun, but it is close to the sea and will usually attract a cooling afternoon sea breeze that funnels up the gorge. At Eastertime, I have always been glad to have a good puffer jacket to keep me warm when belaying; the routes on the other hand, will always keep you warm!

Certa vez um escalador comentou comigo que Poios era o local perfeito se não fosse a marcha de aproximação. Discordo, porque é a caminhada de 15 minutos que torna Poios um local tão bom para visitar, longe das multidões e de quaisquer sinais do homem moderno. A pequena aldeola de Poios é uma mistura de meia dúzia de casas novas, contrastando com celeiros antigos onde seca o milho, tractores velhos cheios de ferrugem, e um cheiro definitivamente muito rural. O caminho desemboca numa grande poça onde moram centenas de rãs, que se refugiam na água quando nos aproximamos. Se se deixar ficar uns momentos, elas tomarão cautelosamente o caminho de regresso às confortáveis posições dos banhos de sol, na lama seca da margem. A partir daqui o caminho pula para a direita e atravessa olivais de pequena estatura, que ilustram bem o trabalho do campo e sua forma de vida um tanto árdua. Mais à frente, uma pequena pirâmide de pedras, indica ao escalador o desvio do carreiro principal vermelho e branco para esquerda, (que se perde muito facilmente). Este carreiro circunda suavemente a colina através do matagal um pouco mais denso, sem nunca lhe impedir a passagem ou molestar as pernas queimadas pelo sol. Então, precisamente quando sente que já andou bastante, a curva abre-se para o formoso vale de Poios com as paredes elevando-se de ambos os lados. Faz lembrar uma mini garganta, e se não se enganou estará ao nível da parede principal. Se se enganou a escalada até à parede vai cortar-lhe a respiração, mas apenas por pouco mais de um minuto.

Esta parede principal é conhecida por "micro-ondas", porque pode queimar e tostar em apenas 90 segundos. Além disso, é tão inclinada que "se" cair acabará por ficar suspenso no ar, rodando lentamente, a cozinhar uniformemente por todos os lados, para ganhar um belo bronze integral. O vale permite escolher diversas paredes. Algumas são pequenas e um pouco frágeis, outras também são pequenas mas de boa rocha, com uma mão-cheia de vias. Sem dúvida que o desenvolvimento dos próximos anos trará bastante mais vias para a rocha das redondezas, contudo, a melhor e mais impressionante já foi equipada e oferece alguma variedade de vias duras e violentas. Há também muitos contrastes entre as vias, desde as paredes técnicas verticais aos extraprumos escarpados em ziguezague e finalmente tectos enormes, que se perdem no espaço. A parede recebe o sol da tarde mesmo em cheio mas, como fica próximo do mar, capta a brisa marítima fresca canalizada pela garganta. Na Páscoa, fiquei sempre satisfeito por ter comigo um bom casaco almofadado para me aquecer ao fazer segurança; as vias, essas pelo contrário mantê-lo-ão sempre quente!

Redinha - Poios - Buracas do Cagimil

Redinha - Poios

Poios Approach Directions:
Park in the village near the big white house. Be careful to park considerately, and look for a place where you will not in the way. Take a track straight on up to a pool where the frogs sunbathe. Follow the marked footpath in red - the GR 26. After a casual 8 mins from the parking, there is a small cairn of stones, take the footpath on the left here. This will bring you out at the same level as the main cliff. If you are going to the shady south side, keep low on the GR 26. The paths up the south side, are very steep.

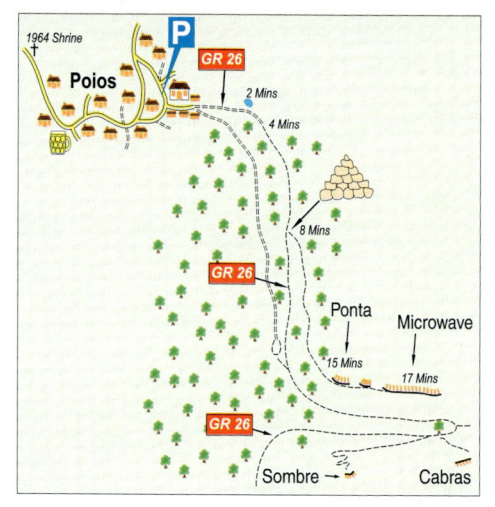

Roads in the Poios area can suddenly turn into gravel tracks on blind bends - watch out!

bealplanet.com

the dynamic company

BEAL THE DYNAMIC COMPANY

For product information and stockist details please contact Lyon Equipment
tel. 015396 25493, email info@lyon.co.uk www.lyon.co.uk

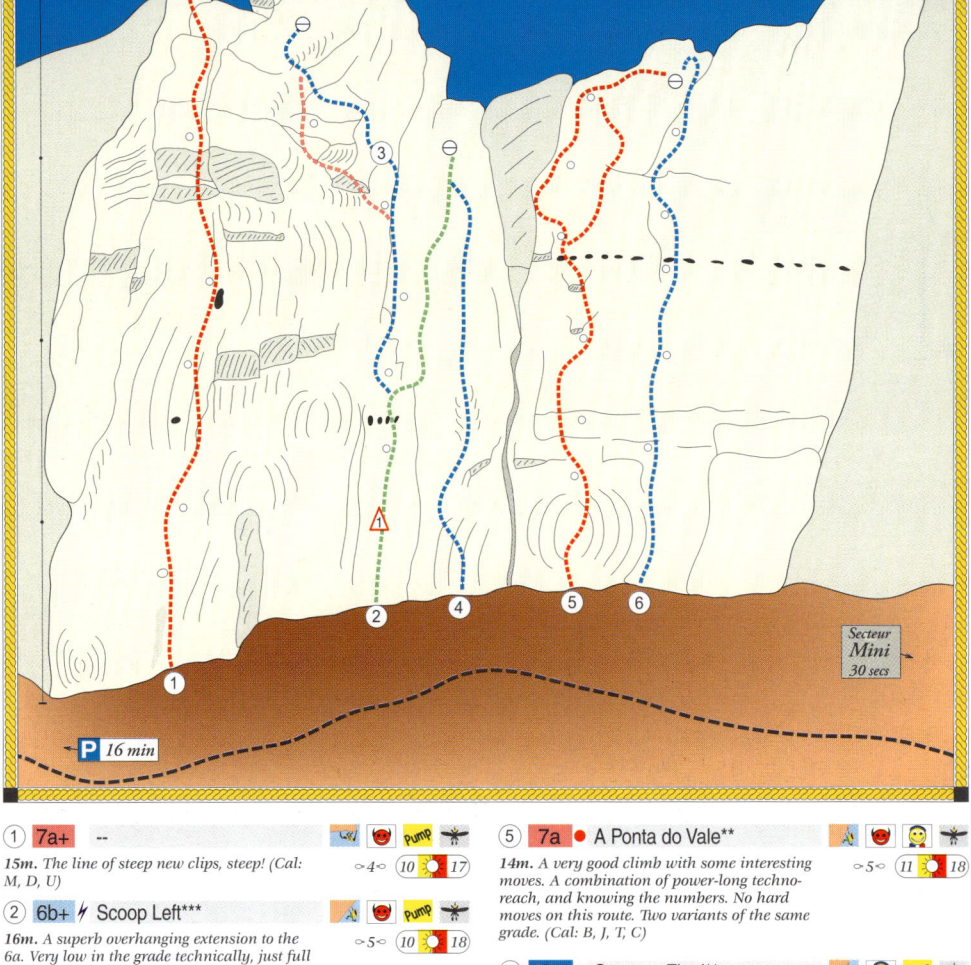

① **7a+** --

15m. The line of steep new clips, steep! (Cal: M, D, U)

② **6b+** ⚡ Scoop Left***

16m. A superb overhanging extension to the 6a. Very low in the grade technically, just full of pump and out there climbing. Joining the roof early is energetic. The finishing jug is bigger than all known jugs. (Cal: C, F, U)

③ **6a** ⚡ Scoop Right*

13m. No hard moves on this at all, just nice and steep - crust infested rock. A delight and pleasant warm up. (Cal: C, F)

④ **6b** ⚡ Arete Wall*

13m. Starting in the bay on the right and using the left edge to start. A bloc move is made to good holds. Steep ground to bring on a pump, but plenty of holds. (Cal: M, O, C)

⑤ **7a** ● A Ponta do Vale**

14m. A very good climb with some interesting moves. A combination of power-long techno-reach, and knowing the numbers. No hard moves on this route. Two variants of the same grade. (Cal: B, J, T, C)

⑥ **6b+** ● Supresa Final**

14m. A very good face climb with lots of sharp holds - perfect for the on-sight climber. Climbing past the belay is generally 6c because you are usually exhausted (Cal: C)

Résumé. This is the first sector that you arrive at - if you come on the high path. Small, but offers a lot for the middle grade climber. Quality routes with some good technical moves.

Ponta do Vale - Mini - Micro-ondas - Cumprida - Galo na testa - Cabras - Sombre

SCOOP LEFT 6b+, Poios; Wobbly

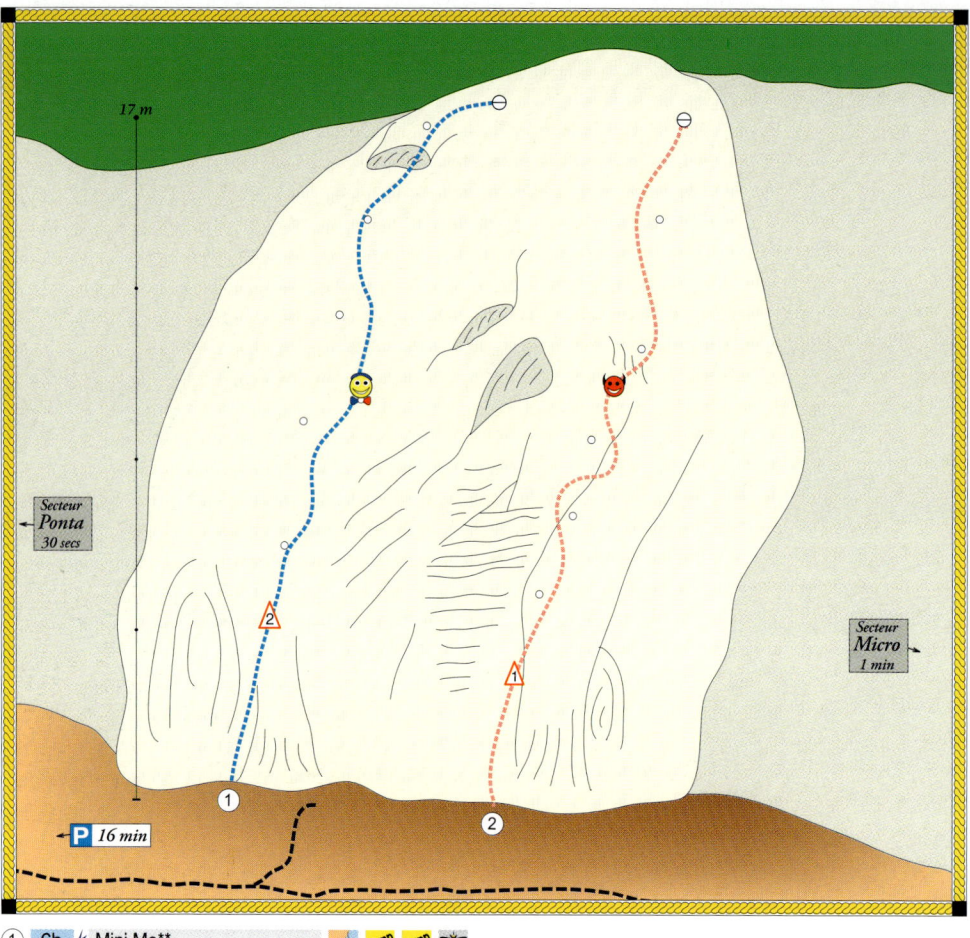

Poios

① **6b** ⚡ Mini Mo**

17m. *A full on stamina jug fest. Scary to the 1st bolt. Keep right for the best moves on the best holds, a lovely route. (Cal: J, C, U)*

② **6c+** ⚡ Steep Bastard**

14m. *If you treat this climb with a beastly full on approach - you are sure to flash it. Definitely worth hanging on in there, lots of fun. (Cal: F, B, D, U)*

Résumé. *A small but very worthwhile little sector. Two contrasting climbs; steep wall and juggy overhang.*

Ponta do Vale - **Mini** - Micro-ondas - Cumprida - Galo na testa - Cabras - Sombre

Microwave sectors - Poios

POIOS

① **6c** ⚡ VGA
25m. Very low in the grade, and might be a soft touch for strong climbers. (Cal: H, S, E)

② **7a+** ⚡ Relógio de Sol**
23m. (Cal: H, S, E)

③ **7a** Reumo Loção p'Melão*
23m. (Cal: H, S, E)

④ **7a** Micro - Ondas*
23m. (Cal: H, S, E)

⑤ **7a+** ⚡ Tubarão com Pêlo
21m. Superb juggy climbing, the only difficulty is when the jugs get too far apart - lunge happily at will. (Cal: H, S, T)

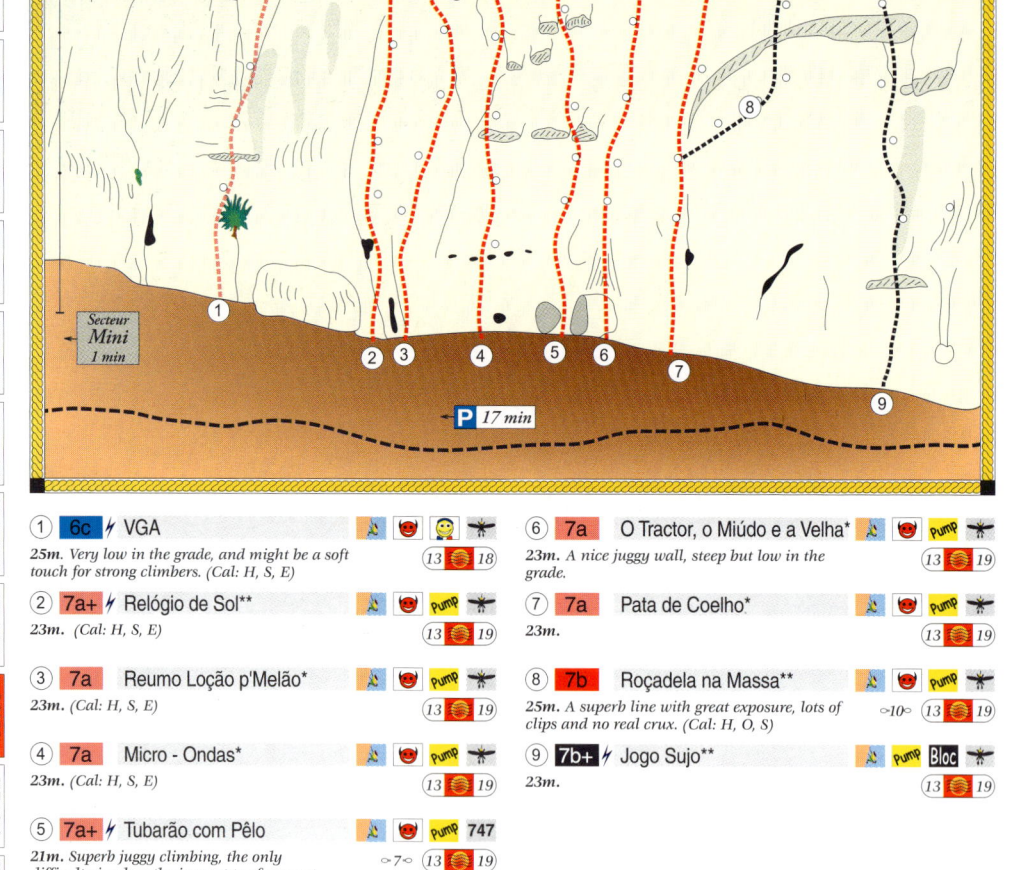

⑥ **7a** O Tractor, o Miúdo e a Velha*
23m. A nice juggy wall, steep but low in the grade.

⑦ **7a** Pata de Coelho*
23m.

⑧ **7b** Roçadela na Massa**
25m. A superb line with great exposure, lots of clips and no real crux. (Cal: H, O, S)

⑨ **7b+** ⚡ Jogo Sujo**
23m.

Résumé. The left side of the giant orange wall, offers plenty of routes on the low 7th grade. All are fairly graded and give a nice day out. Can get very hot here, but few of the routes involve small holds, so chalk up and sweat it out.

Ponta do Vale - Mini - **Micro-ondas** - Cumprida - Galo na testa - Cabras - Sombre

ROÇADELA NA MASSA 7b+, Poios; Jerry Moffatt

POIOS

Secteur Micro

Secteur Gola

25 m.

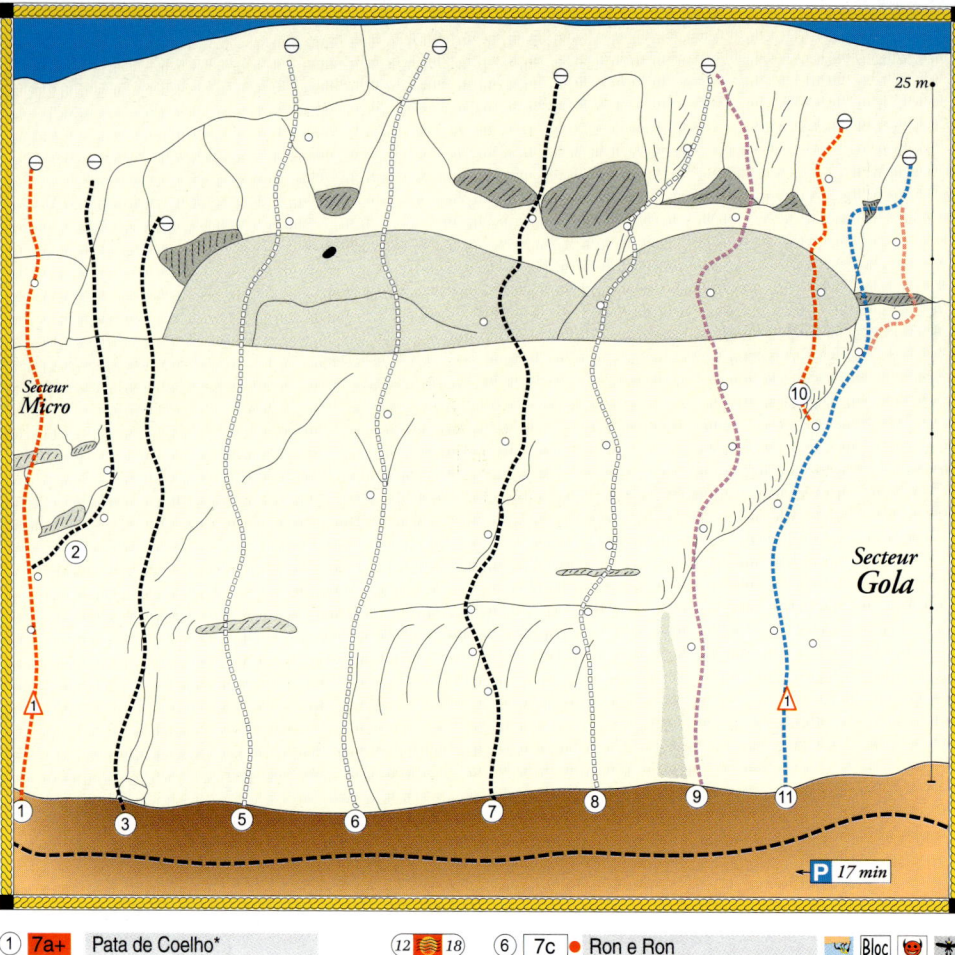

P 17 min

① **7a+** Pata de Coelho*
22m.

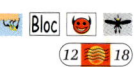

② **7b** Roçadela na Massa**
22m.

③ **7b+** Jogo Sujo** Bloc
22m.

④ **7b+** Trabalhos forçados*
22m.

⑤ **7c** Bola branca*
22m.

Résumé. Not a sector for beginners! Very impressive routes with a mix of long stamina roofs, and individual hard moves. Very spectacular and wild.

⑥ **7c** ● Ron e Ron
23m. Problematic. (Cal: T, H, E)

⑦ **7b+** ⚡ Missao Cumprida***
23m. The superb easy line up through the centre of the grand overhangs. Good holds all the way. (Cal: T, H, E)

⑧ **7c+** ● O Membro***
23m. Roofy. (Cal: H, T)

⑨ **8a+** ● O Mestre Golias

⑩ **7a** ⚡ O Peregrino***
23m. Up for the flash - keep going. (Cal: H, E, S)

⑪ **6c** ⚡ Com esta Máquina é Mel***
22m. Now re-equipped this crux proves quite sensible and pleasant for the onsight. (Go left for the freaky but easier 6b. (Cal: H, E, S)

Ponta do Vale - Mini - Micro-ondas - **Cumprida** - Galo na testa - Cabras - Sombre

MISSÃO CUMPRIDA 7b+, Poios; Ben Moon

PAULO 5b, Poios; Bruno Coelho

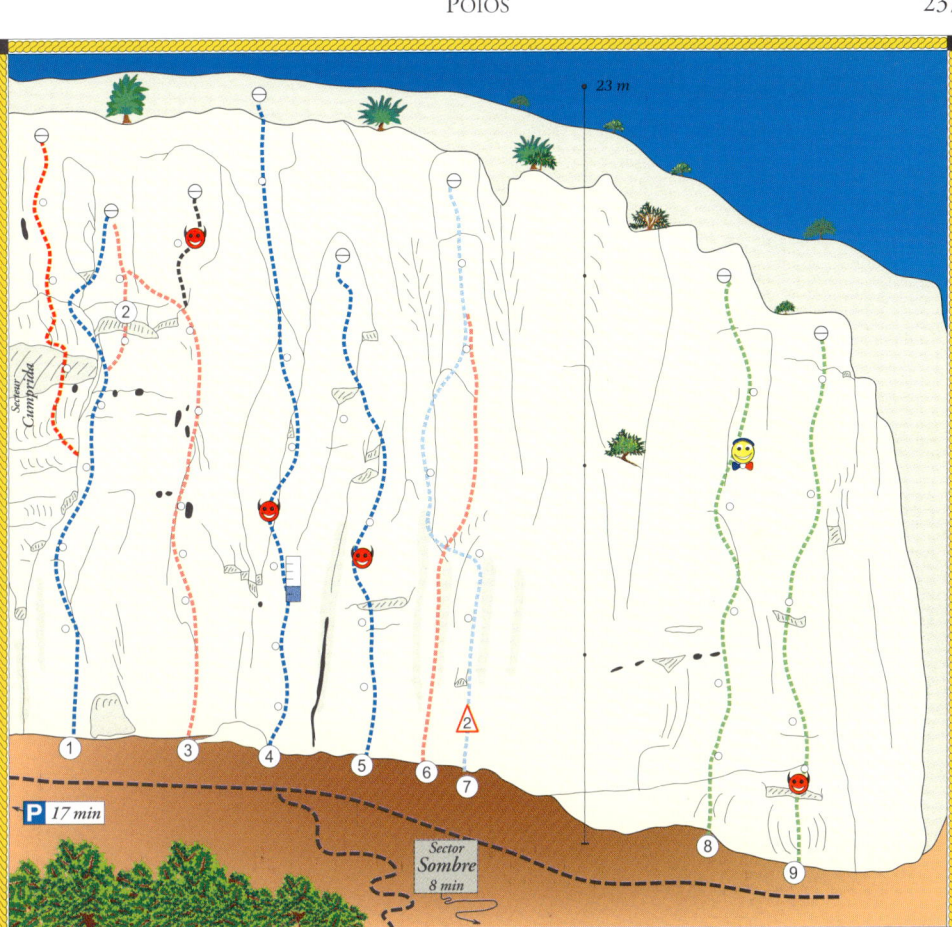

POIOS

① **6b** ⚡ Com esta Máquina é Mel**   747
18m. Climb this in the original way with ease but considerable test of nerve. (Cal: I, H, S)

② **6c** ⚡ Com esta Máquina é Mel***
18m. Direct version with new bolts is straightforward.

③ **6c** ⚡ Via da Inés**
18m. A good route that works well by going left at the top. Take it direct and you get a typical font 6b move. If you can actually clip the bolt whilst doing the move - get on 7c's. (Cal: H,B,E,W)

④ **6b** ⚡ Galo na Testa**   747
19m. A steep and polished power style climb; not really anything hard, but just sustained. A good initiation for the pump., (Cal: E, H, B)

⑤ **6b+** ⚡ 2 em 1***   747
14m. Lots of jugs and then a mono. I hope that you like mono's if you're shorter than 5ft 8". Steep, demanding and pumpy with no shortage of holds. (Badly bolted at present May-03) (Cal: H,B,E,T)

⑥ **6c** ⚡ O Superbio**   T
17m. A good route after you have done Glorioso; taking the opposite line on this section of rock. (Cal: B, I, U)

⑦ **6a+** ⚡ O Glorioso***
17m. This climb hits you hard early on and gives out a good, hard punch. Observe topo for easiest line here. (Cal: B, I, U)

⑧ **5a** ⚡ ?**
17m. A lovely wall on good pockets and plenty of rests. A couple of moves in the middle to make it interesting. (Cal: B, D)

⑨ **5b** ⚡ Paulo***
17m. A very nice introduction to the cliff; good jugs. Quite a difficult first overhang so be prepared. Lovely position. (Cal: C, D)

Résumé. *This is the lovely sector the right of the big giant overhangs. The routes are very sustained for the newcomer to the 6th grade. The position is fantastic, and although the routes are less than 20 metres long; they feel a lot longer. Typical Spanish red rock with good slots, its texture will polish up very highly in the future. (Top can be accessed by walking up to the right, also upper tier with maybe more routes.)*

Ponta do Vale - Mini - Micro-ondas - Cumprida - **Galo na testa** - Cabras - Sombre

Shady South side of the valley, with Cabras sector.

Sector SOMBRE

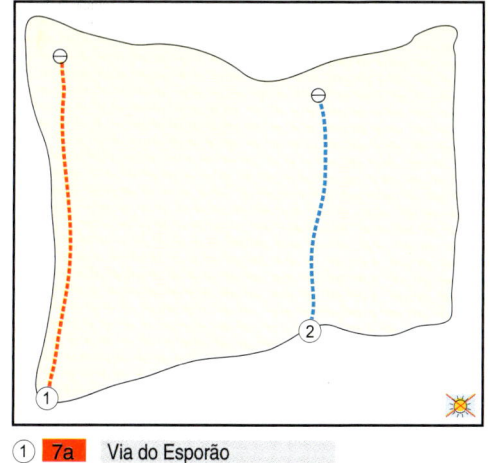

POIOS

① **6a** ⚡ **Cruzada**
10m. A short pocketed wall giving quite an outing for a 6a climber. (Cal: R, F)

② **7a** **A Sombra**
17m. Lots of different ways to skin a cat.

③ **7c** **Última Hora**
17m. Want a surprise - 5 clips in only 5 metres! Must be a 7c. (Cal: M)

④ **7a+** **O Sucateiro**
17m. Hard and sequency with rounded slaps. (Cal: E, H, B)

⑤ **7a** **?**
14m. A lovely pillar in a superb position, good rests on rounded holds. (Cal: M, O)

⑥ **6c** **Só Mais Um**
14m. The short groove may get a few panicking. (Cal: M)

Résumé. *High up on the shady side of the valley. A small bay with a distinct overhang in the middle. Good sport when the other side is too hot and sunny. (Note routes 2,3,4 only have 10 metres of real climbing.)*

① **7a** Via do Esporão
② **6b** As Cabras

Ponta do Vale - Mini - Micro-ondas - Cumprida - Galo na testa - **Cabras** - Sombre

Coimbra is one of the most important cities of Portugal, and is the main communicative focus of the central Portugal region of the Beiras. The city is full of history, and around the 13th century was indeed the capitol. For the visitor, there are many sights to see, ranging from churches and cloisters, to botanical gardens. You should not pass up a visit up to Coimbra University, which is over 700 years old, and full of historical architectural delight and learning. Just to the North of the city is the Buçaco. This is a laid out ancient woodland that has been cultivated with hundreds of exotic plant species, collected with the aid from many Portuguese explorers and looked after by monks; a must to visit for anyone interested in plants. To the Southeast is the small town of Penela with its fine castle that was built at the end of the 11th century. From here you get lovely views of the woody forests of oak, walnut and olives; and an insight to a green and lush, rural interior. Between here and Coimbra are the hills of the Serra do Rabaçal, which gets its name from the village of Rabaçal. This village is name and founder of an excellent mild cheese that is a mixture of sheep and goats milk, and is certainly not to be missed. Only a few kilometres to the north west of Rabaçal, the hills start giving wonderful indications for the climber; among the grass and roots of olive trees, stones of perfect limestone are begun to be seen, almost everywhere.

You might find the village of Casmilo, but alas - may never find the cliffs of Buracas do Cagimil. They are the hidden secret of the Serra. Fortunately today there is a brown tourist sign to Buracas, but this is only an indicator rather than a perfect locator. The track to the gorge is rough, and has left me with a punctured tyre on a previous occasion. The cliff remains hidden and secret, and from glancing at the second smaller cliff on the hillside edge, the unwary might turn back instantly and go to the beach. Crack on I encourage you, the bottom of the tiny gorge is a shady parking spot for a few cars. You then wander around the corner and your heart fills either with excitement on dread – depending on the fitness level of your forearms. The main wall of Buracas is stupendous. It is not in the league of Buoux or Céüse, but in such a small scenic surrounding, it commands a wonderful aspect, and is totally impressive. It is certainly not a cliff for a beginner, but one for the real steep overhang enthusiast. The routes on the smaller north-facing cliff are often forgotten, which is a mistake. They are short, but of good moves and technical merit, and keep good cool shade on blisteringly hot days. If you are feeling weak, it's still worth the visit for one of the most beautiful picnic spots in the world; please really look after it.

Coimbra é uma das cidades portuguesas mais importantes e o principal foco da região das Beiras, no centro de Portugal. A cidade tem uma imensa tradição histórica, e cerca do século XIII foi mesmo a capital. O visitante tem muito para ver, desde igrejas e conventos a jardins botânicos. Não se pode deixar de visitar a Universidade de Coimbra, com cerca de 700 anos, porque é um encanto arquitectónico e uma lição de História. Mesmo a Norte da cidade fica o Buçaco - uma antiga extensão de bosque, cultivada com centenas de espécies de plantas exóticas, que foram recolhidas por inúmeros exploradores portugueses e cuidadas por monges; uma visita obrigatória para quem se interesse por plantas. A Sudeste fica a vilazinha de Penela com o seu formoso castelo construído nos finais do século XI. Dele poderá disfrutar de uma belíssima vista que se estende sobre florestas de carvalhos, nogueiras e oliveiras, e vislumbrar um pouco do interior rural português, sempre verde e viçoso. Separando-nos de Coimbra estende-se a encosta da Serra do Rabaçal, cujo nome deriva da aldeia do Rabaçal. Esta aldeia deu também o nome e origem a um queijo excelente e suave, feito com uma mistura de leite de ovelha e de cabra, que certamente não poderá perder. Apenas a alguns quilómetros a Noroeste do Rabaçal, a orografia começa a dar pistas estupendas aos escaladores; entre a erva e as oliveiras, surgem pedras de calcário perfeito quase por todo o lado.

Pode encontrar a aldeia do Casmilo, mas ah! – pode não encontrar nunca as paredes das Buracas do Cagimil. Elas são o segredo melhor guardado da Serra. Felizmente já existe um sinal turístico castanho para as Buracas, mas apenas aponta uma direcção, não lhe dá a localização exacta. O caminho para o desfiladeiro é bastante rude, e já uma vez me furou um pneu. A parede mantém-se escondida e secreta pelo que, ao olhar para a encosta e vendo a segunda parede tão pequena, qualquer desprevenido dá meia

CIRCUS 8a, Buracas do Cagimil; Ben Moon

Two different views of the Vaca section; it is small but still offers some very good and concentrated climbing, not that easy either.

BURACAS DO CAGIMIL

Redinha - Poios - Buracas do Cagimil

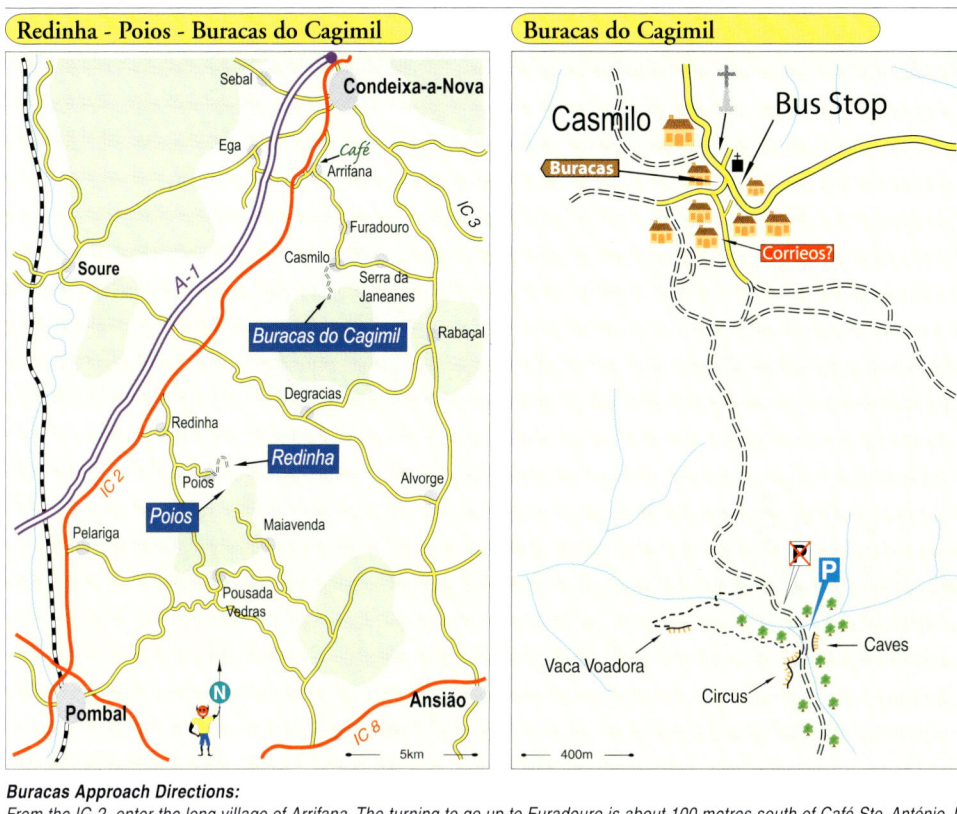

Buracas do Cagimil

Buracas Approach Directions:
From the IC-2, enter the long village of Arrifana. The turning to go up to Furadouro is about 100 metres south of Café Sto. António. It is a narrow road and goes uphill; & at an oblique angle to the main street. (usually no signpost). At 3.5km you get to Furadouro (no sign), the road goes along the valley bottom, then climbs up steeply to Casimilo (no sign). Look for the stone cross, then take the turn on the R opposite the church (behind you there is a new tourist sign to Buracas). After 20 metres turn Left, then pass an old Correios sign. The road turns to a track and leads away, carry on up to the right - going uphill, then as the road swings around to go back to the houses, there is a track on the left. Take this track which goes through an olive grove. This opens out onto a ridge, and a lovely view. 0.6km from the village you will see the cliff of Vaca Voadora. If you want to climb here, please park at the very bottom, where there is good space for parking many cars. *There is a small space near the path for Vaca Voadora, but this is the only space for the farmer, who works the small field and needs to use it. There is also a good footpath from a track on the hill that leads to Vaca Voadora, and does not go across any of the farmers fields - please use it.* The main cliff is only seen after parking your car, and then walking a few metres up the track, a nice surprise. Buracas do Cagimil is a very beautiful and unspoilt area, please respect this lovely area. Stop for a coffee at Arrifana, and use the toilet there, before you come here. Rabaçal is famous for its cheese, which is made from a mixture of sheep and goats milk; it is mild, creamy, and full of beautiful flavour.

Como chegar às Buracas:
Vindo do IC2 entre na povoação de Arrifana. O desvio para o Furadouro fica cerca de 100m a sul do Café Sto. António. É uma estrada estreita que sobe a encosta e forma um ângulo oblíquo com a estrada principal, (não tem nenhum sinal). A cerca de 3.5 Km chega-se ao Furadoro (não tem placa toponímica), e a estrada acompanha o fundo do vale, subindo depois acentuadamente até ao Casmilo (que também não tem placa). Procure o cruzeiro de pedra e a seguir vire à direita na rua oposta à igreja, (atrás de si há um sinal turístico novo que indica as Buracas). Vinte metros à frente vire à esquerda e passe um velho sinal dos Correios. A estrada transforma-se num caminho e segue em frente; continue a subir a encosta sobre a direita e onde o caminho curva de novo em direcção às casas, existe outro à esquerda. Siga este caminho através do olival até chegar a uma cumiada com uma vista deslumbrante, e a cerca de 0.6 Km da aldeia verá a parede da Vaca Voadora. Se pretende escalar nesse sector, por favor desça até mesmo ao fundo onde há espaço suficiente para estacionar vários carros. Existe um recanto junto ao carreiro para a Vaca Voadora mas é o único espaço disponível para o lavrador que cultiva o terreno adjacente e precisa de utilizá-lo. Há também outro bom caminho que conduz à Vaca Voadora, bastando seguir o carreiro que contorna a colina sem atravessar nenhum dos terrenos dos lavradores - por favor utilize-o. A parede principal só se vê após estacionar o seu carro e caminhar alguns metros, proporcionando uma agradável surpresa. As Buracas do Cagimil constituem uma área ainda preservada e de grande beleza, por isso respeite-a. Pare para tomar um café em Arrifana e aproveite para usar os sanitários antes de chegar ao local. Nas redondezas, o Rabaçal é famoso pelo seu queijo que é feito de uma mistura de leite de ovelha e de cabra; é suave, cremoso e tem um belo sabor.

Buracas do Cagimil

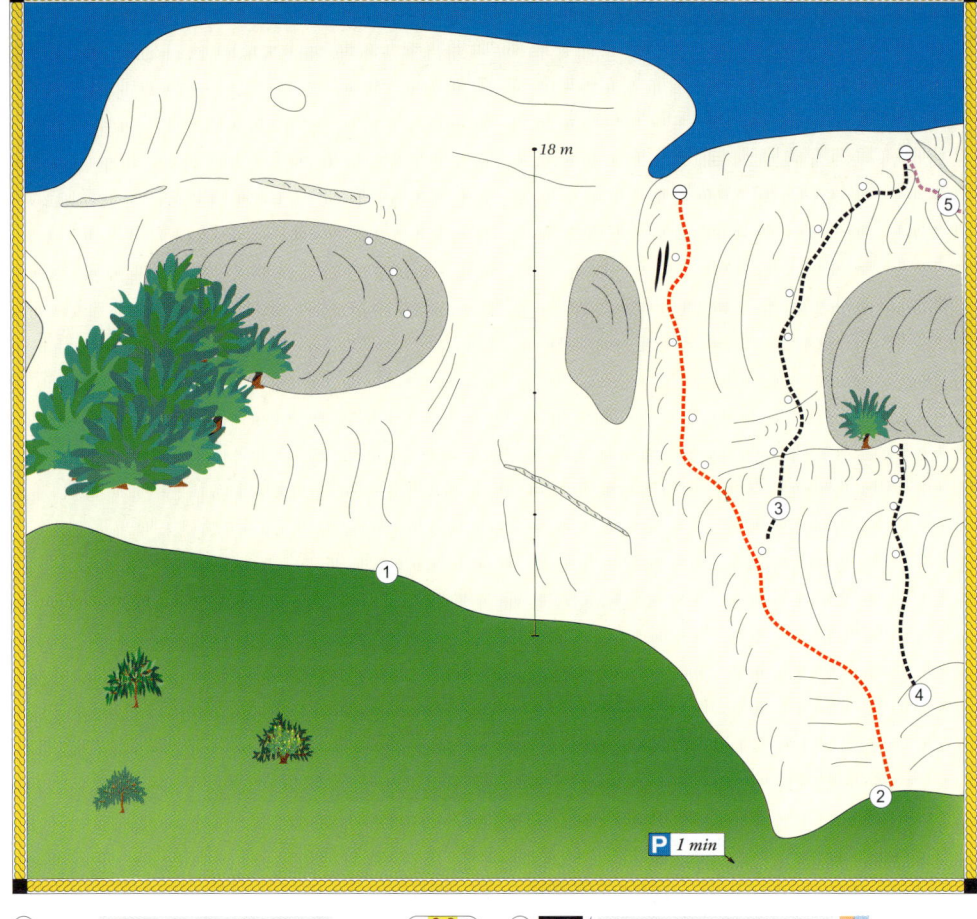

(1) - 07 09

(2) **7a** ⚡ Deixa-me Entrar que Está a Chover* 07 11
18m. Climbing the arête low down is not worth the risk; a fine upper half that comes out at you. (Cal: F, H)

(3) **7b+** ⚡ Cachiba** 07 09
22m. A route that certainly gets steeper and steeper. Climb to conserve energy. (Cal: F, H)

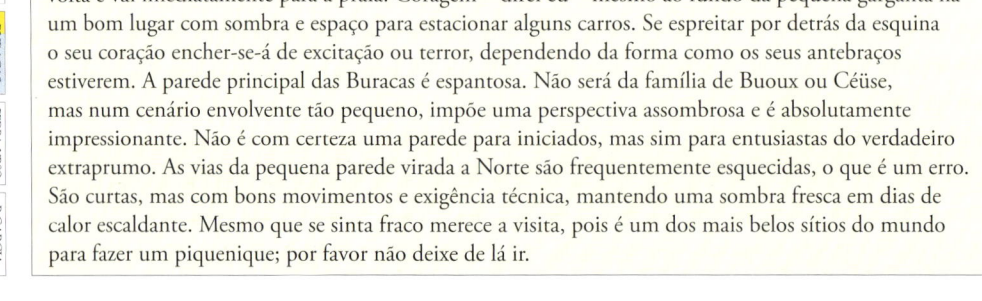

(4) **7?** ⚡
15m. A new line of bolts.

(5) **8a** ● Inumana
18m. Top part of route coming from the right.

Résumé. *The caves to the left of the main Circus wall give some good routes and await more development. The rock is suspect in places, but should clean up. This side does tend to seep a lot in winter, but is really dry in summer and autumn.*

volta e vai imediatamente para a praia. Coragem – direi eu – mesmo ao fundo da pequena garganta há um bom lugar com sombra e espaço para estacionar alguns carros. Se espreitar por detrás da esquina o seu coração encher-se-á de excitação ou terror, dependendo da forma como os seus antebraços estiverem. A parede principal das Buracas é espantosa. Não será da família de Buoux ou Céüse, mas num cenário envolvente tão pequeno, impõe uma perspectiva assombrosa e é absolutamente impressionante. Não é com certeza uma parede para iniciados, mas sim para entusiastas do verdadeiro extraprumo. As vias da pequena parede virada a Norte são frequentemente esquecidas, o que é um erro. São curtas, mas com bons movimentos e exigência técnica, mantendo uma sombra fresca em dias de calor escaldante. Mesmo que se sinta fraco merece a visita, pois é um dos mais belos sítios do mundo para fazer um piquenique; por favor não deixe de lá ir.

BROCA MOLE EM PEDRA DURA 6c/7a, Buracas do Cagimil; José Teixeira

BURACAS DO CAGIMIL

① **7c+** ● Hermanias*
10m. *An endurance route of crimps.*

② **8a** ● Inumana**

③ **7b** Custóias*
8m. *Long reaches between pockets.*

④ **8a+** ● Sem Testemunhas**

⑤ **7b** Equi-thump*

⑥ **8a** ● Equinócio***

⑦ **8a+**

⑧ **8a** ● Circus
20m. *A steep wall that can easily catch you out; then the top wall has a real stopper move. (Cal: B,W)*

⑨ **8a** Os 3 Mentirosos***

⑩ **7b+** ● Bute P'touro***
24m. *Superbly demanding climbing and full on for the grade.*

⑪ **7b** ● Luis***
24m. *Hard and explosive, bloc styles.*

⑫ **7b** ● Desejo Ardente e Cama Fria**
18m. *Low in the grade, still a testing route for the onsight - tricky and awkward. (Cal: H, C, B)*

⑬ **7a** Broca Mole em Pedra Dura***
20m. *A steep groove that can easily catch you out, keep left for the full 7a pump (6c to the right). (Cal: H,O,J,B)*

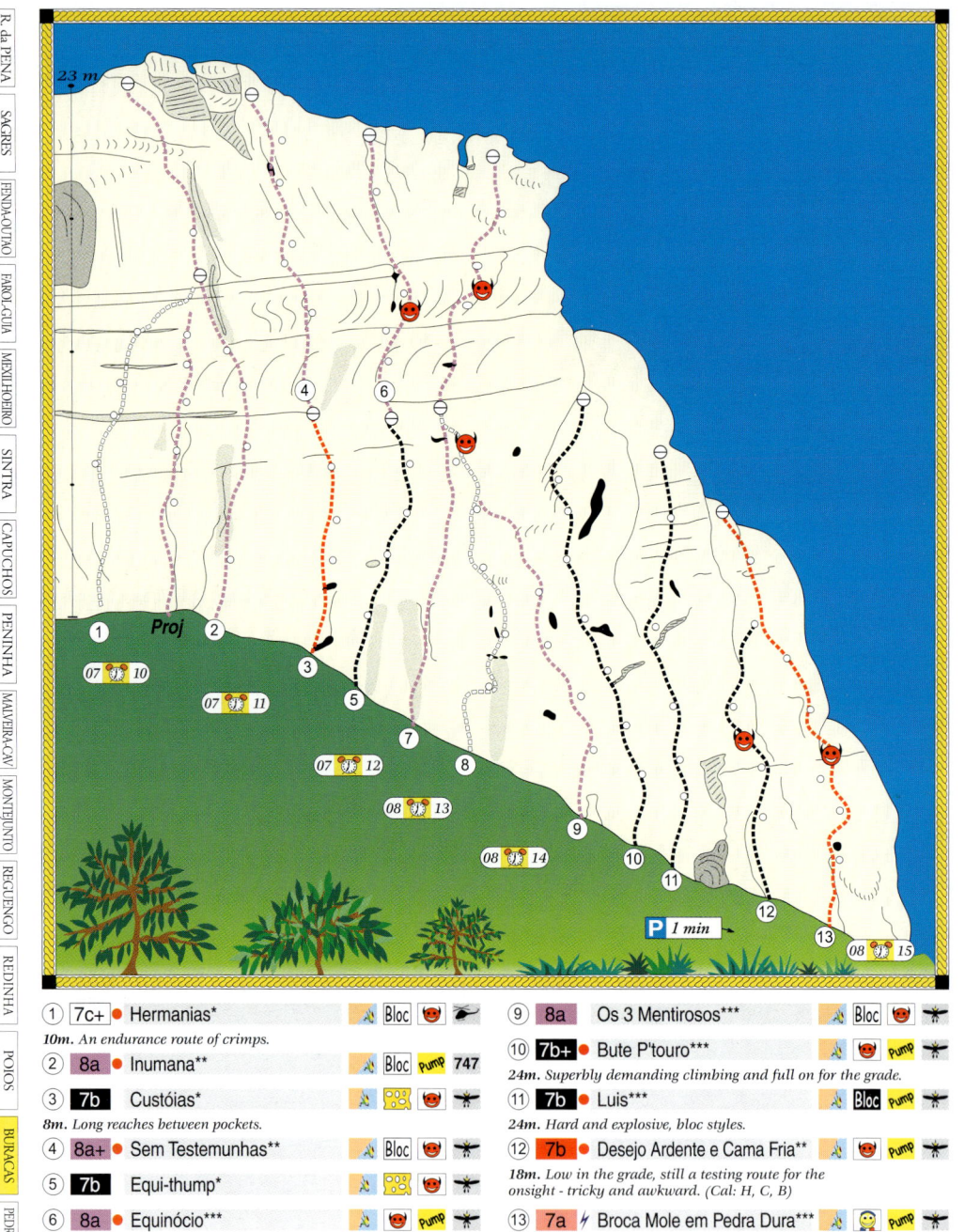

Résumé. *A magnificent wall of superb pockets and unrelenting steepness.*

| Cachiba | Circus | Cave | - | Vaca Voadora |

EQUINÓCIO, Buracas do Cagimil; Jerry Moffatt

CAVE RIGHT 7b, Buracas do Cagimil; Jingo

Buracas do Cagimil

Buracas Do Cagimil

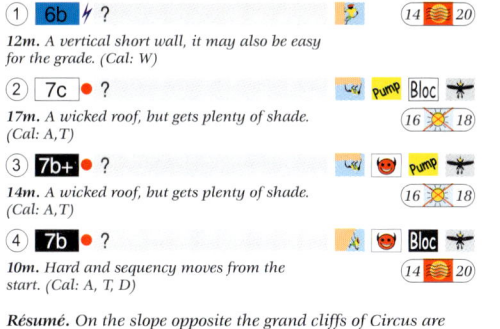

① **6b** ?
12m. A vertical short wall, it may also be easy for the grade. (Cal: W)

② **7c** ?
17m. A wicked roof, but gets plenty of shade. (Cal: A,T)

③ **7b+** ?
14m. A wicked roof, but gets plenty of shade. (Cal: A,T)

④ **7b** ?
10m. Hard and sequency moves from the start. (Cal: A, T, D)

⑤ **7a+** ?
8m. A short way up the left side of the top cave, avoiding the roof on the right. (Cal: W)

⑥ **7c** ?
8m. A wicked roof, but gets plenty of shade. (Cal: A,T)

⑦ **7b+** ?
8m. A wicked roof, but gets plenty of shade. (Cal: A,T)

⑧ **6c+** ?
8m. A short way up the right side to the top cave, sharing belay with no.7. (Cal: W)

⑨ **6a** ?
11m. A short wall to the right. (Cal: W)

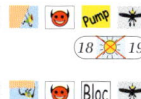

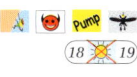

Résumé. On the slope opposite the grand cliffs of Circus are some small caves. These give some really overhanging and desperate small routes. The rock is shattered in places but there may be some more routes here in the future, for the lower grades. The caves do seep so they can be very wet, great for a hot day though. Also a fab picnic spot.

ÀS APALPADELAS NA PAREDE 6c, Buracas do Cagimil; Wobbly

BURACAS DO CAGIMIL

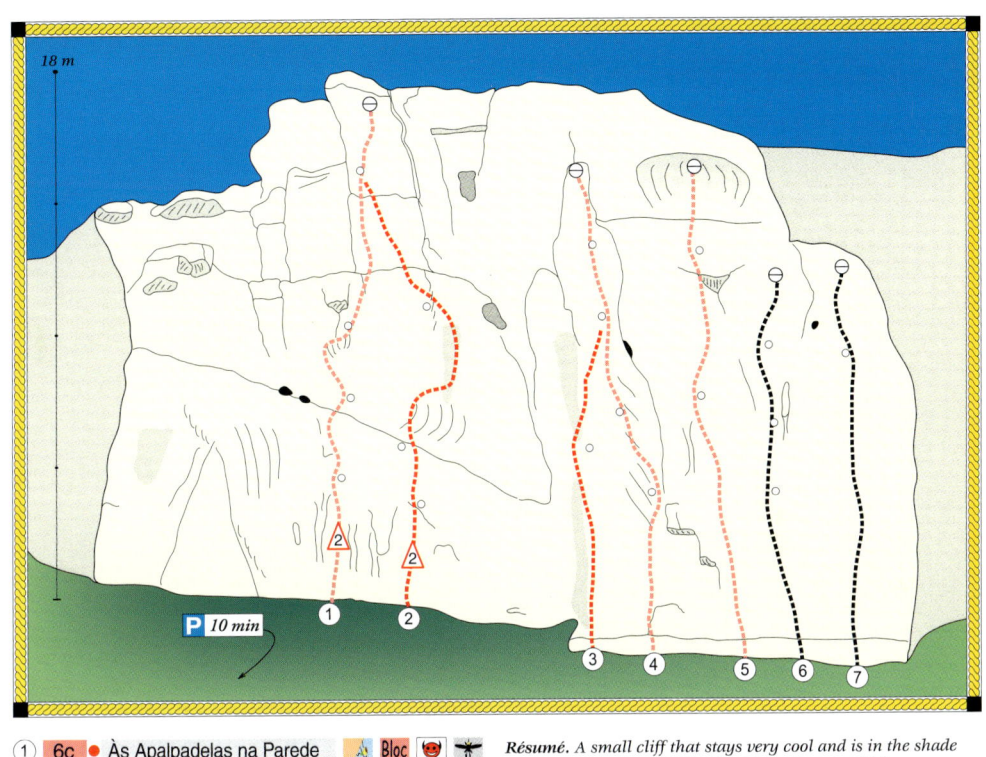

① **6c** ● Às Apalpadelas na Parede Bloc
14m. No surprises where the hard section is. Four jingo moves in a row, only a technical solution keeps the grade down. (Cal: B, M) ○4○ (18) 22

② **7a** ● Eu Sou um Insubmisso Bloc 747
14m. A slightly harder variation and another complete headache onsight. You can also climb direct up the wall at font 6b/c on mono pockets. (Cal: B, M, F) ○5○ (18) 22

③ **7a** Super Vaca Bloc (18) 22

④ **6c+** Vaca Voadora Bloc

⑤ **6c+** Click Bloc

⑥ **7b** Mão Morta Bloc

⑦ **7b** O que está aí é o que se vê* Bloc

8 metres to the right

⑧ **7b** A1 8a no Verdon

15 metres further to the right

⑨ **6c** Realidade Agora a Cores

⑩ ?

Résumé. *A small cliff that stays very cool and is in the shade for most of the day. All the climbs are short and full on, mainly boulder style. Worth a visit if you are strong and don't want stamina routes.*

Cachiba - Circus - Cave - Vaca Voadora

BOREAL

Zorro

THE INCREDIBLE ZORRO, so strong that he can lift a whole boulder with one arm!

Just above the centre of Portugal is the granite mountain range called the Serra da Estrela, with its highest peak of Torre being just short of 2000 metres. It's not going to remind you of the Picos d'Europa or the Alps, but it is high enough to give that grand feeling of scale; with elegant views, sunsets and sunrises. In the central area, there are a few high peaks with substantial cliffs that offer a good selection of traditional classic climbs, popular with weekend climbers. In an exceptionally cold winter, the gullies on these ice up to give some challenging ice routes for the enthusiast. The Serra da Estrela however, offers a lot more to the discerning boulderer than just about anywhere in Portugal. There are lots of hillsides with boulders, and the whole range will not doubt be explored over the next 100 years to give endless problems. So far, the ingredients for the best bouldering can be found at Pedra do Urso – about 7 kilometres north west of Covilhã, in a land of 1000 boulders beneath Penhas da Saúde.

To arrive at Pedra do Urso, you have several options. The best way is most probably to drive to Seia, about 40km SW of Viseu. From here, a beautiful road winds over the top of the Serra da Estrela and gives you a lovely way to see the mountains for the first time. The most practical way to Pedra do Urso, is Via Covilhã and to take the fast motorway. Covilhã is a lovely big town set on the side of a hill, and looks at first glance more like a ski resort, with the it's old centre surrounded by high rise new developments. It has a buoyant University, which gives the town a youthful and vibrant feel, and has all the shops and amenities that you will need. The bars always become busy at night, and will easily put an end to getting up the following morning! (Boudering here is more of an afternoon pastime). From Covilhã the road tortuously winds up the hillside above the town, however - nice and quickly to a gently sloping plateau set at around 1400 metres. This altitude keeps the temperature cool in autumn, winter and spring – with only July and August being roasting hot. The granite is rough and of superb quality. The boulders are often bread shaped stones, which offer undercut problems, both in the sun and the shade; and on occasions do give some scary high balls. The landings in general are good, and a couple of crash pads are sufficient. In this guidebook we cover just one of the areas with around 100 quality problems. In the other areas there are hundreds more problems of all grades, and styles of skin shredding. Like all mountains, you can get some bad weather, but the brutality of mountain granite is going to send you to the bar early, anyway. I hear there is also a wine museum in Covilhã, yum!

Mesmo acima do centro de Portugal ergue-se a cordilheira granítica da Serra da Estrela, com o seu cume, a Torre, pouco abaixo dos 2000 metros. Não vai lembrar-lhe os Picos da Europa nem os Alpes, mas é suficientemente alta para dar aquela esplêndida sensação de espaço, ter paisagens requintadas e a magia do pôr e nascer do sol. Na parte central existem alguns picos mais altos, com paredes importantes, que proporcionam uma boa variedade de escaladas clássicas tradicionais, muito populares entre escaladores de fim-de-semana. Se o Inverno for excepcionalmente frio algumas ravinas congelam, e dão origem a desafiantes vias de gelo para os entusiastas. Contudo, a Serra da Estrela oferece muito mais ao praticante de bloco perspicaz, do que qualquer outro local em Portugal. Há montes de encostas com blocos e a cadeia montanhosa inteira será sem dúvida explorada durante os próximos 100 anos, para dar uma infinidade de problemas. Até agora os ingredientes para o melhor bloco encontram-se na Pedra do Urso – cerca de 7 quilómetros a Noroeste da Covilhã, num terreno com 1000 blocos, logo abaixo das Penhas da Saúde.

Para chegar à Pedra do Urso tem várias opções. O melhor caminho é provavelmente por Seia, cerca de 40km a Sudoeste de Viseu. Daqui parte uma bonita estrada, que serpenteia até ao topo da Serra da Estrela e proporciona uma forma maravilhosa de ver as montanhas pela primeira vez. O caminho mais prático para chegar à Pedra do Urso é através da Covilhã, tomando a auto-estrada. A Covilhã é uma cidade apaixonante, assente numa encosta, e à primeira vista parece mais uma estância de esqui. O seu antigo centro encontra-se rodeado por grandes empreendimentos muito mais recentes. Tem uma Universidade alegre que confere à cidade uma atmosfera jovem e vibrante, e tem também todas a

COVILHÃ MAGIC 6a+, Old Pedra do Urso; Jerry Moffatt

CANNONBALL BOULDER ? The last Great problem, Pedra do Urso-Desert; Jingo (Photo; Jerry Moffatt)

lojas e serviços de que pode necessitar. Os bares tornam-se movimentados à noite, e porão facilmente um fim ao levantar cedo na manhã seguinte! (O bloco aqui é mais um passatempo vespertino). Desde a Covilhã a estrada serpenteia tortuosamente pela encosta sobranceira à cidade – e conduz, de forma rápida e agradável, a um planalto ligeiramente inclinado que se situa sensivelmente a 1400 metros. Esta altitude mantém a temperatura baixa durante o Outono, Inverno e Primavera – sendo apenas Julho e Agosto torridamente quentes. O granito é rugoso e de qualidade excelente. Os blocos são calhaus que têm frequentemente a forma de um pão, pelo que proporcionam problemas extraprumados, tanto ao sol, como à sombra; por vezes assumem também a forma de bolas altas e assustadoras. As aterragens são geralmente boas, por isso um par de crash pads será suficiente. Neste guia cobrimos apenas uma das áreas com cerca de 100 problemas de qualidade. Nas outras áreas, existem mais umas centenas com todos os graus de dificuldade e formas de retalhar a pele. Como em todas as montanhas, pode apanhar mau tempo; de qualquer maneira a brutalidade do granito irá enviá-lo mais cedo para o bar. Ouvi dizer que também há um museu do vinho na Covilhã, yum!

CANNONBALL (Unclimbed), Pedra do Urso; Ben Moon (making it 'look'- ok-ish)

Covilhã

Pedra do Urso

P1 - Penhas da Saúde; 2 km +/-
P1 - Camping Piao; 3.9 km
P1 - Covilhã - 7 km +/-
P1 Altitude 1350m

Camping Pião
Clube de Campismo e Carav. de Covilhã
Apartado 208, 6200 Covilhã
Tel: 275 314 312 & 275 327 932
Situation: 4km WNW of Covilhã
Notes: High up and cool, relaxed,
open and shade but not much grass,
Open: (1/1- 31/12) - Quite big but is quiet
out of summer season.
2 Chalets to rent with one bedroom in each.

Bar: Penhas da Saúde & camping
Shop: Camping & Covilhã
Petrol Station: Covilhã
Supermecado: Covilhã
Nearest climbing shop: Coimbra & Oporto

Tubarão

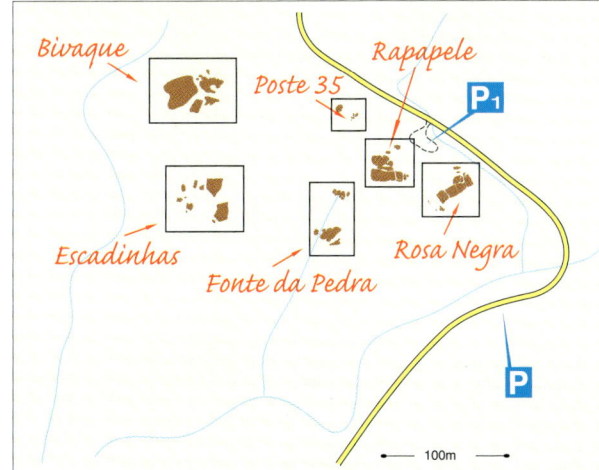

Tubarão Approach Directions:
1). From the A23 autoroute go into Covilhã. You have to go up into the town centre - right up the hill; then follow brown tourist signs to Serra da Estrela. This then goes up the mountain side. As you pass the camping on the left - set you car distance to zero. After 3.9km you will see the parking spot on the left - set about 25 metres back in a bay. This spot is level and good for a picnic also. For the other sectors there are a few smaller places to park, but all are within a few minutes of this spot anyway.

Deserto:
This is a big and spread out area. It takes a good 15 minutes to walk to the end of the good boulders. These get quite high so bring a small rope to throw over the boulder to get down!

Pedra do Urso:
This area has superb views over Covilhã. There are hundreds of problems of all grades, and some spooky high balls.

PEDRA DO URSO

P 4 min

Bivaque

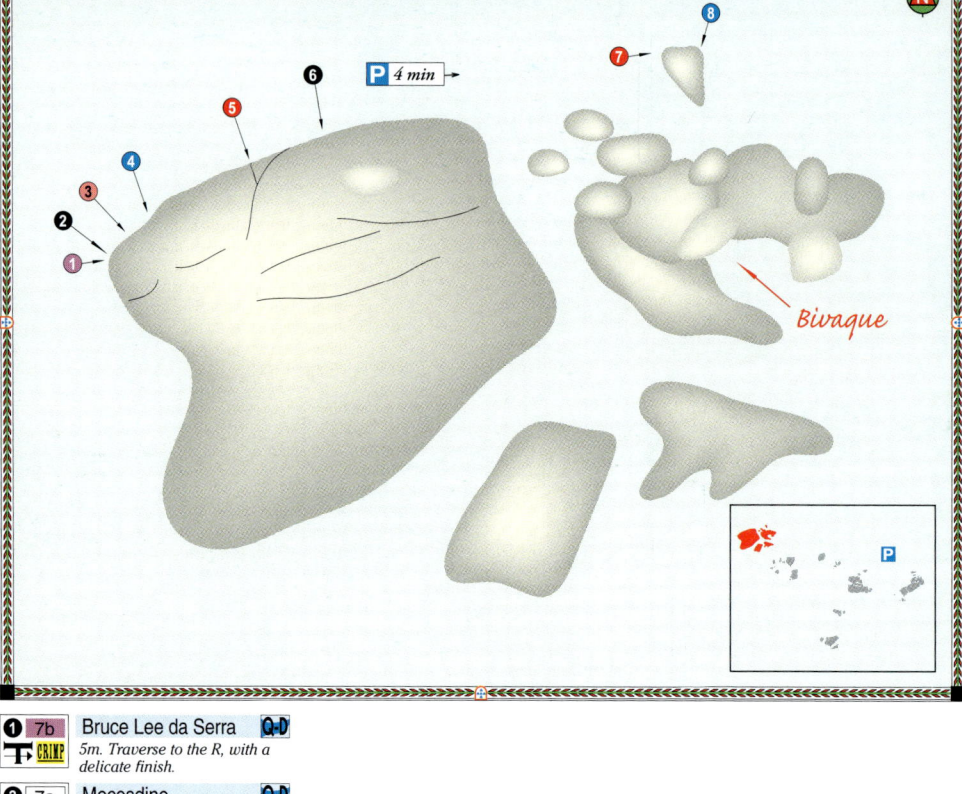

| ① | 7b | Bruce Lee da Serra | Q-D |

CRIMP
5m. Traverse to the R, with a delicate finish.

| ② | 7a | Mecosdino | Q-D |

CRIMP
4m. The obvious break, dyno for lip, then crimp your way over.

| ③ | 5b | Mecostatic |

4m. Excellent simple dyno for huge jugs and mantle .

| ④ | 4c | Exposoto |

?

| ⑤ | 5c | Ode aos Ursos Medrosos |

4m. Nice vertical crack with a strange rock over.

| ⑥ | 6b | Cristaleira |

CRIMP
4m. Crimpy start to a technical finish.

| ⑦ | 6a | Aresta* | Q-D |

3m: SS, the short arête is climbed, keeping on the left.

| ⑧ | 4c | Travessia |

5m. Traverse to the R, ending near Aresta

Bivaque - Escadinhas - Fonte de Pedra - Poste 35 - Rapapele - Pouca Terra - Rosa negro - Zimbre

Pedra do Urso - Desert problem 6a; Jerry Moffatt

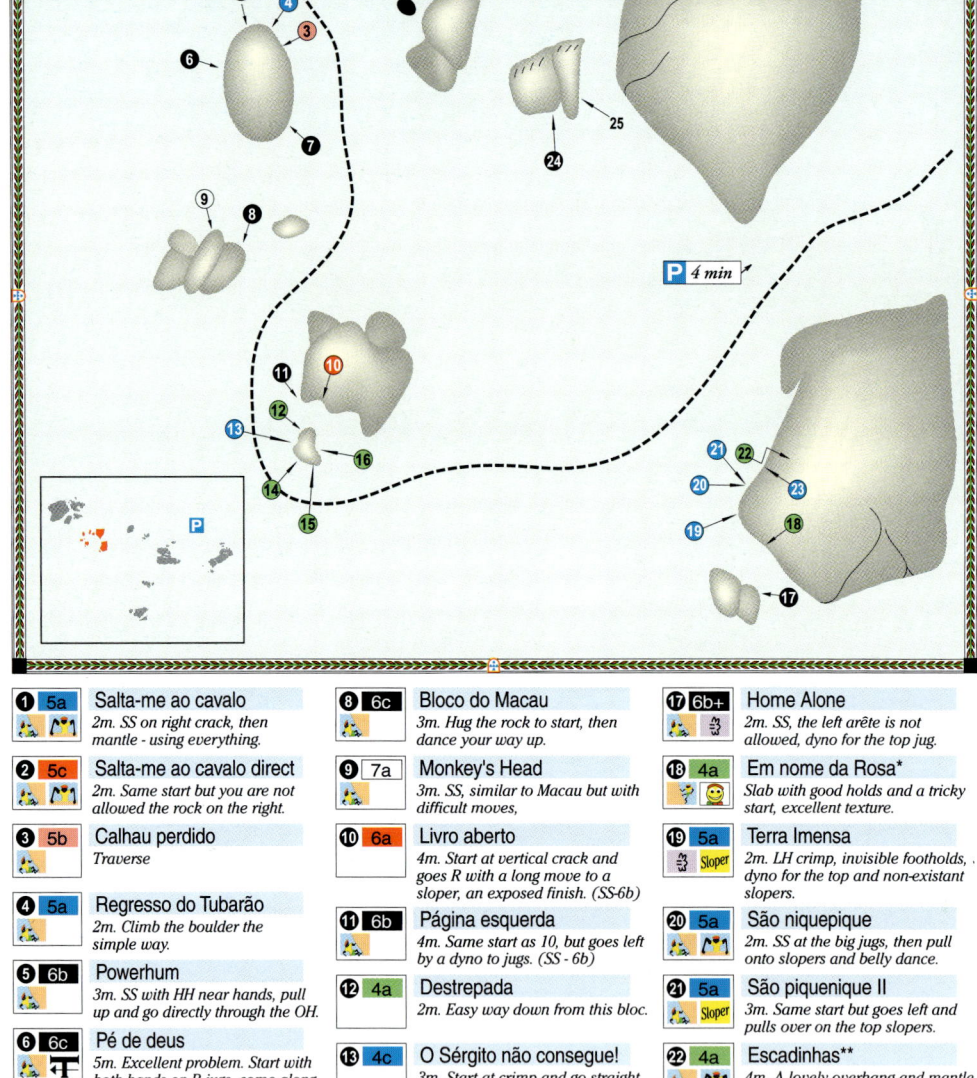

Pedra Do Urso

#	Grade	Name	Description
1	5a	Salta-me ao cavalo	2m. SS on right crack, then mantle - using everything.
2	5c	Salta-me ao cavalo direct	2m. Same start but you are not allowed the rock on the right.
3	5b	Calhau perdido	Traverse
4	5a	Regresso do Tubarão	2m. Climb the boulder the simple way.
5	6b	Powerhum	3m. SS with HH near hands, pull up and go directly through the OH.
6	6c	Pé de deus	5m. Excellent problem. Start with both hands on R jugs, come along the edge of the OH with tiny crimps and crossovers, big jug to tricky way out.
7	6c	Ataque de raiva	4m. SS on big jugs to start, crux at the end.
8	6c	Bloco do Macau	3m. Hug the rock to start, then dance your way up.
9	7a	Monkey's Head	3m. SS, similar to Macau but with difficult moves,
10	6a	Livro aberto	4m. Start at vertical crack and goes R with a long move to a sloper, an exposed finish. (SS-6b)
11	6b	Página esquerda	4m. Same start as 10, but goes left by a dyno to jugs. (SS - 6b)
12	4a	Destrepada	2m. Easy way down from this bloc.
13	4c	O Sérgito não consegue!	3m. Start at crimp and go straight up.
14	4b	Niu	3m. Running start to catch first hold, then mantle.
15	4a	Arexta Xuja	4m. Climb the arête.
16	4a	Laplaque	4m. A very good easy slab.
17	6b+	Home Alone	2m. SS, the left arête is not allowed, dyno for the top jug.
18	4a	Em nome da Rosa*	Slab with good holds and a tricky start, excellent texture.
19	5a	Terra Imensa	2m. LH crimp, invisible footholds, dyno for the top and non-existant slopers.
20	5a	São niquepique	2m. SS at the big jugs, then pull onto slopers and belly dance.
21	5a	São piquenique II	3m. Same start but goes left and pulls over on the top slopers.
22	4a	Escadinhas**	4m. A lovely overhang and mantle.
23	4c	Escadinhas direct	Same start but go directly up.
24	6c	Tusa na Verga	2m. Hard SS.
25		Project	?

ESCADINHAS 4a, Pedra do Urso; Carla Duarte

BRUCE LEE DE LA SERRA 7b, Pedra do Urso-Bivaque; Ben Moon

Pedra Do Urso

1 `4c` **Pica-pica****
4m. Fantastic slab.

2 `5b` **Flecha azul**
?

3 `5c` **Fonte da pedra**
3m. SS on vertical, sloping crack.

4 `4a` **Dia das Mentiras**
2m. A nice and easy climb.

5 **Onda**
An inexplorable wall!

6 `7a+` **Kung Fu da Selva**
4m. Hard SS, with dynos and then a delicate & exposed finish. The real boulder for Kung Fu experts!

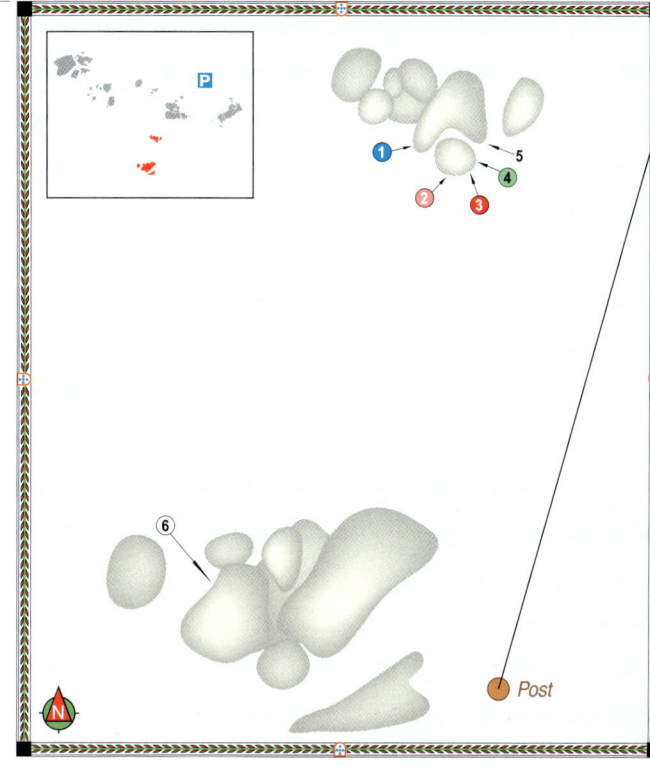

Manuel Franco getting into some heavy brush work, 7a+ and sustained!

Bivaque - Escadinhas - **Fonte de Pedra** - Poste 35 - Rapapele - Pouca Terra - Rosa negro - Zimbre

RAPAPELE 6a - Problem 1-Rapapele, Pedra do Urso; Luis Pinheiro

ZORRO 4c - Problem 1-Rosa Negra, Pedra do Urso; Jingo

Pedra Do Urso

1 `4c` **Acesso domingueiro**
Easiest way to climb this boulder. Characterised by a pile of rocks at the bottom - used by pic-nic weekenders to get up it. Use them.

2 `5a` **Acesso Alpinista**
(Começo saltando para presas) Jump start, then mantle.

3 `4a` **Os 2 Buracos**
Traverse

4 `5a` **1 Buraco**
Starts the same and goes left.

5 `4c` **?**
?

6 `6b` **Cavalo na placa**
3m. Really hard and crimpy slab.

7 `6a` **Bosas 35**
?

8 `4c` **?**
?

9 `5b` **Travessia do tecto com musgo**
3m. SS on the L, traverse to the R and to the lip of the overhang.

10 `4a` **Nariz**
2. SS and exit on the aliens nose!

11 `5a` **Travessia**
Traverse L to R, then mantle on the edge of the boulder.

12 `6a` **Sapatilha 35**
3m. Nice slab/wall.

13 `4a` **?**
?

14 `6a` **Batata 35**
?

Poste 35

Pedra do Urso is one of the great places to have a picnic - on a nice day that is. The gastronomic speciality of the area, is a wonderful cheese 'Queijo de Ovelha.' This is made from the milk of sheep grazing in the Serra da Estrela. It soon warms up in the midday sun, whilst you sample the odd glass of wine. Then you cut into the top of the round and scoop out the soft and smooth cheese.

Bivaque - Escadinhas - Fonte de Pedra - **Poste 35** - Rapapele - Pouca Terra - Rosa negro - Zimbre

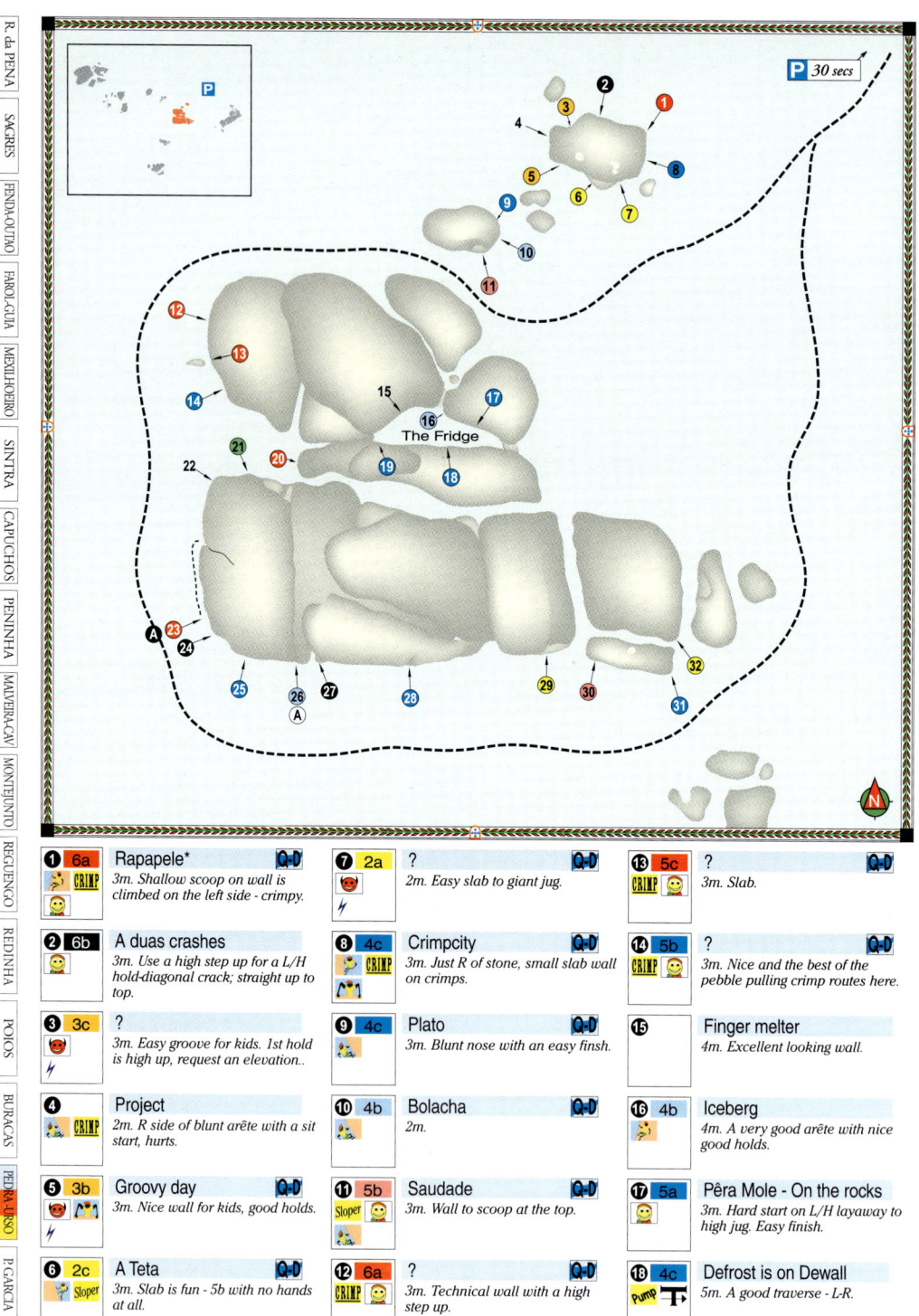

Pedra Do Urso

#	Grade	Name	Description
1	6a	Rapapele*	3m. Shallow scoop on wall is climbed on the left side - crimpy.
2	6b	A duas crashes	3m. Use a high step up for a L/H hold-diagonal crack; straight up to top.
3	3c	?	3m. Easy groove for kids. 1st hold is high up, request an elevation..
4		Project	2m. R side of blunt arête with a sit start, hurts.
5	3b	Groovy day	3m. Nice wall for kids, good holds.
6	2c	A Teta	3m. Slab is fun - 5b with no hands at all.
7	2a	?	2m. Easy slab to giant jug.
8	4c	Crimpcity	3m. Just R of stone, small slab wall on crimps.
9	4c	Plato	3m. Blunt nose with an easy finsh.
10	4b	Bolacha	2m.
11	5b	Saudade	3m. Wall to scoop at the top.
12	6a	?	3m. Technical wall with a high step up.
13	5c	?	3m. Slab.
14	5b	?	3m. Nice and the best of the pebble pulling crimp routes here.
15		Finger melter	4m. Excellent looking wall.
16	4b	Iceberg	4m. A very good arête with nice good holds.
17	5a	Pêra Mole - On the rocks	3m. Hard start on L/H layaway to high jug. Easy finish.
18	4c	Defrost is on Dewall	5m. A good traverse - L-R.

Bivaque - Escadinhas - Fonte de Pedra - Poste 35 - Rapapele - Pouca Terra - Rosa negro - Zimbre

IMPRÓPRIO PARA CONSUMO 6c, Pedra do Urso-Pouca Terra; Ben Moon

OS PORNOGRÁFICOS 5a, Pedra do Urso; Ben Moon

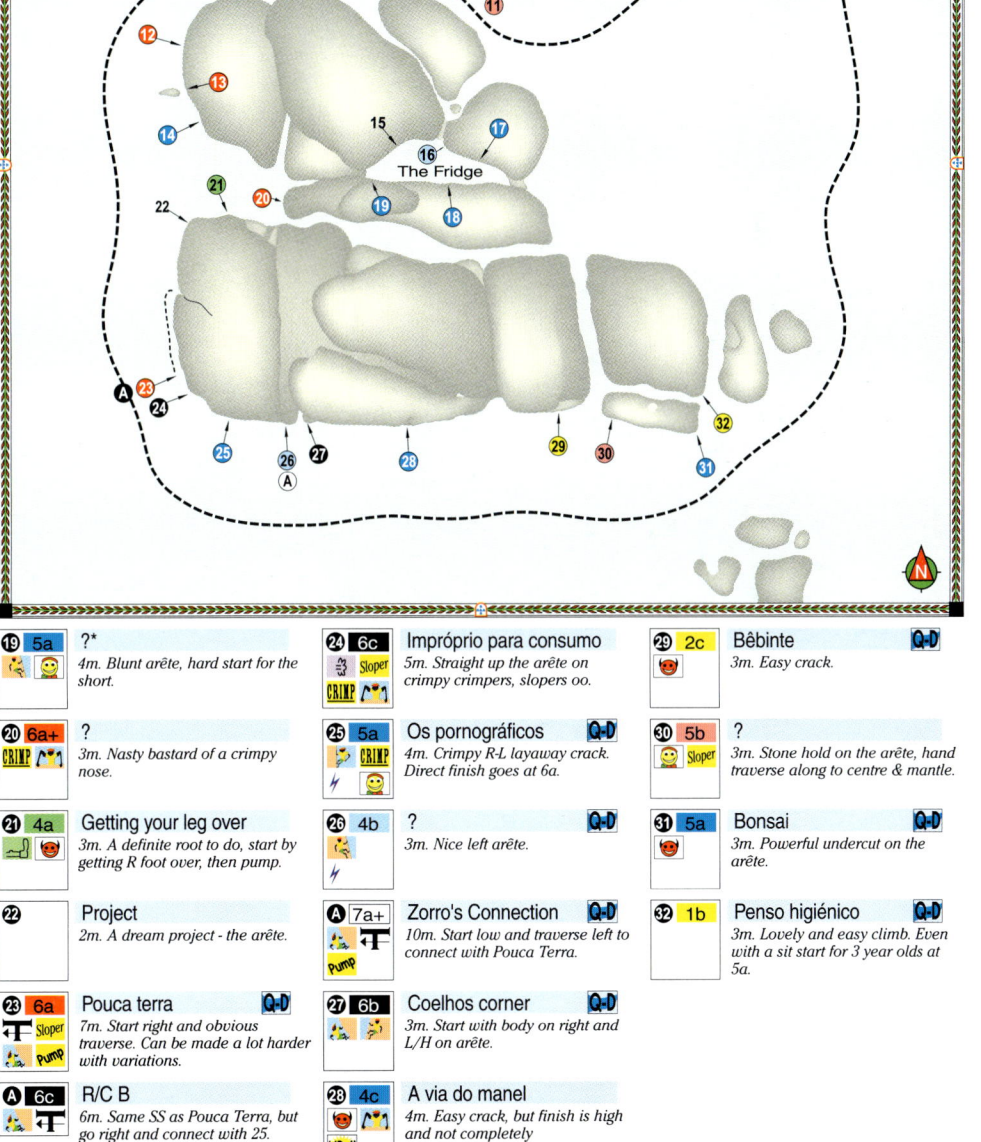

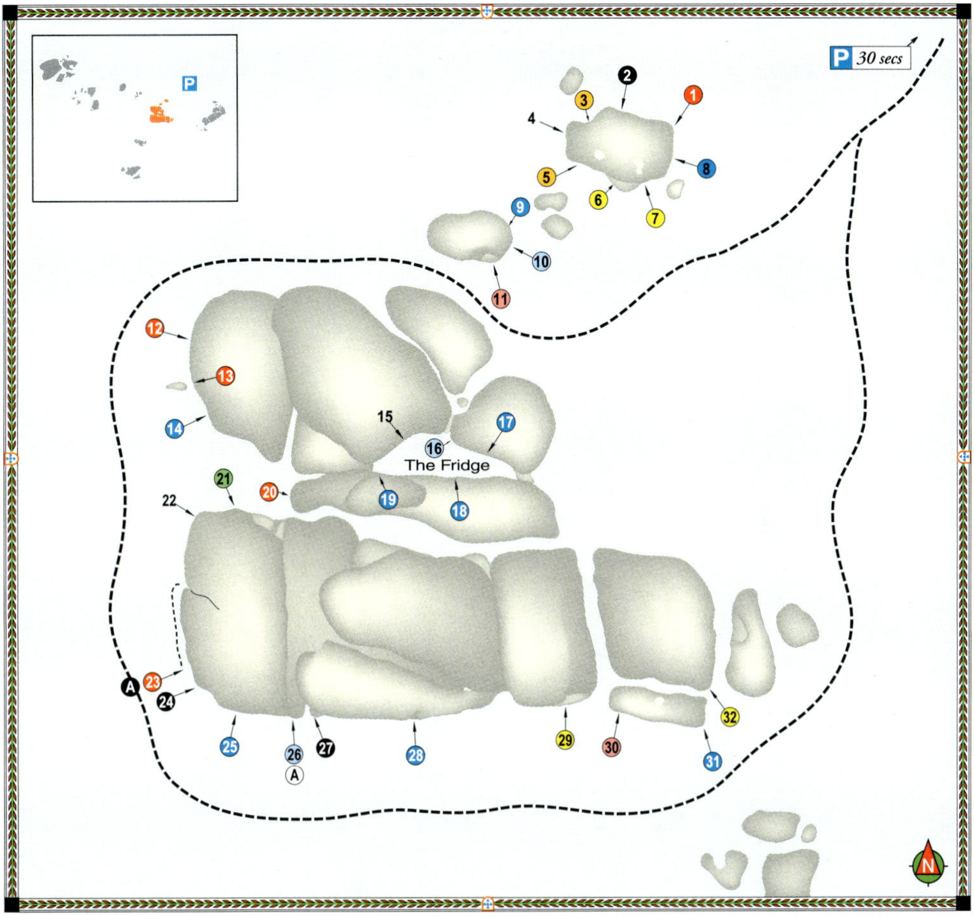

Pedra Do Urso

#	Grade	Name	Description
19	5a	?*	4m. Blunt arête, hard start for the short.
20	6a+	?	3m. Nasty bastard of a crimpy nose.
21	4a	Getting your leg over	3m. A definite root to do, start by getting R foot over, then pump.
22		Project	2m. A dream project - the arête.
23	6a	Pouca terra	7m. Start right and obvious traverse. Can be made a lot harder with variations.
A	6c	R/C B	6m. Same SS as Pouca Terra, but go right and connect with 25.
24	6c	Impróprio para consumo	5m. Straight up the arête on crimpy crimpers, slopers oo.
25	5a	Os pornográficos	4m. Crimpy R-L layaway crack. Direct finish goes at 6a.
26	4b	?	3m. Nice left arête.
A	7a+	Zorro's Connection	10m. Start low and traverse left to connect with Pouca Terra.
27	6b	Coelhos corner	3m. Start with body on right and L/H on arête.
28	4c	A via do manel	4m. Easy crack, but finish is high and not completely straightforward.
29	2c	Bêbinte	3m. Easy crack.
30	5b	?	3m. Stone hold on the arête, hand traverse along to centre & mantle.
31	5a	Bonsai	3m. Powerful undercut on the arête.
32	1b	Penso higiénico	3m. Lovely and easy climb. Even with a sit start for 3 year olds at 5a.

Bivaque - Escadinhas - Fonte de Pedra - Poste 35 - Rapapele - **Pouca Terra** - Rosa negro - Zimbre

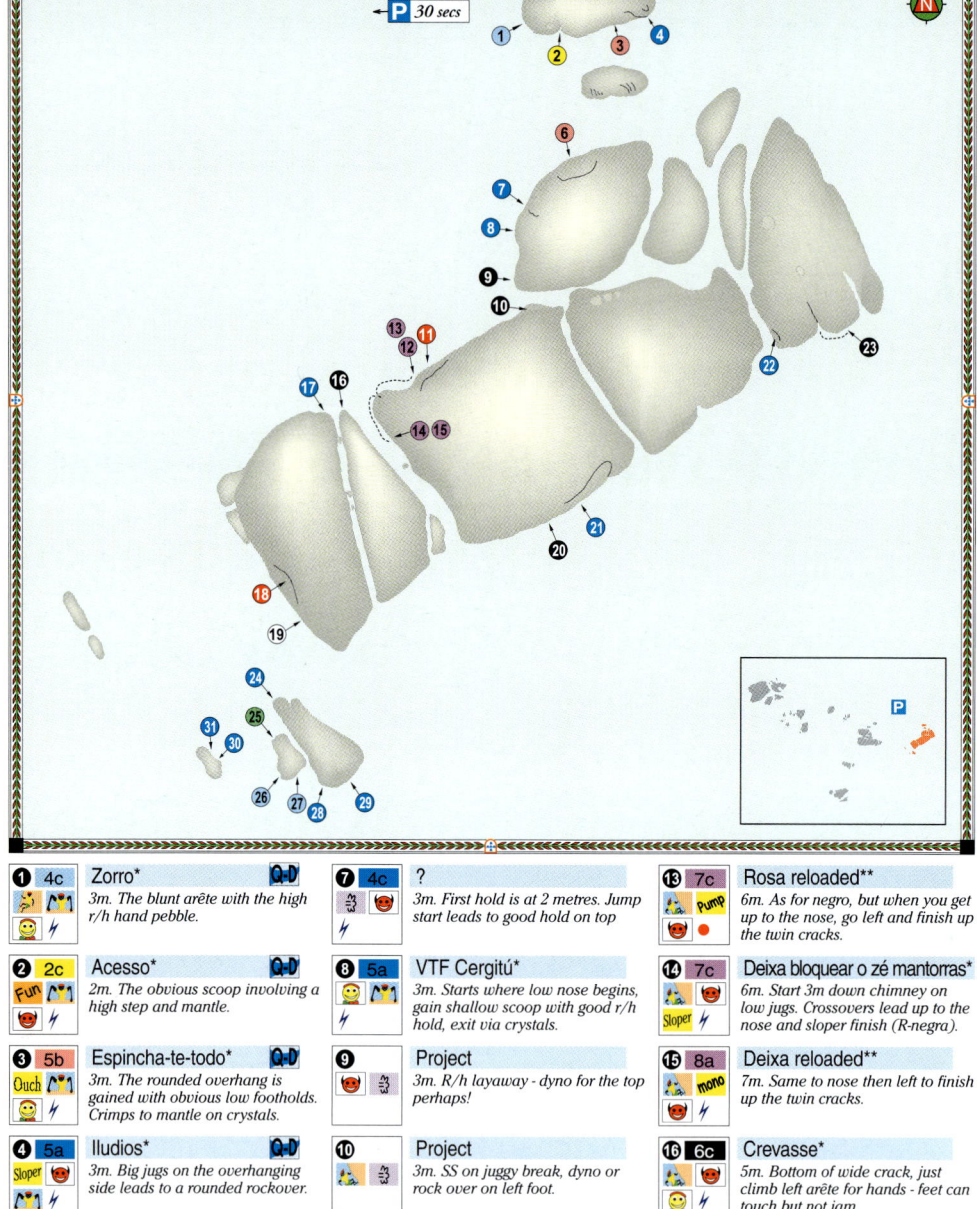

Pedra Do Urso

1 `4c` **Zorro***
3m. The blunt arête with the high r/h hand pebble.

2 `2c` **Acesso***
2m. The obvious scoop involving a high step and mantle.

3 `5b` **Espincha-te-todo***
3m. The rounded overhang is gained with obvious low footholds. Crimps to mantle on crystals.

4 `5a` **Iludios***
3m. Big jugs on the overhanging side leads to a rounded rockover.

5 **Project**
3m. Big overhanging nose is gnarly and rounded - no footholds.

6 `5b` **Poleiro***
3m. Technically gain the scoop, the fight with the crystals to get over the overhanging top.

7 `4c` **?**
3m. First hold is at 2 metres. Jump start leads to good hold on top

8 `5a` **VTF Cergitú***
3m. Starts where low nose begins, gain shallow scoop with good r/h hold, exit via crystals.

9 **Project**
3m. R/h layaway - dyno for the top perhaps!

10 **Project**
3m. SS on juggy break, dyno or rock over on left foot.

11 `6a` **Força do vento****
4m. Start on u-cuts at shoulder height, up to good LH hold, then crystal mantle; SS may be poss.

12 `7b+` **Rosa Negro*****
5m. St on big flake 2m in from chimney. Go rt on crossovers and finish up nose on slopers.

13 `7c` **Rosa reloaded****
6m. As for negro, but when you get up to the nose, go left and finish up the twin cracks.

14 `7c` **Deixa bloquear o zé mantorras***
6m. Start 3m down chimney on low jugs. Crossovers lead up to the nose and sloper finish (R-negra).

15 `8a` **Deixa reloaded****
7m. Same to nose then left to finish up the twin cracks.

16 `6c` **Crevasse***
5m. Bottom of wide crack, just climb left arête for hands - feet can touch but not jam.

17 `5a` **Blue***
4m. Big sloping jug high on R side of crack. Anything allowed - guppy the arête.

ROSA NEGRA 7b+, Pedra do Urso; Ben Moon

A solitary boulder in the Desert sector.

MEIA LUNA 4c, Jerry Moffatt on a full scale High Ball, old sector, Pedra do Urso

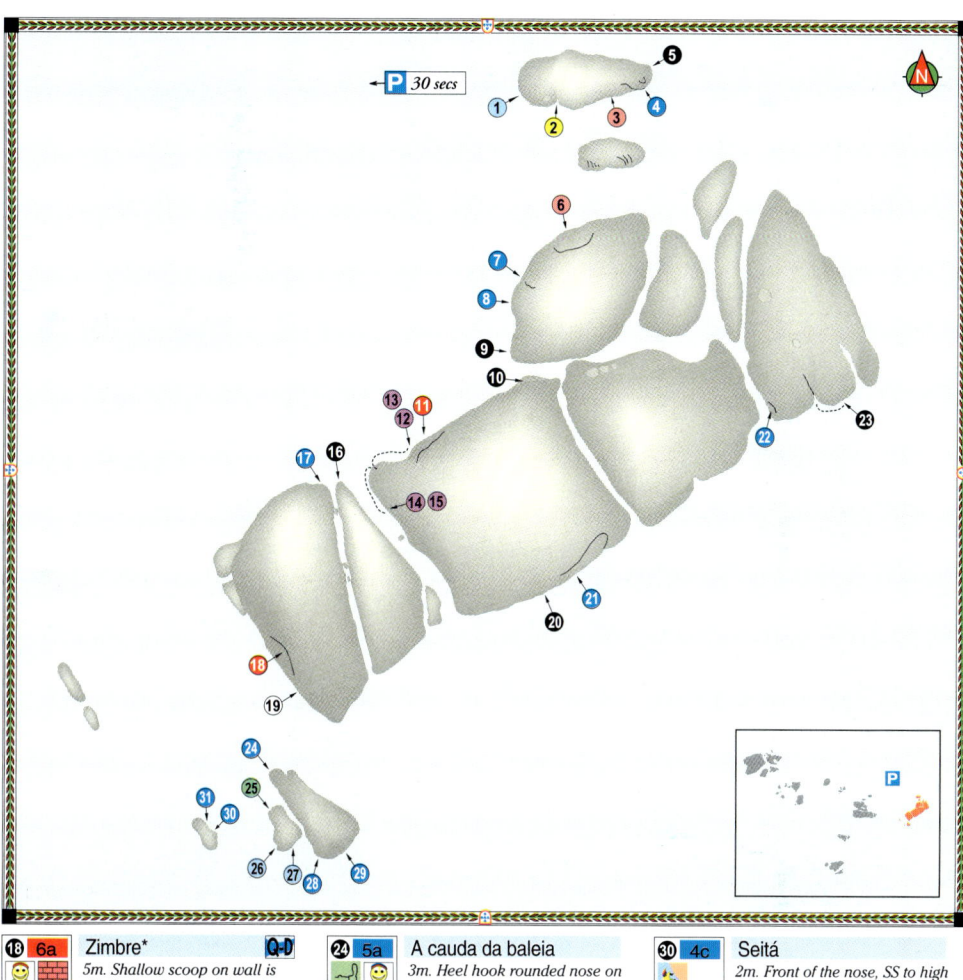

Pedra Do Urso

№	Grade	Name	Description
18	6a	Zimbre*	5m. Shallow scoop on wall is climbed on the left side - crimpy.
19	7a+	Recompensa*	5m. Start 2m left of arête. Jump for sloper at 2,5m; match and go up to the right.
20	6c	A Ostra*	4m. 2m left of curving crack - a crystal plate on the wall. Crimps to a difficult finish.
21	4c	Liquen man**	4m. Easy crack goes right on good holds with pebble footholds.
22	4b	Degrau	3m. Start in the corridor 1 metre back. Jump up to heel hook and rock over.
23	6c	A teia*	5m. Start with hands crossed on slopers and R-HH. Go left and up over nose - do not use L-nose.
24	5a	A cauda da baleia	3m. Heel hook rounded nose on the right - awkward.
25	4a	Alaska	2m. Overhanging short groove - follow jugs up and right, rock over.
26	4b	Salto de Cavalo	2m. Rounded arête on good holds.
27	4b	?	2m. Simple wall, step up on left foot to go up if you can, easier for the tall.
28	5a	?	3m. Rounded wall, pull up on crimps, then giant jug high up. Technical - no footholds. (SS-7a)
29	4c	Boca da baleia	3m. Good footholds for right foot, pull up on crimps and slopers.
30	4c	Seitá	2m. Front of the nose, SS to high L/H crimp, then up to nose top.
31	4c	Seitá variante	6m. Variation finish going under the nose and finishing right.

Bivaque - Escadinhas - Fonte de Pedra - Poste 35 - Rapapele - Pouca Terra - Rosa negro - Zimbre

Penha Garcia

Penha Garcia

1. Placa das Tartarugas
2. Marrocos
3. Placas do Rio
4. Cabeça do Nico
5. Cova do Castelo

Barragem de Penha Garcia

Monfortinho

Monsanto
Castelo Branco

N239

Monfortinho
Espanha

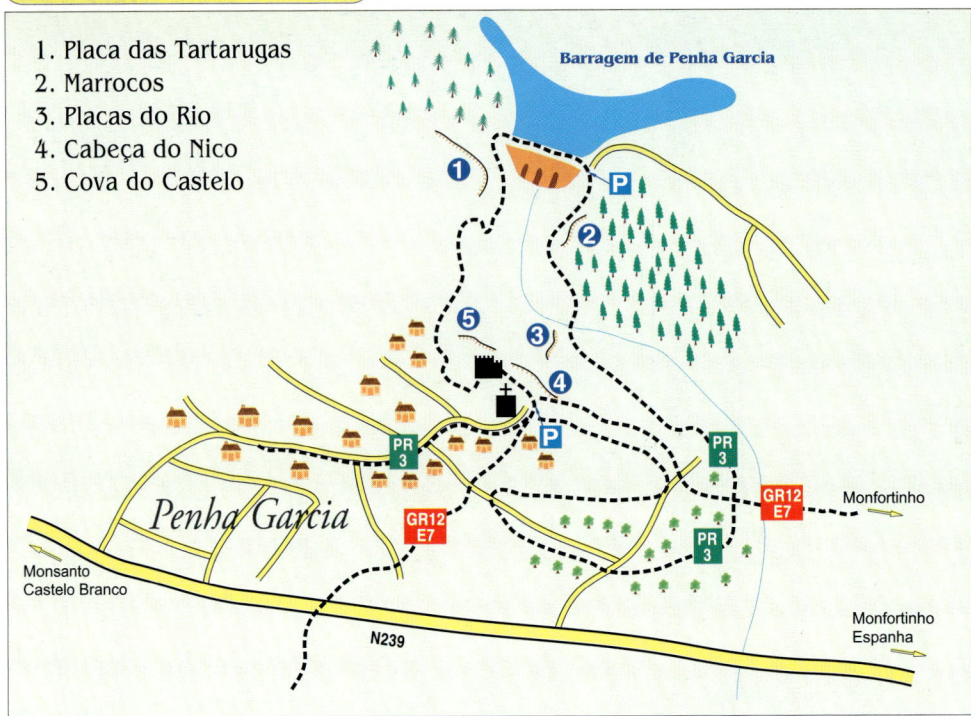

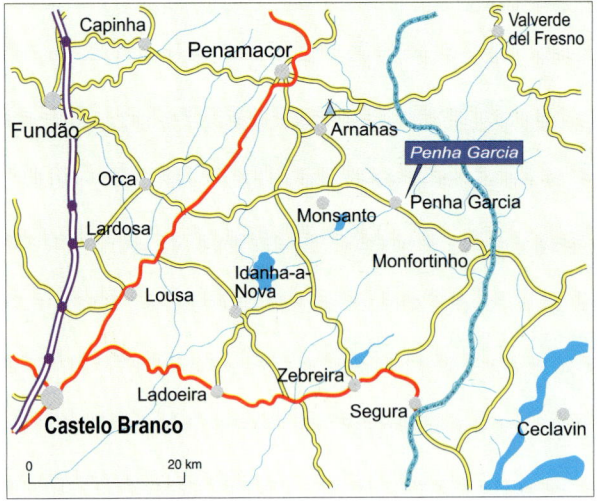

Penha Garcia: Helpful info:
We don't have much detail on these cliffs, since the details came on the back of a piece of paper, very late one night spent in a very busy bar of Covilhã; and with great thanks to the Secção de Montanha of Covilhã who provided us with the information, so that everyone could benefit.

The rock here is quartzite and offers plenty of cracks and small face holds. The routes are very varied and range from 8m up tp 45 metres long. The routes should be quite well equipped with bolts etc.

Tipo de Rocha; quartzito com abundantes fissuras e regletes. Vias; 8-45 metros.
Tipo de escalada: placas técnicas, fissuras e extraprumos atléticos.

Camping Freixal
Aranhas, 6090-565 Penamacor
Tel: 277 385 529 Fax: 277 394 196
3 hectares, 250 places. Open 01/04 - 31/10
www.cm-penamacor.pt
(Penamacor 13km for ATM)

Bar-Cafe: Penha Garcia - "O Nico"
Hotels: Monfortinho

Penha Garcia

#	Grade	Name
1	4c	By the Crack
2	4b	Val de Plaque
3	3c	Carro Vassoura
4	5c	Duplo mortal entortado
5	5b	Passelo das tartarugas
6	5b	Pilar dos cagados
7	6a+	Banho da água fria
8	6b	Bos broca
9	6a	Belchoir
10	5a	Baltazar
11	5c	Rei gaspar
12	5b	Guachinin
13	5c	Vida de lebre
14	6b+	Osso erótico
15	6b	H²0 tinto
16	3b	Terceira idade
17	6a	Pablo Escovar
18	6a	Vinho do casa
19	6b	Vento contra
20	6b+	Palpitações (L2)
21	6a	Turbo escova (L2)
22	6a	Corta Vento (L2)
23	6a	Musgolãndia
24	6b	Capitão Ryobi
25	6b	Casa dos Bicos

Placa das Tartarugas - *Marrocos* - *Plasas do Rio* - *Cabeça do Nico* - *Cova do Caste*

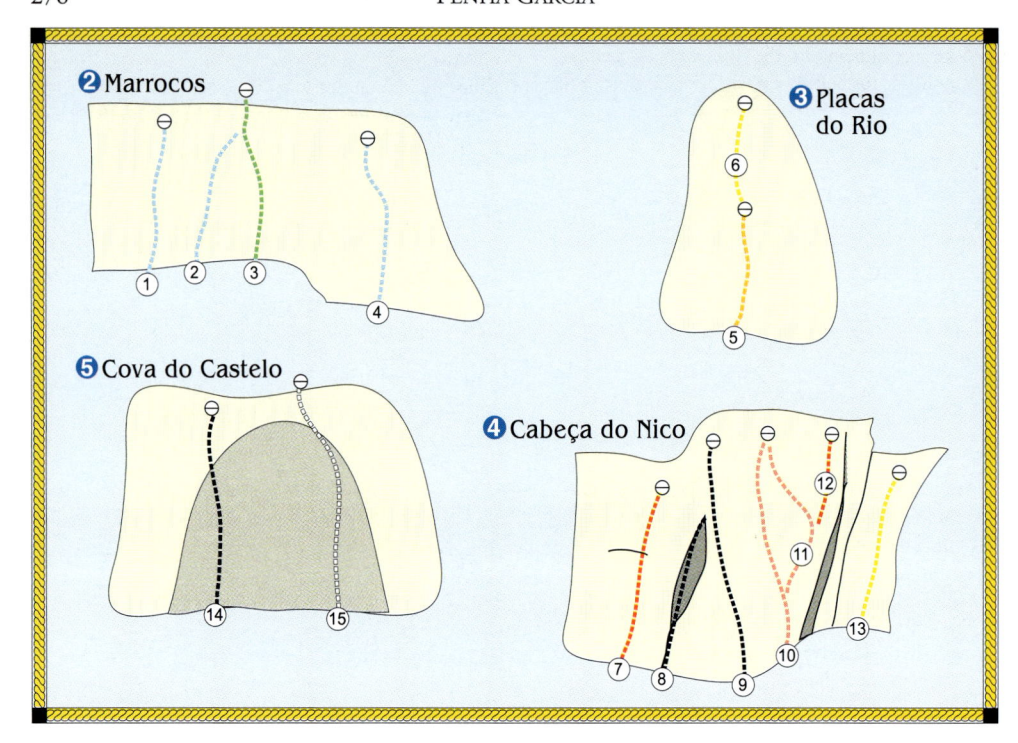

Marrocos
- ① 6a — Marrakech
- ② 6a+ — Casa Blanca
- ③ 5c — Rabat
- ④ 6a — Essauira

Placas do Rio
- ⑤ 4b — A idade não peroda
- ⑥ 3b — PPR (L2)

Cova do Castelo
- ⑭ 7b — de caixão a cova
- ⑮ 7c — Vanila

Cabeça do Nico
- ⑦ 7a — Passage Violet
- ⑧ 7b+ — O Ilusionosta
- ⑨ — Merzuga
- ⑩ 6c — Cabeça do Nico
- ⑪ 6c+ — Raio da velha
- ⑫ 7a — Docinho da casa
- ⑬ 3c — Tapete voador

With special thanks to the clubs who are mainly responsible for bolting and the looking after of the cliffs.

FARO
Nucleo de Montanha da Casa da Junventude de Faro
Rua D. Diogo Mendonça Corte Real nº71
8000 - Faro
PORTUGAL
Tel./Fax.: (00351) 289803802
http://www.ccjf.pt/nm/
nm@ccjf.pt

LISBOA

CASCAIS
Associação de Desportos de Aventura Desnivel
Rua do Estorninho, Loja K,
Quinta da Bicuda
2750-686 Cascais
PORTUGAL
Tel.: (00351) 214847084, Fax: (00351) 214847085
http://www.adesnivel.pt/
info@adesnivel.pt

SINTRA
Grupo de Montanha e Escalada de Sintra
www.gmesintra.com
gmes@gmesintra.com

LEIRA
Associação Pé no Trilho
Rua do Alecrim, nº 206
Vale do Horto
2400 - 828 Azoia - Leiria
PORTUGAL
Fax : (00351) 244 568 539
http://www.penotrilho.com
info@penotrilho.com

FIGUEIRA DA FOZ
Clube de Montanha da Figueira da Foz
Rua Envolvente Monte Alto, 58
BUAROS
3080 FIGUEIRA DA FOZ
clubemontanha@clix.pt

COIMBRA

COVILHA

GUARDA
Clube de Montanhismo da Guarda
Largo do Torreão
6300 GUARDA
Telefone/Fax: (00351) 271 222840
http://www.montanhismo-guarda.pt
clube.montanhismo.guarda@clix.pt

OPORTO
Clube Nacional de Montanhismo
Rua Formosa, 303-2º
4000-252 PORTO
PORTUGAL
Tel./Fax: (00351) 223 321 295
http://www.cnm.org.pt
cnm@cnm.org.pt

SANTO TIRSO
Trampolins de Santo Tirso
C. C. Carneiro Pacheco
Piso 3 - Lj. 23
4780 Santo Tirso
Telefone: 91 9140924

VILLA REAL
Grupo de Montanhismo de Vila Real
Apartado 169
Largo de S. Pedro, Nº 1
5000 Vila Real
PORTUGAL
Tel. / Fax.: (OO351) 259326868
http://gmvr.home.sapo.pt/
gmvr@mail.telepac.pt

CARRAZEDA DE ANSIAES
Clube de Ar Livre do Alto Douro
Rua João José de Freitas, 345
5140-069 CARRAZEDA DE ANSIAES
PORTUGAL
http://www.ansiaes.net/amn
ansiaes@ansiaes.net

Clube Celtas do Minho
Terminal do Ferry-boat
Apartado 68
4920 Vila Nova de Cerveira Minho
PORTUGAL
Telef: (00351) 251 794 784
Fax: (00351) 251 794 784
http://www.celtasdominho.com/
celtasdominho@celtasdominho.com

We had a lot of people telling us about different types of calcaire, such as, urgonien, jurassic, cretaceous, etc. The fact is, that generally only geologists know anything about rock, and their descriptions have simply nothing to do with climbing. We instead looked at the general different effect of CALCAIRE, with climbing interest: Such as:- slipperyness - which we all hate; rounded texture - good for worn skin; sharp 'cimai' teeth - bad for worn skin, etc. We then distilled all the different types to a reasonable quantity - 25, and gave them a letter each. Nobody, except 'those typical retentives,' were going to remember the letters. So we decided to use the first letter from the name of a cliff, where that type of rock is present. It's never going to be perfect, since many cliffs have quite a few different types of calcaire, and some are not precise examples. However, we feel it is a lot more useful than just saying 'calcaire.' We hope it works as a quick to use reference system. The graphic icons on the cover will help, but the photos on these 4 pages, should help even more.

A - Alaro

B - Buoux

C - Cimai

D - Dolomiti

E - Erto

Calcaire - Limestone

279

F - Finale

G - Gréolières

H - Hochkogel

I - Ith

J - Jaraba

K - Kreutzfels

L - Saint Llorenç de Montgai

CALCAIRE - LIMESTONE

M - Malham Cove

N - Gorges du Nesque

O - Oillaskoa

P - Pouponne

Q - Quié

R - Rosenstein

Calcaire - Limestone

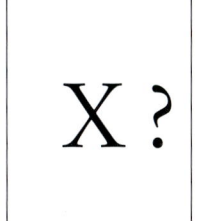

S - Stoney Middleton

V - Vignettes

T - Troubat

U - Ubrieux

W - Water-Cum-Jolly

X ?

Y - Yenne

Z - Zwergenschloß

	English	Français	España	Portugal	
😈	Powerful climbing-Big holds, steep rock	Puissant - Bonnes prises, dévers	Escalada atlética - cazos, roca vertical	Escalada atlética. Boas presas	😈
🙂	Technique, balance and experience required	Technique, équilibre et expérience nécessaires	Técnica, requiere equilibrio y experiencia	Escalada Técnica requer equilíbrio e experiência	🙂
●	A redpoint climb, difficult to read or onsight	Point Rouge - A grimper de préférence avec plusieurs essais	-	Leitura Difícil	●
⚡	Onsight flash, good holds should be straightforward	Eclair bleu - Doit être possible à vue	-	Leitura Fácil	⚡
⚠2	Warning, first bolt is high up, clip stick useful	1 triangle - Le 1er goujon est très haut placé	-	Danger	⚠2
∽9∽	Number of bolts to clip with quickdraws	Nombre de dégaines nécessaires	-	Numero quickdraws	∽9∽
⊖	Proper lower off point, at your own risk	Cercle - Relais avec point de moulinette	-	Ponto de moulinete	⊖
▽	Abseil point, difficult friction, poor lower off	Triangle - Point de rappel, pas de moulinette	-	Ponto de Rappel	▽
🗑	Complete choss, not worth a visit	Ne vaut pas la peine de visiter	Fracaso, no merece la pena	Non bello	🗑
≪	A wonderful view, often in the mountains	Vue magnifique, souvent en montagne	Maravillosas vistas, a menudo entre montañas	Vista fabulosa Zona de montanha	≪
✺	A beautiful natural setting, countryside	Joli site naturel, campagne	Marco natural, campo	Paisagem de beleza natural	✺
S/A	Mostly sport routes, but nuts should be carried	Terrain sportif, plus coinceurs.	Mayoritariamente deportiva, pero es conveniente llevar empotradores	Principalmente vias desportivas Devem levar-se entaladores	S/A
A/S	Natural protection mainly, with some bolts	Protection naturelle, quelques broches	Seguros naturales, con algunos parabolts	Protecções naturais Pouco equipamento fixo	A/S
A	Terrain adventure - roofs are done with aid	Terrain adventure !!!!!!!	Terreno de aventura - techos con ayuda	Terreno de aventura Tectos em artif	A
N	Natural protection only, no pegs or bolts	Protection naturelle, aucune broche	Sólo con autoprotección, sin spits ni parabolts	Vias não equipadas	N
C	Czech style - only knots on slings, insitu bolts	Czech style	Estilo checo - sólo nudos en anillas, en lugar de parabolts	Sem equipamento Só pontes de rocha	C
T	Top roping, and you may need slings	Corde a la tête	Top-rope, pudiendo necesitar anillas	Top Rope Levar anéis	T
≡	Via ferrata in the nearby area, good fun	Via ferrata à proximité, divertissant	Vía ferrata en la zona, muy divertido	Via Ferrata próxima	≡
⤴	Very well protected crux, bolt above move	Mouvement clé très bien protégé	Muy bien protegido el paso clave, parabolt por encima del paso	Crux bem protegido	⤴
✹	A good 2 metre fall from crux will be expected	Du mouvement clé chute de 2 mètres possible	Puedes caer dos metros desde el paso clave	Queda de 2 metros possível no crux	✹
747	A whopper fall 5-10 metres - wheeeee	Longue chute de 5-10 mètres	Sartenazo de 5 a 10 metros	Possível queda de 5-10 metros	747
✎	If you fall !! you will go a very long way, 30 metres	Si vous tombez, énorme chute de 30 mètres	Si caes, tendrás un gran vuelo, 30 metros	Queda muito longa Até 30 metros	✎
👻	A very scary cliff, will completely terrify you	Falaise qui vous donnera la chair de poule	Pared escalofriante, te aterrorizará...	Parede aterrorizante	👻
△	General warning, loose rock, wear helmets etc.	Roche instable, portez un casque	Precauciones generales, roca suelta, llevar casco, etc.	Rocha solta Levar capacete	△
⊘	No climbing during the restriction please	Pas d'escalade pendant la période de restriction	No escalar durante las restricciones	Não escalar no período de restrição	⊘
🐦	Climbing restrictions for bird nesting season	Restrifications pour nidification	Restricciones de escalada por nidificación	Restrições de escalada por nidificação	🐦
🔫	Shooting season - you may get shot!	Période de chasse - attention aux balles perdues	Temporada de caza - te pueden disparar	Perigo de tiros no período de caça	🔫
90db	A rating for car traffic noise 30-99 db	Côte pour les bruits de circulation 30-99 db	Intervalo de ruido de coches, entre 30 y 99 db	Ruido de trafeco Entre 30-99 db	90db
90db	Really loud river noise	Rivière très bruyante	Ruido de río realmente fuerte	Ruído de água corrente	90db
Zzz	A very quiet crag	Une falaise très calme	Zona muy tranquila	Zona muito tranquila	Zzz
●●●	Humidity warning, often on overcast days	Attention à l'humidité surtout les jours couverts	Cuidado humedad, a menudo nublado	Humidade frequente em dias encobertos	●●●
☢	Nuclear reactor closeby watch out!	Réacteur nucléaire proche - Attention!	Reactor nuclear en las cercanías. ¡Cuidado!	Reactor nuclear Nas proximidades	☢
△	Open field - camping, no facilities at all	Camping dans un champ, aucun équipement	Campo abierto - escasez de servicios	Acampamento selvagem sem serviços	△
△	Very basic camping, with toilets and water	Camping de base avec toilettes et eau	Camping básico, con baños y agua	Parque de campismo básico Com água e casas de banho	△
△	Normal campsite, hot showers, basic	Camping avec eau chaude, douches	Camping normal, agua caliente, básico	Parque de campismo com água quente	△
△	Excellent campsite with shop, bike hire, etc.	Excellent camping avec magasins, location vélos	Camping excelente, con tienda, alquiler de bicis, etc.	Parque de campismo completo Compras, aluguer de bicicletas,,	△
△	Amazing, top facilities, swimming pool, dancing	Camping de luxe avec piscine, discothèque	Impresionante, todo tipo de servicios, piscina, baile	Parque de campismo excelente Piscina, discoteca, etc.	△
(F)	Languages used in a guidebook	Langues utilisées dans le guide	Idiomas utilizados en la guía	Idiomas utilizados no guia	(F)

English	Français	España	Portugal
Boulders for good bouldering	Bons blocs	Buenos boulders	Bons boulders blocos
Slab climbing	Dalle	Escala en placa	Escalada em placa
Vertical, climbing - bad for resting	Vertical - pas de repos	Escalada vertical, sin reposos	Escalada vertical sem repousos
Leaning rock, the wrong side of vertical	Le - Ooohmph	Roca desplomada, el lado malo de la vertical	Rocha extraprumada
Really leaning and steep rock, grottos	grottos	Muy vertical, incluso desplomada, cuevas	Extraprumos com grutas
Roof climbs, or sections with roofs	Toit ou sections avec toit	Techos, o secciones con techos	Tectos
Sea cliff climbing above the water	Falaises, escalade au-dessus de la mer	Acantilado en el que se escala sobre el agua	Falésia sobre o mar
You must swim to the route, or take a boat	Rejoindre la voie à la nage ou par bateau	Hay que nadar hasta pie de vía o coger un bote	Acesso somente com barco ou a nado
Approach by abseil	Approche en rappel	Aproximación rapelando	Acesso por rappel
A chimney	Cheminée	Chimenea clásica	Chaminé
Very pocketed rock	Roche avec beaucoup de trous - gruyère	Roca muy agujereada - como un queso	Rocha com muitos buracos
An arête, here shown climbed on the right	Une arête, montrée ici à droite	Arista, aquí se muestra escalada por la derecha	Aresta escalada pela direita
A mantleshelf, no holds to pull over on	Un rétablissement aucune prise pour la sortie	Paso de mostrador, sin agujeros para traccionar	Passo de prateleira Sem presas para traccionar
Foot lock, hooking a heel to do a problem	Le technique - pour le pied	Talonaje para resolver el paso	Bloqueio de calcanhar
A real friction problem, no good holds	Beaucoup d'adhérence, aucune bonne prise	Paso de adherencia sin buenos agarres	Aderência pura
Dynamic lunge, leaping for holds	Mouvement dynamique Sauter pour les prises	Lanzamiento dinámico para encontrar los agarres	Lançamento movimento dinâmico
A climb with corners and grooves	Une voie avec dièdres et cannelures	Escalada con aristas y fisuras	Escalada com arestas E diedros
Fine thin edges, painful to the fingertips	Briques - Réglettes fines et douloureuses	Regletas	Con reglette
Forearms get really pumped, endurance	Force - Muscles mis à l'épreuve	Sustentar	Continuidade
A nice route, good for kids and beginners	Une belle voie pour les enfants	Divertirse	Bonito
Slippery like a banana skin, glass	Banane - Très glissant et poli	Resbaladizo	Escorregadio
A lot of balance moves and is technical	Equilibre -Utilisation de l'équilibre plutôt que la force	adherencia	Placca Technica
Crux moves will have a single finger pocket	Mono - Mono-doigt	mono	mono
Hand cracks, jamming and fist engaging	Fissure - Fissure avec coincement de main	Fissura de manos	Fessura-mano
Very hard bloc-crux move, stopper move	Bloc - Un mouvement très, très difficile	paso de decisión	Pass-di forza
A route which wakes up to morning sunshine	Une voie avec le soleil le matin	Una vía para madrugar	Via com sol pela manhã
A route in the sun all day	Une voie avec le soleil toute la journée	Vía al sol durante todo el día	Via ao sol durante todo o dia
A route with the sun in the afternoon	Une voie avec le soleil l'après-midi et soir	Vía para no madrugar, sol hasta tarde	Via com sol ao final do dia
A route that keeps out of the sun	Une voie non exposée au soleil	Vía en sombra	Via sempre a sombra
Trees in the area to give shade in summer	Arbres qui donnent de l'ombre en été	Arbolado que da sombra en verano	Via com bastantes sombras
Limestone; All seabed sedimentary fossils	Calcaire sédimentaire, fossiles	Caliza, toda llena de fósiles sedimentario	Calário sedimentar
Granite; all quality from white hard - brown poor	Granit	Granito; de todas las calidades, desde el blanco duro al marrón más pobre	Granito de todas as qualidades
Green hard gneiss, often in natural folds	Gneis	Gneis verde duro, a menudo en fallas	Gneiss
Free parking normally	Parking gratuit normalement	Parking gratuito habitualmente	Estacionamento gratuito
Pay parking, have coins for slot machines	Parking payant avec horodateurs	Parking de pago, ten monedas para las máquinas	Estacionamento pago Trazer moedas para parquímetro
General spot height for a high point	Point de altitude	Visión general de la zona desde un punto alto	Vista geral da zona de um ponto alto
Currency accepted	Devises acceptées	Se acepta efectivo	Moedas aceites
Credit cards	Cartes de crédit	Tarjetas de crédito	Cartões de crédito aceites

	Deutschland	Česká	Japan	
😀	Athletische Kletterei - große Griffe, steiler Fels	silové lezení - velké chyty, strmé lezení	パワークライミング　ガバ　前傾壁	😀
🧑	Klettertechnik und Gleich- gewichtsgefühl nötig	technika, rovnováha a zkušenosti jsou nutné	テクニカルクライミング、バランス系、垂壁、スラブ	🧑
●	rotpunkt deutlich leichter als onsight	nejlépe lezitelné stylem RP	レッドポイントに最適	●
⚡	gute Onsight-Route	vhodná cesta pro OS	オンサイトに適す	⚡
⚠2	Vorsicht vor dem 2. Haken!	první jištění vysoko	1本目のボルト高い	⚠2
∽9∽	Anzahl der benötigten Expressschlingen	počet expresek	必要なドロー数	∽9∽
⊖	Umlenkung ist geeignet zum Ablassen	místo vhodné pro spouštění	ロワーダウン可能	⊖
▽	hier muss abgeseilt werden, ablassen nicht möglich	slanovací bod nevhodný pro spouštění	下降注意。懸垂など	▽
🗑	Totaler Müll, kann man vergessen	špatné lezení, nestojí za návštěvu	良くない　行く価値無し	🗑
≪	Schöne Aussicht, oft in den Bergen	nádherný výhled, často v horách	眺めが非常に良い	≪
✹	Landschaftlich reizvolles Gebiet	nádherná příroda, prostředí, krajina	自然が豊富	✹
S/A	V.a. Sportkletterrouten, aber Klemmkeile nötig	převážně sportovní cesty, ale nutno dojistit	ほとんどがボルトルート、　ただしナチプロ類も必要	S/A
A/S	V.a. selbst abzusichern, mit ein paar Bohrhaken	převážně ne přírodní jištění, občas nýty	ほとんどがナチプロ、部分的にボルト	A/S
A	Abenteuergelände - in Dächern Technorouten	dobrodružné cesty, stropy se lezou s umělými pomuckami	冒険的、エイドも混ざる	A
N	Komplett selbst abzusichern	pouze přírodní jištění, bez nýtu a skob	ナチプロのみ、ボルト類は一切無い	N
C	Tschechischer Stil - nur Ringe und Knotenschlingen	český styl - pouze smyčky a kruhy	旧東ドイツスタイル、プロテクションはスリングのみ	C
T	Toprope, eventuell Schlingen nötig	top rope, možná budete potřebovat smyčky	トップロープ、スリングは持参	T
🪜	Spaßiger Klettersteig in der Nähe	nedaleko via ferrata (klettersteig), dobrá zábava	岩場にハシゴや橋が　かかって遊べるエリアあり	🪜
🚁	Sehr gut abgesicherte Schlüsselstelle	velmi dobře zajištěná oblast, nýty na každém kroku	プロテクション非常に良し、核心部はボルト下	🚁
🦟	An der Schlüsselstelle ist ein Sturz von 2 Metern drin	bezpečné pády kolem 2 metru	プロテクション良し、核心部は2m以内の墜落	🦟
747	Große Sturzweite: 5-10 Meter	pády 5-10 metru	5-10mの墜落の可能性あり	747
✒	Megasturz möglich: bis 30 Meter	pokud spadnete, tak se docela proletnete, pády až 30 metru	30m程度の大墜落の　可能性あり	✒
👻	Moralisch sehr anspruchs- volles Gebiet	hruzostrašná skála, určitě vás vyděsí	恐怖感満点のエリア	👻
△	Vorsicht! Brüchiger Fels, Helm nötig.	všeobecné varování, zvětralá skála, volné bloky, helma nutná, atp.	要注意、脆い岩　ヘルメット必携など	△
⊘	Bitte während Vogelschutz- zeiten nicht klettern	zákaz lezení v době omezení	クライミング禁止期間あり	⊘
🕊	Kletterverbot während der Vogelbrutzeit	omezení lezení v období hnízdění ptáku	鳥の巣がある期間は　クライミング禁止	🕊
🔫	Jagdsaison - Vorsicht Lebensgefahr!	strelecká sezóna - mužete být zastřeleni!	狩のシーズンあり　撃たれるかも！	🔫
90db	Starker Verkehrslärm	hluk aut kolem 30-99 db	車の騒音あり　30-99db	90db
90db	Sehr lauter Fluss	velmi hlučná řeka	川の音が大きい	90db
Zzz	Sehr ruhiges Gebiet	velmi klidá oblast	とても静かな岩場	Zzz
☔	Fels bei bedecktem Himmel oft feucht	varování ohledně vlhkosti, často během zamračených dnu	湿気高し、特に海風の日	☔
☢	Atomkraftwerk in der Nähe	nedaleko atomový reaktor - pozor!	近くに核施設あり	☢
△	Campingplatz ohne sanitäre Einrichtungen	otevřená plocha pro táboření, žádné sociální zařízení	ただの原っぱのキャンプ場、施設は何も無い	△
△	Einfacher Campingplatz mit Toiletten und Wasser	tábořiště se základním vybavením - toalety a voda	シンプルなキャンプ場　トイレと水はある	△
△	Normaler Campingplatz mit heißen Duschen	kemp se základním vybavením - teplá voda, sprchy	普通のキャンプ場　お湯の出るシャワーあり	△
△	Guter Campingplatz mit Einkaufsmöglichkeit etc.	vynikající kemp s obchodem, pujčovnou kol atd.	とても良いキャンプ場　売店などもある	△
△	Luxus-Campingplatz mit Swimming pool etc.	nadstandardní vybavení - bazén, diskotéka	豪華なキャンプ場　プールなど何でもある	△
F	Im Kletterführer verwendete Sprachen	jazyky použité v pruvodci	ガイドブックで記載されている　言語	F

Deutschland	Česká	Japan
Gute Boulderfelsen	dobré bouldrování	ボルダリングエリアあり
Plattenkletterei	plotnové lezení	スラブ
Klettern in senkrechtem Fels, kaum Ruhepunkte	kolmé lezení - špatné pro odpočívání	垂壁
Überhängender Fels	ukloněná skála do převisu	薄被りの傾斜
Stark überhängender und steiler Fels, Höhlendächer	velmi ukloněná skála, strmé lezení, jeskyně	前傾壁、ケイブ
Dachkletterei, oder Teilbereiche mit Dächern	lezení ve stropech nebo části cest vedou stropem	ルーフ、もしくはルーフ部分あり
Routen direkt über dem Meer	lezení na mořských útesech nad vodou	シークリフ
Schwimmend oder per Boot zum Einstieg	k cestě je nutné doplavat nebo si vzít lodičku	ルートまで泳ぐかボートが必要
Per Abseilen zum Einstieg	přístup ke slanění	取りつくのに懸垂下降が必要
Klassischer Kamin	klasický komín	チムニー
Sehr löchriger Fels - wie Schweizerkäse	skála s kapsami - jako ementál	ポケットホールドがたくさん
Grat, hier auf der rechten Seite beklettert	hrana, zde lezena zprava	カンテ
Mantlemove, keine Griffe zum Hochziehen	římsa bez chytu	マントル
Foothook	stup pro zaháknutí paty	ヒール、トゥフック
Reibungsproblem, gute Griffe sind Mangelware	kroky na tření, žádné dobré chyty	フリクションクライム、ホールドなし
Dynamischer Zug, Griff anspringen	dynamické kroky k chytum	ランジ
Verschneidungskletterei	lezení v koutě, žlebem	コーナー
schmerzhaft scharfe Leisten	ostré lišty	鋭いエッジホールド
dicke Unterarme garantiert	vytrvalostní lezení	パンプする持久系
nette Kinderroute	pěkná cesta pro děti	子供でも楽しめる
polierter Marmor	oklouzané	磨かれていてツルツル
technisch anspruchsvolle Kletterei	více technické než silové lezení	バランス系
Einfingerlöcher	jednoprstové dírky	ワンフィンガーポケット
Handriss	spára	クラック
knallharte Einzelstelle	boulderové místo, těžký krok	ボルダームーブ
Route mit Morgensonne	na cestu svítí slunce pouze ráno	朝から日が当る
Route ganztags sonnig	na cestu svítí slunce celý den	1日中、日当たり良し
Route mit Nachmittags- oder Abendsonne	na cestu svítí slunce pouze odpoledne a večer	午後から日向
Route liegt immer im Schatten	na cestu nikdy nesvítí slunce	1日中日陰
Im Sommer Schatten durch Bäume	v létě je cesta ve stínu stromu	夏は日陰のアリア
Marine Kalke	vápenec; všechny usazené fosílie z mořského dna	石灰岩　二子山、備中と同じ
Granit; von weiß und hart bis braun und brüchig	žula; všech kvalit od bílé tvrdé po hnědou měkkou	花崗岩　小川山と同じ
Grüner harter Gneis, oft gefaltet	zelená tvrdá rula	チャート系
Parken normalerweise gebührenfrei	obvykle park. zdarma	通常は駐車無料
Parken gegen Gebühr, Münzen nötig	placené parkování, připravte si mince do park. hodin	有料駐車場 小銭が必要な場合もある
Höhe über dem Meeresspiegel	nadmořská výška nejvyššího místa	標高
Fremdwährungen werden akzeptiert	hotovost akceptována	使用可能通貨
Kreditkarten	kreditní karty	クレジットカードOK

Jerry Moffatt being very co-operative during a photo shoot.

Wobbly on a walkabout, looking for a good spot to camp.

BEACH FUN TIME PAGE

Travel - Holiday Checklist

Item	Check	Check	Relevant details
Tickets & credit card used to pay (E)			
Car hire details & agreement			
Money - Euros for Portugal			
Travellers Cheques			
Main Credit Card			
Reserve - Credit Card			
Passport - check expiry date			
E111 - health form			
Health insurance policy			
Reverse charge - phone numbers			
Mobile phone & charger (int.-roam)			
Camera & Charger (Plug adaptor)			
Film & memory cards			
Rope - short & bag			
Rope - long			
Harness			
Quickdraws			
Descender			
Gri Gri			
Rock shoes			
Chalk Bag			
Crash Pad & beer towel			
Guidebooks			
Compass, torch & penknife			
Rucksack			
Tent			
Sleeping bag			
Sleeping mat			
Cooker			
Pots			
Plates			
Cutlery			
Clothes			
Wash bag & beach towel			
Warm jacket			
Sun tan lotion & lip salve			
Shades			
Sun umbrella			
Mosquito rep (not really needed)			
Wet suit - Atlantic is cold			
Surf board			
Internet details & email access code			
Travel guides and books			
Local language dictionary			
[Sharp objects - in big luggage]			
Emergency contact numbers			